Eighteenth-Century Popular Culture

EIGHTEENTH-CENTURY POPULAR CULTURE

A SELECTION

EDITED BY

John Mullan and Christopher Reid

OXFORD

UNIVERSITY PRESS

OXFORD

UNIVERSITY PRESS

Great Clarendon Street, Oxford OX2 6DP

Oxford University Press is a department of the University of Oxford.
It furthers the University's objective of excellence in research, scholarship,
and education by publishing worldwide in

Oxford New York

Athens Auckland Bangkok Bogotá Buenos Aires Calcutta
Cape Town Chennai Dar es Salaam Delhi Florence Hong Kong Istanbul
Karachi Kuala Lumpur Madrid Melbourne Mexico City Mumbai
Nairobi Paris São Paulo Shanghai Singapore Taipei Tokyo Toronto Warsaw
and associated companies in Berlin Ibadan

Oxford is a registered trade mark of Oxford University Press
in the UK and certain other countries

Published in the United States
by Oxford University Press Inc., New York

British Library Cataloguing in Publication Data

Data available

Library of Congress Cataloging in Publication Data

Data available

ISBN 0-19-871134-4
ISBN 0-19-871135-2 (Pbk.)

1 3 5 7 9 10 8 6 4 2

Typeset by Best-set Typesetter Ltd., Hong Kong
Printed in Great Britain
on acid-free paper by
Biddles Ltd,
Guildford and King's Lynn

For Kazuko Hatano

ACKNOWLEDGEMENTS

In the course of compiling this book we have drawn on the research strengths of a number of institutions. We are particularly grateful to have been granted access to eighteenth-century material in the following collections: the Library of the Society of Antiquaries, the Bodleian Library, the British Library, the Buckinghamshire Record Office, Cambridge University Library, the Gilbert Library (City of Dublin Public Libraries), Gloucestershire Record Office, the Guildhall Library, the Institute of Historical Research, the Centre for Kentish Studies, Lambeth Palace Library, the libraries of Lincoln College, Oxford and Christ Church, Oxford, the Newberry Library, the Public Record Office, the library of Queen Mary and Westfield College, London University Senate House Library, Toronto Public Library (Osborne Collection of Early Children's Books), and the library of University College London. Passages from the diary of Samson Occom are excerpted from Leon Burr Richardson, *An Indian Preacher in England* © 1933 by the Trustees of Dartmouth College, by permission of the Provost's Office, Dartmouth College, and the University Press of New England. Every effort has been made to trace and contact copyright holders prior to publication. If notified, we undertake to rectify any errors or omissions at the earliest opportunity.

A number of friends and colleagues have helped us in the preparation of this anthology. We are especially grateful to Markman Ellis, Stephen Gill, David Goldthorpe, Shelley Hermes, Elizabeth James, Catherine Jones, Leya Landau, John Mason, Lori McLeod, John Oliphant, Stephen Priddy, Alison Shell, John Sutherland, Glyn Williams, and to participants in the Polite and Popular Culture MA course and the Eighteenth-Century Reading Group at Queen Mary and Westfield College.

Finally, we are indebted to Andrew Lockett, Jason Freeman, and Sophie Goldsworthy who, as successive editors at the Oxford University Press, initiated, encouraged, and stayed with this project. We also thank Matthew Hollis for helping us to bring it to a conclusion.

CONTENTS

LIST OF ILLUSTRATIONS

INTRODUCTION

1

IN February 1754 George Woodward, the rector of East Hendred in Berkshire, wrote to his uncle complaining of the scarcity of new reading-matter in his rural parish: 'I believe, if good S^r. Charles [Grandison] had not so opportunely come to our Relief, we sh^d. have degraded our Taste so far, as to have borrow'd Valentine & Orson from ye Gentry in ye Kitchen, where he is Conn'd over every Night with wonderful Pleasure.'[1] Woodward comments wryly, and in the expectation that he will be understood, on a structural division between cultures. While the clergyman's family gathers in the parlour to read the latest volume of Richardson's novel and follow the fortunes of its polite and pious hero, the occupants of the kitchen read, and re-read, *The History of Valentine and Orson*, one of the most enduringly popular chapbook narratives. Statements like Woodward's, which confidently visualize a culture divided along strictly hierarchical lines, are not uncommon in contemporary sources. They cannot, however, be accepted uncritically as a reflection of social reality. Indeed, they may reflect a desire on the part of the educated to sharpen the supposed distinctions. As we shall see, Woodward's letters raise issues of interpretation which are likely to confront anyone seeking to locate and illustrate popular culture in the eighteenth century. How credible is Woodward's division of culture into polarities of high and low? What was the extent of interaction between these supposedly separate spheres? Of what value are these reports of popular culture, highly mediated as they are, and written from the viewpoint of a condescending if not actively hostile witness?

In thinking through these questions it is natural to begin with Peter Burke's influential survey of cultural relationships in the early modern period, where

---

[1] George Woodward to George London, Centre for Kentish Studies (Maidstone), U771 C7/23. Selections from this correspondence have been published in *A Parson in the Vale of White Horse: George Woodward's Letters from East Hendred 1753–1761*, ed. Donald Gibson (Gloucester, 1982).

they are systematically addressed. Burke identifies two distinctive spheres of culture: 'the great tradition', a closed and learned culture 'transmitted formally at grammar schools and at universities', and 'the little tradition', or popular culture, which was disseminated and acted out in market-places, taverns, and other places of common assembly.[2] Burke does not simply map these traditions on to social groupings, but rather argues that they are complexly related. 'The great tradition' was exclusively the terrain of the educated elite, but popular culture was also in effect a common culture since for much of the period the privileged classes were active participants in it. While a distinction between the cultures of the ordinary and the elite is therefore fundamental to Burke's account, this is neither a simple nor a static polarity. Indeed, his explanatory scheme allows for (and stresses) significant interaction between the cultural spheres, regional, religious, and gendered variations within popular culture, and the processes of cultural change. According to Burke's chronology, it was in the seventeenth and, especially, the eighteenth centuries that the polite progressively disengaged themselves from 'the little tradition'. 'By 1800', he claims, 'in most parts of Europe, the clergy, the nobility, the merchants, the professional men— and their wives—had abandoned popular culture to the lower classes, from whom they were now separated, as never before, by profound differences in world view.'[3] At the same time, popular culture came under direct attack from the agents of moral reform, while profound changes in the economy created new kinds of expectation and desire which existing cultural forms were unable to satisfy.

Burke's account, which presents what has come to be known as the 'bi-polar' view of early modern culture, has provoked considerable debate. While no one could doubt its cogency, a number of alternative emphases and approaches have been proposed (see 'References and Further Reading', 1, below). Predictably, perhaps, much of the discussion has focused on the explanatory value of the bi-polar model itself. According to Burke's critics, that model oversimplifies a complex social picture. Martin Ingram, for instance, argues that notwithstanding Burke's refinements and qualifications, his model 'makes it hard to do justice to the infinite gradations of the social hierarchy (and in particular to the middling social groups who straddled the world of the elites and of the common people), to the cultural variations to be found at any point on the social spectrum, to regional variations or to gender differences'.[4] Similar reservations have frequently been expressed in recent studies. According to this view, the bi-polar

---

[2] Peter Burke, *Popular Culture in Early Modern Europe*, rev. edn. (Aldershot, 1994), 28.

[3] Ibid. 270.

[4] Martin Ingram, 'From Reformation to Toleration: Popular Religious Cultures in England, 1540–1690', in Tim Harris (ed.), *Popular Culture in England, c.1500–1850* (1995), 95. (Unless otherwise stated, London is the place of publication.)

model is predisposed to find opposition rather than interaction between the popular and the elite. Furthermore, it underestimates the extent to which the two spheres may themselves have been internally divided. Tim Harris illustrates the revisionary case well when he offers the example of those whose religious beliefs cut across the presumed divisions between elite and popular culture. 'Poor Anglicans', he suggests, may have 'possessed a stronger sense of cultural identity with upper-class Anglicans . . . than they did with people from a similar social background who did not share their religious leanings'.[5]

A second strand of the debate involves the kinds of questions which historians can productively ask about cultural practices and artefacts. For instance, we might take as our point of departure the social distribution of cultural forms: that is to say, we might ask whether a given form—chapbook, newspaper, procession—was characteristically 'popular' or 'polite'. For some, however, to put the question in these terms is to take for granted the very divisions which historical enquiry is supposed to prove. An alternative approach, associated in particular with the historian Roger Chartier, offers another way of thinking about cultural difference. Instead of investigating the typical patterns of distribution of cultural goods among specific social groups (street ballads for the common people, classical texts for the elite) Chartier looks at 'differentiated uses and plural appropriation of the same goods, the same ideas, and the same actions'.[6] Ballads, printed on single sheets and sold by street singers and by hawkers at fairs, were produced in their thousands in the eighteenth century. How differently might they have been read by those who collected them in their closets and those who came upon them pinned to an alehouse wall? And what can these differences tell us about the role of culture in shaping social distinctions?

The tendency of much recent work in the field, then, has been to question the idea that cultural identities in the eighteenth century (and indeed in the early modern period as a whole) were defined by clear and recognized boundaries separating the high from the low. In place of Burke's twin foci of 'unity and variety' in popular culture, current work insists on difference and plurality. As one leading practitioner has put it, the keywords of the moment in cultural history are 'ambiguous, complex, contradictory, divided, dynamic, fluid, fractured, gendered, hybrid, interacting, multiple, multivalent, overlapping, plural, resistant, and shared'.[7] A major question raised by this distrust of totalizing theories and models is whether the very concept of popular culture is still sustainable: whether it can coexist with the fragmenting emphases on division and difference. At what point does a pluralist approach to culture render popular culture redundant as an explanatory category? Does the now

---

[5] 'Problematising Popular Culture', in Harris, *Popular Culture in England*, 19.
[6] Roger Chartier, *The Cultural Uses of Print in Early Modern France* (Princeton, NJ, 1987), 6.
[7] Barry Reay, *Popular Cultures in England 1550–1750* (1998), 1.

1. *Coblers Hall*, *c.*1750, this impression *c.*1800. Popular ballads and prints are displayed on the walls of the workshop. See Sheila O'Connell, *The Popular Print in England 1550–1850* (1999), 80. © The British Museum

fashionable formulation 'popular culture*s*' simply displace or evade these questions?

In considering these debates it is instructive to look at the example of the eighteenth century, not least because in an important sense it is in that period that their origins lie. As we show in our opening chapter, the eighteenth century saw a progressive sharpening, more marked, say, in 1770 than in 1710, of the distinctions and categories which came to construct the idea of popular culture. One of the social consequences of the process of commercialization (which we examine in more detail later in this introduction) was to intensify polite anxieties about cultural distinctions. When culture can be bought and sold, taste becomes an increasingly useful social marker. We catch something of this when we look at the terms used, then and now, to describe the culture of ordinary people. What we now, deliberately employing a neutral or even approbatory vocabulary, call 'popular' culture the educated in the eighteenth century categorized in inherently judgemental terms as 'vulgar' or 'low'.[8]

George Woodward's contrast between the reading-matter of the parlour and the kitchen helpfully illustrates how these distinctions could be constructed, for

[8] For an extended account of these issues, see Morag Shiach, *Discourse on Popular Culture: Class, Gender and History in Cultural Analysis, 1730 to the Present* (Cambridge, 1989).

on closer inspection his opposition turns out to be less clearly marked than it appears at first sight. A taste for Richardson, for example, was not confined to a social or cultural elite. Indeed, from a polite perspective some of the cultural materials which he worked up into his highly didactic novels must have seemed decidedly low. On reading *Sir Charles Grandison*, the aristocratic Lady Mary Wortley Montagu remarked witheringly to her sister that 'I beleive this Author was never admitted into higher Company, and should confine his Pen to the Amours of Housemaids and the conversation of the Steward's Table, where I imagine he has sometimes intruded, thô oftner in the Servants' Hall'.[9] The son of a joiner, Richardson composed stories for the entertainment and instruction of his schoolfellows, including one 'on the Model of Tommy Potts,' a chapbook which he recalled rewriting as the fable 'of a Servant-Man preferred by a fine young Lady (for his Goodness) to a Lord, who was a Libertine'.[10] Richardson's first publications, which appeared more than twenty years after he entered trade as a printer, were a pocket companion for the instruction of apprentices and a practical letter-writing manual designed, as he put it, to 'be of Use to those Country Readers who were unable to indite for themselves'.[11] His first novel *Pamela*, an enormous publishing success, developed directly from these utilitarian and moralizing materials. Richardson allows his heroine, a virtuous serving-maid who resists her master's attempts at seduction and is rewarded with his hand in marriage, to tell her own story in a series of devout and dutiful letters to her honest and humbly born parents. He gave his two later novels more refined social settings but without necessarily implying a more fashionable readership. Indeed, a contemporary reviewer found a troubling disparity between the social world of novels like *Grandison* and Burney's *Evelina* and the world of the audience they were most likely to reach:

Lords and ladies cannot afford to spend their *precious* time in reading novels . . . The purchasers of novels, the subscribers to circulating libraries, are seldom in more elevated situations than the middle ranks of life.—The subjects of novels are, with a dangerous uniformity, almost always taken from superior life . . . What effect has this upon the readers? They are convinced that happiness is not to be found in the chilling climate of low life, nor even . . . in the temperate zone of middle life.—Rank alone contains this unknown good, wealth alone can bestow this coveted joy.[12]

[9] *The Complete Letters of Lady Mary Wortley Montagu*, ed. Robert Halsband, 3 vols. (Oxford, 1965–7), iii. 96.

[10] *The Richardson–Stinstra Correspondence*, ed. William C. Slattery (Carbondale, Ill., 1969), 27. For the chapbook *The Lover's Quarrel or Cupid's Triumph, being The Pleasant History of Fair Rosamund of Scotland* (otherwise known as 'Tom Potts') see Margaret Spufford, *Small Books and Pleasant Histories: Popular Fiction and its Readership in Seventeenth-Century England* (Cambridge, 1981), 246–7.

[11] *Richardson–Stinstra Correspondence*, 28.

[12] *The Critical Review: Or, Annals of Literature*, 46 (1778), 203–4.

There is evidence to suggest that *Clarissa* offered instruction and pleasure (albeit of a different kind) to readers well below the level of the elite. Thomas Turner, a Sussex shopkeeper, and his wife were spiritually strengthened by reading the novel together in the 1750s, while surviving booksellers' records show that some of its volumes were borrowed (and presumably read) by provincial servants.[13]

Although we do not hear the voices of Woodward's domestic servants or his children, and little of his wife's, the letters show that the cultural life of the rectory was more complex—in some ways more diversified, in some ways more connected—than his more categorical statements suggest. Take the issue of literacy, for instance. It is obvious from remarks which Woodward makes about the education of his children that the social divisions between the polite parlour and the plebeian kitchen are complicated by divisions based on gender. The early reading experiences of his son and daughter have much in common: both are reported to have responded sympathetically to 'ye History of Joseph & his Brethren' (quite possibly the chapbook of that name rather than the Old Testament text). But Woodward's expectations of their attainments in literacy significantly diverge. As he tells his uncle, 'there is not so great a Necessity in getting girls forward in their Books as Boys; for They will be most of their time at home, and have but one Language to Learn'. Although he praises his wife as 'a very good Divine' and values her willingness to enter into the discussion of spiritual topics, it seems that these discussions are typically initiated by his practice of reading aloud from religious texts on Sundays and feast-days.[14]

Yet a practice which sustains or creates dependency can be understood in another sense as one which forges links, both within and across cultural boundaries. Communal reading, often thought of as a practice confined to the semi-literate or unlearned, was evidently a common event in East Hendred. The volumes of *Sir Charles Grandison* which rescued Woodward from the vulgarity of the chapbook were borrowed from a neighbouring archdeacon who read the novel to his family each evening for three hours at a time. The archdeacon maintained strict control of the reading process, insisting that he alone would be permitted to perform. Nevertheless, this practice did mean that access to texts, which were scarcely abundant even among the polite of East Hendred, was in some sense shared. Richardson's novels are often cited in support of the argument that in the eighteenth century reading became an increasingly private experience. A portrait by Joshua Reynolds shows his niece absorbed in *Clarissa*,

---

[13] Naomi Tadmor, ' "In the even my wife read to me": Women, Reading and Household Life in the Eighteenth Century'; Jan Fergus, 'Provincial Servants' Reading in the Late Eighteenth Century', in James Raven, Helen Small, and Naomi Tadmor (eds.), *The Practice and Representation of Reading in England* (Cambridge, 1996), 162–74 and 202–25.

[14] Centre for Kentish Studies, U771 C7/163 (24 Nov. 1761), C7/58 (15 Nov. 1755), C7/36 (28 Sept. 1754). *Parson in the Vale of White Horse*, ed. Gibson, 25.

deeply engaged by an epistolary method which draws the reader into the inte-
rior scenes of the characters' minds.[15] But this representation of reading must be
qualified by the evidence (by no means confined to Woodward's letters) that
eighteenth-century readers thought of novels, including Richardson's, as orally
performative texts. When the archdeacon read *Grandison* his audience was in all
probability confined to his immediate family, but orality does not always respect
or confirm cultural boundaries. The servants in Woodward's kitchen may not
have had the opportunity of reading Richardson, but if the evidence of his letters
is to be believed they did encounter Fielding. In December 1760 Woodward
proudly reports that his son, then about 12 years old, is 'reading ye History of
Tom Jones', while his sister 'listens to it with great Attention, being one of his
Audience in ye Kitchen'.[16]

What, then, of the chapbook culture which stands at the opposite pole of
Woodward's contrast? Although he defines his own sphere in opposition to the
low culture of the kitchen, Woodward himself acknowledges that the boundaries
of taste are more permeable than the walls of the rectory which seem to fix them.
Necessity, he concedes, may sometimes lead the polite to participate in the pleasures of the common people. Even in the eighteenth century this would not have
been an especially unusual or eccentric gesture. There are a number of records
of highly educated readers and collectors of chapbooks, of whom James Boswell
is the best known. In his *London Journal* (1762–3) he tells how

some days ago I went to the old printing-office in Bow Church-yard kept by Dicey,
whose family have kept it fourscore years. There are ushered into the world of literature *Jack and the Giants*, *The Seven Wise Men of Gotham*, and other story-books which
in my dawning years amused me as much as *Rasselas* does now. I saw the whole
scheme with a kind of pleasing romantic feeling to find myself really where all my old
darlings were printed. I bought two dozen of the story-books and had them bound up
with this title, *Curious Productions*.[17]

In the eighteenth century the firm of Dicey, whose Cheapside offices Boswell
visited, was a leading player at the popular end of the market for literature, and
was especially known for its production of chapbooks.[18] Along with ballads and
almanacs, chapbooks were the most affordable form of print, and consequently
the form most likely to be present in plebeian households. In general terms they
can be described as small, paper-covered books, often sold unstitched and uncut
by hawkers (otherwise known as chapmen or flying stationers) together with

---

[15] *Miss Theophila Palmer Reading 'Clarissa Harlowe'* (1771). See Ellis Waterhouse, *Reynolds* (1973),
plate 55.

[16] Centre for Kentish Studies, U771 C7/147.

[17] *Boswell's London Journal 1762–1763*, ed. Frederick A. Pottle (1950), 299.

[18] See Victor E. Neuburg, 'The Diceys and the Chapbook Trade', *The Library*, 5th ser. 24 (1969),
219–31.

other cheap and affordable goods. What more precisely qualifies as a chapbook is, however, less easy to define. Taking price as her 'decisive criterion', Margaret Spufford excludes from the category texts exceeding seventy-two pages which would have cost more than 6*d*., though she acknowledges that some of these longer items were advertised for sale as chapbooks in contemporary trade-lists.[19] Many eighteenth-century examples run to twenty-four pages and cost 2*d*. or less: our topical example in Chapter 6 was shorter (eight pages) and cheaper (priced at 1*d*.). Chapbooks had no fixed generic content: condensed chivalric romances, pious tracts, jest books, folk-tales, abridged novels (including both *Robinson Crusoe* and *Moll Flanders*[20]), criminal narratives, reports of sensational events, and collections of recipes were all printed in chapbook form. Anticipating an audience with diverse reading skills, most chapbooks support their narratives with quite liberal use of woodcut illustration and seem often to have been used as teaching aids. Both the quantity and the range of chapbook output are indicative of the increasing strength of popular print culture. As early as 1664 an inventory of a London printer found a stock of approximately 90,000 chapbooks in his warehouse. At about the time when Boswell visited the offices of the Diceys the company was advertising 150 chapbook titles in its catalogue.[21] A distribution system which took the itinerant sellers on extended circuits through the country and to favoured sites such as markets and fairs made chapbooks widely accessible. Taken together, the evidence suggests 'the existence of a flood of print seeping into the most obscure rural areas', as Michael Harris puts it.[22]

What, then, may have attracted polite readers like Boswell to this material? Pat Rogers describes the episode at Bow churchyard as an example of Boswell's 'literary slumming' (comparable, perhaps, to his compulsive visits to London's poorest prostitutes), but he also notes his 'genuine affection' for the chapbook texts.[23] Boswell, like others of his rank and background, was a consumer of 'popular' literature in the form both of chapbooks and of the criminal lives we illustrate in Chapter 5. What these works meant to him, however, was something quite specific. The association with childhood in polite anecdotes of reading is recurrent and telling. Children of all ranks probably did make up a large part of the chapbook audience, but the simplicity which charms Boswell is

[19] Spufford, *Small Books*, 130–1.
[20] On Defoe and the chapbook see Pat Rogers, *Literature and Popular Culture in Eighteenth-Century England* (Brighton, 1985), 162–97.
[21] Spufford, *Small Books*, 98; Neuburg, 'The Diceys and the Chapbook Trade', 223.
[22] Michael Harris, 'A Few Shillings for Small Books: The Experience of a Flying Stationer in the Eighteenth Century', in Michael Harris and Robin Myers (eds.), *Spreading the Word: The Distribution Networks of Print 1550–1850* (Winchester, 1990), 92.
[23] Rogers, *Literature and Popular Culture*, 165.

not only the simplicity of childhood but a simplicity he attributes to popular culture itself.

Margaret Spufford cites Edmund Burke as another man of letters who acknowledged a familiarity with the world of the chapbook.[24] Replying to a speech in the Commons in 1787 he joked that 'It reminded him pretty strongly of Palmerin of England, Don Bellianis of Greece, and other books of that romantic nature, which he had formerly lost much time in reading.'[25] Although Burke may have in mind longer versions of these neo-chivalric romances than Spufford herself is prepared to categorize as chapbooks, it is clear from other comments made by Burke that he thinks of them as outside the usual cultural orbit of the educated classes. In his early work, *A Philosophical Enquiry into the Origin of our Ideas of the Sublime and Beautiful* (2nd edn., 1759), he compares *Don Bellianis* (a chapbook version of which was published by the Diceys) and Virgil's epic poem the *Aeneid* in the course of an argument about the foundations of the faculty of taste:

It is true, that one man is charmed with Don Bellianis, and reads Virgil coldly; whilst another is transported with the Eneid, and leaves Don Bellianis to children. These two men seem to have a Taste very different from each other; but in fact they differ very little. In both these pieces, which inspire such opposite sentiments, a tale exciting admiration is told; both are full of action, both are passionate, in both are voyages, battles, triumphs, and continual changes of fortune. The admirer of Don Bellianis perhaps does not understand the refined language of the Eneid, who if it was degraded into the style of the Pilgrim's Progress, might feel it in all its energy, on the same principle which made him an admirer of Don Bellianis.[26]

This interestingly assumes that the same person might read the popular romance and the classical epic, but more importantly Burke seems to argue for a similarity of aesthetic appeal. Yet as the discussion develops he reintroduces, by the book door as it were, the notion of taste as a distinguishing faculty.[27] Taste is founded not only on the socially undifferentiated resources of natural sensibility but also upon a capacity for judgement and aesthetic discrimination which has to be learned. As Burke puts it, 'it is for the most part in our skill in manners, and in the observances of time and place, and of decency in general, which is only to be learned in those schools to which Horace recommends us, that what is called Taste, by way of distinction, consists'.[28] The occupants of George Woodward's

---

[24] Spufford, *Small Books*, 75.

[25] A. P. I. Samuels, *The Early Life, Correspondence, and Writings of Edmund Burke* (Cambridge, 1923), 46.

[26] *A Philosophical Enquiry into the Origin of our Ideas of the Sublime and Beautiful*, ed. J. T. Boulton (1958), 20–1.

[27] See Tom Furniss, *Edmund Burke's Aesthetic Ideology: Language, Gender and Political Economy in Revolution* (Cambridge, 1993), 68–88. [28] Burke, *Philosophical Enquiry*, 23.

parlour and kitchen might read the same chapbook, but this would not prove a uniformity of taste. The distinction is maintained and measured by what the readings yield. Burke's discussion suggests that if the educated reader finds pleasure in *Don Bellianis* it must be a pleasure derived from the recollection of earlier readings:

In the morning of our days, when the senses are unworn and tender, when the whole man is awake in every part, and the gloss of novelty fresh upon all the objects that surround us, how lively at that time are our sensations, but how false and inaccurate the judgments we form of things? I despair of ever receiving the same degree of pleasure from the most excellent performances of genius which I felt at that age, from pieces which my present judgment regards as trifling and contemptible.[29]

In these comments we catch a glimpse of an important eighteenth-century idea about popular culture which we illustrate in more detail in our opening chapter. Popular culture becomes of interest to the educated partly because it reminds them that something has been lost in the desirable progress towards civility. When Boswell recognizes his 'old darlings' in Dicey's office the 'pleasing romantic feeling' he experiences is a recognition of that loss. But as Rogers comments, 'there is no sign that Boswell's liking for the popular forms in any way affected his judgment of what constituted literature, or how the high forms should be assessed'.[30] The admiration for the simplicity of popular ballads which Addison declared earlier in the century did not compromise his larger project of disseminating polite taste as the basis of social distinction.

    It is symptomatic of the problems involved in work on popular culture that we can be less certain of what chapbooks meant to their primary users. Woodward's condescending remark that *Valentine and Orson* 'is Conn'd over every Night with wonderful Pleasure' suggests not only repeated readings but also perhaps the committing of narrative to memory. What evidence survives from those outside the elite puts these culturally specific reading practices in a more positive light. Writing of his childhood in the 1750s Thomas Holcroft, the son of a shoemaker who had fallen upon hard times, recalled the gift of 'two delightful histories . . . which were among those then called Chapman's Books . . . Parismus and Parismenes, with all the adventures detailed in the Seven Champions of Christendom, were soon as familiar to me as my catechism, or the daily prayers I repeated kneeling before my father.' Holcroft's intense valuing of these chapbooks, which he seems to have carried about him for some years, is in part explained by his observation that this was a time when 'a book, except of prayers, or of daily religious use, was scarcely to be seen but among the opulent,

---

[29] Burke, *Philosophical Enquiry*, 25.
[30] Rogers, *Literature and Popular Culture*, 165.

or in the possession of the studious'.[31] We might conjecture that the relation of the reader to the chapbook in a culture where print was scarce was different from that of the reader for whom it was plentiful. Holcroft's testimony suggests that conning over a chapbook every night was not necessarily a sterile exercise. It could yield both the pleasure of familiarity and the discovery of new meanings, forging close links between the chapbook narrative and the reader's developing sense of self.

This is not to suggest that a chapbook text can in itself give us unproblematic access to an authentically 'popular' mentality. Peter Burke rightly warns that

The books which the chapmen carried round had often been composed by priests, nobles, doctors and lawyers, sometimes centuries earlier . . . There is . . . a whole chain of mediators between a particular text and the peasants whose attitudes it is supposed to express, and we cannot assume that the peasants passively accepted the ideas expressed in the texts any more than contemporary viewers believe all they see on television.[32]

Neither at the point of composition nor at the point of reception can they be thought of as exclusively popular objects. Furthermore, the very diversity of the material organized in chapbook form makes it difficult to draw general conclusions about the ways in which they may have been appropriated and understood. The chapbook version of *Valentine and Orson* retains the courtly settings, chivalric codes, and improbable plot devices of the original French romance which it abridges. It would be difficult to imagine a narrative more remote from the everyday concerns of a middling or plebeian readership (which may, of course, have been the basis of its popular appeal). By way of contrast, two other frequently reprinted chapbooks, *Thomas Hickathrift* and *Long Meg of West-minster*, are firmly rooted in English plebeian life. The lowly but resourceful protagonists of these tales rely upon their physical strength and native ingenuity in their struggles against those who seek to exploit them or who contravene what they understand to be the moral norms of the community. Hickathrift, a specifi-cally fenland hero who sells his labour at hiring fairs, defeats a giant who has been preying on the people and denying them their rights of way, divides the giant's lands between himself and the rural poor, encloses an estate and a deer park for his family, and founds a new church to commemorate his feat. Long Meg, in many ways Tom's female equivalent, is a serving-maid who pits her unusual strength against a succession of abusive authority figures (bailiffs and constables, for instance) and foreigners who cross her path. A practised cross-dresser, she enjoys humiliating her rivals by theatrically revealing her gender as they signal

---

[31] *Memoirs of the late Thomas Holcroft*, 3 vols. (1816), i. 13, 136. See David Vincent, *Literacy and Popular Culture: England 1750–1914* (Cambridge, 1989), 197–8.
[32] Burke, *Popular Culture*, 73.

their submission. Her own submission to her husband, however, is final and stark.[33]

Differences in education, rank, and gender would no doubt have led the occupants of Woodward's parlour and kitchen to make sense of these chapbook narratives in different ways. Few records of such readings survive, and those that do, while revealing, are not necessarily typical. The utopian activist Thomas Spence, one of nineteen children born to a Newcastle netmaker and his wife, a stocking seller, suggested to his readers that chapbook tales could disclose informative political allegories:

> the stories of enormous and tyrannical giants, dwelling in strong castles, which have been thought fabulous, may reasonably be looked upon as disguised truths, and to have been invented as just satires upon great lords. For, if those fabulous monsters were said to eat the people and their children, your real monsters really eat their meat and the savour out of every enjoyment . . . These are the monsters, or giants, that the world want to be rid of. The extirpation of these should employ the philanthropic giant-killers, the deliverers of mankind.[34]

When Spence was writing in the 1790s, just beyond the period covered by our own selections, what we might think of as popular literacy had become an urgent political issue. The politically conservative Hannah More, who was on good terms with the Dicey family of chapbook fame, exploited the forms of popular literature in order to reach an audience which it was now thought to be important to influence. For example, her poem *The Riot; or, Half a Loaf is better than No Bread* (1795) was distributed both in ballad and chapbook form with a view to countering the radical political opinions of Thomas Paine. But as Peter Burke has reminded us, ordinary readers could not be relied upon to be passive readers. Referring in his autobiography to Hannah More's tracts, the agricultural labourer Joseph Mayett complained that 'their Contents were Cheifly to perswade poor people to be satisfied in their situation and not to murmur at the dispensations of providence for we had not so much punishment as our sins deserved'. Such works, he concluded grimly, 'drove me almost into despair for I Could see their design'.[35]

2

We have seen how George Woodward's contrast between the worlds of the parlour and the kitchen simplifies, or masks, more complex cultural interactions.

---

[33] For further discussion of these chapbooks see Spufford, *Small Books*, 244–9. Versions of them can be found in *Chapbooks of the Eighteenth Century*, ed. John Ashton (1882; repr. Skoob Books, n.d.).

[34] Spence, *A Further Account of Spensonia*, in *Pig's Meat; or, Lessons for the Swinish Multitude*, 3 vols. (1793–5), ii. 209. See Olivia Smith, *The Politics of Language, 1791–1819* (Oxford, 1984), 101–3.

[35] *The Autobiography of Joseph Mayett of Quainton (1783–1839)*, ed. Ann Kussmaul (Aylesbury, 1986), 70.

As rector of the parish he was in any case obliged almost *ex officio* to cross what he understood as a cultural divide. Rural clergymen were unusually, and perhaps awkwardly, positioned at an interface between cultures. Literate, and often learned, as the public representatives of the Established Church they were expected to bring the benefits of enlightenment and politeness to their supposedly benighted parishes. On the other hand, they were also viewed as the custodians of local memory and traditions which still centred on the parish church, a role expressed in their participation in calendar customs and communal festivities. Many clergymen (though not, on the evidence of his letters, Woodward himself) were expected to take a lead in the annual perambulation at Rogationtide which renewed the communal memory of the ancient bounds of the parish.[36] It is no accident, then, that antiquarianism, which might be understood as a way of making sense of these distinct if not contradictory roles, found so many recruits among the eighteenth-century clergy. As we show in our opening chapter, antiquarians like the Newcastle clergyman Henry Bourne were among the most important mediators of popular culture in the eighteenth century. They were not, of course, impartial witnesses. Popular culture was of interest to them primarily as a survival. Properly understood it preserved a valuable record of the customs of the past, but its interpreters felt bound to condemn the irrationality and superstition which disfigured it in the present.

We find similarly mixed feelings towards ordinary parish life in George Woodward's letters. On one occasion he tells his uncle of the leading role he played in initiating the celebrations held at East Hendred to mark the British victory at Louisburg in 1758. It was the rector who spread news of the triumph and supplied the bellringers with ale, with the result that 'the Whole Parish was soon got together' and the night was spent in acts of collective and noisy rejoicing. Woodward again seems to identify himself with the common culture of the village when he describes the festivities which greeted the coronation of George III: 'there was a Sheep roasted whole, & money given for Drink, with Ringing of Bells all day long, and Bonfires &c: at Night; so you see S^r., we of Great Hendred are none of your Little Folks, when we have a mind to exert ourselves'. It is not a simple matter to catch the tone here, however, and Woodward's profession of parish pride may well be touched by irony. Certainly he often writes of the ordinary villagers of East Hendred and its neighbourhood as if they belong to an alien culture or exist in a parallel world. He expresses distaste at the prospect of the 'Rustick Mirth' of a forthcoming tithe feast which he is obliged by custom to attend. As we show in Chapter 6, he ridicules the superstitious beliefs of those among his flock who were troubled by the reform of the calendar in 1752. He even describes servants, in the language of scientific classification, as 'an Order

[36] See Bob Bushaway, *By Rite: Custom, Ceremony and Community in England 1700–1880* (1982), 81–8. On polite involvement in rural popular culture see Robert Malcolmson, *Popular Recreations in English Society 1700–1850* (Cambridge, 1973).

of our Species, that we can't well do without'. In a letter which is especially revealing of his attitude towards the beliefs of the unlearned, Woodward describes how in the course of a journey to Devizes in 1754 he struck up a conversation with two countrymen about the origins of Silbury Hill. Having requested 'ye Story of it', one of them replied:

> why, S^r. one King Silby was buried there, & all ye Soldiers carried a Hatful of Earth & throw'd it upon him; & That made ye Hill: ay, says I, that King Silby was a famous Man, & I dare say his Soldiers had larger Heads than ordinary, or else a common Hatful apiece w^d. not have done ye Business; 'tis very true S^r. answer'd Both my new Acquaintance at once; so with a hearty Laugh on both Sides we took our Leaves of one another: & as I rode along, I c^d. not but wonder at ye Ignorance & Simplicity of the Greater part of our Species, who so easily credit whatever is told 'em as Truth.

We might reach different conclusions about the episode, or at least wish that Woodward had asked some additional questions. Where did the countrymen get their information? How widely shared was their belief that Silbury Hill is an enormous burial mound? What was the meaning of their laughter? Could it have been that they laughed because Woodward had been credulous enough to believe that they believed the story they had told him? Without the independent testimony of the countrymen the encounter remains frustratingly (and typically) inconclusive, though Woodward's own condescension at least is abundantly clear.[37]

These episodes from Woodward's letters illustrate some of the problems of mediation which bedevil the historical study of popular culture. It is with good reason that Peter Burke's description of early modern popular culture as 'an elusive quarry' has become a catchphrase among those working in the field. Burke gives a full account of the problems of method involved in his project and he stresses that popular culture is for the most part mediated by learned commentators like Woodward. Nevertheless, he continues to believe that 'we can find out a good deal about the popular culture of this period by more or less indirect means'.[38] Other commentators are more sceptical. Bob Scribner finds that, compared with other forms of historical enquiry, the methodological difficulties inherent in the mediation of popular culture are almost intractable. He warns that, although 'We may recognise that all sources distort, and attempt to make allowance for it . . . we must also ask whether there are unacceptable levels of distortion which defy making allowance, where there is so much "noise" that it will drown out any "popular" voice.'[39]

---

[37] Centre for Kentish Studies, U771 C7/107 (2 Sept. 1758), C7/162 (24 Oct. 1761), C7/111 (30 Dec. 1758), C7/102 (15 Apr. 1758), C7/39 (9 Nov. 1754).

[38] Burke, *Popular Culture*, 65.

[39] Bob Scribner, 'Is a History of Popular Culture Possible?', *History of European Ideas*, 10 (1989), 177.

Of course, our own project, which presents a selection of documents illustrating what has come to be known as 'popular culture' in the eighteenth century, must be especially alive to these difficulties. As we have seen, much of the written record of popular culture in the period originates not 'within' that culture but 'outside' it. It is represented, whether it be with approval, condescension, or hostility, from the perspective of the polite. In that sense, the voice of the 'popular' is rarely, if ever, immediately accessible: it is typically encountered in organs of official discourse and report, or disseminated in publications addressed to a predominantly polite audience. Tim Harris's suggestion that 'since the sources tell us about the interaction of elite and popular culture, maybe we should make the nature of that interaction the focus of our study' therefore has a good deal to recommend it.[40] At the same time, it seems important not to be drawn into conceiving of popular culture within too static a framework, as an irreducible remnant or version of pastoral which has escaped articulation and the forces of change. It might be more productive to think in terms of a process of cultural negotiation between the popular and the polite in which the meaning of those terms is constantly in play. After all, 'politeness' itself was neither a simple nor a stable category in the eighteenth century. Some of those who valued it most were least secure in their possession of it. It was not exclusively the property of those whom we label, perhaps too readily, 'the polite'. Lawrence Klein has shown the importance of ideas of politeness for the social identities of the 'plebes' (by which, however, he means the urban middling sort rather than the labouring poor).[41] Codes of politeness, inculcated by means of conduct manuals, provided shopkeepers and servants with a 'cultural literacy' which facilitated their dealings with social superiors. But this non-elite politeness was not just crudely imitative or merely an abject sign of dependency. The skills of politeness were fashioned in the everyday acts of self promotion, emulation, and bargaining which made up commercial life itself. Politeness may also have offered an empowering model for those who wished to challenge the elite monopoly on political power without adopting the unruly ethos of less respectable forms of radicalism.

The methodological difficulty of prising the polite away from the popular can in this sense be historically instructive. What came to be called polite culture in the eighteenth century established itself by fending off or significantly refining popular forms and by instituting new kinds of distinction when the popular seemed to press too close. A familiarity with popular genres is everywhere apparent in the canonical writers of the first half of the century. Augustan satirists

---

[40] Harris, *Popular Culture in England*, 10.
[41] Lawrence Klein, 'Politeness for Plebes: Consumption and Social Identity in Early Eighteenth-Century England', in Ann Bermingham and John Brewer (eds.), *The Consumption of Culture 1600–1800: Image, Object, Text* (1995), 362–82.

delighted in the ironic and unpredictable effects which could be forced out of collisions between the high and low. Swift, for example, burlesqued one of the most widely disseminated of all printed items, the almanac (see Chapter 4), exploited the genre of the last dying speech of the condemned criminal (see Chapter 5), and mimicked the demotic vocabulary of forms of street literature such as ballads and hawkers' cries.[42] This is not to say that popular culture as such is the primary satirical target of these texts. Indeed, in one sense, as Pat Rogers has argued, 'high' culture in this period pays a backhanded tribute to its 'lower-class cousin' by tapping its energies and borrowing its devices. The chosen victims of Pope's Grub Street satire the *Dunciad* are not so much the unlettered as the popularizers of culture who, in Rogers's words, 'straddle the world of fashion and the alleys of Smithfield, who unite high life and low art' and thereby degrade the standards of literature.[43] It is no accident, then, that distaste for popular culture is most keenly expressed in the literary forms such as novels, periodicals, and criminal biographies which were considered to be closest to it. The author (possibly Defoe) of the *True and Genuine Account of the Life and Actions of the late Jonathan Wild* (1725) quite elegantly acknowledges that he has foreseen his work's commercial potential (its acceptability to the world, as he puts it), but immediately distances it from those rival efforts (with which it might all too easily be identified) produced by 'our Hackney *Grub-street* Writers, upon the old Pick-pocket Principle of Publishing any Thing to get a Penny'.[44] This rejection of what might be thought 'low' or 'vulgar' becomes all the more important at this time as the producers of polite culture try to disengage a desirable property of popularity (the commercially rewarding appeal to a large, unknowable audience) from an undesirable one (a pandering to vulgar tastes and an accessibility to those with no special qualification).

These tensions are well illustrated by a remark which Frances Burney made shortly after the publication of *Evelina*, her first, and highly successful novel:

I have an exceeding odd sensation when I consider that it is now in the power of *any* and *every* body to read what I so carefully hoarded even from my best friends, till this last month or two,—and that a work which was so lately lodged, in all privacy in my bureau, may now be seen by every butcher and baker, cobler and tinker, throughout the three Kingdoms, for the small tribute of three pence.[45]

---

[42] See his *Bickerstaff Papers* and *The Last Speech and Dying Words of Ebenezer Elliston*, in *The Prose Works of Jonathan Swift*, ed. Herbert Davis, 14 vols. (1939–68), ii. 139–70 and ix. 37–41; *Verses made for Women who cry Apples, &c.*, in *The Poems of Jonathan Swift*, ed. Harold Williams, 3 vols. (Oxford, 1937), iii. 951–3.

[43] Rogers, *Literature and Popular Culture*, 30.

[44] *The True and Genuine Account of the Life and Actions of the late Jonathan Wild* (1725), p. v.

[45] *The Early Diary of Frances Burney, 1768–1778*, ed. Annie Raine Ellis, 2 vols. (1907), ii. 215.

The 'small tribute' which Burney imagines these plebeian readers forking out would not have been nearly enough to *buy* the three volumes of *Evelina* when the novel was published in 1778. In the 1770s bound volumes of novels usually cost 3*s*. each, with paper-covered volumes priced at 2*s*. 6*d*. More realistically, Burney means that her novel, with its merciless ridicule of shopkeeper vulgarity, will reach an unknown (and, she clearly fears, unrefined) public through the expanding network of circulating libraries. Even so, her comments must be viewed with some caution. Circulating libraries, sometimes run from small provincial bookshops, certainly increased the readership for fiction in the second half of the eighteenth century, but in general subscriptions seem to have been far from cheap.[46] As we have seen, there is evidence that some servants found it within their means to borrow volumes of *Clarissa* from small provincial circulating libraries, but remarks like Burney's probably exaggerate the extent to which these new forms of distribution brought such books within the orbit of a readership below the middling sort. Nevertheless, such expressions of alarm are surely revealing in their own way. They point to the shifting nature of cultural boundaries in the eighteenth century when relations between the popular and the polite were negotiable and, therefore, constantly being redrawn.

Recent work has done much to show how this process of negotiation defined and reconstituted the sphere of high culture in the eighteenth century in the face of increasing participation by the middling ranks in the discussion and marketing of art.[47] But much of the best and most challenging specialist work on popular culture deals either with the period before 1700 or with the rather different cultural scene after 1790. In the chapters which follow we have chosen to focus on what is sometimes known as the 'short' eighteenth century, spanning the period between 1700 and 1780. For long regarded as a historiographical backwater, in the last two decades this period has been at the centre of vigorous and sometimes heated debate among historians (see 'References and Further Reading', 3, below). A key area of dispute is the extent to which eighteenth-century England can be characterized as a 'commercial' society, driven by the skills and appetites of an increasingly prosperous and self-confident middle class. An important strand of historical writing about the period (best represented, perhaps, by the work of Paul Langford and John Brewer) explores, and largely confirms, the self-image of the English as 'a polite and commercial

---

[46] See James Raven, *Judging New Wealth: Popular Publishing and Responses to Commerce in England, 1750–1800* (Oxford, 1992), 51; id., 'From Promotion to Proscription: Arrangements for Reading and Eighteenth-Century Libraries', in Raven, Small, and Tadmor, *The Practice and Representation of Reading*, 175–201.

[47] See David Solkin, *Painting for Money: The Visual Arts and the Public Sphere in Eighteenth-Century England* (New Haven, 1993); John Brewer, *The Pleasures of the Imagination: English Culture in the Eighteenth Century* (1997).

people'. According to this view, 'a commercial middle class' was the most dynamic group in society and a major beneficiary of a period of economic expansion which raised disposable incomes and thereby created a growing market for household goods and for an impressive range of leisure and luxury items. For some these changes in patterns of consumption were so profound and so novel as to bring into being a new kind of society marked by a decisive shift in the conditions of material life. These developments, it is argued, had a transformative effect on the social identities and cultural values of the middling sort. In short, the period witnessed 'the birth of a consumer society' which was more individualistic, more secular in its outlook, and more mobile than the world it had left behind. The socially unifying influences of religious allegiance, the vocabulary of deference, and the rule of custom declined as those with money to spend came to see themselves, and those whose manners they wished to emulate, above all as participants in a market for worldly services and goods. The driving forces (if not quite the heroes) of this newly commercialized world were entrepreneurs like Jonathan Tyers, the proprietor of Vauxhall, who put the musical, pastoral, and culinary entertainments of the pleasure garden within reach of anyone with the ability to pay. Indeed, if a single image could illustrate this interpretation of eighteenth-century society it might be that of Vauxhall Gardens, situated on the outskirts of the capital city, patronized by a socially mixed audience of primarily urban pleasure-seekers whose entrance fee of 1s. bought them the opportunity to engage in the polite but competitive arts of Georgian self-fashioning.

This version of eighteenth-century social history has not gone unchallenged. Jonathan Clark finds in the thesis of commercialization all the errors of what has been called 'present-minded' history: a way of understanding the past as an anticipation of the present which misreads the eighteenth century as 'essentially modern' and consequently neglects the social and clerical elites whose 'Anglican', 'aristocratic', and 'monarchical' view of the world dominated and unified Georgian England.[48] Equally hostile, though quite different in substance, is E. P. Thompson's bi-polar social model, which divides culture into patrician and plebeian spheres of influence, denies the middling ranks a leading role, and focuses primarily on rural living. Thompson sees plebeian culture in the eighteenth century as articulate, assertive, and 'robust', but also as defensive, reactive, and even conservative. What it reacted against were the forces of change which extended the laws of the market into rural social relations and threatened a culture governed by custom. Ordinary villagers, preoccupied by their struggle to secure the means of subsistence, 'might have been surprised to learn that they belonged to a "consumer society"' he comments sardonically.[49] In fact, much of

---

[48] Clark, *English Society 1688–1832* (Cambridge, 1985), 7.
[49] Thompson, *Customs in Common* (1991), 22.

the historical work on commercialization deals primarily with its impact on middling and fashionable society, leaving unexplored the changes it may have made to the material circumstances—let alone the self-perceptions—of those below that level. A recent study of pauper inventories finds a surprisingly wide range of domestic goods in the homes of the labouring poor by the end of the eighteenth century, but stresses that the extent to which they 'had bought into "the culture of consumerism" either mentally or literally remains unclear'.[50]

These debates are of importance to our own selection because they suggest alternative ways of conceiving popular culture's interaction with social and economic change. According to one view, accounts of popular culture have characteristically distorted their object of study. Because they are founded on the myth of 'a fall from a society that was "traditional", customary, organic and precapitalist to one that was modern, individualistic, commercial and capitalist', they are predisposed to resist the idea that commercialization could have been anything other than a baneful influence.[51] On the contrary, it is argued, eighteenth-century popular culture was overwhelmingly a beneficiary of change: the development of commercial society enriched rather than destroyed it, creating new possibilities for leisure and a wider audience for the pleasures of the imagination, while allowing many of the existing cultural institutions (fairs and alehouses, for example) to adapt and indeed flourish. One response to these disagreements would be to decline to accept the oppositions in which they are so often couched. We might conjecture that the effects of commercialization could be destructive or liberating, that popular identities could typically be shaped by an ethos of consumption or by an ethos of custom depending on where (country or city?) or when (1710 or 1770?) one looks. Let us then see for the final time what the example of East Hendred can tell us. How keenly were the forces which changed popular culture in the eighteenth century felt in Woodward's rural parish? How closely integrated into national networks of information were his ordinary parishioners and how responsive were they to great events?

East Hendred could in no sense be described as a 'closed' culture, but Woodward's letters show that its social life was in large part shaped by local and customary forms. Relationships within the rectory, and between the rectory and the parish at large, were confirmed by his household's very own festive calendar. Woodward's Christmas celebrations, for example, always began on 28 December because that was his wife's birthday. In 1753 he tells his uncle that 'Three of yᵉ Principal farmers & their Wives' had been invited 'to eat minc'd Pie, & play

[50] Peter King, 'Pauper Inventories and the Material Lives of the Poor in the Eighteenth and Early Nineteenth Centuries', in Tim Hitchcock, Peter King, and Pamela Sharpe (eds.), *Chronicling Poverty: The Voices and Strategies of the English Poor, 1640–1840* (1997), 183.

[51] J. M. Golby and A. W. Purdue, *The Civilisation of the Crowd: Popular Culture in England 1750–1900* (1984), 11.

at cards' at the rectory on that day, and reports that their visit will be returned later in the season. On New Year's Day he held what he called his 'Grand Rout', clearly an occasion for unifying the household, 'when y[e] lower part of y[e] House is to be well season'd with Tobacco'. This cluster of festivities was regularly brought to a close on 17 January (Twelfth Day, according to the old calendar) by a visit to a neighbouring archdeacon and his wife whose wedding anniversary fell on that day. The Woodwards repaid the favour each year on 16 July, that being their own wedding anniversary. These last two events, positioned neatly at either end of the year, were 'Two grand festivals in y[e] Hendred Calendar', as Woodward puts it good-humouredly. As he well knew, the parish calendar was much more socially inclusive than this. A key local event, which centred on the church but extended into many secular aspects of village life, was the church's annual festival of commemoration which was celebrated in early May. Eighteenth-century clergymen often condemned these feasts, or 'wakes' as they were often known, as occasions for drunkenness and sexually loose behaviour. Woodward notes the popularity of Hendred feast among 'y[e] young Folks', but seems unperturbed by the prospect that 'y[e] greatest part of [the] Week will be Dedicated to Sports & Jollity'.[52]

In some respects, then, Hendred culture seems to have been characteristically local, self-contained, and parish-centred. When Richard Gough completed a history of the Shropshire village of Myddle in 1702 he presented it in the form of a history of the pews in his parish church and the families who occupied them.[53] In Hendred too the influence of the parish, as a focus of identification and belonging, remained strong. In a letter of April 1753 Woodward describes how after an absence of three weeks he proceeded through the village in his chaise 'amidst y[e] Bows & Court'sies of y[e] Parish, & y[e] Ringing of y[e] Bells, to welcome my Return'. Even allowing for the possibility of self-congratulation, the role of the spiritual head of the parish as a force of social cohesion seems clear. But if Hendred was parish-centred, it was not necessarily an inward-looking community. Its communications with important towns and cities—Oxford, Abingdon, Reading, Salisbury, London—were extensive and improving: Woodward notes the benefits brought by the completion in 1760 of a new turnpike road to Oxford. These roads were also the conduits of an expanding print culture. Books, as we have seen, were not exactly plentiful in Hendred, but Woodward was a sub-

[52] Centre for Kentish Studies, U771 C7/21 (29 Dec. 1753), C7/31 (13 July 1754), C7/103 (6 May 1758).

[53] Richard Gough, *The History of Myddle*, ed. David Hey (Harmondsworth, 1981). On the continuing importance of parish identity, see D. M. Palliser, 'Introduction: The Parish in Perspective', in S. J. Wright (ed.), *Parish, Church and People: Local Studies in Lay Religion 1350–1750* (1988), 5–28; John Walsh and Stephen Taylor, 'Introduction: The Church and Anglicanism in the "Long" Eighteenth Century', in John Walsh, Colin Haydon, and Stephen Taylor (eds.), *The Church of England c.1689–c.1833* (Cambridge, 1993), 1–64.

scriber to the *Critical Review*, one of the first periodicals to offer an extensive account of recent publications, and he received newspapers through the postal system three times a week. Furthermore, he acted as a kind of informal local distribution point, circulating his newspapers among a group of his parishioners. His letters make it clear that this had become a regular arrangement. 'We had yᵉ News by yᵉ Sunday's Post', he wrote in September 1758, shortly after the British victory at Louisburg, 'and as our Chief Politicians are always impatient for News

2. *The Blacksmith lets his Iron grow cold attending to the Taylor's News* (1772). The title alludes to Shakespeare, *King John*, IV. ii. 193–5. The portrait on the wall (possibly of John Wilkes) and the printed newspaper indicate the contemporary interest. © The British Museum

every Post-Night, I immediately sent it to 'em at ye Blacksmith's hard by, where the Committee generally sitts for ye Dispatch of Business'. We hear more about the membership of this news-hungry 'Committee' in other letters. In December 1757 Woodward tells his uncle that he has sent the news of a recent Prussian victory to the forge where 'ye Politicians of ye Village'—the blacksmith, a wheelwright, an exciseman, and 'two or three Farmers'—'assemble & debate Matters of ye greatest Importance to ye Nation'. Despite Woodward's condescension, the members of 'this Illustrious Junto', as he calls it, were in East Hendred terms clearly men of influence. They received the news from Woodward and then played a pivotal role in deciding how the village should respond to events. Victories and coronations may have been celebrated according to traditional forms—bonfires, bells, the roasting of sheep, and the firing of guns—but the newspaper press was changing the ways in which such events were made public and understood.[54]

We make no apology for drawing so extensively on newspaper reports in the selections which follow. As recent studies have shown (see 'References and Further Reading', 2, below), the miscellaneous quality of the newspaper's contents and the extent of its social reach made it an exceptionally important instrument for cultural transmission and interaction. If the 'news' itself was not exactly an eighteenth-century invention—printed newsbooks and handwritten newsletters had been in circulation from the 1620s—it was in the eighteenth century that the newspaper began to take on many of its familiar functions and forms. The growth of the newspaper press (and indeed of eighteenth-century print culture in general) is usually dated from the lapsing of the Licensing Act, which strictly regulated the right to print and provided for pre-publication censorship, in 1695. A large number of newspapers, some of them very short-lived, were founded in the course of the century. The first daily paper, the *Daily Courant*, was published in 1702, and at about the same time the first provincial papers began to appear. The number of titles fluctuated significantly, but in the mid-1740s, to give one example, it appears that there were around forty provincial weeklies and a total of eighteen London newspapers, issued in daily, tri-weekly, or weekly form. Periodic increases in stamp duty, which raised the price of newspapers from 2d. in 1725 to 6d. by 1797, may have significantly depressed circulation. In the course of the century the newspaper became the single most important medium for the circulation of information and opinion. From the outset, foreign news figured prominently in its columns, alongside a variety of domestic items: activities at court and in the fashionable world, parliamentary affairs, crime, promotions, bankruptcies, and the price of bread. Poems, essays, and letters submitted by

---

[54]   Centre for Kentish Studies, U771 C7/8 (Apr. 1753), C7/140 (30 Aug. 1760: turnpike road), C7/75 (20 Oct. 1756: newspapers), C7/107 (2 Sept. 1758), C7/97 (3 Dec. 1757).

readers were frequently printed, making the newspaper an important forum for public debate. Advertisements for books, schools, recreational events, medicines, domestic and luxury goods, and services were an important source of revenue and filled an increasing proportion of newspaper space as the century progressed. Christine Ferdinand's research into the *Salisbury Journal* reveals an increase in the number of advertisements from an annual average of about 300 in the 1730s to nearly 2,500 in the 1760s, with advertisements for books, real estate, and medicines making up half or more of the total each year.[55]

The newspapers which Woodward read, and then passed on to the committee at the forge, seem to have been London tri-weeklies. He received them through the postal service which brought London newspapers within the reach of readers throughout the country; in the capital itself they could be acquired from booksellers, coffee-houses, and hawkers. East Hendred would also have fallen within the distribution networks of provincial weeklies such as *Jackson's Oxford Journal*, the *Reading Mercury and Oxford Gazette*, and the *Salisbury Journal*, whose proprietors employed newsmen for carriage to rural areas and appointed agents in towns which came within their spheres of influence. These could be surprisingly extensive: in 1750 the printer of the *Salisbury Journal* claimed that his paper was *'being circulated Weekly in great Numbers, throughout the Counties of* Hants, Wilts, *and* Dorset, *with Parts of* Berks, Gloucester, *and* Somerset, *and the Isles of* Wight, Purbeck, Jersey, *and* Guernsey'.[56] The extent of the social circulation of newspapers in the eighteenth century is more difficult to assess. Much polite comment is decidedly hostile towards the newspaper, which it derides as a vulgar form read by the socially low. The newspaper, in George Crabbe's poem of that name (1785), is a poisoner of social virtue, an enemy of literature, and a leveller of taste:

> To you all readers turn, and they can look
> Pleas'd on a paper, who abhor a book;
> Those who ne'er deign'd their Bible to peruse,
> Would think it hard to be deny'd their News;
> Sinners and saints, the wisest with the weak,
> Here mingle tastes, and one amusement seek . . .
>
> (ll. 227–32)[57]

Among the humbler readers of newspapers Crabbe pictures the rural freeholder who leaves 'the little hut that makes him free' (l. 178) for a local alehouse where 'he delights the weekly News to con, | And mingle comments as he blunders on'

[55] Ferdinand, *Benjamin Collins and the Provincial Newspaper Trade in the Eighteenth Century* (Oxford, 1997), 193. [56] Ibid. 106.
[57] Text from George Crabbe, *The Complete Poetical Works*, 3 vols., ed. Norma Dalrymple-Champney and Arthur Pollard (Oxford, 1988), i. 177–96.

(ll. 183–4). The supposed political susceptibilities of this class of reader made them the focus of contemporary attacks on newspapers. A frequent complaint was that newspapers were dangerously irresponsible in bringing political information (especially in the form of reports of parliamentary proceedings) to the notice of readers who were culturally unqualified to understand it. Addressing the Commons in 1738, Sir William Yonge predicted gloomily that 'you may soon expect to see your votes, your proceedings and your speeches printed and hawked about the streets'.[58] Arguing much the same case sixty years later, William Windham advised the House that

> the great mass of the readers of newspapers were not the most discerning class of society, nor was it to be expected they should be so, for the advertisements and other articles of which a newspaper was composed were often interesting chiefly to the lower orders of the community. They were for this very reason carried every where, read every where, by persons of very inferior capacities, and in common alehouses and places frequented chiefly by those who were least of all accustomed to reflection, to any great mental efforts.[59]

Recent discussions of the question of readership have suggested that we should treat such statements with caution. Speaking at a time of profound political crisis, Windham was no doubt seeking to alarm his audience, and his pronounced political conservatism may well have coloured his account. The social character of newspaper readers was almost certainly much more varied than Windham suggests and, as historians of the press have stressed, the newspaper would have appealed in particular to the interests and values of the middling sort of consumer. Nonetheless, as the example of East Hendred shows, the readership of newspapers could be socially quite broad. The rector passed his papers on to the leading village craftsmen, who may in turn have brought their contents to the attention of other parishioners, perhaps by reading them aloud. By such means, and through their availability at alehouses, coffee-houses, and other places of recreation, newspapers circulated more widely than the raw sales figures suggest. At the same time, the miscellaneous character of the newspaper made it peculiarly open to different forms of appropriation. The foreign news and reports of intrigue among the political elite may have implied a reader with specialist knowledge, yet readers with a diverse range of interests and literary skills could find it informative and entertaining in different ways (as, of course, they still do).

It seems probable, then, that, like the wider process of commercialization (of which it was in many ways a typical product), the newspaper had complex effects on popular culture. In one sense it was certainly an instrument of change. Its

---

[58] *The Parliamentary History of England*, ed. William Cobbett, 36 vols. (1806–20), x. 801.
[59] Ibid. xxxiv. 162.

advertisements stimulated new desires for goods and suggested opportunities for material and cultural self-improvement, its parliamentary reports gave readers a new sense of political agency, and its accounts of military campaigns in distant lands helped to create the consciousness of empire which we explore in our final chapter. Moreover, the newspaper's attitudes towards the customs, beliefs, and practices which made up what is sometimes called 'traditional' popular culture were often critical and reforming. As we show in Chapter 6, newspapers often saw themselves as agents of enlightenment and were quick to ridicule 'superstitions' such as the belief that the Glastonbury Thorn blossomed on Christmas Day. Yet, as another example from Glastonbury suggests, the columns of the newspaper could also be used to disseminate and repackage traditional beliefs. The legend that a spring of water near Glastonbury Tor commemorated Joseph of Arimathea's burial of the Holy Grail there was given new life in 1751 when a local man claimed to have been miraculously cured of his ailments by drinking the Glastonbury waters on seven successive Sundays. While some newspaper reports poured scorn on the story, others printed testimonials which lent support to the original claim. Replying to a critical account which appeared in the *Whitehall Evening Post*, Henry Fielding wrote a long letter to the *General Advertizer* in defence of the waters. It seems clear that Fielding, a Glastonbury man by birth, genuinely believed that the waters had extraordinary virtues. It is equally clear that he saw they had a potential for profit. He ensured that the Universal Register Office, a thoroughly modern enterprise which he had founded with his half-brother in order to advance commercial interests through the circulation of information, should enjoy the right to supply Londoners with the waters at a charge of 'fourteen pence a bottle, two-pence back when the bottle was returned'.[60]

Newspapers, then, could sell tradition, just as they could sell horses, hats, and almanacs. They could promote customary events such as fairs by publicizing their latest attractions. Reports of local beliefs could be conveyed nationwide by improved systems of information, leaving neither untouched by the process. Popular culture in the eighteenth century was not static, then, nor, as has sometimes been implied, was it necessarily the victim of economic and technological change. Yet the contrary view, that popular culture was characteristically a participant in, and beneficiary of, change must itself be tested against the record of local experiences and meanings. Woodward's parishioners may indeed have begun to think of themselves as consumers, but without necessarily relinquishing existing identities and attachments. Their enthusiastic celebrations of victories over the French show that it was important to them to share in a sense of

[60] M. C. Battestin, 'Fielding and the Glastonbury Waters', *Yearbook of English Studies* (1980), 205. For a valuable discussion of the Universal Register Office, see Miles Ogborn, *Spaces of Modernity: London's Geographies 1680–1780* (New York, 1998), 201–30.

national belonging. No doubt they also identified themselves with their work-places in the village and with their occupations as maidservants, blacksmiths, wheelwrights, and the like. Not least, perhaps, when they worshipped in Woodward's church, or dressed up each May for the annual feast, they continued to think of themselves as members of Hendred parish. Our selection shows some of the ways in which these identities remain consistent in this period of considerable cultural change. We hope that it also gives a sense of that change, and in particular of the framing of new distinctions between the popular and the polite.

REFERENCES AND FURTHER READING

Unless otherwise stated, London is the place of publication.

1. General and Period Studies

Peter Burke's *Popular Culture in Early Modern Europe*, rev. edn. (Aldershot, 1994) is the best starting-point for work in the field. Issues raised by his account are helpfully discussed in two recent period studies: Tim Harris (ed.), *Popular Culture in England, c.1500–1850* (1995) and Barry Reay, *Popular Cultures in England 1550–1750* (1998). J. M. Golby and A. W. Purdue, *The Civilisation of the Crowd: Popular Culture in England 1750–1900* (1984) offers a critique of the supposed 'conservatism' of much historical work on popular culture. On questions of method and approach see in particular Stuart Hall, 'Notes on Deconstructing the Popular', in Raphael Samuel (ed.), *People's History and Socialist Theory* (1981), 227–40; Bob Scribner, 'Is a History of Popular Culture Possible?', *History of European Ideas*, 10 (1989), 175–91; and Morag Shiach, *Discourse on Popular Culture: Class, Gender and History in Cultural Analysis, 1730 to the Present* (Cambridge, 1989). For the idea of appropriation which informs much current debate see especially Roger Chartier, 'Culture as Appropriation: Popular Cultural Uses in Early Modern France', in S. Kaplan (ed.), *Understanding Popular Culture: Europe from the Middle Ages to the Nineteenth Century* (Berlin, 1984), 229–53, and id., *The Cultural Uses of Print in Early Modern France* (Princeton, NJ, 1987). The importance of custom in eighteenth-century popular culture is considered in R. W. Malcolmson, *Popular Recreations in English Society, 1700–1850* (Cambridge, 1973); Bob Bushaway, *By Rite: Custom, Ceremony and Community in England 1700–1880* (1982); and E. P. Thompson, *Customs in Common* (1991). Among studies which deal largely with periods outside the eighteenth century but raise pertinent issues, see in particular Barry Reay (ed.), *Popular Culture in Seventeenth-Century England* (1985), and David Vincent, *Literacy and Popular Culture: England 1750–1914* (Cambridge, 1989).

2. Literature and Popular Culture

Relations between the 'high' and 'low' in eighteenth-century literature and art are discussed in Pat Rogers, *Literature and Popular Culture in Eighteenth-Century England*

(Brighton, 1985), and in Ronald Paulson, *Popular and Polite Art in the Age of Hogarth and Fielding* (Notre Dame, Ind., 1979). General and thematic surveys which contain relevant material include Victor Neuburg, *Popular Literature: A History and Guide* (Harmondsworth, 1977); id., *Popular Education in Eighteenth-Century England* (1971); and Leslie Shepherd, *The History of Street Literature* (Newton Abbot, 1977). On conditions of writing, publishing, and reading see Pat Rogers, *Grub Street: Studies in a Subculture* (1972); Isobel Rivers (ed.), *Books and their Readers in Eighteenth-Century England* (Leicester, 1982); James Raven, *Judging New Wealth: Popular Publishing and Responses to Commerce in England, 1750–1800* (Oxford, 1992); and James Raven, Helen Small, and Naomi Tadmor (eds.), *The Practice and Representation of Reading in England* (Cambridge, 1996). Philip Pinkus, *Grub Street Stripped Bare* (1968) is a full and entertaining selection of eighteenth-century texts. Some of the best work on popular forms covers earlier or later periods but is nonetheless of relevance to the eighteenth century: see especially Margaret Spufford, *Small Books and Pleasant Histories: Popular Fiction and its Readership in Seventeenth-Century England* (Cambridge, 1981); George Deacon, *John Clare and the Folk Tradition* (1983); and Tessa Watt, *Cheap Print and Popular Piety 1550–1640* (Cambridge, 1991). John Ashton (ed.), *Chap-Books of the Eighteenth Century* (1882; repr. Skoob Books, n.d.), prints a number of Dicey texts and title-pages; see also Susan Pedersen, 'Hannah More Meets Simple Simon: Tracts, Chapbooks, and Popular Culture in Late Eighteenth-Century England', *Journal of British Studies*, 25 (1986), 84–113, and Michael Harris, 'A Few Shillings for Small Books: The Experiences of a Flying Stationer in the Eighteenth Century', in Michael Harris and Robin Myers (eds.), *Spreading the Word: The Distribution Networks of Print 1550–1850* (Winchester, 1990), 83–108. There are a number of collections of street ballads which include eighteenth-century material: among the more recent are John Holloway and Joan Black (eds.), *Later English Broadside Ballads*, 2 vols. (1975, 1979); Roy Palmer, *A Ballad History of England: From 1588 to the Present Day* (1979); and id., *The Sound of History: Songs and Social Comment* (Oxford, 1988). The eighteenth-century newspaper has received a good deal of scholarly attention: Bob Harris, *Politics and the Rise of the Press: Britain and France, 1620–1800* (1996) is an excellent introduction to the newspaper's readership and cultural impact. Jeremy Black presents a detailed survey in *The English Press in the Eighteenth Century* (1987); accounts of the provincial press are given in G. A. Cranfield, *The Development of the Provincial Newspaper, 1700–1760* (Cambridge, 1962) and R. M. Wiles, *Freshest Advices: Early Provincial Newspapers in England* (Columbia, Oh., 1965). There is a detailed account of the *Salisbury Journal* in Christine Ferdinand, *Benjamin Collins and the Provincial Newspaper Trade in the Eighteenth Century* (Oxford, 1997). For specialist studies of the London press see Michael Harris, *London Newspapers in the Age of Walpole: A Study in the Origins of the Modern English Press* (1987), and Bob Harris, *A Patriot Press: National Politics and the London Press in the 1740s* (Oxford, 1993). On visual culture in the eighteenth century see especially John Brewer, *The Common People and Politics 1750–1790s* (Cambridge, 1986) and Sheila O'Connell, *The Popular Print in England 1550–1850* (1999).

3. Historical Debate

Three leading contributions to a vast literature make a fascinating exercise in contrasts: J. C. D. Clark, *English Society 1688–1832: Ideology, Social Structure and Political Practice During the Ancien Regime* (Cambridge, 1985); Paul Langford, *A Polite and Commercial People: England 1727–1783* (Oxford, 1989); and E. P. Thompson, *Customs in Common* (1991). Review articles offer a helpful introduction to the historiographical arguments: see, for example, J. C. D. Clark, 'Eighteenth-Century Social History', *Historical Journal*, 27 (1984), 733–88; Linda Colley, 'The Politics of Eighteenth-Century British History', *Journal of British Studies*, 25 (1986), 359–79; Frank O'Gorman, 'The Recent Historiography of the Hanoverian Regime', *Historical Journal*, 29 (1986), 1005–20; Joanna Innes, 'Jonathan Clark, Social History and England's "Ancien Regime"', *Past & Present*, 115 (1987), 165–200; J. C. D. Clark, 'On Hitting the Buffers: The Historiography of England's Ancien Regime', *Past & Present*, 117 (1988), 195–207; Roy Porter, 'English Society in the Eighteenth Century Revisited', in Jeremy Black (ed.), *British Politics and Society from Walpole to Pitt* (1990), 29–52; W. A. Speck, 'Will the Real Eighteenth Century Stand Up?', *Historical Journal*, 34 (1991), 203–6; Peter King, 'Edward Thompson's Contribution to Eighteenth-Century Studies: The Patrician-Plebeian Model Re-examined', *Social History*, 21 (1996), 215–28.

A major stimulus to the debate about the 'commercialization' of eighteenth-century society was given by Neil McKendrick, John Brewer, and J. H. Plumb, *The Birth of a Consumer Society: The Commercialization of Eighteenth-Century England* (1982). Two later collections develop these arguments from a number of perspectives, some of them revisionist or critical: John Brewer and Roy Porter (eds.), *Consumption and the World of Goods* (1993), and Ann Bermingham and John Brewer (eds.), *The Consumption of Culture 1600–1800: Image, Object, Text* (1995). The middling sort, whose relation to popular culture is both important and problematic, have received a good deal of recent attention: see, for example, J. Barry and C. Brooks (eds.), *The Middling Sort of People: Culture, Society and Politics in England, 1550–1800* (1994), and Margaret Hunt, *The Middling Sort: Commerce, Gender, and the Family in England 1680–1780* (Berkeley and Los Angeles, Calif., 1996). For a recent attempt 'to get as close as possible to the words and worlds of the poor' in the period covered by our selection see Tim Hitchcock, Peter King, and Pamela Sharpe (eds.), *Chronicling Poverty: The Voices and Strategies of the English Poor, 1640–1840* (1997).

USING THE SELECTION

As we have seen, the meanings and value of the concept of 'popular culture' have been vigorously debated by historians and cultural theorists. Yet the textual sources from which such arguments and enquiries might be developed are, for the eighteenth century, largely inaccessible to the majority of readers. The purpose of our selection is to address this need by presenting an annotated sequence of documents of the period illustrating what has come to be known as 'popular culture'. We hope that it exemplifies both the difficulties of using that category and its practical and intellectual advantages.

Our approach to organizing this material is unusual and calls for some explanation. Rather than attempting to present the selections along thematic lines (under such headings as 'work', 'leisure', 'the family', 'religion', and so on), we have chosen to focus on *occasions*, sequences of events that illustrate, and bring to life, such themes. After our opening selection of eighteenth-century views of popular culture each chapter offers a case-study, and consequently a more or less continuous narrative which we hope will make sense in its own terms. One function of these occasions is to focus and test out the models and explanations of popular culture which have been discussed in our introduction. Naturally, the ways in which we have chosen to select and present these episodes bear the imprint of our own thinking. Nonetheless, we believe that the material illustrates the fluidity and complexity of cultural interactions in the eighteenth century and can support a variety of alternative interpretations and conclusions. In annotating this material our aim has been to steer a middle course, offering enough information in our introductions, shorter prefaces, and notes to make the episodes accessible without overwhelming them with editorial comment. Spelling has not been modernized but some of the obscurer occurrences have been glossed. We have generally avoided the use of the term *sic*, which would soon have become intrusive. Unless otherwise stated, the dates given are as in our original texts. Until the reform of the calendar in 1752 (our topic in Chapter 6) the year officially began on 25 March. In each chapter we give a bibliography of key secondary sources and suggestions for further reading which we hope will assist those who wish to develop particular interests beyond the material selected here. The chapters are arranged in roughly chronological order. We begin at the start of the century with one of the half-bemused descriptions of the non-polite classes which fill Ned Ward's trips to the Town and end, seventy years later, with the troubled reflections of a visiting native American whose 'trips' have bridged continents and cultures.

1

EIGHTEENTH-CENTURY VIEWS OF POPULAR CULTURE

THE Introduction discussed how appropriate our ideas about popular culture might be when applied to the eighteenth century, and noticed that collisions of the polite and the popular—the elegant and the vulgar—are characteristic of much 'high' culture of the earlier part of the period. The energies of some visual art (Hogarth, above all) and much literature (Pope's *Dunciad*, Gay's *The Beggar's Opera*, Fielding's fiction) derive from such collisions. But how did writers of the period attempt to document popular culture, and what did they call it when they found it? This chapter presents a sample of efforts to describe a culture below the polite world to which the writers themselves belonged.

There were many discussions of poverty and the poor in the eighteenth century, and these were often vividly argumentative or anxious. Most notoriously Mandeville, in *The Fable of the Bees*, but also writers like Henry Fielding and John Brown, argued about how the lives of the poor were improved or blighted by the growth of a commercial economy.[1] These writings, which we might call 'economic' or 'political', were certainly interested in the behaviour of the labouring classes. They do not, however, give any reader—of the time or now—a sense of the lives, customs, or pleasures of the poor, or of the proximity of the poor and the propertied. Nowhere is there a Mayhew for the eighteenth century. Yet there were ways in which the culture of the propertyless and uneducated was represented to polite readers, and some of these are epitomized below.

It seems natural to begin, as we have done, with an eighteenth-century sub-genre whose whole appeal lay in its supposed knowledge of 'low life', and of the odd encounters of 'high' and 'low': the 'Spy' books, of which the most famous and influential is Ned Ward's *The London Spy*. As Ward's title declares, this is a type of urban writing: the narrator has explored the streets and dubious resorts of the capital, and reports back on them as if he were a traveller to exotic, and perhaps dangerous, regions. Ward provides a guide to a city whose life was

---

[1] See Henry Fielding, *An Enquiry into the causes of the Late Increase of Robbers* (1751) and John Brown, *An Estimate of the Manners and Principles of the Times* (1757).

characterized by the mingling of the polite and the vulgar, the rich and the poor, where the narrator can move instantly from a description of Dryden's funeral in Westminster Abbey to 'Some passages of Hackney coachmen in quarrelling'. It is all described as a life that is intimately known to the author (though, one should note, not to the narrator). This sense of the urban writer as guide has its polite apotheosis as Addison and Steele's 'Mr Spectator', who purports to frequent the same coffee-houses that Ward visited, but does not linger in fairs and street markets like him. (See Chapter 3 for a further example of Ward's characteristic reportage, a description of Bartholomew Fair.)

The premise of *The London Spy*, as of many of the works it influenced, is that its narrator is a stranger to the urban alleyways. In the first part of Ward's account, a 'scholar' from the countryside tells us how, tiring of his reclusive pursuit of knowledge ('a fig for St Augustine and his doctrines, a fart for Virgil and his elegance, and a turd for Descartes and his philosophy'), he develops an 'itching inclination' to visit London. He arrives in 'our metropolis' with 'wonder and amazement' and encounters 'an old schoolfellow' who is already familiar with many of the mysteries of urban life. He walks the streets with this friend, who points out oddities and cures him of his innocent perplexities. Thus he is drawn to what he sees, but can remain distant from it. We might note that this allows the 'Spy' to be disgusted by or disdainful of what he observes. The extract below describing Rag Fair is not troubled by any sympathy for the poor. Indeed, throughout his writings Ward expresses a lively contempt for the follies and vices of the poor, even as he records them; he was later to write a long satirical poem, *Vulgus Britannicus*, which is mostly taken up with an attack on the political and religious enthusiasms of 'the Rabble'—'the Rude *Vulgi*'.

Ward's fiction of the ingenuous tourist relies on the reader's implicit trust that the author (as opposed to the narrator) is in fact well versed in the city's habits and peculiarities, especially those which offend against propriety. The idea of an innocent abroad in London is used in many 'guides' to the capital (and, we might note, is continually exploited in eighteenth-century novels). Tom Brown, who sometimes collaborated with Ward, employed the same fiction for his tour of London in *Amusements, Serious and Comical* (1.2). In this case, he took on 'the Genius of an *Indian* . . . who had never seen any thing like what he sees in *London*'. The last of the extracts (1.6) in the section on 'Urban Low Life', from the late eighteenth century, is still using the character of the wide-eyed visitor to London, though more decorously than *The London Spy*. It is taken from *The Complete Modern Spy, for the present Year, 1781*. This 'candid and minute review of the inhabitants of this immense metropolis, with a scrutiny of their customs, manners and passions', as its preface puts it, features an unworldly narrator who is conducted through London's alleys by 'Mr. Ambler', a denizen of the metropolis. Thus we are introduced to the city's 'Secret, Nocturnal, and Diurnal Transactions'. The title-page advertises the work as 'Exhibiting a great Variety of Scenes of Midnight Entertainment and curious Adventures in high, low, and middling Life, which are at this Period performed and carried on by the various inhabitants of London', and sounds more or less ironical when it adds to its enticing list of topics ('Gaming-Houses, Bagnios, and other Nunneries, Night-Houses, Jelly-Houses, Taverns . . .'), a promise to provide 'suitable Reflections to the Unwary'. The book is distinguished by some notably sentimental encounters with prostitutes, who tell their stories of cheated innocence to the appreciative narrator and his companion.

Other 'guides' purport to give cautionary descriptions of urban culture for the benefit of those unfamiliar with it. Into this category falls *The Town Spy: or, A View of London and Westminster . . . Written by a Foreigner* (1.3). The idea of instructing country folk on the town's wicked ways might have been merely a useful fiction. One thinks this when one reads, for example, in the preface to *The Country Spy; or, A Ramble thro' London* (not excerpted here), probably from the mid-eighteenth century, that it has been written by a countryman for fellow 'Country Men', 'to entertain them during the long and tedious Winter Nights, and to caution them against their being ensnared in the Traps and Follies that are artfully laid to catch the *Unwary*'. It is difficult not to recall the preface to Defoe's *Moll Flanders*, with its straight-faced recommendation of the sequence of Moll's 'Depredations upon Mankind' as 'so many warnings to honest People to beware of them, intimating to them by what Methods innocent People are drawn in, plunder'd and robb'd, and by Consequence how to avoid them';[2] or the prefatory claims of *The London Spy* that its readers might read it in order to 'learn the better to avoid those snares and practised subtleties which trepan many to their ruin'.

The frontispiece of *The Frauds of London Detected; or, a Warning Piece Against the Iniquitous Practices of the Metropolis* (1.5) shows an anxious countryman bidding farewell to his two children as they set off for London, and handing them each a copy of this very book, which 'will show | "The Paths where Vice and Ruin go"'. It extends the conceit of instructional and cautionary purposes avowed by earlier spy-guides to the capital and modernizes an old tradition of 'coney-catching' literature. It purports to give a 'just, true, and accurate Account of the many atrocious Artifices, Tricks, Seductions, Stratagems, Impositions and Deceptions, which are daily committed in and about *London* and *Westminster*'. There is an alphabetical catalogue of the tricks of various conmen, pimps, and thieves beginning with 'BAWDS'. We give an excerpt from this section, and from 'GAMBLERS', where one finds the characteristic mix of high and low cultures at the cock-fight, and 'LOTTERY OFFICE KEEPERS' (a small example of the copious lottery literature of the period). The work continues with chapters on Pimps, Pickpockets, Receivers of Stolen Goods,

---

[2] *Moll Flanders*, ed. David Blewett (Harmondsworth, 1989), 40.

Spungers, Sharpers, Swindlers, Setters (those who trick men into marrying 'heiresses' who have, in fact, no money, and then profit from the enforced articles of separation), Smugglers, Shoplifters, Trappers (who blackmail men who have once slept with a prostitute by claiming they are the fathers of their bastard children), Whores, Way-layers, Waggon-hunters (who 'lure and entice country maidens, on their arrival in London, to their houses of ill fame'), and finally 'JEW DEFAULTERS'.

All these descriptions of London 'low life' are, in fact, about the meetings and combinations of high and low. This is particularly true of *The Town Spy*, which is clearly influenced by Ned Ward. It tells us, for instance, about 'the Quality and their Servants at St *James's*', while a description of the peculiarities of London's lawyers is succeeded (topographically, as well as thematically) by the habits of 'the Mercers of *Ludgate Hill*'. Ward taught later writers that London's streets lead to incongruities and surprising parallels. His narrator goes through London parish by parish, remarking on the absurdities of all ranks. In a coffee-house, an aristocrat receives obsequious attention from his impecunious companion; at dinner with 'a *Shopkeeper* in this Parish' he observes the 'Grief' of a family whose beer-seller neighbours have appeared at church in finer clothes than them. In the parish of St Giles, the 'crafty *Projector*', extracting money for an imaginary investment scheme, works alongside the 'Ladies' from the 'Pleasure-houses', who ply their trade 'as publickly as the *Sollicitors* do their Clients at *Westminster*'. As in many a satire, the different classes are energetically parisitic upon each other, and the vocabularies of high and low mingle. As much as Gay or Fielding, the author of this guided tour enjoys elevated terms applied to grubby subjects. When we get to Newgate, for example, we are told: 'St. SEPULCHRES Parish is noted for a large *Monastery*, to which great Numbers resort daily, and live retired from the World, insomuch that every six Months they are forced to send away divers on their Pilgrimage to Parts beyond the Seas, to make room for other recluse Persons.'

The accounts of 'low life' from which we have taken extracts may be written with real knowledge of the city, but they are most notable for their satirical relish. Often the proportions of record and satire are impossible to decide. 'Low life' is a literary category as much as a social one. This is clearly the case with Thomas Legg's *Low-life: or one half of the world knows not how the other half live*, probably from the 1750s (1.4), a teeming study of the London streets in mid-century. It should be grist to any social historian's mill, though it has remained—as far as we know—in obscurity. The stylistic debts that it might owe to Brown's *Amusements* (1.2)—which itself owes something to the first of Juvenal's *Satires* and is an imitation of a French work (see below)—and the fact that *Low-life* has a structure that alludes to Hogarth's *Four Times of the Day* (there is an opening 'Address to the ingenious and ingenuous Mr. Hogarth'), might also warn off the historian and represent rather clearly the difficulties that we face with some of the most interesting accounts of popular culture from this period. How much of this is invented? (Several of the details in our extracts, however credible, can hardly have been *seen* by the implied observer.) Its receptiveness to the oddness, variety, and levelling proximities of London life is characteristic of writing of the period. And the work's very existence (it went through three editions) testifies to a kind of appetite amongst readers for pictures of low life—even if they were conventionally obliged to disapprove of what interested them.

The London of these pseudo-guidebooks, the 'spies', is full of thieves and crime. Indeed, it would sometimes seem that, inasmuch as educated readers of the period have a sense of there being a popular culture, they think of it in terms of criminality and licentiousness. The language of criminals is certainly one of the fascinations of writers on 'low life' in the eighteenth century (as it still is). In the early eighteenth century, not only were tales of crimes and criminals popular, but glossaries of the 'canting' speech of criminals were common we give some brief extracts from these: 2.1–2.3. Often lives and lexicons were combined. So, for instance, a representative criminal autobiography of 1708 *Memoirs of the Right Villainous John Hall* ('Penn'd from his Mouth some time before his Death'), begins with 'An Interpretation of the Several Qualities of Rogues'—a glossary of different kinds of thief.[3] Such argot does crop up in literature of the early eighteenth century, notably in some of Defoe's fiction and Gay's drama. Some of the criminal 'lives' of the period, and in particular dramatized versions of the exploits of criminals, exhibit this same fascination (see, for instance, the excerpt from *The Quaker's Opera* in Chapter 5).

It is significant that this interest in the vocabulary of 'canting' was embodied in one of the century's most peculiar and intriguing works of reference, Francis Grose's *Classical Dictionary of the Vulgar Tongue*, first published in 1785. In this work, the recording of the language of crime was made semi-respectable by an established antiquarian. Grose, a fellow of the Society of Antiquaries, had already published a miscellaneous collection of antiquarian observations, *The Antiquarian Repertory* (1775) and the first numbers of his *Antiquities of England and Wales* (1773–87), illustrated by himself (he was an accomplished draughtsman). The son of a wealthy Swiss jeweller, he used the money that he inherited from his father to support his lifelong antiquarian enthusiasms. By the late eighteenth century, antiquarianism was itself more self-confident, and Grose's work was dedicated to showing that, as he explains in the introduction to *The Antiquarian Repertory*, 'every man is naturally an Antiquarian' because every man has a sense of locality. One work illustrating this is his *Provincial Glossary* of 1787 (see 3.3), which also discovered much idiomatic talk of crime, particularly in the

---

[3] See Philip Pinkus, *Grub Street Stripped Bare* (1968), 289.

'local proverbs' of London. The 'vulgar tongue' was in every way, for Grose, unpolite. It is worth noting that his obituary in the *Gentleman's Magazine* cele-brated his antiquarian researches but affirmed that 'it would have been to his credit to have suppressed' his *Classical Dictionary*.[4]

Other eighteenth-century antiquarians had come to take an interest in what we might call 'popular culture', although they were usually careful not only to take a lofty attitude towards it but also, more importantly, to treat it as if it came from the mists of time. Popular culture, in the compilation of Newcastle clergyman Henry Bourne, *Antiquitates Vulgares*, was inherently antique. The 'common people' did indeed still practise certain customs and repeat certain cer-emonies, but these were the relics of distant times and beliefs, understood better by the learned antiquarian than by the people themselves. Bourne was interested in the origins of apparently immemorial rituals and supposedly timeless super-stitions. In particular, as will be evident in the extract from his survey given below (3.1), he was interested in the entangling of 'heathenish' with Christian customs. This gives his antiquarianism a strong moralistic impulse; he is quite explicit that his work aims at the 'regulation' of 'sinful' practices.

It is notable that, in the 1770s, John Brand still found it necessary to justify his interest in 'Popular Antiquities' when he issued a newly annotated version of Bourne's work. While 'the enlightened Understandings of Men in the *Eighteenth* Century', as he puts it in his preface (see 3.2), may have made antiquarian researches respectable, these researches are likely to find some of their objects ridiculous. Francis Grose also takes a condescending attitude in his 1787 *Provin-cial Glossary* (3.3), even if his rhetoric carries some sense of regret that, in an age of 'news-papers and stage-coaches', popular rural proverbs and superstitions are likely to die out. The kinds of popular idiom and belief that Grose collects are remnants, arranged in a museum by the dedicated researcher (Grose gathered much information on energetic walking tours) who has dug them out of their local soil.

By the end of the century, the growing respectability of antiquarianism and local history allowed for the glimmerings of an interest in popular culture that we can almost recognize. This is particularly the case in the work of Joseph Strutt, an antiquarian who had trained as an engraver and, like Francis Grose, would continue to use his skills to illustrate his antiquarian works. Strutt's first book had been his *Regal and Ecclesiastical Antiquities of England* (1773), but he soon turned to a wider interest in 'the English people', producing between 1774 and 1776 his *Compleat View of the Manners, Customs, Arms, Habits, &c. of the Inhabitants of England*, a historical survey 'from the arrival of the Saxons'. Com-posed in the 1790s, his most influential work was his last (he died in 1802): *Glig-*

---

[4]   *The Gentleman's Magazine*, 1 (June 1791), 493.

gamena . . . or the sports and pastimes of the people of England (see 3.4). In the introduction to this he sounds more like a social historian than a moralist: 'In order to form a just estimation of the character of any particular people, it is absolutely necessary to investigate the sports and pastimes most generally prevalent among them.' Nationalism allows 'the people' to be treated with a certain kind of respect.

Strutt does, however, write from the vantage-point of a polite age, looking back on less enlightened times—even if those times might be only fifty years distant. Discussing bull-baiting, cock-fighting, and bear-baiting, for instance, Strutt says, 'The ladies of the present day will probably be surprised to hear, that all, or the greater part of these barbarous recreations, were much frequented by the fair sex, and countenanced by those among them of the highest rank and most finished education.' He is referring to the sixteenth and seventeenth centuries, but he is capable of describing early eighteenth-century London as if it were a primitive place, where the educated classes were all too close to the vulgar. Once the popular and the elegant were intertwined; now they are separate. One might argue that this separation, clearly defined in Strutt's work, makes possible the birth of a modern idea of popular culture.

Elsewhere in the eighteenth century, an interest in popular culture is an aspect of what is now often called 'primitivism'. There is much discussion of non-polite poetry, especially of ballads, which, by the end of the century, are positively fashionable. The final section of this chapter presents a brief selection of writing about ballads. Three well-known essays by Addison on the subject in the *Spectator* (nos. 70, 74, and 85)—not excerpted here—amount to the earliest sustained critical writing on ballads, setting the terms for later eighteenth-century discussions of 'popular' verse. It is important to recognize that, while Addison's arguments for the merits of ballads were unusual for his time, his enjoyment of ballads was rather less odd. As Albert Friedman has shown, it may be that from the sixteenth to the early eighteenth centuries 'the critical code would not admit the ballad regularly into the discussion of poetry', yet 'a lively and intimate interest in the ballad' was common amongst 'literary men'.[5] Without any special justification, ballads had continued to be published in certain kinds of miscellany through the seventeenth and early eighteenth centuries.[6]

Ballads are interesting curiosities for the man of taste, but do not undermine Addison's refined values. One important fact about ballads, of course, is that they are antiquities. They may be currently known and repeated, but they are elements of an essentially timeless popular culture. Yet, in one important respect, they do turn the polite gentleman's taste to the habits and attachments of the vulgar. For Addison, as later for Edmund Burke in his *Philosophical Enquiry into*

---

[5] Albert B. Friedman, *The Ballad Revival: Studies in the Influence of Popular on Sophisticated Poetry* (Chicago, 1961), 9.   [6] Ibid., ch. 5.

the Origin of our Ideas of the Sublime and the Beautiful, 'the remarkable fact about the ballad was its hold on the common people'.[7] The first of Addison's essays has a motto taken from Horace's *Epistles* (2. 1. 63): *Interdum vulgus rectum vident*—'sometimes the people get it right'. The educated reader would have known that the line is completed by 'est ubi peccat' '. . .—sometimes they blunder'. The unstated half of the line is closer to polite truism: vulgar judgement is invariably foolish. Addison was using the motto to acknowledge, with some small show of audacity, that he was about to argue something heterodox. On his travels, Mr. Spectator has delighted in 'hearing the Songs and Fables that are come from Father to Son, and are most in vogue among the common People of the Countries through which I passed'.[8] He takes his own pleasure to indicate that the enjoyment of ballads by 'a Multitude', even if 'they are only the Rabble of a Nation', must suggest that these compositions can have some 'Perfection of Simplicity of Thought' that even the gentleman might relish. He takes as an example 'The old Song of Chevy Chase' ('the favourite Ballad of the common People of England') and spends the rest of the paper giving 'a Critick upon it, without any further Apology for so doing'.

In this essay, and in a subsequent issue published four days later (no. 74, 25 May 1711), Addison sets out to demonstrate that 'the Sentiments in that Ballad are extremely natural and poetical, and full of the majestick Simplicity which we admire in the greatest of the ancient Poets'.[9] He even risks comparing the depiction of martial virtues in 'Chevy Chase' with passages from the *Aeneid*. 'I feared my own Judgment would have looked too singular on such a Subject, had not I supported it by the Practice and Authority of Virgil', Addison has Mr. Spectator explain.[10] Two weeks later (no. 85, 7 June 1711) he is dealing with the merits of ballads again, this time praising 'the old Ballad of the Two Children in the Wood, which is one of the Darling Songs of the Common People'.[11] 'There is even a despicable Simplicity in the Verse; and yet, because the Sentiments appear genuine and unaffected, they are Able to move the Mind of even the most polite Reader with inward Meltings of Humanity and Compassion.' Without diverging from proper codes of taste, some of 'the most refined Writers of our present Age' can take pleasure in reading ballads.

Addison's celebrations of 'simplicity' were mocked or attacked by some (see excerpts 4.1 and 4.2 below), but went on being cited by supporters of ballads until the late eighteenth century. In one of the century's earliest important anthologies, *A Collection of Old Ballads* (1723) (see 4.3) the introduction to 'Chevy Chase' cites the 'very accurate Criticism upon it' in the *Spectator*.

[7] Friedman, *The Ballad Revival*, 183.
[8] *The Spectator*, ed. Donald F. Bond, 5 vols. (1965; repr. Oxford, 1987), i. 297.
[9] Ibid. 315–16.   [10] Ibid. 321–2.   [11] Ibid. 362.

Thomas Percy refers to the same essay in the preface to his *Reliques of Ancient English Poetry*, citing Addison, alongside Dryden and Dorset, as one of those leading critics who have thought that the 'artless graces' of ballads 'compensate for the want of higher beauties, and if they do not dazzle the imagination, are frequently found to interest the heart'.[12] Addison is still the supportive authority cited in Thomas Evans's preface to his collection of 1777, *Old Ballads, Historical and Narrative, with Some of the Modern Date*. Most of the preface to this influential anthology consists of passages first from the *Spectator* 'in favour of the rude and unpolished efforts of the English muse in its infant state', and then from John Aikin's *Essays on Song-Writing* (see 4.5).

The most important work of the century for the status of ballads was Thomas Percy's *Reliques of Ancient English Poetry*, which was first published in 1765. Percy's preface to this collection sounds a chord that can be heard in the lesser-known pieces given below. 'In a polished age, like the present, I am sensible that many of these reliques of antiquity will require great allowances to be made for them.' There is nothing truly primitivist about Percy's antiquarianism; he believes implicitly in 'the gradual improvements of the English language and poetry from the earliest ages down to the present'. Indeed, he famously made his 'reliques' more satisfactory by rewriting them for his polite readers. This may now seem extraordinary, but, as Albert Friedman puts it, 'the respect which the *Reliques* won for popular poetry led eventually to higher standards in ballad-editing, against which the *Reliques* itself came to be measured and found seriously deficient'.[13] Most significantly, Percy created a taste for 'popular' verse that was to lead, in one way, to *Lyrical Ballads*.

Percy's sense of the 'popular' is still at some remove from Wordsworth's, however. Consider the use of the words 'popular' and 'the people' in these two statements from the preface to the *Reliques*: 'such specimens of ancient poetry have been selected as either shew the gradation of our language, exhibit the progress of popular opinions, display the peculiar manners and customs of former ages, or throw light on our earlier classical poets'; these 'are of great simplicity, and seem to have been meerly written for the people'.[14] 'Popular opinions' here are those of the uninformed or uneducated. Whatever is composed for 'the people' is unrefined and unsophisticated (and normally beneath the notice of Percy's polite readers). But then the 'popular' culture that Percy seems to record is to be taken as distant in time—worth preserving and reading because it is 'ancient'. There is no room for an interest in any active, contemporary popular culture.

---

[12] Thomas Percy (ed.), *Reliques of Ancient English Poetry* (1765), p. x.
[13] Friedman, *The Ballad Revival*, 209.   [14] *Reliques*, pp. ix–x.

After Percy, an interest in ballads becomes part of the official, polite culture. Thomas Evans, in his preface to *Old Ballads, Historical and Narrative*, comments that defences of such collections are, by the time that he writes in the 1770s, hardly needed; 'the taste of the times' has now turned to these compositions, and the refined reader now recognizes the importance of their preservation. Implicitly acknowledging the main influence on this 'taste', Evans refers any reader wanting to know about the significance of ballads to Percy's *Reliques*. (The opening page of each of the four volumes of his own collection proclaims that it contains ballads 'None of which are inserted in Dr. Percy's Collection'.) Even Joseph Ritson, who was to attack Percy for his corruption of his texts, defers to the *Reliques*, directing interested readers of his *Pieces of Ancient Popular Poetry* (1791) (see 4.6) to Percy's prefatory 'essays on English Minstrels'. One catches in Ritson, often an aggressive antagonist of what he saw as the complacently genteel culture of English antiquarianism, a different sense of what the 'popular' might mean. He is interested in compositions that will have 'few charms in the critical eye of a cultivated age'.[15] In his irascible manner, Ritson points the way to a powerful new idea: that popular culture might be valuable as an alternative to the official culture.

REFERENCES AND FURTHER READING

A useful introductory anthology of eighteenth-century writings on the poor, the social order and crime is Stephen Copley (ed.), *Literature and the Social Order* (1984). Ned Ward's *The London Spy* is available in an edition by Paul Hyland (East Lansing, Mich., 1993); his career is surveyed in Howard William Troyer's *Ned Ward of Grubstreet: A Study of Sub-Literary London in the Eighteenth Century* (Cambridge, Mass., 1946). The most detailed survey of the eighteenth-century literature of crime is Lincoln Faller's *Turned to Account: The Forms and Functions of Criminal Biography in Late Seventeenth- and Early Eighteenth-Century England* (Cambridge, 1987); further reading is suggested in Chapter 5 of this book. For antiquarianism in the eighteenth century, Joan Evans, *A History of the Society of Antiquaries* (Oxford, 1956) is indispensable. Richard M. Dorson, *The British Folklorists: A History* (1968) places Bourne, Brand, and Strutt in a longer tradition of antiquarianism, and measures their influence on nineteenth-century folklore studies. The interest in the period in canting and the 'vulgar tongue' is described in Jonathon Green, *Chasing the Sun: Dictionary-Makers and the Dictionaries They Made* (1996), particularly chapters 5 and 14. An overview of the history of attitudes to ballads is Albert B. Friedman, *The Ballad Revival: Studies in the Influence of Popular on Sophisticated Poetry* (Chicago, 1961), while useful introductions to the place of the ballad in changing currents of taste in the late eighteenth century are Maximillian E. Novak, 'Primitivism', in H. B. Nisbet and Claude Rawson

---

[15] Joseph Ritson, *Pieces of Ancient Popular Poetry* (1791), p. vi.

(eds.), *The Cambridge History of Literary Criticism*, vol. iv: *The Eighteenth Century* (Cambridge, 1997) and Nick Groom, *The Making of Percy's Reliques* (Oxford, 1999), Ch. 2.

1. URBAN LOW LIFE

The London Spy (1.1) first appeared in eighteen monthly parts, published between November 1698 and May 1700. It appeared 'Compleat' in 1703. Further editions were published in 1704, 1706, 1709, and 1718. Its success is marked by the fact that, after 1700, Ward styled himself 'the Author of the London Spy' on the title-pages of his subsequent works. Ward himself lived until 1731, ending his days as an innkeeper and a bit-part player in Alexander Pope's *Dunciad*. We have here used the first edition of 1703. The extracts are taken from Part XIV, in which the 'Spy' and his friend wander 'quite out of our knowledge' into Wapping, close to the Thames, where they encounter various 'Salt-water kind of Vagabonds'. They eventually visit 'a Famous Amphibious House of Entertainment, compounded of one half *Tavern*, and t'other *Musick-House*'. The animated sarcasm of Ward's description of this is characteristic, high and low meeting in his very style. We also give an extract from the same part where the two wanderers come upon Rag Fair, a glimpse of the lives of London's poorest.

The second set of extracts (1.2) is taken from Tom Brown's *Amusements, Serious and Comical*, published in 1700. It is an imitation of Dufresny's *Amusements, sérieux et comiques*, published two years earlier. As this might suggest, Brown, though a Grub Street hack, was also an educated writer; he had been to Christ Church, Oxford, and had once planned to become a clergyman. Most of the *Amusements* is concerned with the behaviour—and the follies—of the politer classes, at the theatre, in the park, in the City. It includes, however, this crowded image of street life. Next (1.3) come passages from *The Town Spy: or, A View of London and Westminster . . . Written by a Foreigner*. Its title-page lists booksellers in Bristol, Worcester, Hereford, Ross-on-Wye, Cirencester, Devizes, Cardiff, Monmouth, Gloucester, and Northampton, and adds that it might also be purchased from 'the Men that carry the News'. It should be noted, however, that *The Town Spy* is a but slightly revised version of *A View of London and Westminster: or, The Town Spy* (1728), which is likely to have sold to urban readers. Then, as now, those who lived in London also needed—or enjoyed—guides to the city. In the first extract we are in the parish of St Mary's, where the narrator finds that undertakers congregate. Next we visit the parish of St Dunstan's to observe the prostitutes at work. Prostitution figures a good deal in this cynical, vivid tour of London's parishes. The grave of an infamous prostitute, Sally Salisbury ('that great and wonderful Woman Sarah Salisb—y') being worthier of remark to the 'spy' than any other tomb of the once famous. In a final paragraph we are in the parish of St James's Clerkenwell, and the 'spy' is referring to the prisons in the parish, and the popularity amongst readers of the supposed 'lives' and 'confessions' of their inmates.

Thomas Legg's *Low-life: or one half of the world knows not how the other half live* (1752?) (1.4) is 'a true description of a Sunday, as it is usually spent within the Bills of Mortality', each chapter being given over to one representative hour. Every chapter is a stream of detail, without paragraph breaks, full of juxtapositions and encounters that will seem half-familiar to readers of the imaginative literature of the period. Yet there is a particularity of detail here that is often convincingly factual (even if designed to be typical). The work went through two further editions: a second edition 'with very large additions', undated but perhaps from 1755, and a third edition of 1764. *The Frauds of London Detected; or, a Warning Piece Against the Iniquitous Practices of the Metropolis* (1.5) is undated, but the first edition is dated 1770 in the British Library catalogue. Its author is 'Richard King', almost certainly a pseudonym. *The Complete Modern Spy, for the Present Year, 1781* (1.6), though supposedly 'written by a gentleman of fortune', is 'Revised, corrected, and improved' by this same 'Richard King, Esq.'. It includes a series of tavern scenes, one of which, featuring some striking amateur drama, is given here. Its account of the performance, in an inn near Tyburn, of several great scenes from high tragedies suggests, once more, why it is difficult to separate out 'popular culture' from the culture of the polite and educated. It might be noted, however, that the narrator treats with amused disdain the debasement of the drama that he has watched.

1.1   From *The London Spy*, Part XIV, 1st coll. edn. (1703)

As soon as we came to the Sign of the Spiritual Helmet, such as the High Priests us'd to wear when they bid defiance to the Devil, we no sooner enter'd the House, but we heard Fiddlers and Hautboys, together with a Hum-drum Organ, make such incomparable Musick, that had the Harmonious Grunting of a Hog been added as a Bass to the ravishing Concert of Caterwauling Performers, in the height of their extasie, the unusualness of the sound could not have render'd it to a Nice Ear more engaging. Having heard the Beauty and Contrivance of the Publick Musick Room, as well as other parts of the House, very highly Commended, we agreed first to take a view of that which was likely to be most Remarkable. In order to which we ascended the Grades, and were usher'd into a most stately Appartment, Dedicated purely to the Lovers of *Musick, Painting, Dancing*, and *t'other thing too*. No Gilding, Carving, Colouring, or good Contrivance, was here wanting to Illustrate the Beauty of this most Noble Academy; where a good Genius may Learn with safety to abominate Vice; and a bad Genius, with as much danger to Practice it. The Room, by its compact Order and costly Improvements, looks so far above the use its now converted to, that the Seats are more like Pews than Boxes; and the upper-end being divided by a Rail, looks more like a *Chancel* than a *Musick-Loft*: That I could not but imagine it was built for an *Oaten* Meeting-House, but that they have for ever destroy'd the Sanctity of the Place by putting an Organ in it, round which hung a great many pretty Whimsical Pictures, more particularly one, wherein was describ'd the solemnity formerly us'd at *Horn Fair*, which, at first, I took (till I was unde-ceiv'd) for an Assembly of Grave Citizens going to deliver a Petition to a Court of Common-Council, to desire 'em to make a By-Act, or an Act by the by, to prevent Cuckold-making. There were but few Companies in the Room; the most Remarkable Person was a Drunken Commander, who plucking out a handful of Money, to give the Musick Sixpence, dropt a Shilling, and was so very Gener-ous, that he gave an officious Drawer, standing by, half a Crown for stooping to take it up.

The Master finding we were much pleas'd with the Order and Beauty of his Room of State, was so Civil to ask us to see his House, whose kind offer we very readily Embrac'd, following him into several Cleanly and very Delightful Rooms, furnish'd for the Entertainment of the best of Company; and to render 'em the more Diverting, had so many Whimsical Figures Painted upon the Pannels, that you could look no way but you must see an Antick, whose Posture would provoke Laughter as much as the *Dumb-Man* in the *Red-Cap*, when his Brains were agitated with a Cup of Porters Comfort. When he had show'd us the most costly part of his Tippling Conveniency, he brought us into the Kitchen, which was Rail'd in with as much Pomp, as if nothing was to be Dress'd in it but a Dinner for a Prince. Over-head hung an Harmonious Choir of *Canary-Birds*, Singing; and under them a parcel of Sea-Gulls, Drinking; who made such ordi-nary Figures, in so fine a Room, that they look'd as homely as a *Bantam Ambas-sador* in one of the King's Coaches. From thence he Ushered us Down stairs into a *Subterranean* Sanctuary, where his *Sunday* Friends may be protected from the Insolence of the *Church-Wardens*, who every *Sunday* like *Good Christians* break the *Sabbath* themselves, to have the *Letchery* of Punishing others for the same Fault. Round this *Sot's Retiring Room*, were painted as many *Maggots* as ever crawl'd out of an old *Cheshire Cheese*; in one Pannel a parcel of Drunken Women Tormenting the Devil, some plucking him by the Nose, like *St. Dunstan*; some Spewing upon his Worship; and others endeavouring to piss his Eyes out; and many such-like Whimsies. But the most remarkable of all was the *Bonana-Tree*, which bears an Evil Fruit, of which Women are most wonderful Lovers: Beneath its Umbrage are a great number of the kind Sex, contending for the Wind-falls;

and some are so unreasonable, that notwithstanding they have gathered up more than they are able to stick in their Girdles, yet exert the utmost of their strength in endeavouring to shake the Tree: some measuring what they had pick'd up by their Spans, to try whether the Size was Standard; others Quarrelling for those of the largest Growth, like so many Sows for a great Apple; in which condition we left 'em to dispute the matter, and return'd up Stairs, where we Drank a Quart of good Red, thank'd the Master for his Civility and so departed the House, which may very justly be Stil'd by such who Love good Wine, and a Pleasant Room to sit in, *The Paradise of* Wapping . . .

From thence we Rambled on, like a couple of Sweetners in search of a Country Gudgeon, who thro' Greediness of Gain, would Bite at his share in a drop'd Half Crown, a Gilded Ring, or Rug and Leather, till we came to a Heathenish part of the Town, distinguish'd, as we found by Enquiry, with the applicable Title of *Knock-Verges*, adjoining to a *Savory* place, which, in Ridicule of Fragrant Fumes that arise from the Musty Rotten Rags, and Burnt Old Shoes, is call'd by the Sweet Name of *Rosemary Lane*; where such a Numberless Congregation of Ill-favoured Maukins were gather'd together with their Hand-Baskets, that we thought a Fleet of *French* Protestants had been just arriv'd, and were newly come on Shore with Bag and Baggage, to implore the Charity of *English* well disposed Christians, to shelter them from the Terrible Persecution of *Rags*, *Lice*, and *Poverty*: But upon a true Inquisition into the meaning of this Tatter'd Multitude being Assembled in this surprizing manner, we were inform'd by a little Draggle-Tail Flat-Cap, it was *Rag-Fair*, held every Day from between two and three of the Clock in the Afternoon, till Night; where all the Ragg-pickers in Town, and such as swop Earthen Ware for old Apparel, also the Cryers of *Old Satin*, *Taffaty* or *Velvet*, have Recourse to sell their Commodities, to *Cow-Cross* Merchants, *Long-Lane* Sharpers, and other Brokers, who were as busy in Raking into their Dunghills of old Shreds and Patches, and examining their Wardrobes of decay'd Coats, Breeches, Gowns, and Petticoats, as so many Cocks upon a pile of Horse-dung, Scraping about the Filth to find an Oat worth picking at; or like a Parsons Hog on a Monday Morning, routing about a Church-yard to find a S—nce worth biting at.

The adjacent Magistrates, we were inform'd, has us'd the utmost of their endeavours to suppress their Meeting, but to no purpose; for their *Number* bids defiance to all Molestation, and their *Impudence* and *Poverty* are such, that they fear neither Goal nor Punishment. You may see the very scum of the Kingdom in a Body consisting of more *Ragged Regiments*, than ever, I believe, was muster'd together at any other Rendezvous since the World's Creation.

From Tom Brown, *Amusements, Serious and Comical* (1700)   1.2

Amusement III

London is a World, by it self. We daily discover in it more new Countries, and surprizing Singularities, than in all the Universe besides. There are among the *Londiners* so many Nations differing in Manners, Customs, and Religions, that the Inhabitants themselves don't know a quarter of them. Imagine then what an *Indian* wou'd think of such a Motly Herd of people, and what a Diverting Amusement it would be to him, to examine with a Traveller's Eye, all the Remarkable Things of this Mighty City. A Whimsy now takes me in the Head, to carry this Stranger all over the Town with me: No doubt but his Odd and Fantastical Ideas, will furnish me with Variety, and perhaps with Diversion.

Thus I am resolv'd to take upon me the Genius of an *Indian*, who has had the Curiosity to Travel hither among us, and who had never seen any thing like what he sees in *London*. We shall see how he will be amazed at certain things, which the Prejudice of Custom makes to seem Reasonable and Natural to us . . .

At first Dash the confused Clamours near *Temple Bar*, Stun him, Fright him, and make him Giddy.

He sees an infinite Number of different *Machines*, all in violent Motion. Some Riding on the Top, some Within, others Behind, and *Jehu* in the Coach-Box before, whirling some Dignify'd Villain towards the *Devil*, who has got an Estate by Cheating the Publick. He Lolls at full Stretch within, and half a Dozen Brawny Bulk-begotten Foot-men behind.

In that *dark* Shop there, several Mysteries of Iniquity have seen the *Light*, and its a sign our Saviour's Example is little regarded, since the Money-changers are suffer'd to live so near the *Temple*. To'ther side of the Way directs you to a House of a more sweet smelling Savour than its Owner's Conscience, and you can no sooner prepare your self to make Water near his Back Window, but you shall have an obliging Female look thro' her Fingers to take the Dimensions of the *Pipe* that emits it. Here stands a shopkeeper, who has not Soul enough to wear a Beaver Hat, with the Key of his Small Beer in his Pocket, and not far from him, a stingy Trader who has no Small Beer to have a Key to. One side of the Way point you out a Bookseller turn'd Quack, with his *Elixirs* and Gally-pots ready to poison old *Galen*, and the rest of his Wormeaten Men of Physick's Works, which have taken no other Air than what blows upon his *Stall*, since they unhappily fell into his hands; and to'ther directs you to a Divinity-monger, who to the D—of St. P—'s immortal Credit, is ready to attest, that there is one living that has got Money by him, and can prove any Man's Opinion to be Heterodox, and incon-sistent with that of the Christian Church, if he believes otherwise.

Some Carry, others are Carry'd: *Make Way there*, says a Gouty-Leg'd Chairman, that is carrying a Punk of Quality to a Mornings Exercise: Or a *Bartholomew*-Baby Beau, newly Launch'd out of a Chocolate-House, with his Pockets as empty as his Brains. *Make Room there*, says another Fellow driving a Wheel-Barrow of Nuts, that spoil the Lungs of the City Prentices, and make them Wheeze over their Mistresses, as bad as the Phlegmatick Cuckolds their Masters do, when call'd to Family Duty. One Draws, another Drives. *Stand up there, you blind dog*, says a Car-man, *Will you have the Cart squeeze your Guts out?* One Tinker knocks, another Bawls, *Have you brass Pot, Iron Pot, Kettle, Skilit, or a Frying-Pan to mend*: Whilst another Son of a Whore yelps louder than *Homer's* Stentor, *Two a Groat and Four for Six Pence Mackerel!* One draws his mouth up to his Eats, and Howls out, *Buy my Flawnders*, and is followed by an Old Burly Drab, that Screams out the sale of her *Maids* and her *Sole* at the same Instant.

Here a Sooty Chimney-Sweeper takes the Wall of a Grave *Alderman*, and a *Broom-Man* Justles the *Parson* of the Parish. There a Fat Greasie *Porter* runs a Trunk full Butt upon you, while another Salutes your Antlers with a Flasket of *Eggs* and *Butter*. *Turn out there you Country Put*, says a *Bully*, with a Sword two Yards long jarring at his Heels, and throws him into the Channel. By and by comes a *Christning*, with the *Reader*, screwing up his mouth to deliver the Service *alamode de Paris*, and afterwards talk immoderately nice and dull with the Gossips, and the *Midwife* strutting in the Front, and Young Original Sin as fine as fip-pence, follow'd with the Vocal Musick of *Kitchen-Stuff ha'you Maids*; and a damn'd *Trumpeter* calling in the Rabble to see a Calf with Six Legs and a Top-knot. There goes a Funeral, with the Men of Rosemary after it, licking there Lips after their three Hits of White, Sack and Claret, at the House of Mourning, and the Sexton walking before, as Big and Bluff as a *Beef-Eater* at a Coronation. Here's a *Poet* scampers for't as fast as his Legs will carry him, and at his Heels a Brace of *Bandog Bayliffs*, with open mouths ready to Devour him, and all the Nine Muses; and there an *Evidence* ready to spew up his *false Oaths* at the sight of the common *Executioner*.

1.3 From *The Town Spy: or, A View of London and Westminster . . . Written by a Foreigner* (Gloucester, 1729)

I take the Business of a *Dead-monger* to differ little from that of a *News-monger*, as depending in a very great measure upon Intelligence. There is *Tom Busy*, who is a most indefatigable Man this Way, has told me, that he has, e'er now, paid as dear for his Informations as a *Foreign Minister* or a *General* of an army. It seems their first Correspondents are the *Coachmen* and *Footmen* of the most eminent and practising Physicians, who daily deliver in a *Paper* called the *Joyful List*, containing an account of the Quality and Maladies of the Persons who fall under their Master's Visitation, together with an Account of the Progress of their respective Diseases. Their Prices are as follows, *vz.*

	s.	d.
For the News of the first Fit of an Apoplexy	00	06
For the second Fit, ditto	01	06
For the third and last Fit.	02	06
For a Small Pox, *if the Party be attended by two or three*		
Physicians	01	00
For a Cold, and the Prospect of a Fever	00	04
For a high Fever, the standing Price all the Town over	01	06
For a DEATH	05	00

If any of these can sound the Servants of the *sick Person*, and learn that Part of the *Will* relating to the *Funeral*, 'tis not at all amiss, but if it happens to be a *private Interment*, the News is too bad to be reported.

Their other Correspondents are the *Chairmen*, who by their constant Attendance upon the *greater* Sort, are very useful Hands. These *Low-heel'd* Gentlemen shall watch as impatiently for the Gasp of a Person of Quality, as a *Jew* for an Opportunity to debauch his *Maid*; and the *Porter* at the Door no sooner gives out the Word DEAD, than these *human Horses* are fled Express to all the *burial Offices* in Town, it being the constant Custom for every one of them to pay for the Intelligence, tho' they *miss the Job*.

. . . *Ram-Alley*, one of the *Temple* Avenues, a Place which I'm told, is the Night-Scene of a good deal of obscure Gallantry among Serjeants Clerks, and Judges Footmen; a Market, where *Half-pence* pass in current Payment; and Abundance of dirty Love is hung out to Sale *ready made*, and at reasonable Rates. I remember a pleasant Adventure which happen'd to the Master of a Vessel (newly come ashoar) in the Latitude of this Place, who *spy'd* and *came up* with a pretty young Wench, rigg'd in a round-ear'd Cap and Housewife's Apron, and in her Hand a large Key, as of an outer Door; equipt with these Tokens of a Servant in the Neighbourhood, he began to give *Chase*, and endeavour'd to *speak with her*: The poor Innocent kept off, as if she had been really afraid, but stood in with the *Trade Wind* for *Bolt and Tun Creek*; the Captain crowded all his Sail, and *standing directly after her*, he soon came to an *Anchor a thwart her Hawse*. But the next Day was oblig'd to have *Poop examin'd by an able Surgeon*, who upon viewing his Case, pronounced it as handsome a *P—x* as he had observ'd throughout the whole Course of his Practice.

These *fair Traders*, who appear by Moon-light, and retail by Inch of Candle, range themselves in due Order, at most of the Doors and Bulks of *this*, and of the other principal Streets in the City; for when other Trades-People think fit to finish and shut their Shops in, their Business begins, and they commonly keep open till Twelve and One in the Morning. One of these indefatigable Damsels tells me, she pays a certain cruel Shopkeeper in *Fleet-street* half a Crown a Night for her Stand, prompt Payment, besides certain *Perquisites*; and that this poor Drudge is many times made *Wife* and *Widow* Twenty-five times in an Evening, so fickle and unstable the Minds of Man and Woman-kind.

. . . there are two *Colleges*, in which are taught several Sciences, as the *Kid Laye* the *File Laye*, &c. and the *Students* by their Proficiency in these Arts, often render themselves very famous to Posterity; and much Industry has been us'd lately to collect *Memoirs* and *Narratives* of the Lives of the *Defunct Fellows*, being Histories that are greatly admired now a-days. Vast Numbers that have been here educated, are now on their Travels beyond Sea, and the Custom being to tarry *seven* or *fourteen* Years, they usually return largely furnish'd with Foreign Knowledge.

1.4   From [T. Legg,] *Low-Life: Or One Half of the World Knows Not How the Other Half Live* (1752?)

HOUR I. *From Twelve o'Clock on* SATURDAY *Night, to One o'Clock on* SUNDAY *Morning.*

The Salop-Man in *Fleetstreet* shuts up his Gossiping Coffee-House. Journeymen Barbers entertaining themselves for the ensuing Day's Employment, about *St. Giles's, Spittle-Fields, Rag-Fair,* the *Fleet,* the *Mint,* and other Poverty-stricken Parts of the Town. Watchmen taking Fees from House-Breakers, for Liberty to commit Burglaries within their Beats, and at the same Time promise to give them Notice, if there is any Danger of their being taken,—or even disturbed in their Villainies. Masters of Night-Houses getting up, (after having been in Bed a little while, under Pretence of arising in the Morning to serve their Customers). Hackney Coachmen full of Employment about *Charing-Cross, Covent-Garden,* and the *Inns of Court,* carrying to their respective Habitations such People who are either too drunk or too lazy to walk. Poor Tradesmens Wives hanging about their Husbands at little Ale-Houses, to secure some Money to support their Family, before it is all lost at Whist, Cribbage, Putt and All-Fours. Pawnbrokers Shops very full of Men and Women, who are bringing Cloaths to a new Lodging, and fetching them from their last Week's Habitation. Bawds setting Pimps for Spies at the Avenues to their Houses, to give them timely Notice of the City Marshals or Constables coming to search their Houses for disorderly Company. Victuallers carrying the Scores of Tradesmen, such as Coachmakers, Carpenters, Smiths, Plaisterers, Plumbers, and others in the Building Branch of Business, to the Pay-Tables in order to clear their last Week's Reckoning, and if possible to get a Trifle paid off from an old Score. Gangs of Robbers dividing themselves into Parties, some of whom go to the Watch-House to make the Constable and Watchmen drunk, while the others break open Houses, rob them, and make off with their Booty undiscover'd. Regular Publicans, and such as live in Fear of Informations, making awry Faces, and giving smart Words to Sleepers, noisy Fools and Drunkards, to get them out of their Houses. The Markets begin to swarm with the Wives of poor Journeymen Shoemakers, Smiths, Tinkers, Taylors, &c. who come to buy great Bargains with little Money. Servants of Taverns and Coffee-Houses cleaning out their Drinking Rooms with light Hearts, being glad they have finished their Weeks Work, and can add two Hours to their usual Rest when they go to Bed. *Dark-House-Lane* near *Billingsgate* in an Uproar with Whores, Custom-House-Officers, Sailors Wives, Smugglers, and City-Apprentices, waiting to hear the High-Water Bell ring, to go in the Tilt-Boat to *Gravesend*. Persons of Quality ordering their Chairmen to carry them to publick Gaming-Tables. Ballad-Singers who have encumber'd the Corners of Markets several Hours together, repairing to the Houses of appointed Rendezvous, that they may share with Pick-Pockets what had been stolen from the Croud of Fools which stood about them all the Evening. Masters of Cooks Shops going to the several Markets, especially *Leadenhall, Clare,* and *Newgate*, and buying large Quantities of indifferent Meat, for very little Money. Fidlers, Harpers, and other itinerant Musicians, in great Esteem at the Publick-Houses in back Alleys, Courts, Yards, &c. in playing Hornpipes and Jiggs to nimble-footed, noisy, drunken Fools. Constables marching thro' their Liberties with long Staves in their Hands, attended by several Watchmen who are out on Duty at their respective Stands. Beadles of Parishes and Precincts very great Men in the Constables Absence, by sitting in their Chairs, drinking their Liquor, and deciding what Squabbles are brought before them. Gangs of Gypsies near *London,* robbing Gentlemens and Farmers Hen-Roosts and Pig-Styes, immediately killing and putting what they steal into Bags, and making off with their Booty. Poor People who have been in Bed some Time, and are thoroughly warm, groping about for their Tinder-Boxes, that they may strike a Light in order to go a Bugg-hunting . . . The *Post-Boy* Publick-House in *Sherborn-Lane* near the *Post-Office*, full of Post-Boys who are regaling themselves with Brandy, Rum, Beer, Geneva, and Bread and Cheese, while the Gentlemen of that Office are sweating over large Candles, and preparing the several Mails to go to all parts of

Great-Britain, Ireland, and other Places in his Majesty's Dominions. The unhappy Lunaticks in *Bethlehem*-Hospital in Moorfields, rattling their Chains, and making a terrible Out-cry, occasioned by the Heat of the Weather having too great an Effect over their rambling Brains.

———————

1.5   From Richard King, *The Frauds of London Detected; or, a Warning Piece Against the Iniquitous Practices of the Metropolis* (1770?)

BAWDS

These old Bawds frequent our modern Conventicles, and other public places, with a young Nun (as they call them) under their arm, whose business is, while the old beldam is mocking religion with uplifted eyes and hypocritical prayers, the young sinner is ogling some man fit for their purpose. Service done, they return; on being accosted by the person in view, the old woman stumbles, falls down, or faints, as best suits her purpose; the gentleman assists her, offers his arm, or a coach to convey her home; which accepted, she makes apology for the trouble she gives him, desires her daughter to thank the gentleman for his great care of her mother, which she does, and, if near, squeezes him by the hand, or otherwise shows a forwardness to be better acquainted with him. On their arrival at her hotel, the stranger is invited in, and desired to partake of a collation always in readiness for that purpose; which done, on some frivolous excuse or another, the old lady leaves the room, and the young couple to their machinations, which are variegated according to the perspicacity and adroitness of the visitant; the Nun having her different cues either to be forward, shy, or otherwise, as may best suit the interest of her employer, and allure the gallant into the snare laid for him, which seldom fails of success.

To enumerate the different arts and wiles made use of by the Bawd to decoy the innocent of both sexes, to explain the various stratagems, detect the many frauds, and set to view the scenes of wickedness pursued and exhibited under and by her direction and cognizance would fill a large volume; therefore I shall content myself with laying down some rules and observations thereon, whereby the reader, if a countryman, may escape the trap prepared for him . . .

GAMBLERS

. . . Cock-fighting, of all games, is surely one of the most barbarous, and a scandal to the practitioners who follow it, both high and low; for, notwithstanding its antiquity as a diversion in England, it is now become a disgrace to humanity; and surely none but the most notorious gamblers can be elated therewith, or give a sanction to barbarity that even shudders the Indian to hear of. At these scenes of cruelty the greatest depredations are committed by the attendants thereon, the most prophane and wicked expressions made use of, the most horrid and blasphemous oaths and curses denounced against Fortune for the loss of an odd battle, with a jargon of disconsonant tongues as hard to be understood, and in as great confusion, as that at Babel, composes the group; among whom are to be found my Lord in dispute with a Butcher, and his Grace with the Farrier, all hail fellows well met. From these, and other meetings of the like nature, let me dissuade my readers, where nothing is to be obtained but at the expence of humanity, and to the discredit of Christianity.

LOTTERY OFFICE KEEPERS

. . . For several years past these Lottery Office Keepers have had an ample share in imposing on the town, and cheating the country, by vending of books, handkerchiefs, and other things of little value, with shares of tickets, said to be impending, or then drawing, in the State Lottery, with a note of hand, importing, that if No. 45 should come a prize of 20,000£. the bearer of that ticket would be intitled to 50£. and so for other prizes in proportion; by this means thousands were taken in with their eyes open, (such an itch has the world for gambling) and paid thrice the value for the commodity they purchase (allured by the hopes of a prize in the lottery) than its real worth.

On the drawing of the lottery the lower part of the creation, who were concerned in the above schemes for enriching themselves, would quit their labour and industry, and repair to the Guildhall, to be present at the drawing, in expectation of every next number called being theirs, when twenty thousand to one of their getting a prize of 10£. Some few have been so lucky as to get the 20,000£. and 10,000£. but I never knew that they received the sum stipulated for payment, in the promissory note given for that purpose. On the contrary, I have seen the Office Keeper's windows and shops demolished, by a deluded and justly enraged mob, who have been ruined by the purchase of tickets, shares, chances, and insurances thereon.

The Keepers had a custom, a day or two before the finishing the drawing, to shut up their shops and decamp, for fear of being brought to account for their cheats and roguery, practised on the ignorant and unthinking. The countryman, hearing that he had a prize in the lottery, hastened up to town, at no small expence, to receive the money due thereon; when, to his great sorrow, there was no Keeper to be found, but, as an alleviation of his grief, he saw hundreds deceived as well as himself.

To such an height were these Lottery Officers carried (as they called themselves) that you might purchase shares and chances at six pence a piece, one of which is worth observing: An advertisement appeared in the Morning Chronicle, intimating that shares and chances were to be disposed of at Fuller's Eating-house, in Wych-street, and tickets insured; that whosoever bought six pennyworth of beef, would be presented with a ticket, and a note of hand to receive the sums inserted therein, if the number of the ticket was drawn a prize of 20,000£. &c. and told you, that this was the most rationable of all schemes hitherto projected, as the purchaser, at least, would have, for his six pence, three pennyworth of meat, besides a chance in the Lottery.

1.6　From *The Complete Modern Spy, for the Present Year*, 1781

A SPOUTING CLUB

After an interval of a few minutes, during which two of the members, whom Mr. Harry said were esteemed quite *capital*, made their appearance in the characters of Tamerlane and Bajazet, in the scene where the latter is brought in chains before the victor. We were indeed in one sense *entertained* with this performance, which was as great a burlesque on *tragedy* as if it had been intended to answer that purpose.

Omar forgot his message, and after going back to fetch it, could scarcely deliver it so as to be understood. It seems the Tartar was a *Grecian*, i.e. an Irishman; but the two sultans were both of our own growth . . . As to Bajazet, he sometimes repeated inwardly with a sort of grumbling, as if he had been muttering a sort of wayward spell; at other times he tore the passion to rags; and when he addressed Tamerlane in those words, which should be uttered with supreme contempt,

'Make thy demands to those that own thy pow'r;'

he clinched his fist, which he shook full in the face of the conquering Tartar, who was obliged to take this insult patiently, though he had a monstrous large sabre by his side, and all his guards attending.

Tamerlane was very tame when he demanded,

'—Where slept the thunder
That could have arm'd this idol deity?'

but put himself into a violent passion when he repeated the cool philosophic remark,

'Causeless to hate, is not of human kind.'

As to the concluding lines of the act,

> 'Above the worthless trophies man can raise,
> And with herself, herself the goddess pays:'

These beautiful verses he recited with the tone of a schoolboy, giving every word a false emphasis, and went off, sawing the air with his hands. At his exit he received a thundering clap from the company.

Romeo and Juliet next made their appearance, but such a *matchless* pair I never saw. Romeo was frequently asleep, till Juliet awaked him by the affected violence of her love, when he threw himself into some very unnatural attitudes, and ranted away, in order to make amends for his former apathy.

After this scene, Lothario and Horatio made their appearance, the former of which committed a barbarous murder upon the character which he pretended to represent. Repeating the following line with the most improper emphasis, he expressed himself thus,

'Ha! dost thou know ME, that *I am* Lothario?' 'To be sure (said a young fellow who sat near the stage, as it was called) I never saw you before—and that *you* are Lothario, I must beg your pardon, when I observe that I should never have suspected even that you were his representative, but that you have been so obliging as to tell us so.'

The hero stopping short while the person above mentioned made this pertinent remark, only said, 'D——n you, sir, you shall be remembered for this interruption,' and then went on with his massacre till he got a hearty cuff from a bloated Horatio, and two or three thrusts in the stomach from Altamont, after which he died most triumphantly, without any signs of regret for the murder he had committed.

A scene in Macbeth next claimed our attention, in which the Scotch tyrant spoke the west-country dialect so strong, and was otherwise so disagreeable, that (being a new performer) he was hissed by the majority of the audience.

The plaintive Monimia, and boisterous Polydore, were the next who favoured us with an exhibition. Monimia had got her lesson tolerably perfect, but repeated it like a charity child. Polydore was for ever out, and besides had such an impediment in his speech, and an appearance so unpromising, that he received several marks of disapprobation.

The son of our landlord was now given to understand that *his* scene was coming on. This made us give great attention: and it seemed that the members thought him of consequence; for the curtain was dropped during the space of some minutes, and at length Pierre and Jaffier opened upon us. As to Pierre, he was really very decent, and but for some unnatural pauses, might have passed for a tolerable actor. Jaffier was performed by our new friend, Mr. Harry; but I was sorry to see that the youth had mistaken his talents, and instead of appearing the tender, injured person, loaded with misfortunes, he strove to vie with Pierre in boldness and exertion, and thus perverted the very meaning of the part; yet he received unmerited applauses, some of which were possibly bestowed on him out of a compliment to the landlord his father . . .

The entertainments for the evening being now concluded, at near six in the morning, I thought of departing, when Mr. Ambler went forward to the stage, and took the liberty of following the fair Violante into the dressing-room. In the mean time the gallant, gay Lothario, having quitted his stage dress, came up to the landlord, and demanded, in a peremptory [accent], who it was that had affronted him? Before the person to whom he had applied could give an answer, the aggressor stood forth, and declared he was the man that had interrupted the gentlemen; but he could not think any sensible man could be angry at receiving an indication of his inabilities in a line he was not bred to. 'You may be a very worthy man, sir (added he) but I profess I think you a very bad player. However, if I have hurt your feelings in any respect, I am very sorry for it.' The stage hero not relishing this calm and sensible address, began blustering aloud, 'You sc——l (says he) how durst you interrupt any one?' 'I paid my money (replied the other) and had a consequent right to give my opinion in any way I chose.'

'You are a liar,' cried the spouter, and made a blow at him with a stick he had in his hand; but the other evading the stroke, returned it, and brought him to the ground. When he arose, he was in a more pacific disposition, and having experienced the force of his adversary, was inclined to be satisfied. Our host also interposing his good offices, peace was restored.

2. THIEVES AND THEIR ARGOT

As discussed in the introduction to this chapter, the interest in crime in the eighteenth century is often an interest in the language of criminality. Lexicons of 'canting' vocabulary were common, and samples of these are given below. Authorship of most of these works is and will remain entirely obscure. Francis Grose published his *Classical Dictionary of the Vulgar Tongue* anonymously, but with antiquarian credentials that would allow him to lay claim to it retrospectively.

From *The Life and Death of the English Rogue; or his Last Legacy to the*   2.1
World. Containing Most of his Notorious Robberies, Cheats and Debaucht
Practices. With a Full Discovery of a High-way Rogue; Also Directions to All
Travellers, How to Know Rogues, and How to Avoid Them. And an Infallible
Rule How to Take Them, When Rob'd by Them. Directing all Inn-keepers,
Chamberlains and Ostlers, How to Distinguish Rogues from Honest Guests.
The Manner of his Being Apprehended and his Behaviour in Prison, which was
Very Remarkable. To which is Added an Alphabetical Canting Dictionary;
English Before the Canting for the Better Understanding of Mumpers and
Maunders, Priggers and Prancers, Rum Pads and Rum Padders (London,
n.d.)

B

    Bar-boy, *Squeeker*
    Beadle of Bridewell, *Floging cove*
    Better, *Benor*
    Bridewell, *Naskin*
    Begger born, *Clapperdogeon*
    Boghouse or Privy, *Croppinken*
    Bed, *Libedge*
    Bottle, *Bounsing cheat*
    Begg, *Maund*
    Beggers, *Maunders*
    Bread, *annam*
    Be careful of what you say, *Stow your whilds and plant 'em*
    Bridle, *Nabgirder*
    Bolt or Shackles, *Cramprings*
    Body, *Quarron*
    Base or Roguish, *Queer*
    Bacon, *Ruff Peck*
    Bastard, *Stall-whimper*
    Brokers, *Fencing Cully*
    Belated, *Hoodwinkt*
    Blind men, *Gropers*
    Barn, *Skippers*
    Bar of an Ale-house or Tavern, *Touting ken*
    Be wary, *Stow your whids*
    Brokers shop, *Scallen ken*
    Beaten, *Chaft*
    Breast, *Heaver* . . .

[We are then given descriptions of the various types of thieves: Anglers, Palliards, Priggers, Fraters, and those below.]

Whip-jacks

Whip-jacks, are counterfeit Mariners, who talk of nothing but Sea-fights, Drowning, and Ship-wracks; they have always a counterfeit Pass or Licence, which they call a Gybe, and with this they Cheat the Country; telling them of their great Losses, and that they beg only for something to carry them home: but in the way, they will not stick to heave a Booth; that is, to rob a Booth at a Fair, or some on the Road. These Rogues have learn'd all the Sea terms, so that they often cheat those that have been at Sea.

Mumpers

Mumpers, are both Male and Female, a genteeler sort of Beggers, they scorn to beg for Food, but Money or Cloaths; the Money they lay out to pamper the Gut, and the Cloaths they sell to re-imburse the Pocket: Sometimes they appear in the Habit of some decay'd Gentleman, and then he pretends what a great Sufferer he hath been for his Majesty; sometimes he appears with an Apron before him, and a Cap on his Head, and begs in the nature of a broken Tradesman, who having been a long time sick, has spent all his Stock, and now is so weak that he cannot work.

Of Dommerars

Dommerars, are such as Counterfeit themselves Dumb; they have an Art to rowl their Tongues up into the Roof of their Mouths, so that you cannot see it.

Of the Night-walker and Diver

I cannot well part these two; for she that is a Diver, or Pick-pocket, is an infallible Stroler or Night-walker; this Occupation is contrary to all others; for she opens her Shop-windows when all other Traders are about to shut up: the Night approaching she rigs her self in the best manner she can, with some apparent outward Ensign of her Profession; having weighed Anchor and quitted her Port, she steers her course for some principal Street, as Cheapside, or Cornhill and the Bridge-walks: With a gentle Breeze she first sails slowly on one side of the way, and if she meets never a Man of War she tacks and stands away for the other side. But if it be a well-built Frigat, she is laid aboard before, and made fast with Grapleings, and presently rummaged in the Hold; sometimes she shears off and leaves the Man of War on Fire.

You may know her by her brushing you, and staring you in the Face, and by her often halting in the Street, and gazing about her, or looking after some that she hath brusht; but the most infallible sign, is her asking of Questions, As, I pray Sir, what is it a Clock? Or, which is the way to such a place; for I am a great stranger here.

If you pick her up, 'tis a thousand to one but she will give something whereby you shall have cause to remember her as long as you live; besides 'Tis a thousand pound to a penny but she picks your Pocket into the Bargain.

From *The Triumph of Wit: or, the Canting Dictionary. Being the Newest and* 2.2 *Most Useful Academy: Containing the Mystery and Art of Canting, with the Original and Present Management Thereof, and the Ends to Which it Serves and is Employed. Illustrated with Poems, Songs, and Various Intrigues in the Canting Language, with the Explanation, &c.* (Dublin, n.d.)

The *Fraters* are such as forge Briefs or counterfeit Patents, pretending to beg for decay'd Hospitals, Losses by Fire, and the like; but have been so often detected and punished, that scarce any thing but the Name remains at this Day; for it being a publick fraud, 'tis more narrowly pry'd into than those that are personal and private.

The *Paillards* or *Clapperdogeons*, are those that have been brought up to beg from their Infancy, and frequently counterfeit Lameness, making their Legs, Arms and Hands appear to be sore, and very nauseous, with Cream and Blood, Butter and Soap, Ointment and Corrosives, and sometimes by putting on counterfeit lame Legs, and false wither'd Arms, making horrible wry Faces, and setting off their Story of being Shot, Burnt, scalded, perished with the Evil, and the like; with a lamentable Voice, and for the most part they carry Children about with 'em, which they frequently hire of poor Nurses for so much a Week, the better to move Compassion: but if you strictly enquire into their Lameness, you will find it nothing but a counterfeit of their own devising, and their Sores so slight, that in a Day or two they'd cure of themselves, did they not apply Corrosives.

The *Glimmerers* are such as go up and down a Maunding, under Pretence they have been undone by Fire, and for the most part have a forg'd Certificate with many names, insinuated to those of the Minister, Justice, and Church-Wardens of some remote Parish; pretending great Losses, when indeed their whole Life has been the begging Trade.

The *Mumpers* is the general Beggar, Male and Female which lie in the Cross-ways, or Travel to and fro, carrying for the most part Children with them, which generally are By-blows, and delivered to them with a Sum of Money, almost as soon as born.

As for the Women that attend those strolling Gypsies and Beggars, those that are married after their Fashion, are called Antem-morts; the Dells are young Wenches that yet retain their Maidenheads, which by their Custom they must sacrifice to the *Upright-Man* [their chief], before they can be free with the Brotherhood.

The *Dixies* are such as are prostituted to any, and are no other than common Whores of the kind, among the Brotherhood, and consequently to any Person, if Advantage offers; and for the most part they have the Art of diving into the Pockets of such Cullies they ensnare.

The *Stroling Morts* are such as pretend to be Parsons Widows, or to be born Gentlewomen, and by Marrying against the Consent of their Parents, by Losses and Sicknesses are utterly ruined and undone, telling a lamentable Story, to stir up the Minds of the hearers to compassionate their Sufferings.

The *Baudy Baskets* are such as wander up and down with a Basket under their Arm, and a Child at their Backs, pretending to sell Toys and Trifles, and so beg or steal, as they see Occasion, and find Opportunity.

The *Kitchen Morts* are the little Girls that run in the Hands of these Gypsies and Beggars, or are carried at their Backs in Blankets.

And these are the chief of the Gang, who from their Head Rendezvous set out twice a Year and scatter all over *England*.

. . . A Cheat	Napper
A Coach	Ratler
A Chamber-Pot	Jacum-gag
A Constable	Harmanbeck
Coach-beggars	Ratling-mumpers
A Cloak bag	Roger
A Candlestick	Glimstick
Fire	Glimmer
Cut the Cloak bag	Flick the Roger
Corn	Grannam
A Cluster of Grapes	Rum boozing Welts
A Crust	Crackler
A Crafty Fellow	Clincher
A Crutch	Lifter
A Church	Autem
To Cheat	Bite
A [C]ow	Mower
A Coat	Mishtopper
Counterfeit	Confeck
A Coachman	Smacking Cove

To copulate	Wap
Cheese	Case
A Cloak	Togeman
The Country	Deaufaville
Carriers	Deaufaville stampers
[C]hoaked	Frummagem'd
Chickens	Cackling-cheats
A Dog	Bugher
A Drawer of Wine	Rump-hooper
Day, or Day-break	Lightmans
Duck	Quacking-cheat
Drunk	Nazzy
A Drunkard	Nazzy cove
Drusy	Peeping
Drink	Booze
To enter a House	Dup
Eyes	Olges or Glaziers
Ends of Gold and Silver	Spangles
Dumb	Cauk . . .

Besides the stroling Beggars and pretended Egyptians, there are others that use the Cant, who are most of the Town Thieves; or such as harbour about London, and are distinguished by several canting Names and Titles, *viz.*

The High-Pad, or Highway Man. The Low-Pad, or Foot-robber, The Budge, who makes it his business to run into Houses, and takes what comes first to Hand. The Diver, or Pick-Pocket. The Bulk, or one that is his Assistant, in creating Quarrels by Jostling, &c. to gather a crowd that the diver may have the better opportunity to effect his Purpose. The Jilt is one that pretending business in a Tavern or Alehouse, takes a private Room, and with Pick locks opens the Trunks or Chests, and taking what he can conveniently, locks 'em again, pays his reckoning and departs. The prigger of prancers is one that makes it his Business to steal Horses. The Ken-miller is one that robs Houses in the Night-time, by breaking them open, or getting in at the Window, and seldom goes alone. The File is the same with the Diver, tho' for the most part he goes without the Bulk, and was formerly known by the Title of the Bang-nipper, because with a Horn thumb and a sharp Knife, he used to cut the Pockets clear off, with all that was in them. The Shoplifts are commonly Women, who go into Shops under pretence of buying, and seeming very difficult to be pleas'd, find an opportunity to slip some Garment, piece of silk of stuff, &c. into the coat, Bag, or other private conveyance, with which they are seldom unfurnished. The Angler is one that takes a Quarry of Glass out of a casement, and so opening it, with a long Pole and

Hook, at the end on't, pulls to him what he can conveniently reach, without entering the House. But enough of these Varlets that like the Egyptian Locusts, pester the Nation, there being no remedy effectual to put an end to their Rogueries but the Gallows; wherefore not to trouble the Reader with a story of their many Villanies, and by what Means they atchieve them, all of them being witty and ingenious in Mischief; I shall conclude this Discourse with a song very suitable to the Purpose . . .

2.3   From *A New Canting Dictionary: Comprehending All the Terms, Ancient and Modern, Used in the Several Tribes of Gypsies, Beggars, Shoplifters, Highwaymen, Foot Pads, and All Other Clans of Cheats and Villains. Interspersed with Proverbs, Phrases, Figurative Speeches, &c. Being a Complete Collection of All that has been Publish'd of That Kind. With Very Large Additions of Words Never Before Made Public. Detecting, Under Each Head or Order, the Several Tricks or Pranks Made Use of by Varlets of All Denominations; and Therefore Useful for All Sorts of People (Especially Travellers and Foreigners) to Enable Them to Secure their Money and Preserve their Lives. With a Preface, Giving an Account of the Original Progress, &c. of the Canting Crew; and Recommending Methods for Diminishing these Varlets, by Better Employment of the Poor. To Which is Added a Complete Collection of Songs in the Canting Dialect* (London, 1725)

Preface

. . . no Country in the World, has within it self, better Opportunities than England, to imploy and make useful the Poor of all Degrees, and of every Age and Sex, by means of our Woollen and other our numerous Manufactures: And that notwithstanding these Native Advantages, no Country in the World abounds so much with Vagrants and Beggars; insomuch that it is impossible to stir abroad in the Streets, to step into any of the Shops in London, or to take the Air within two or three Miles of this great Metropolis, but one must be attack'd with the clamorous and often insolent, Petitions of Sturdy Beggars and Vagabonds, who, by proper Regulations, might be made equally useful to themselves and the Publick . . .

[There follows an encomium on the use of workhouses in Holland.]

How many poor Souls are almost daily reclaimed from their vicious Courses, by this Means, and saved from utter Destruction, and render'd usefull Members of the Common wealth! And how many Robberies, Murders, and Invasions of

Private Right are hourly prevented! . . . this, I have Reason to believe, might be done at a much easier Expence than is at present levied for the Maintenance of the Poor by the Rates and Assessments of every Parish, which raise a Sum so immense, that 'tis the Admiration and Astonishment of all the World, that England should be so over-run with Beggars . . .

CLICK, to Snatch. *I have Clickt the Nab from the Cull*; I whipt the Hat from the Man's Head. *Click the rum Topping*. Snatch that Woman's fine Commode, or Head-Dress.

CLICKER, the Shoe-maker's Journey-man, or Servant that cuts out all the Work. Among the *Canters*, used for the Person whom they intrust to divide their Spoils, and proportion to every one his Share.

CLICKET, Copulation of Foxes, and thence used in a *Canting* Sense, for that of Men and Women; as, *The Cull and the Mort are at Clicket in the Dyke*.

CLICKETTING, The Act of Fruition; as *He has pick'd up the Blowse, and they are pik'd into that Smuggling-Ken a Clicketting*.

CLINKER, a crafty Fellow.

CLINKERS, the Irons Felons wear in Gaols.

CLIP, as, *To Clip the Coin*, to diminish or impair it. *To Clip the King's English*, not to speak plain, when one's drunk.

CLOAK-TWITCHERS, Villains, who formerly, when Cloaks were much worn, us'd to lurk, in and by dark Places, to snatch them off of the Wearer's Shoulders; as now their Descendants of the Tribe, do by Peruques, Hats, &c. *The Thirty-third Order of Villains*.

CLOD-HOPPER, a Ploughman.

CLOUD, Tobacco. *Will you raise a Cloud?* Shall we smoak a Pipe?

CLOVEN, *Cleave* or *Cleft*, used in a *Canting* Sense, to denote a young Woman who passes for a Maid, and is not one.

CLOUT, a Handkerchief.

CLOY, to Steal. *Cloy the Clout*; to steal the Money.

CLOYERS, Thieves, Robbers, Rogues.

CLOYING, Stealing, Thieving, Robbing; also fulsom or satiating.

CLOWES, Rogues.

CLUCK, the Noise made by Hens, when they sit upon their Eggs to hatch; or when they wou'd have Eggs put under them for that purpose. Whence 'tis used in a *Canting Sense*, to signify a Wench's Propension to Male-Conversation, by her Romping and Playfulness; when they say, *The Mort Clucks*; or, *You may know what she'd be at, by her Clucking*.

CLUMP, a Heap or Lump.

CLUMPISH, Lumpish.

CLUNCH, a clumsy Clown, an awkward or unhandy Fellow.

CLY, Money. *To cly the Jerk*, to be Whipt. *Let's strike his Cly*; let's get his Money from him. Also a Pocket, as, *Filed a Cly*, Pick'd a Pocket.

COACH-WHEEL, as, *A Fore-Coach-Wheel*, Half a Crown. *A Hind-Coach-Wheel*, a Crown or Five-shilling Piece . . .

FILE-*Cloy*, a Pickpocket, Thief or Rogue; the same as File.

FILLUP, as, *To give Nature a Fillup*; to give a Loose to Women or Wine.

FIRE-*Ship*, a Pockey Whore.

FIRKIN *of foul Stuff*, a very homely, coarse, corpulent Woman.

FLAG, a Groat; *The Flag of Defiance is out*, (among the Tarrs) the Fellow's Face is very red, and he is drunk.

FLAM, a Trick or Sham Story.

FLANDERS-*Fortunes*, of small Substance.

FLANDERS-*Pieces*, Pictures that look fair at a Distance, but coarser near at Hand.

FLAP-DRAGON, a Clap or Pox.

FLASH, a Periwig. *Rum Flash*, a long, full, high-priz'd Wig. *Queer Flash*, a sorry weather-beaten Wig, not worth Stealing, fit only to put on a Pole, or dress a Scare-Crow.

FLASH-*Ken*, a House where Thieves use, and are connived at.

FLAW'D, Drunk.

FLEECE, to Rob, Plunder or Strip.

FLESH-*Broker*, a Match-maker; also a Bawd; between whom is but little Difference, for they both (usually) take Money.

FILIBUSTIERS, *West-Indian* Pirates, or Buccaneers, Free-booters . . .

[The most animated feature of the 'dictionary' is a certain strain of sardonic euphemism, as in the following examples.]

COLLEGE, *Newgate*.

FRENCHIFIED, Clapt or Poxt.

GOLD-*Finders*, Emptiers of Jakes.

HIGH *Tide*, when the Pocket is full of Money.

LOOKING-*Glass*, a Chamber-pot.

MAIDEN-*Sessions*, when none are hang'd.

MOTHER, a Bawd.

PROVENDER, Money taken from any one on the Highway.

[Amongst the collection of songs is the following.]

. . . the notable Exploits and Escapes of the late notorious *John Shepherd*, who became, for the Time, so much the Talk and Entertainment of the Town, that the polite Gentlemen of a certain *Theatre*, thought it worth their while to lay aside *Heroicks*, and learn the *Canting Dialect*, and from being the awful Representatives of ancient Heroes and Monarchs, thought fit, for the Diversion of their Audiences, and to shew the Universality of their Genius, and the low Station of Life, misbecame their Capacity and Profession, to suffer themselves to dwindle into the Characters of *Sharpers* and *Pickpockets*; and accordingly the Town was presented with a Night Scene in *Grotesque Characters*, wherein that unhappy Felon's Misfortunes were re-acted, under the Title of *Harlequin Shepherd*, for the Publick *Emolument*; which was pompously embellish'd with the Expence of New Scenes, painted from the Real Places of Action: To some of these celebrated Wits, it seems, the whole *Canting Fraternity*, are obliged for the following Song, sung on the Stage, as they tell us, by FRISKY MOLL, the supposed Representative Mistress of *Shepherd*, on Occasion of his being retaken the second Time: The Explanation of the Canting Terms whereof, may be found in the foregoing *Vocabulary*.

From Francis Grose, *A Classical Dictionary of the Vulgar Tongue* (1785)   2.4

Preface

The many vulgar allusions and cant expressions that so frequently occur in our common conversation and periodical publications, make a work of this kind extremely useful, if not absolutely necessary, not only to foreigners, but even to natives resident at a distance from the metropolis, or who do not mix in the busy world; without some such help, they might hunt through all the ordinary Dictionaries, from Alpha to Omega, in search of the words, 'Black legs, lame duck, a plumb, malingeror, nip cheese, darbies, and the new drop,' although these are all terms of well-known import, at New-market, Exchange-alley, the City, the Parade, Wapping, and Newgate. The fashionable words, or favourite expressions of the day, also find their way into our political and theatrical compositions; these, as they generally originate from some trifling event, or temporary circumstance, on falling into disuse, or being superseded by new ones, vanish without leaving a trace behind, such were the late fashionable words, a Bore and a Twaddle, among the great vulgar, Maccaroni and the Barber, among the small; these too are here carefully registered.

   The Vulgar Tongue consists of two parts: the first is the Cant Language, called sometimes, Pedlar's French, or St. Giles's Greek; the second, those Burlesque Phrases, Quaint Allusions, and Nick-names for persons, things and places, which from long uninterrupted usage are made classical by prescription . . .

The second part or burlesque terms, have been drawn from the most classical authorities; such as soldiers on the long march, seamen at the cap-stern, ladies disposing of their fish, and the colloquies of a Gravesend-boat; many heroic sentences, expressing and inculcating a contempt of death, have been caught from the mouths of the applauding populace, attending those triumphant processions up Holborn-hill, with which many an unfortunate hero, till lately finished his course, and various choice flowers have been collected at executions, as well those authorized by the sentence of the law, and performed under the direction of the sheriff, as those inflicted under the authority and inspection of that impartial and summary tribunal, called the Mob, upon the pick-pockets, informers, or other unpopular criminals.

In the course of this work many ludicrous games and customs are explained, which are not to be met with in any other book: the succession of the finishers of the law, the abolition of the triumph or ovation of Holborn-hill, with the introduction of the present mode of execution at Newgate, are chronologically ascertained; points of great importance to both the present and future compilers of the Tyburne Chronicle.

To prevent any charge of immorality being brought against this work, the Editor begs leave to observe, that when an indelicate or immodest word has obtruded itself for explanation, he has endeavoured to get rid of it in the most decent manner possible; and none have been admitted but such, as either could not be left out, without rendering the work incomplete, or, in some measure, compensate by their wit, for the trespass committed on decorum. Indeed respecting this matter, he can with great truth make the same defence that Falstaff ludicrously urges in behalf of one engaged in rebellion, viz. that he did not seek them, but that, like rebellion in the case instanced, they lay in his way, and he found them.

The Editor likewise begs leave to add, that if he has had the misfortune to run foul of the dignity of any body of men, profession, or trade, it is totally contrary to his intention; and he hopes the interpretations given to any particular terms that may seem to bear hard upon them, will not be considered as his sentiments, but as the sentiments of the persons by whom such terms were first invented, or those by whom they are used . . .

ABBESS, or LADY ABBESS, a bawd, the mistress of a brothel.
ABEL-WACKETS, blows given on the palm of the hand with a twisted handkerchief, instead of a ferula; a jocular punishment among seamen, who sometimes play at cards for wackets, the loser suffering as many strokes as he has lost games.
AN ABIGAIL, a lady's waiting maid.
ABRAM, naked, (cant).

ABRAM COVE, a cant word among thieves, signifying a naked or poor man, also a lusty strong rogue.

TO SHAM ABRAM, to pretend sickness.

ACADEMY, or PUSHING SCHOOL, a brothel. The floating academy, the lighters on board of which those persons are confined, who by a late regulation are condemned to hard labour, instead of transportation. Campbell's academy, the same, from a gentleman of that name, who had the contract for finding and victualling the hulks or lighters.

ACCOUNTS, to cast up one's accounts, to vomit.

ACT OF PARLIAMENT, a military term for small beer, five pints of which, by an act of parliament, a landlord was formerly obliged to give to each soldier gratis.

ACTEON, a cockold, from the horns planted on the head of Acteon by Diana.

ADAM'S ALE, water.

ADAM TILER, a pickpocket's associate, who receives the stolen goods, and runs off with them, (cant).

ADDLE PATE, an inconsiderate foolish fellow.

ADDLE PLOT, a spoil sport, a mar all.

ADMIRAL OF THE BLUE, who carries his flag on his mainmast, a landlord or publican wearing a blue apron, as was formerly the custom among gentlemen of that vocation.

ADRIFT, (sea phrase) loose, turned adrift, discharged.

AFFIDAVIT MEN, knights of the post, or false witnesses, said to attend Westminster Hall and other courts of justice, ready to swear any thing for hire, distinguished by having straws stuck in the heels of their shoes.

AFTER-CLAP, a demand after that first given in has been discharged, a charge for pretended omissions.

AGAINST THE GRAIN, unwillingly, it went much against the grain with him, i.e. it was much against his inclination, or against his pluck.

AGOG, ALL-A-GOG, anxious, eager, impatient.

AGROUND, stuck fast, stopped, at a loss, ruined, like a boat or vessel aground.

AIR AND EXERCISE, he has had air and exercise, i.e. he has been whipped at the cart's tail, or as it is generally, though more vulgarly, expressed, at the cart's a—se.

ALE DRAPER, an alehouse keeper.

ALL-A-MORT, struck dumb, confounded.

ALL NATIONS, a composition of all the different spirits sold in a dram shop, collected in a vessel, into which the drainings of the bottles and quartern pots are emptied.

ALSASIA THE HIGHER, White Fryers, once a place privileged from arrests for debt, as was also the Mint, but suppressed on account of the notorious abuses committed there.

ALSASIA THE LOWER, the Mint in Southwark.

ALSASIANS, the inhabitants of White Fryers, or the Mint.

ALTAMEL, vide Dutch reckoning, a verbal or lump account, without particulars, such as are commonly produced at bawdy houses, spunging houses, &c.

ALTITUDES, the man is in his altitudes, i.e. he is drunk . . .

3. ANTIQUARIANISM

Henry Bourne's interest in popular customs was unusual for his times, and might, in some part, be explained by his own humble background. Born in 1696, he was the son of a tailor, and was apprenticed to a glazier, until released at the behest of friends of the family. He was then educated at Newcastle Grammar School and Christ's College, Cambridge, before becoming curate of All Hallows, Newcastle, a position he held until his early death in 1733. When he died he was working on a history of Newcastle, which was published by his widow in 1736. The extract from his *Antiquitates vulgares* (3.1) illustrates most of the characteristics of his study, including censoriousness in the name of Christian orthodoxy. Popular customs are usually ancient, and as 'heathenish' remnants are sometimes to be tolerated with condescension, sometimes to be rooted out (his very next chapter is 'Of the Twelfth Day; how observed: The wickedness of observing the Twelve Days after the common Way'.) It has been necessary, in the passages given below, to omit the often lengthy footnotes in which Bourne parades his authorities. Usually these consist of Latin quotations from the ancient authors mentioned in the text.

Bourne's work was taken up half a century later by John Brand. He reprinted Bourne's work in its entirety, complete with his own, often supercilious and sometimes scathing, 'Addenda'. As will be apparent, he had a strongly anti-Catholic bent and an inclination to see 'popular Notions and vulgar Ceremonies' as relics from the times before the Reformation. 'No Bondage seems so dreadful as that of Superstition', he writes. He understands popular culture in terms of that 'Bondage'. We give passages from his General Preface and from sample 'Observations'. The second of these takes up (dismissively) the topic of carols discussed by Bourne. The work was eventually highly influential; it was reprinted in 1813, expanded and revised, by Sir Henry Ellis, and would have a second life as a source book for nineteenth-century enthusiasts for 'folklore'. Francis Grose also drew on Bourne and Brand for his *Provincial Glossary* (3.3).

From Henry Bourne, *Antiquitates Vulgares; or, the Antiquities of the Common* 3.1
People **(Newcastle, 1725)**

Preface

The following Sheets are a few of that vast Number of *Ceremonies* and *Opinions*, which are held by the Common People; such as they solely or generally observe. For tho' some of them have been of National and others perhaps of universal Observance, yet at present they would have little or no Being, if not observed among the Vulgar.

I would not be thought a Reviver of old Rites and Ceremonies to the Burdening of the People, nor an Abolisher of innocent Customs, which are their Pleasures and Recreations: I aim at nothing, but a Regulation of those which are in Being amongst them, which they themselves are far from thinking burdensome, and abolishing such only as are sinful and wicked.

Some of the Customs they hold, have been originally good, tho' at present they retain little of their primitive Purity; the true Meaning and Design of them, being either lost, or very much in the Dark through Folly and Superstition. To wipe off therefore the Dust they have contracted, to clear them of Superstition, and make known their End and Design, may turn to some Account, and be of Advantage; whereas observing them in the present Way, is not only of no Advantage, but of very great Detriment.

Others they hold, are really sinful, notwithstanding in outward Appearance they seem very harmless, being a Scandal to Religion, and an encouraging of Wickedness. And therefore to aim at abolishing these, will I hope be no Crime, tho' they be the Diversions of the People.

As to the Opinions they hold, they are almost all superstitious, being generally either the Produce of Heathenism; or the Inventions of indolent *Monks*, who having nothing else to do, were the Forgers of many silly and wicked Opinions, to keep the World in Awe and Ignorance. And indeed the ignorant Part of the World is still so aw'd, that they follow the idle Traditions of the one, more than the Word of GOD; and have more Dependence upon the lucky Omens of the other than his Providence, more Dread of their unlucky ones, than his Wrath and Punishment.

The regulating therefore of these Opinions and Customs, is what I propos'd by the following Compositions, whatever has been suggested to the contrary: And as to the Menaces of some, and the Censures of others, I neither fear nor regard them. I shall be always ready to own any Mistake, and in what I justly may, to vindicate my self . . .

CHAP. XV

Of the Christmas Carol, an ancient Custom: The common Observation of it very unbecoming

As soon as the Morning of the *Nativity* appears, it is customary among the common People to sing a *Christmas-Carol*, which is a Song upon the Birth of our Saviour, and is generally sung with some others, from the Nativity to the Twelveth-Day, the Continuance of *Christmas*. It comes, they say, from *Cantare*, to sing, and *Rola*, which is an Interjection of Joy: For in ancient Times, the Burden of the Song, when Men were Merry, was *Rola, Rola*.

This kind of Songs is of an Ancient standing: They were sung early in the Church it self, in memory of the Nativity, as the many HYMNS for that Season manifestly declare: *Tertullian* says, it was customary among the Christians, at their Feasts, to bring those, who were able to sing, into the Midst, and make them sing a Song unto GOD; either out of the Holy Scripture, or of their own Composing and Invention. And as this was done at their Feasts, so no doubt it was observed at the great Feast of the Nativity; which Song, no Question of it, was to them, what the *Christmas-Carol* should be to us. In after Ages we have it also taken notice of: For *Dunand* tells us, That on the Day of the *Nativity*, it was usual for the Bishops of some Churches to sing among their Clergy, in the Episcopal House, which Song was undoubtedly a *Christmas-Carol*.

The Reason of this Custom seems to be an Imitation of the *Gloria in Excelsis*, or *Glory be to GOD on High*, &c. which was sung by the Angels, as they hovered o'er the Fields of *Bethlehem*, in the Morning of the Nativity. For even that Song, as the learned Bishop *Taylor* observes, was a Christmas-Carol. *As soon*, says he, *as these blessed Choristers had sung their Christmas-Carol, and taught the Church a Hymn, to put into her Offices for Ever, in the Anniversary of this Festivity; the Angels*, &c.

Was this performed with that Reverence and Decency, which are due to a Song of this Nature, in Honour of the Nativity, and Glory to our LORD, it would be very commendable; but to sing it, as is generally done, in the midst of *Rioting and Chambering, and Wantoness*, is no Honour, but Disgrace; no Glory, but an Affront to that Holy Season, a Scandal to Religion, and a Sin against CHRIST . . .

Another old Custom at this Time, is the wishing of a *good New-Year*, either when a New-Year's Gift is presented, or when Friends meet, or when a New-Year's Song is sung at the Door; the Burden of which is, *we wish you a happy New-Year* . . .

Now the Original of this Custom is Heathenish, as appears by the Feasting and Presents before mentioned, which were a Wish for a good Year. And it was customary among the Heathens on the Calends of *January*, to go about and sing a *New-Year's Song. Hospinian* therefore tells us, That when Night comes on, not only the Young, but also the Old of both Sexes, run about here and there, and sing a Song at the Doors of the wealthier People, in which they wish them a *happy New-Year.* This he speaks indeed of the Christians, but he calls it an exact Copy of the Heathens Custom.

But however I cannot see the Harm of retaining this ancient Ceremony, so it be not used superstitiously, nor attended with Obscenity and Lewdness. For then there will be no more in it, than a hearty Wish for each others Welfare and Prosperity; no more Harm, than wishing a good Day, or good Night; than in bidding one GOD *speed*; or than in wishing to our Friend, what *Abraham's* Servant did to himself, *O LORD GOD of my Master* Abraham, *I pray thee send me good speed this Day.*

There is another Custom observed at this Time, which is called among us *Mumming*; which is a changing of Clothes between Men and Women; who when dress'd in each others Habits, go from one Neigbour's House to another, and partake of their *Christmas-Cheer*, and make merry with them in Disguise, by dancing and singing, and such like Merriments.

This is an Imitation of the *Sigillaria*, or Festival Days which were added to the ancient *Saturnalia*, and observed by the Heathens in *January*; which was a going in Disguise, not publickly, or to any indifferent Place, but privately, and to some well known Families.

This kind of Custom received a deserved Blow from the Church, and was taken Notice of in the Synod of *Trullus*; where it was decreed, that the Days called the *Calends*, should be intirely strip'd of their Ceremonies, and the Faithful should no longer observe them: That the publick Dancings of Women should cease, as being the Occasion of much Harm and Ruin, and as being invented and observed in honour of their Gods, and therefore quite averse to the Christian Life. They therefore decreed, that no Man should be Cloathed with a Woman's Garment, no Woman with a Man's.

It were to be wish'd, this Custom, which is still so Common among us at this Season of the Year, was laid aside; as it is the Occasion of much Uncleanness and Debauchery, and directly opposite to the Word of GOD. *The Woman shall not wear that which pertaineth unto a Man, neither shall a Man put on a Woman's Garment; for all that do so, are Abomination unto the LORD thy GOD.*

From John Brand, *Observations on Popular Antiquities* (1777)   3.2

The General Preface

Tradition has in no Instance so clearly evinced her Faithfulness, as in the transmitting of vulgar Rites and popular Opinions.

Of these, when we are desirous of tracing them backwards to their Origin, many lose themselves in Antiquity.

They have indeed travelled down to us through a long Succession of Years, and the greatest part of them, it is not improbable, will be of perpetual Observation: for the generality of Men look back with superstitious Veneration on the Ages of their Forefathers: and Authorities, that are grey with Time, seldom fail of commanding those filial Honours, claimed even by the Appearance of hoary old Age.

Many of these it must be confessed are mutilated, and, as in the Remains of antient Statuary, the Parts of not a few of them have been awkwardly transposed: they preserve, however, the principal *Traits*, that distinguished them in their origin.

Things, composed of such flimsy Materials as the Fancies of a Multitude, do not seem calculated for a long Duration; yet have these survived Shocks, by which even Empires have been overthrown, and preserved at least some *Form* and *Contour* of Identity, during a Repetition of Changes, both in Religious Opinions, and in the Polity of States.

But the strongest Proof of their remote Antiquity, is, that they have outlived the general Knowledge of the very Causes that gave Rise to them.

The Reader will find in subsequent pages an union of Endeavours to rescue many of these Causes from Oblivion. If, on the Investigation, they appear to any so frivolous as not to have deserved the Pains of the Search, the humble Labourers will avoid Censure, by incurring Contempt. How trivial soever such an Enquiry may seem to some, yet all must be informed that it is attended with no small share of Difficulty and Toil.

A Passage is to be forced through a Wilderness intricate and entangled: few Vestiges of former Labours can be found to direct us; we must sometimes trace a tedious retrospective Course, perhaps to return at last weary and unsatisfied, from the making of Researches, fruitless as those of some antient enthusiastic Traveller, who ranging the barren *African* Sands, had in vain attempted to investigate the hidden Sources of the *Nile*.

Rugged and narrow as this Walk of Study may seem to many, yet *Fancy* (who shares with *Hope* the pleasing Office of brightening a Passage through every *Route* of human Endeavour) opens from hence to Prospects, enriched with the choicest beauties of her magic Creation.

The prime Origin of the superstitious Notions and Ceremonies of the People is absolutely unattainable; we despair of ever being able to reach the Fountain Head of Streams which have been running and increasing from the Beginning of Time. All that we aspire to do, is only to trace backwards, as far as possible, the Courses of them on those Charts, that remain, of the distant Countries from whence they were first perceived to flow.

Few, who are desirous of investigating the popular Notions and vulgar Ceremonies in our Nation, can fail of deducing them in their first Direction from the Times when Popery was our established Religion.

We shall not wonder that these were able to survive the Reformation, when we consider, that though our sensible and spirited forefathers were, upon Conviction, easily induced to forgo religious Tenets, which had been weighed in the Balance, and found wanting; yet were *the People* by no means inclined to annihilate the seemingly innocent Ceremonies of their former superstitious Faith.

These, consecrated to the Fancies of Men, by a Usage from Time immemorial, though erazed by public Authority from the *written Word*, were committed as a venerable Deposit to the keeping of *oral Tradition*: like the *Penates* of another *Troy*, recently destroyed, they were religiously brought off, after having been snatched out of the smoking Ruins of Popery . . .

The Common People, confined by daily Labour, seem to require their proper Intervals of Relaxation; perhaps it is of the highest political Utility to encourage innocent Sports and Games among them. The Revival of many of these, would, I think, be highly pertinent at this particular Season, when the general Spread of Luxury and Dissipation threatens more than at any preceding Period to extinguish the Character of our boasted national Bravery. For the Observation of an honest old Writer, Stow, (who tells us, speaking of the May-games, Midsummer-Eve *Rejoicings*, &c. antiently used in the Streets of London, 'which open Pastimes in my Youth being now supprest, worse Practices *within Doors* are to be feared)', may be with singular propriety adopted on the most transient Survey of our present popular Manners.

Mr. Bourne, my Predecessor in this Walk, has not, from whatever Cause, done Justice to the Subject he undertook to treat of. Far from having the Vanity to think that I have exhausted it, the utmost of my Pretensions is to the Merit of having endeavoured, by making Additions, to improve it. I think him, however, deserving of no small share of Praise for his imperfect Attempt, for 'much is due to those, who first broke the Way to Knowledge, and left only to their Successors the Task of smoothing it.'

New Lights have arisen since his Time. The English Antique has become a general and fashionable Study; and the Discoveries of the very respectable Society of Antiquaries have rendered the Recesses of Papal and Heathen Antiquities easier of access . . .

Elegance of Composition will hardly be expected in a Work of this Kind, which stands much less in need of Attic Wit, than of Roman Perseverance, and *Dutch* assiduity.

I shall therefore offer some Discoveries, which are peculiarly my own; for there are Customs yet retained here in the North, of which I am persuaded the learned of the Southern part of the Island have not heard, which is, perhaps, the sole Cause why they have never before been investigated.

In perusing the subsequent Observations, the candid Reader, who has never before considered this neglected Subject, is requested not to be rash in passing Sentence, but to suspend his Judgment, at least, till he has carefully examined all the evidence; by which Caution I do not wish to have it understood that our Determinations are thought to be infallible, or that every Decision here is not amenable to an higher Authority. In the mean time Prejudice may be forewarned, and it will apologize for many seemingly trivial Reasons, assigned for the beginning and transmitting of this or that *Notion* or *Ceremony*, to reflect, that what may appear foolish to the enlightened Understandings of Men in the *Eighteenth* Century, wore a very different Aspect when viewed through the Gloom that prevailed in the *seventh* or *eighth* . . .

When I call to remembrance the *Poet of Humanity*, who has transmitted his Name to Immortality, by Reflections written among the little Tomb-stones of the Vulgar, in a Country Church-Yard; I am urged by no false Shame to apologize for the seeming Unimportance of my Subject.

The Antiquities of the Common People cannot be studied without acquiring some useful Knowledge of Mankind. By the chemical Process of Philosophy, even Wisdom may be extracted from the Follies and Superstitions of our Forefathers.

The *People*, of whom Society is chiefly composed, and for whose good, Superiority of Rank is only a Grant made originally by mutual Concession, is a respectable Subject to every one who is a Friend of Man.

Pride, which, independent of the Idea arising from the Necessity of civil Polity, has portioned out the human *Genus* into such a variety of different and subordinate *Species*, must be compelled to own that the lowest of these derives itself from an Origin, common to it with the highest of the Kind. The beautiful Sentiment of *Terence*:

'*Homo* sum, *humani* nihil a me alienum puto.'

may be adopted therefore in this Place, to persuade us that nothing can be foreign to our Enquiry, which concerns the smallest of the Vulgar; of those *little ones*, who occupy the lowest Place in the political Arrangement of human Beings.

[From 'Observations on Chapter VIII' (*Of visiting Wells and Fountains . . .*)]

. . . I have frequently observed Shreds, or Bits of Rags, upon the Bushes that over-hang a *Well*, in the Road to Benton, a Village in the Neighbourhood of Newcastle. It is called the *Rag Well*. This Name is undoubtedly of a very long standing: The Spring has been visited for some Disorder or other, and these *Rag-offerings* are the Reliques of the then prevailing popular Superstition.—Thus Mr. Pennant tells us, they visit the Well of Spey, in Scotland, for many Distempers, and the Well of Drachaldy for as many, offering small Pieces of Money and *Bits of Rags* . . .

Mr. Shaw, in his History of the Province of Moray, tells us, that true rational, Christian Knowledge, which was almost quite lost under Popery, made very slow Progress after the Reformation;—that the prevailing Ignorance was attended with much Superstition and Credulity; Heathenish and Romish Customs were much practised; *Pilgrimages to Wells* and Chapels were frequent, &c.—We had a remarkable Well of this Kind at Jesmond, at the Distance of about a Mile from Newcastle.—One of our principal Streets is said to have its Name from an *Inn* that was in it, to which the *Pilgrims*, that flocked hither for the Benefit of the *supposed* holy Water, used to resort.

[From 'Observations on Chapter XV' (*Of the Christmas-Carol, an antient Custom*). Brand prints an old Scottish carol, which he calls sarcastically 'a *precious Relique*']

It is hardly credible that such a Composition as this should ever have been thought serious. The Author has left a fine *Example* in the *Art* of *Sinking*. Had he *designed* to have rendered his Subject ridiculous, he could not more effectually have made it so; and yet we will absolve him from having had the smallest Degree of any such Intention.

In the *Office* where this Work is printed, there is preserved an *hereditary* Collection of *Ballads*, numerous almost as the celebrated one of *Pepys*.—Among these (the greatest Part of which is worse than Trash) I find several *Carrols* for this Season; for the *Nativity*, St. Stephen's Day, Childermass Day, &c. with *Alexander* and the *King of Egypt*, a *mock Play*, usually acted about this Time by *Mummers*. The *Stile* of them all is so *puerile* and *simple*, that I cannot think it would be worth the Pains to invade the Hawkers' Province, by exhibiting any Specimens of them.

———

From Francis Grose, *A Provincial Glossary, with a Collection of Local* 3.3 *Proverbs, and Popular Superstitions* (1787)

Preface

The utility of a Provincial Glossary to all persons desirous of understanding our ancient poets, is so universally acknowledged, that to enter into a proof of it would be entirely a work of supererogation. Divers partial collections have been occasionally made, all which have been well received, and frequently re-printed; these are, in this work, all united under one alphabet, and augmented by many hundred words collected by the Editor in the different places wherein they are used; the rotation of military quarters, and the recruiting service, having occasioned him to reside for some time in most of the counties in England . . .

As the Local Proverbs, all allude to the particular history of the places mentioned, or some ancient custom respecting them, they seem worth preserving, particularly as both the customs and many of the places alluded to are sliding silently into oblivion. For these Local Proverbs I have consulted Fuller's Worthies, Ray, and a variety of other writers, many of whose explanations I have ventured to controvert, and, I hope, amend.

The Popular Superstitions, likewise, tend to illustrate our ancient poems and romances, Shakspear, in particular, drew his inimitable scenes of magic from that source; for, on consulting the writers on that subject, it will be found he has exhibited the vulgar superstitions of his time. Indeed one cause of these scenes having so great effect on us, is their calling back to our fancies, the tales and terrors of the nursery, which are so strongly stamped on our tender minds, as rarely, if ever, to be totally effaced; and of these tales, spite of the precaution of parents, every child has heard something, more or less.

The different articles under this head, that are collected from books, are all from the most celebrated authors on the subject. Among them are King James I, Glanvil, Dr. Henry More, Beaumont, Aubrey, Cotton Mather, Richard Baxter, Reginald Scot, and Bourne's Popular Antiquities, as augmented by Mr. Brand.

Other articles on this subject, and those not a few, have been collected from the mouths of village historians, as they were related to a closing circle of attentive hearers, assembled in a winter's evening, round the capacious chimney of an old hall or manor-house; for, formerly, in counties remote from the metropolis, or which had no immediate intercourse with it, before news-papers and stage-coaches had imported scepticism, and made every plowman and thresher a politician and free-thinker, ghosts, fairies and witches, with bloody murders, committed by tinkers, formed a principal part of rural conversation, in all large assemblies, and particularly those in Christmas holydays, during the burning of the yule-block . . .

Local Proverbs: London

. . . St. Giles's breed; fat, ragged and saucy.

The people of that parish, particularly those resident in Newton and Dyot-streets, still retain their rags and impudence, but do not seem remarkable for their embonpoint; perhaps the proverb only meant to indicate that they did not wear down their flesh by hard labour, in which case lazy, ragged, and saucy, would have been a better description of them.

He will ride backwards up Holborn-hill.

He will come to be hanged. Criminals condemned for offences committed in London and Middlesex, were, till about the year 1784, executed at Tyburn, the way to which from Newgate, was up Holborn-hill. They were generally conveyed in carts (except such as had interest to obtain leave to ride thither in a coach) they, I mean those in carts, were always placed with their backs towards the horses, it is said out of humanity, that they might not be shocked with a view of the gallows till they arrived under it; though some think the mode of riding was to increase the ignominy.

He will faint at the smell of a wall-flower.

Intimating that the person so spoken of had been confined in the gaol of Newgate, formerly stiled the wall-flower, from the wall-flowers growing up against it.

He may wet his knife on the threshold of the Fleet.

Said of persons who are not in debt, as they may go into prison without danger of being detained. This proverb, however, is sometimes used in a different sense, on seeing a person newly come to a great fortune, and spending it extravagantly, it naturally occurs, that by such proceedings, he may wet his knife on the threshold of the Fleet, which may be done as well on one side as the other of the iron grates. The Fleet takes its name from a small brook running by it.

A cockney.

A very ancient nick-name for a citizen of London. Ray says, an interpretation of it is, a young person coaxed or cocquered, made a wanton, or nestle-cock, delicately bred and brought up, so as when arrived at man's estate, to be unable to bear the least hardship. Another, a person ignorant of the terms of country oeconomy, such as a young citizen, who, having been ridiculed for calling the neighing of a horse laughing, and told that was called neighing, next morning, on hearing the cock crow, to shew instruction was not thrown away upon him, exclaimed to his former instructor, how that cock neighs! whence the citizens of London have ever since been called cock-neighs, or cockneys . . .

3.4   From Joseph Strutt, *Glig-gamena*, 1st edn. (1801)

Book III. Pastimes usually exercised in Towns and Cities, or Places adjoining to them.

The PUPPET-SHOWS usually made their appearance at great fairs, and especially at those in the vicinity of the metropolis; they still continue to be exhibited in Smithfield at Bartholomew-tide, though with very little traces of their former greatness; indeed, of late years, they have become unpopular, and are frequented only by children. It is, however, certain, that the puppet-shows attracted the notice of the public at the commencement of the last century, and rivalled in some degree the more pompous exhibitions of the larger theatres. Powel, a famous puppet-show man, is mentioned in one of the early papers of the Spectator, and his performances are humorously contrasted with those at the Opera House. At the same time there was another motion-master, who also appears to have been of some celebrity, named Crawley; I have before me two bills of his exhibition, one for Bartholomew Fair, and the other for Southwark Fair. The first runs thus: 'At Crawley's Booth, over against the *Crown Tavern* in *Smithfield*, during the time of *Bartholomew Fair*, will be presented a little *opera*, called the *Old Creation of the World*, yet newly revived; with the addition of *Noah's flood*; also several fountains playing water during the time of the play.—The last scene does represent *Noah* and his *family* coming out of the ark, with all the beasts two by two, and all the fowls of the air seen in a prospect sitting upon trees; likewise over the ark is seen the sun rising in a most glorious manner; moreover, a multitude of angels will be seen in a double rank, which presents a double prospect, one for the sun, the other for a palace, where will be seen six angels ringing of bells.—Likewise machines descend from above, double and treble, with *Dives* rising out of hell, and *Lazarus* seen in Abraham's bosom, besides several *figures* dancing *jiggs*, *sarabands*, and *country dances*, to the admiration of the spectators; with the merry conceits of squire *Punch* and Sir *John Spendall*.' This curious medley was, we are told, 'completed by an entertainment of singing, and dancing with several naked swords, performed by a child of eight years of age.' In the second bill, we find the addition of 'the ball of *little dogs*;' it is also added, that these celebrated performers had danced before the queen and most of the quality of England, and amazed every body.

  XIX. The subjects of the puppet-dramas were formerly taken from some well known and popular stories, with the introduction of knights and giants; hence the following speech in an old comedy: 'They had like to have frighted me with a man dressed up like a gyant in a puppet show.' [A footnote tells us this is from *The Humorous Lovers*, printed in 1617.] In my memory, these shows consisted of a wretched display of wooden figures, barbarously formed and decorated, without the least degree of taste or propriety; the wires that communicated the motion to them appeared at the tops of their heads, and the manner in which they were made to move evinced the ignorance and inattention of the managers; the dialogues were mere jumbles of absurdity and nonsense, intermixed with low immoral discourses passing between Punch and the fiddler, for the orchestra rarely admitted of more than one minstrel; and these flashes of merriment were made offensive to decency by the actions of the puppet.

XX. The introduction, or rather the revival of *pantomimes*, which indeed have long disgraced the superior theatres, proved the utter undoing of the puppet-show men; in fact, all the absurdities of the puppet-show, except the discourse, are retained in the pantomimes, the difference consisting principally in the substitution of living puppets for wooden ones; but it must be confessed, though nothing be added to the rationality of the performances, great pains is taken to supply the defect, by fascinating the eyes and ears; and certainly the brilliancy of the dresses and scenery, the skilful management of the machinery, and the excellence of the music, in the pantomimes, are great improvements upon the humble attempts of the vagrant *motion-master*.

XXI. In the present day, the puppet-show man travels about the streets when the weather will permit, and carries his motions, with the theatre itself, upon his back! The exhibition takes place in the open air; and the precarious income of the miserable itinerant depends entirely on the voluntary contributions of the spectators, which, as far as any one may judge from the squalid appearance he usually makes, is very trifling . . .

XXVIII. Bull and bear-baiting is not encouraged by persons of rank and opulence in the present day; and when practised, which rarely happens, it is attended only by the lowest and most despicable part of the people; which plainly indicates a general refinement of manners and prevalency of humanity among the moderns; on the contrary, this barbarous pastime was highly relished by the nobility in former ages, and countenanced by persons of the most exalted rank, without exception even of the fair sex. When queen Mary visited her sister the princess Elizabeth during her confinement at Hatfield-house, the next morning, after mass, a grand exhibition of bear-baiting was made for their amusement, with which, it is said, 'their highnesses were right well content.' The same princess, soon after her accession to the throne, gave a splendid dinner to the French ambassadors, who afterwards were entertained with the baiting of bulls and bears, and the queen herself stood with the ambassadors looking on the pastime till six at night.

4. BALLADS

The first of the extracts below appeared in a pamphlet written by Tory hack William Wagstaffe in direct and mocking response to Addison's famous critique of 'Chevy Chase'. It attempts to play upon standard views about the inferiority of the popular and the vulgar. After his sardonic opening, given in the first of the paragraphs below, Wagstaffe embarks on some 'Observations' on Tom Thumb, 'a Performance not unworthy the Perusal of the Judicious, and the Model superiour to either of those incomparable Poems of Chevy Chase or The Children in the Wood'. When he considers the 'Miracle of a Man' who was the ballad's author, he turns the ridicule on the antiquarians. There follows a sustained, ironic celebration of the expressive powers of the ballad, and a series of supposedly flattering comparisons between it and Virgil. This concludes with sideswipes at two well-known hack writers of the day, Thomas D'Urfey and John Dunton (appropriately tasteless connoisseurs of such verse) and one of the most frequently ridiculed antiquarians, Dr John Woodward (often a victim of Pope's and Swift's satires).

John Dennis's rejoinder to Addison, represented in the next group of excerpts (4.2), was written immediately after the publication of the second of Addison's essays. It was not, however, published until 1721, by which time Addison was dead, as was any immediate controversy caused by his arguments. It is addressed to Henry Cromwell, who had apparently written to Dennis asking whether the *Spectator* papers were serious or ironical. At the heart of the essay, Dennis argues against the misapplication of the observation in the *Spectator* that 'Human Nature is the same in all reasonable Creatures, and whatever falls in with it, will meet with Admirers among Readers of all Qualities and Conditions'. He concludes by quoting Horace at some length, finding that the great poet advised other poets not to try to please 'the Multitude'. Ballads did appeal to a polite readership, however, as is evident from the number of collections like *A Collection of Old Ballads* (1723–5), from the preface of which a brief extract is given (4.3).

David Herd's *Ancient and Modern Scottish Songs, Heroic Ballads, etc Collected from Memory, Tradition, and Ancient Authors* (4.4) first appeared in 1769, building on the interest generated by Percy's *Reliques*. Herd did actually collect ballads from country folk, although he neglected to indicate which were these, and which were copied from books. His defence of ballads, in an extract from his preface, shows how sentimentalism could be adapted to this fashion for 'simple' verse. The excerpt from John Aikin's *Essays on Song-Writing* (4.5) is taken from the third edition of the work (Dublin, 1777). The bulk of this volume is taken up by 'A collection of such English songs as are most eminent for poetical merit'. These are lyrics (sorted into the categories 'Pastoral', 'Descriptive', and 'Witty') by authors of the seventeenth and eighteenth centuries. Those from whom he has taken most are Congreve, Prior, Shenstone, and Anna Laetitia Barbauld (his sister). His defence of ballads is, in fact, a prelude to an anthology of elegantly simple verse, and a kind of explanation of the lyric impulse as such. The chapter ends with extracts from the preface to Joseph Ritson's *Pieces of Ancient Popular Poetry*, which aggressively opposes ballads to 'the artificial refinements of modern taste'.

From William Wagstaffe, *A Comment Upon the History of Tom Thumb* 4.1 (1711)

It is a surprising thing that in an Age so Polite as this, in which we have such a Number of Poets, Criticks and Commentators, some of the best things that are extant in our Language shou'd pass unobserv'd amidst a croud of inferiour Productions, and lie so long buried as it were, among those that profess such a Readiness to give Life to every thing that is valuable. Indeed we have had an Enterprising Genius of late, that has thought fit to disclose the Beauties of some Pieces to the World, that might have been otherwise indiscernible, and believ'd to have been trifling and insipid, for no other Reason but their unpolish'd Homeliness of Dress. And if we were to apply our selves, instead of the Classicks, to the Study of Ballads and other ingenious Composures of that Nature, in such Periods of our Lives, when we are arriv'd to a Maturity of Judgment, it is impossible to say what Improvement might be made to Wit in general, and the Art of Poetry in particular: And certainly our Passions are describ'd in them so naturally, in such lively, tho' simple, Colours, that how far they may fall short of the Artfulness and Embellishments of the *Romans* in their Way of Writing, *yet cannot fail to please all such Readers as are not unqualify'd for the Entertainment by their Affectation or Ignorance* . . .

   I have consulted Monsieur *Le Clerk*, and my friend Dr. *B—ly* concerning the Chronology of this Author, who both assure me, tho' Neither can settle the Matter exactly, that he is the most ancient of our Poets, and 'tis very probable he was a *Druid*, who, as *Julius Caesar* mentions in his *Commentaries*, us'd to deliver their Precepts in Poetry and Metre. The Author of *The Tale of a Tub*, believes he was a *Pythagorean* Philosopher, and held the *Metempsichosis*; and Others that he has read Ovid's *Metamorphosis*, and was the first Person that ever found out the Philosopher's Stone. A certain Antiquary of my Acquaintance, who is willing to forget every thing he shou'd remember, tells me, He can scarcely believe him to be Genuine, but if he is, he must have liv'd some time before the *Barons* Wars; which he proves, as he does the Establishment of Religion in this Nation, upon the Credit of an old Monument . . .

I know there are some People that cast an Odium on me, and others, for point-ing out the Beauties of such Authors, as have, they say, been hitherto unknown, and argue, That 'tis a sort of Heresie in Wit, and is like the fruitless Endeavours of proving the Apostolical Constitutions *Genuine*, that have been indisputably *Spurious* for so many Ages: But let these Gentlemen consider, whether they pass not the same Judgment on an Author, as a Woman does on a Man, by the gayety of his Dress, or the gaudy Equipage of his Epithets. And however they may call me *second-sighted*, for discerning what they are Blind to, I must tell them this Poem has not been altogether so obscure, but that the most refin'd *Writers* of this Age have been delighted with the reading it. Mr. *Tho. D'Urfey*, I am told, is an Admirer, and Mr. *John Dunton* has been heard to say, more than once, he had rather be the Author of it than all his Works.

How often, *says my Author*, have I seen the Tears trickle down the Face of the Polite *Woodwardius* upon reading some of the most pathetical Encounters of *Tom Thumb*! How soft, how musically sorrowful was his Voice! How good Natur'd, how gentle, how unaffected was the Ceremonial of his Gesture, and how unfit for a Profession so Merciless and Inhuman!

———————

4.2 From John Dennis, *Original Letters, Familiar, Moral and Critical*, 2 vols. (1721)

From 'To H—C—Esq; Of Simplicity in Poetical Compositions, in Remarks on the 70th Spectator'

. . . Has he not himself observed in the 134th Tatler, that there are Exercises and Diversions which universally please the Rabble, which yet Men of Quality or Education either despise or abhor? Such are the Shrove-Tuesday and Bear-Garden Diversions, which he there particularizes. I have known a Country Fidler who has been the Delight of three Counties, tho' he could never play the Truth of one Tune; and a Sign-Post Painter, who has been the Admiration not only of the Rabble, but even of most of the Squires of the North of England. I appeal to the Booksellers, who in this Case ought to be Judges without Appeal, whether more of the common People do not approve of Quarles and Bunyan than esteem Chevy Chase. Therefore 'tis plain that Author could not design that the period above-mentioned should run thus,

For 'tis impossible that any thing should be universally tasted and approved of by a Multitude, tho' they are only the Rabble of a Nation, which has not in it some peculiar Aptness to please and gratify the Minds of Men of Quality and Education . . .

Can he be so dull and so absurd as not to know how to distinguish between what Human Nature is, and what Human Nature should be? Human Nature was Human Nature before the Fall, and 'tis Human Nature now 'tis degenerated from that perfect Virtue and that unclouded Knowledge, which it enjoy'd before. 'Tis the Business and Design of Education to endeavour to retrieve in some measure the Loss that Human Nature has sustain'd by the Fall; and to recover some Measure of Knowledge and Virtue. Now Heroick Poetry is an Imitation of Human Nature exalted, and Comedy is an Imitation of Human Nature depraved. What can be more absurd than to conclude, that because the Rabble, that is, such as never had any Education, are tolerable Judges of Human Nature depraved, that therefore they are Judges of Human Nature exalted, of which none can be Judges but they who have had the best Education? And therefore not only the Rabble, but an universal Nation has been mistaken in their Judgments of Poets and Poetry, when the Judgments have been made, before that Nation came to be sufficiently cultivated . . .

From *A Collection of Old Ballads* vol. 1 (1723)   4.3

[The title-page prints these lines from Rowe's tragedy *Jane Shore*]

> Let no nice Sir despise the hapless Dame,
> Because Recording BALLADS chaunt her Name.
> Those Venerable Ancient Song-Enditers
> Soar'd man a Pitch beyond our modern Writers.
> With rough Majestic Force they mov'd the Heart,
> And Strength and Nature made amends for Art.

[The preface goes on to argue that Pindar, Anacreon, Horace, Cowley, and Suckling were all ballad-writers.]

The Ballad-Makers are a more ancient, more numerous, and more noble Society than the boasted Free-Masons; and Duke upon Duke will witness, that People of considerable Fashion have thought it no Disgrace to enroll themselves in this Worshipful Society.

Nor have these antique Songs ever been without their Admirers. When Thebes was sack'd, Pindar was spar'd for the Sake of his Works; and Alexander wept, to think his Age did not afford so clever a Ballad-singer as Homer had been, to record his Actions to Posterity.

It was the Custom of these Song Enditers thus to transmit to their Children the glorious Actions which happen'd in their Days. And I believe it never was used more than amongst the English in Times of old. For we may very reasonably suppose, that one half at least of their Works are lost; and we have still one half of whatever is remarkable in History, handed down to us in Ballads.

———————

4.4   From David Herd, *Ancient and Modern Scottish Songs, Heroic Ballads, etc Collected from Memory, Tradition, and Ancient Authors*, 2nd edn. (1776)

Preface

The common popular songs and national music, as they form a favourite entertainment of the Gay and the Chearful, seem likewise to merit some regard from the Speculative and Refined, in so far as they exhibit natural and striking traits of the character, genius, taste and pursuits of the people. And trivial as his idea of a song may be, the statesman has often felt this paultry engine affecting the machine of government; and those who are versant in history can produce instances of popular songs and ballads having been rendered subservient to great revolutions both in church and state.

Every nation, at least every ancient and unmixed nation, hath its peculiar style of musical expression, its peculiar mode of melody; modulated by the joint influence of climate and government, character and situation, as well as by the formation of the organs. Thus each of the states of ancient Greece had its characteristic style of music, the Doric, the Phrygian, the Lydian mood, &c. and thus the moderns have their distinct national styles, the Italian, the Spanish, the Irish, and the Scottish. That predilection so natural for every production of one's own country, together with the force of habit, a certain enthusiasm attendant upon music, and perhaps sometimes the principle of association, whereby other agreeable ideas are mingled and always called up to the mind together with the musical air, has ever induced people to prefer their own national music to that of others: and we are seldom at a loss for arguments in support of this real or fancied preeminence. Strongly biassed, however, as our judgements must be by the powerful prejudices mentioned above, it would seem that the question concerning the comparative merit of the respective styles of national melody is a question of much difficulty and little importance . . .

. . . it may be permitted [the editor] to observe, that the merit both of the poetry and the music of the Scots songs is undoubtedly great; and that the peculiar spirit and genius of each is so admirably adapted to each other, as to produce, when conjoined, the most enchanting effect on every lover of nature and unaffected simplicity. For the characteristical excellence of both, he apprehends, is nearly the same, to wit, a forcible and pathetic simplicity, which at once lays strong hold on the affections; so that the heart itself may be considered as an instrument, which the bard or minstrel harmonizes, touching all its strings in the most delicate and masterly manner! Such is the character of the pathetic and sentimental songs of Scotland, which may with truth be termed, *the poetry and the music of the heart*. There is another species, to wit, the humorous and comic, no less admirable for genuine humour, sprightly naivete, picturesque language, and striking paintings of low life and comic characters; the music whereof is so well adapted to the sentiment, that any person of a tolerable ear upon hearing it, feels a difficulty in restraining a strong propensity to dance.

From John Aikin, *Essays on Song-Writing*, 3rd edn. (1777)　　　　　　　　4.5

The rude original pastoral poetry of our country furnishes the first class in the popular pieces called ballads. These consist of the village tale, the dialogue of rustic courtship, the description of natural objects, and the incidents of a rural life. Their language is the language of nature, simple and unadorned; their story is not the wild offspring of fancy, but the probable adventure of the cottage; and their sentiments are the unstudied expressions of passions and emotions common to all mankind.

Nature, farther refined, but still nature, gives the second class of pieces containing the sentimental part of the former, abstracted from the tale and rural landscape, and improved by a more studied observation of the internal feelings of passion and their external symptoms. It is the natural philosophy of the mind, and the description of sensations. Here love appears in all its variatious forms of desire, doubt, jealousy, hope, despair; and suggests a language, rich, strong, and figurative. This is what may strictly be called the pathetic in poetry.

The third class is formed upon an artificial turn of thinking, and the operation of the fancy. Here the sentiments arise from cool reflection and curious speculation, rather than from a present emotion. They accordingly require enlivening by ingenious comparison, striking contrast, unexpected turns, a climax finishing in a point, and all the pleasing refinements of art which give the denominations of ingenious and witty to our conceptions . . .

Many of the antient ballads have been transmitted to the present times, and in them the character of the nation displays itself in striking colours. The boastful history of her victories, the prowess of her favourite kings and captains, and the wonderful adventures of the legendary saint and knight errant, are the topics of the rough rhyme and unadorned narration which was ever the delight of the vulgar, and is now an object of curiosity to the antiquarian and man of taste. As it is not my design to collect pieces of this sort, which is already done in a very elegant manner by Dr. Percy, in his *Reliques of antient English poetry*, I shall proceed to consider the ballad more as an artificial than a natural species of composition . . .

4.6   From Joseph Ritson, *Pieces of Ancient Popular Poetry* (1791)

Preface

The venerable though nameless bards whom the generosity of the public is now courted to rescue from oblivion and obscurity, have been the favourites of the people for ages, and could once boast a more numerous train of applauding admirers than the most celebrated of our modern poets. Their compositions, it may be true, will have few charms in the critical eye of a cultivated age; but it should always be remembered, that, without such efforts, humble as they are, cultivation or refinement would never exist, and barbarism and ignorance be eternal . . .

Any enquiry, it is presumed, after the authors of these fugitive productions is at present impossible. It can only be conjectured that they were written (or, more accurately speaking, perhaps, imagined and commited to memory) by men, who made it their profession to chant or rehearse them, up and down the country, in the trophyed hall or before the gloomy castle, and at marriages, wakes and other festive meetings, who generally accompanyed their strains, by no means ruder than the age itself, with the tinkling of a harp, or sometimes, it is apprehended, with the graces of a much humbler instrument. . . . they seem to have been more attentive to temporary applause or present emolument than to future fame, of which they had possibly no idea, and, while they consigned their effusions to the casual protection of an auditors memory, were totally ignorant whether they were remembered or forgotten. The consequence is that while we are indebted for those which remain to accident and good fortune, numbers have perished, not less, and possibly even more, worthy of preservation . . .

It is not the editor's inclination to enter more at large into the nature or merits of the poems he has here collected. The originals have fallen in his way on various occasions, and the pleasing recollection of that happyest period of which most of them were the familiar acquaintance, has induced him to give them to the public with a degree of elegance, fidelity and correctness, seldom instanced in republications of greater importance. Every poem is printed from the authority refered to, with no other intentional license than was occasioned by the disuse of contractions, and a regular systematical punctuation, or became necessary by the errors of the original, which are generally, if not uniformly, noticed in the margin, the emendation being at the same time distinguished in the text. Under these circumstances, the impression is commited to the patronage of the liberal and candid, of those whom the artificial refinements of modern taste have not rendered totally insensible to the humble effusions of unpolished nature, and the simplicity of old times; a description of readers, it is to be hoped, sufficiently numerous to justify a wish that it may never fall into the hands of any other.

2

RELIGIOUS ENTHUSIASM:
THE FRENCH PROPHETS,
1707–1711

DURING the first half of the eighteenth century religious dissenters, having acquired some degree of toleration, looked to gain respectability, and the groups they formed became less like sects and more like denominations. The activities of the so-called French Prophets are an instructive exception to this quest for absorption. Their own prophecies, and visions of the coming Millennium, speak of the need of many Protestants for a more 'enthusiastic' religion than the official Anglicanism or the dissenting alternatives. The followers of the group that is the topic of this chapter were in search of 'inspiration', both metaphorically and literally. Their leaders—the actual Prophets—would put them in direct contact with the divine will. The inspired utterances that they produced were usually predictions of the end of a sinful world—a world in which the true Christian spirit was almost extinguished, and in which religious institutions merely parodied practices of sincere devotion. They were bearers of news of the Millennium.

In the early eighteenth century 'enthusiasm' was one of the most pejorative of labels. It still activated the memory of civil and religious war half a century earlier, and it was readily used to characterize forms of religious experience not contained by the Church of England. It referred to any conviction of direct communication with God. Those who were uneducated or politically subversive were thought to be particularly susceptible to 'enthusiasm'. It was therefore often seen as a potentially 'popular' self-delusion—in some accounts, literally an energy that spreads through crowds. One of the texts that describes the dangers of 'enthusiasm' in this way is the third earl of Shaftesbury's *Letter concerning Enthusiasm* (1708), which was directly provoked by the activities of the French Prophets. Indeed, even though these activities are rarely discussed in histories of religion, they preoccupied many contemporary commentators. In his *Review*, Daniel Defoe finds himself perplexed by the Prophets' strange predictions, and on several occasions discusses their claims of inspiration. Jonathan Swift mocks and exploits these claims in the first of his satires on the almanac-maker John

Partridge, the *Bickerstaff Papers*, while Partridge's rival almanac-maker, George Parker, mocked the non-fulfilment of one of their prophecies in the chronology that was printed every year near the front of his almanac (see Chapter 4). In one of the prestigious Boyle Lectures, William Whiston took them to task. Such writers were interested in the Prophets because they were challenging as well as ludicrous—because they appeared to speak for needs unsatisfied by contemporary Christian institutions.

As the name suggests, the French Prophets had their origins amongst Huguenots fleeing persecution in France. Refugee leaders of the so-called 'Camisard' rebellion in southern France began arriving in London in 1706. These millenarian Protestants had fought a guerrilla war for several years against the military and clerical authorities of Languedoc and Dauphiné, and had attracted followers with their prophecies and inspired visions of the triumph of their religion, and the demise of Roman Catholicism. In England, although disowned and eventually hounded by fellow Huguenot refugees, they began to attract new followers. In May 1707 there appeared translations both of the prophecies of Elias Marion, the most important of the Camisards, and of François-Maximilien Misson's *A Cry from the Desart*, an account of the group's spiritual and military struggles. These were translated and published thanks to the efforts of two leading English 'Prophets': John Lacy, a well-to-do Presbyterian, and Sir Richard Bulkeley, a virtuoso and member of the Royal Society. Lacy himself began speaking in tongues in the summer of 1707 (his divinely inspired pronouncements initially being spoken in Latin), and soon had miraculous powers of healing claimed for him by other members of the group. These included Anglicans as well as dissenters, and appealed to many who were well educated, like Lacy himself, and even devotees of (supposedly rational) Newtonian natural philosophy, like the leading 'Prophet' Nicholas Fatio de Duillier.

To their English followers, the Camisard refugees were divinely inspired prophets. To John Lacy, they spoke of a 'glorious Dispensation, touching the Vocation of the *Jews*, the Conversion of all Nations, the Destruction of Antichrist, an universal Holiness to the Lord, and in fine, the Kingdom of God on Earth'.[1] Lacy published their 'Warnings', along with justifications sensitive to the accusation of 'enthusiasm'. The 'Warnings' were utterances made under the influence of the Holy Spirit, and were accompanied by seizures and palpitations: 'The Agitations of Body being the outward sign given of the Time, when the Word of the Lord comes into, or his Spirit over-rules the Mouth of the Person.'[2]

---

[1] *A Cry from the Desart: Or, Testimonials of the Miraculous Things Lately Come to Pass in the Cevennes, Verified upon Oath, and by Other Proofs* (1707), 2nd edn., preface dated 9 June 1707, p. v.

[2] Ibid., p. x.

Prophetical Warnings of Elias Marion was subtitled 'Discourses Uttered by him in London, under the Operation of the Spirit and Faithfully taken in Writing, whilst they were spoken'. It was to be followed by volumes containing the 'Warnings' of some of his English followers. All predict the end of worldly things, and the Second Coming.

The prophetic inclinations of this sect were both what was most ridiculous and what was most compelling about its claims. A tradition within dissenting Protestantism that had only recently become dormant was being reactivated. Predicting divine intervention in the affairs of men drew special attention to the group, but also threw it into crisis. When one of its members, Thomas Emes, died in December 1707, several Prophets prophesied his resurrection, and even named the date on which it would occur. On Thursday, 27 May 1708 the London newspaper *The Flying Post*, after providing its usual reports on the continental war, its details of the arrivals and departures of ships from major British ports, and its summary of stock prices, included this:

Tuesday last great crowds of People flock'd to Bunhill Fields, to see whether the pretended Prophets would come to raise Dr. Emms from the dead, according to their predictions, but none of them thought fit to appear, so that 'tis hoped there's an end of that unaccountable Infatuation which has made so much noise of late, since they themselves own'd before, that this would be decisive whether it were real Inspiration or a Delusion they were under.[3]

It might seem strange to have expected miracles in Queen Anne's London, but the very language in which the newspaper dismisses the 'unaccountable Infatuation' registers the appeal of such expectation. It was an appeal that was 'popular' not only because it reached across the usual barriers of rank and education, but also because it was at its most lively in public displays of inspiration. Although these displays touched off theological controversy and debate, it was not by such debate that the sect acquired new members. Like religious enthusiasts in any age, they were to know God's will directly, unmediated by specially privileged or skilled interpreters.

REFERENCES AND FURTHER READING

On the intellectual varieties of Orthodoxy and Enlightenment in the early eighteenth century, see John Redwood, *Reason, Ridicule, and Religion: The Age of Enlightenment in England 1660–1750* (1976); J. W. Packer, *The Transformation of Anglicanism* (Manchester, 1969); and Margaret Jacob, *The Newtonians and the English Revolution*

---

[3]   *The Flying Post: Or, The Post-master*, no. 2040, Tuesday, 25 – Thursday, 27 May 1708.

1689–1720 (Ithaca, NY, 1976). The last of these indicates how millenarianism could accompany, rather than oppose, new scientific arguments. For the importance of millennial prophecies to Protestants see Norman Cohn, *The Pursuit of the Millennium*, 3rd edn. (New York, 1970). Studies of popular beliefs in the powers of prophecy and the Second Coming tend to focus on the seventeenth century: notable examples are Christopher Hill, *The World Turned Upside Down* (1972) and Bernard Capp, *The Fifth Monarchy Men: A Study in Seventeenth-Century Millenarianism* (1972). Although it only touches upon the period of the French Prophets, the widest-ranging study of such beliefs is Keith Thomas, *Religion and the Decline of Magic* (1971), especially chapter 5, while R. A. Knox, *Enthusiasm: A Chapter in the History of Religion* (Oxford, 1950) spans the seventeenth and eighteenth centuries and devotes a chapter to the French Prophets. The one full-length study of this group is Hillel Schwartz, *The French Prophets: The History of a Millenarian Group in Eighteenth-Century England* (Berkeley and Los Angeles, Calif., 1980). This book builds on Schwartz's earlier *Knaves, Fools, Madmen, and that Subtile Effluvium* (Gainesville, Fla., 1978), which concentrates on the opposition to the Prophets and the contemporary medical explanations given for their inspired displays. It contains an excellent bibliography of writings for and against the group. This is particularly useful because it includes the libraries where most of these items are to be found. Finally, Charles Domson, *Nicholas Fatio de Duillier and the Prophets of London* (New York, 1981) is an intellectual biography of one of the leading Prophets, who was also, for a time, a close associate of Isaac Newton.

1. INSPIRATION

The most important publications undertaken by the Prophets were not arguments; they were transcriptions of inspired utterances. In extracts 1.1 and 1.2 first Elias Marion and then John Lacy describe the symptoms that attend divine inspiration. As Hillel Schwartz has recorded in *The French Prophets*, the convulsions into which these religious enthusiasts fell when they were 'inspired' provoked fascination as well as ridicule, as contemporaries tried to find explanations for these displays, other than mere fraudulence. Passage 1.3 is taken from an anonymous pamphlet that worriedly credits the power of the Prophets to 'inspire' curious onlookers. Public displays of inspiration continued to be what most attracted potential followers, and what most nettled those who wrote against the French Prophets, as in the final eye-witness account of these displays, 1.4.

1.1   From *The French Prophet's Declaration; Or, an Account of the Preachings, Prophecies, and Warnings of Elias Marion Truly Translated from the Original, Taken from his Own Mouth in Writing* (1707)

'The Declaration of *Elias Marion*'

When the Spirit of God is about to seize me, I feel a great Heat in my Heart and the parts adjacent; which sometimes has a shivering of my whole Body, going before it: At other times I am seiz'd all at once, without having any such preceding Notice. As soon as I find myself seized, my Eyes are instantly shut up, and the Spirit caused in me great Agitations of Body, making me to put forth great Sighs and Throbings, which are in short, as I were labouring for Breath. I have also frequently very hard Shocks, but yet all this is without Pain, and without hindering me of the freedom of thinking. I continue thus about a quarter of an Hour, more or less, before I utter one Word. At last, I feel that the spirit forms in my Mouth the Words which he will have me pronounce, which are almost always accompanied with some Agitations, or extraordinary Motions, or at least with a great Constraint. Sometimes it is so, that the first word that I am to speak next, is already formed in my own Idea; but I am very often ignorant how that very Word will end, which the Spirit has already begun. And it has happened sometimes, that when I thought I was going to pronounce a Word, or a Sentence, it proved to be only a meer intriculate sound that was formed by my Voice. During all the time of these Visits I always feel my Spirit extreamly enlarged toward my God . . .

Written at London, March 31, 1707
Elias Marion

1.2   *From The Prophetical Warnings of John Lacy, Esq; Pronounced Under the Operation of the Spirit; and Faithfully Taken in Writing, When They Were Spoken* (1707)

The bodily Impressions . . . began by a preternatural Course of Breathing; then my Head came to be agitated or shaken violently and forcibly, and with a very quick Motion horizontally, or from Side to Side: Then my Stomach had Twitches, not much unlike a Hyccop, afterwards my Hands and Arms were violently shaken, at length a Struggle or Labouring in the Wind-pipe, and sometimes a sort of Catching or Twitches all over my Body; and for about a Week before my Speaking, I observed my Tongue was now and then moved involun-

tarily, as were also my Lips, my Mouth and Jaw severally; all which preparation
of the bodily Organs I found attended with a constant Elevation of my Soul to
God.

———

From *A Warning Concerning the French Prophets. Being Advice for Those 1.3
That Go After Them, to Take Heed Lest They Fall into Fits, as They Do, and
Others Have Done, by Often Seeing and Continuing Among Them* (1707)

IT was but a few days ago I went to make a Visit to a Neighbour, a very worthy
Gentleman, and yet a Follower of these Prophets of whom, as I have had, and
have a true and great value for the Sincerity of his Heart to God, in seeking his
Glory and the Publick Good: so now I have a deep sorrow and Grief of Soul,
upon my seeing him to fall suddenly, in talking with me, into a horrid shaking
Convulsion-fit. I observe, in reading something of these Mens Papers, that it is
the method among them, that Persons are for some months under Probation, by
such Agitations, before they come to *Speak*. Alas! what a Dispensation is this,
with which the Quakers begun, but let it off. Oh that a Man of such Reason in
his Discourse and Writing, as this Gentleman, should think that to be trans-
form'd into a Brute for an hour or more should be the way to become a *Prophet*!
I was offended, and God (I think) is offended, that when his gracious and good
Spirit descended down on Christ as a *Dove*, these Men should be for bringing
him down as a *Vulture*, to rear and make them in pieces in the Communication
of it to them.

And what are these Agitations or Convulsions, and from whence do they
come? It is a Question with the Physician, *An Imaginatio creat Morbis?* Whether
Imagination begets Diseases. Let the Question be turn'd hither, and I am persuaded in the Affirmative. Here is Example and Proof of it. No, some may say,
these shakings are above Nature, and must be from some Spirit, and that Spirit
is a good Spirit or a bad Spirit, that is, from God or the Devil: But I deny the
Argument; it is from a Man's own Spirit, possess'd with Imagination. I have
twice observ'd it. These Motions are indeed strange, but not beyond human
strength, even their own, and what Imagination may cause. The tone there is in
Imagination, as to the Effects it has both on a Man's own self, and upon others,
is so great that what is true will not be believ'd when it is told. It is from Belief,
such a Belief as consists in a strong and peremptory Imagination (not Historical
or Justifying) that Miracles are wrought. Oh that my honour'd Friend had never
been drawn in to see others in these Fits, and hear their sayings! for then he
wou'd have continu'd to look to his Estate as a wise Gentleman, and serv'd his
Generation as a godly Christian. As one gapes seeing another gaping, and as one

Grape does *liorem ducem*, get Rot and Infection from its Fellow; so does a Man, thoroughly imprest by the Sight of these Persons in such Agitations (as it hath happened to others upon their seeing some in a Fit of the *Mother* or *Falling-Sickness*) fall into the same (even when they know not how) by a kind of irresistible Imitation . . .

But let us stay a while until we see more, that is, the *Gift* of Tongues, and healing Diseases, and doing such Miracles as were done by the Apostles, added to these *Extasies*, which these Men expect, and profess their Expectation thereof, tho they thereby have expos'd themselves to Open Trial and Shame if it come not to pass; but withal, shown their simplicity and Innocence in such Delusion and Credulity, as a sober Man may smile at and pity, rather than be envy'd at and persecute, seeing the Proof is so near at hand; and if contrarily it should indeed come to pass, we must all then confess them Prophets. In the mean time I remember *Gamaliel*'s good Counsel, and wish to God this good Neighbour of mine had been one that had taken it; that is, to have *refrain'd from these Men, and let them alone* (at least till then) as others are fit from his Example to be advis'd: *If the Work be of God, it cannot be overthrown; if it be of Men, it will come to nothing.*

1.4   **From *The French Prophets Mad Sermon, as Preacht Since their Sufferings at their Several Assemblies Held in Baldwins Gardens, at Barbican, Pancras-Wells, and Several Other Places In and About London* (1707)**

THE First that spoke was a *French* Prophet, sitting in an Elbow Cane Chair, shaking his Head, moving his Body, and Stamping with his Feet, as if he was in a Convulsion Fit, and shaking his Fingers as if he had no Joints; but at last cried out *Hoc, Hoc, Hoc*; and then again, saying, Awake, Ah you drousy stiff-necked People, *Hoc, Hoc, Hoc, Hoc.* A stander by asked the Prophet what he stamp'd for? He cryed *Hoc, Hoc*, that he stamped the Wicked of the Earth under his Feet; and so continued for above half an Hour, and so sat still.

The Second Prophet that spoke, was *Mr. Dutton*, a Lawyer of the *Temple*, standing up and shaking his Head and spreading out his Hands, and beat them on their Table, crying *Ah, Ah, Ah, Ah, Ah*, for a pretty while, and said: The Day of the Lord is near at hand, my Brethren, and so sat down.

The Third Prophet was *John Lacy*, Esq; sitting in a Cane Chair, leaning backwards, moving and lifting up his Body, and shaking his Head as if he was mad, crying *Oh, Oh, Oh, Oh, Oh, John* and Elius, but he quoted no Scripture for what he said, *Oh, Oh, Oh, Oh*, the *Actions exterior of the Holy Spirit upon* Balaam, Saul, *and the Prophets, with, and upon* David, *who was the Son of the Drunkards,*

Oh, Oh, Oh, Oh, shaking his Head as if it were loose, and Sweated mightily: To force People to receive their Benedictions, is their premeditated Practice; of which *Mr. Lacy* himself is an Instance, whose own Son refusing to accept a Blessing, he was so inrag'd at him for being so unlucky a Precedent to others, that he knockt his Sons Head against the Wainscot, and struck him so severely upon his Mouth with his Fist, that he beat out one of his Teeth, and made his Head and Face swell in an extraordinary manner; this Relation is sign'd by *S.L.*

A little Prophet about Ten years of Age, fell a shaking, stamping, and throwing his Arms abroad, saying, *Ah! Ah! Oh!* for some time. I am come to tell you, if you don't leave off your Scoffing, and come over to us in time, the Gate will be shut against you, and you shall not enter therein.

And in a little time a She Prophet about Seven Years of Age, fell a shaking and nodding her Head, *Oh! Oh! Oh!* and when that Fit was over, fell a Cursing, as the little Boy did. It frighten'd the Spectators.

On *Sunday* the 16th of *November*, they assembled in *Barbican*, and several of the Prophets began to shake and nodded their Heads, Arms, and Legs, as if they were Mad, crying, *He, Ha*, one after another, for most part of the Day; some in *English*, and some in *French*; but about Three in the Afternoon, one of the Prophets fell a shaking in a most dreadful manner, *Oh, Oh.*

Oh accustom your selves to fear, and Reverence, and Decency in your Assemblies, Oh, Oh. For when ye set ill Examples, and others, following your Examples, will draw down my Judgements upon their Heads, can you expect to escape? O ye are all vile Worms in my Sight. When I give a Law, 'tis the Duty of every Soul to obey that Law. He that does his Endeavours, *Oh, Oh*, his utmost Endeavours to keep that Law, he shall be safe.

Another Prophet fell a shaking his Head, and cry'd, I am come to tell you, I am the Man that comes to tell you, I will cure the Blind, and make the Dumb to speak, the Deaf to hear, *Oh, Oh*, the Crooked strait, and the Lame to walk: I will do it very suddenly, you shall see it, *Oh, Oh*, in a very little time: Presently after the Mob began to pull down the Seats and break the Windows, and turn'd all the Prophets out of their Assembly, and fastened the Doors. The same Night Mr. *Dutton* the Lawyer went all the way up *Holbourn*, crying like a Madman, Halleluja, Halleluja; and singing of Psalms.

We thought good to insert this Relation of Mrs. *Betty Gray*, an Impostor, an Angel of Light, for they so call her, went with Mr. *Lacy* and another Prophet to Mrs. *Gray*'s Kinswoman's House at *Westminster*; and coming out of Doors there came a Dove and sat on her shoulder, and flew into the *Pallace-Yard* on the top of a Coach; which she followed, and took that Coach the Dove was on, and Mr. *Lacy* and the other Prophet followed her into the Coach, and the Dove followed them in; she bid the Coachman drive her where the Dove did light, which was in *Lumbard-street* in the City; the Dove flew out of the Coach on a Paint-House, and so they did all light and went into the House; but no sooner they were there, the Dove flew up Stairs into the Room to them; they fell a shaking, crying, Oh, Oh, till they were both tired with the Spirit; till they could stand no longer. *This they have Printed in their own Books.*

2. MOCKERY

Those who claimed such inspiration quickly attracted satire. Passage **2.1**, a broadside, probably from 1707, is a clever mock-prophecy directed at the extreme wishfulness of those envisioning the Second Coming. Its very existence is evidence that the activities of the Prophets were widely known and the matter of popular interest and satire. Another of the attacks upon the Prophets—*The Honest Quaker: Or, the Forgeries and Impostures of the Pretended French Prophets and Their Abettors Expos'd in a Letter from a Quaker to his Friend, Giving an Account of a Sham-Miracle Perform'd by John L-y Esq; on the Body of Elizabeth Gray, on the 17th of August Last* (1707)—commented: 'It is a Matter of Wonder, that in so Learned an Age, and among so wise, so discerning, and so penetrating a Nation as Ours is, Imposters have daily the Confidence to set up.' The attack on the 'Imposters' was taken up in the twice-weekly journal *The Rehearsal*. The issue for Wednesday December 3rd, 1707 (**2.2**) consists of a dialogue between 'Country-man' and 'Rehearsal' concerning matters of pressing religious and political significance. The next month (**2.3**) *The Rehearsal* returned to the attack, telling the usefully ingenuous 'Countryman' about the forces behind an 'Invasion of the Authority of the Church'.

2.1   *The French Prophet. Or, a New Touch of the Times* (n.d.)

> I am an old Prophet, and newly come over,
>   To tell you the Truth I was born in France,
> Last Monday was Se'nnight I landed at Dover,
>   The Truth is the Truth, and is no Romance:
> Then chear up your Hearts, your Spirits raise,
>   And remember the Nation is now in its Prime;
> Then let us be jolly, and drown Melancholly,
>   I warrant, brave Boys, we have golden Times.
> When the name of Cuckold is quite forgot,

And Wheat shall be sold for a Groat the Coomb;
When Drunkards forget to handle their Pot,
   And the City of London is joined to Rome:
When Vintners neglect to use their Chalk,
   And Poets forget to make their Rhimes,
When Pimps are all rotten, and whoring forgotten,
   I'll warrant, &c.

When Conscience is prized more than Gold,
   And the Tower of London runs upon Wheels;
When fractious old Women forget to scold,
   And the Monument has a fine Ring of Bells:
When Norwich Castle goes to Christ Church,
   And all for to hear St. Peter's Chimes;
When Lovers leave lying, and Birds leave off flying,
   I'll warrant, &c.

When Cucumbers grow upon Sycamore Trees,
   And Knavery is turn'd out of Doors;
When a Miss of the Town refuses a Crown,
   And Swearing and Lying are used no more;
When a Quack doth come to visit a Whore,
   And the Kingdom of England is all of one Mine;
When Pigs forget grunting, and Cats ride a hunting,
   I'll warrant, &c.

When Landlords they reduce their rents,
   And Taylors make their Bills too short;
When Bakers make their Bread too large;
   And are made to stand in the Pillory for't;
When a Welshman eats no toasted Cheese;
   I'll warrant, &c.

When Malice and Envy are laid quite aside,
   And honestly lov'd by rich and poor;
When Charity's lov'd more than Pride,
   And Millers forget to take Toll any more:
When Sailors refuse to take their Pay,
   And the Rich to the Poor grow loving and kind;
When Women leave Washing, and Cows go a Fishing,
   I'll warrant, &c.

When Maids chuse a single Life,
   And will not be married at twenty Years;
When Eels have got Legs, like Shoemakers Pegs,
   And Willow Trees bear Warden Pears:

When Sugar and Salt are both of a Taste,
  And Misers become both free and kind;
And Candlemas falls on the Eleventh of May,
  I'll warrant, &c.
When Houses are with Pancakes til'd,
  And Vinegar runs like Water Springs;
When Mankind are all of a Mind,
  And England is blest with a King or a Queen,
When Cocks ride out in Boots and Spurs,
  And Mackerel are catch'd without Net or Line;
When the Cheats of the Nation are quite out of Fashion
  I'll warrant, &c.
When Paul's Church goes for a Man of War,
  Mann'd with old Women to fight for the Nation;
When Bakers forget to gripe the Poor,
  And Whoring is clearly out of Fashion;
When Beaus they do a hunting ride.
  And Winter is past without Frost or Rhime:
These Things they may be, but few will them see,
  Until the Devil is grown lame and blind.

2.2 From *The Rehearsal*, 2/17 (3 December 1707)

(7) *Countryman*. I was t'other day, *Master*, at *Barbican* to see our *English Camis-ars* a *Prophesying*, and there I saw *Beaux*, Men as well Dress'd as any in the *Mall*, with Long Furbulo'd *Wiggs* and *Swords* by their Sides, Creeping upon their *Knees*, in most Humble Manner, to two or three Paultry *Wenches* (who were *Hopping* about the Room, and *Screaming*) to Receive their *Blessing*. For they say, these *Prophets* and *Prophetesses* can *Bless*.

Rehears. And if I am not misinform'd, there are some of *Quality*, at t'other End of the Town, who send for those *Girls*, and submit to be *Blessed* by them. And this is a Just *Judgement* upon those who Ridicule *Religion*, and employ their *Wits* to make a *Jest* of the *Church* and all her *Institutions*, who *Laugh* at the *Bless-ing* of a *Bishop*; and at the same time are let down so low as to seek it from an *Oyster-Wench*!

Country-m. This is shewing their *Wisdom* to Purpose! But may not any one *Bless* another; that is, Pray for the *Blessing* of *God* upon him?

(8) *Rehears.* Yes, *Country-man*. But it is a very different thing from *Blessing* in the *Name* of the *Lord*, for that is an *Authoritative* Act, and Requires a *Commis-*

sion from *God*; for who otherwise can *Act* in His *Name*? This is the very Defini-
tion of a *Priest*, Deut. x. 8. *To stand before the Lord to Minister unto Him, and to
Bless in His Name.* And St. *Paul* argues the Greatness of *Melchisodec* above
Abraham, from *Melchisodec*'s Blessing him, for, says the *Apostle*, Heb. vii. 7.
Without all Contradiction, the less is Blessed of the Better.

   And hence it is Common with *Heresiarchs*, and the Setters up of New *Sects* to
assume this *Authority* to themselves. *Fox* the first *Bishop* of the *Quakers*, and
Lodowick Muggleton both took upon them to *Bless* and to *Curse*. And thus our
New *Camisers*, both *Men* and *Women*!

<hr style="width:20%">

From *The Rehearsal*, 2/29 (17 January 1707)   2.3

There were no Profess'd *Deists*, who throw off all *Revelation*, and set up what
they call *Natural Religion* in its place. For *Natural Religion* and *Deism* are the
self same thing. None then said he had been in an Higher *Heaven* than that into
which *Christ* has Ascended, as I have heard *Jean Leads* the Mother of the
Philadelphians say. None then *Blasphemn'd* so loud as our *Camisar-Quakers*
who not only say they are sent by *God,* and speak in his *Name*, which is the stile
of the *Prophets*, but they Assume His *Person*, and say He speaks by moving their
Organs, without their own Consent or Knowledge, and that He speaks in them,
and to themselves, as well as to others. A Person of Veracity told me he saw one
of them, in their *Meeting*, take another of them by the Arm, and looking Broad
in his Face, said, *Do you* not *acknowledge me to be the Eternal and ever-living
God?* To which the other Answer'd, falling down and Trembling, *I do acknowledge you to be the Eternal and Ever-living God.* Their Excuse is, That it is
not Themselves who speak the Words, but *God* who speaks in them. But this
Aggravates the *Blasphemy* instead of lessening it.

3. THE RESURRECTION OF THOMAS EMES

<hr style="width:20%">

In December 1707, shortly after three of the Prophets had been placed on the
Pillory at Charing Cross for prophane prophecy, Dr Thomas Emes, a leading
member of the group, fell ill. His death on 22 December was followed, a
month later, by the publication of a text recording the predictions (see 3.1) of
his fellow Prophets that he would be resurrected.

   John Potter predicted that the resurrection would take place on 25 May

1708. Clearly the predictions became widely known, and a month before this date we find Daniel Defoe in the *Review* advising 'the Readers of this Paper in this Particular, Hold them to the Point, it was their own Offer, that if this did not come to pass, they would own they were deluded'.[4] The annalist Narcissus Luttrell reported: 'The 25th instant being the day which Mr. Lacy some time since prophesied that Dr. Emes, who died about Christmas last, should be raised from the dead, two regiments of our train'd bands are ordered upon the guard during the holydayes, to prevent any disorder which may happen by the mobb on that occasion.'[5] The prophecy was widely enough known for it to be the focus of many of the considerable number of books, pamphlets, and broadsides that were beginning to appear in opposition to the Prophets. The next pamphlet (3.2) must have been published shortly before the day fixed for Emes's resurrection.

Disputes grew amongst the Prophets themselves about the likelihood of Emes's resurrection, and most of the leaders of the group, including John Lacy, made sure that they were not in London on the date at which it should have taken place. However, Abraham Whitrow and others did attend the graveside, along with (according to one contemporary witness) some 20,000 spectators. Emes's failure to rise from the dead inevitably provoked both dissension amongst the Prophets themselves, and further attacks from their critics. Extract 3.3 is from one of the several explanatory defences offered by the group's leaders.

Unsurprisingly, the episode continued to be used by satirists, like the anonymous author of the mocking response from which passage 3.4 is taken, or the composer of the broadside which is given in its entirety in 3.5. The Emes affair, and the activities of the French Prophets in general, were even made the subject of a play, *The Modern Prophets; or New Wit for a Husband*, by Thomas d'Urfey. In this play, the Prophets are confidence tricksters who live off (and dramatically reveal) the credulity of several of the characters—in particular the gullible Squire Whimsey. The main prophet, Betty Plotwell, is the standard deceiver of comic drama of the period, who declares to a collaborator: 'I'm a rare Actress, you must know, and perform my Rants, and my Groans, my Flights and my Fancies with exact Method.' Her fellow Prophets are depicted as a mixture of Jesuits and Jacobites. In the second act, from which passage 3.6 is taken, Betty acts out her 'inspiration', and sings the 'Prophet's Song'. The other characters who feature in the extract are Ned, the Squire's nephew; Lord Noble, the 'Witty and Generous' aristocrat who will help expose the Prophets; Fidelia, virtuous daughter of the chief 'Sham Prophet', Zekiel Magus; Clora, her friend; and Mrs Guiacum, 'Widow to a late Physician, one of the Prophets'. In an obvious reference to the Emes

---

[4]   Daniel Defoe, *Review*, 5/12 (24 Apr. 1708), 46.
[5]   Narcissus Luttrell, *A Brief Historical Relation of State Affairs from September 1678 to April 1714. In Six Volumes* (Oxford, 1857), vi. 307.

affair, Mrs Guiacum talks, in this scene, of having prepared her husband's dinner in readiness for his resurrection.

But what Defoe called 'the affair of raising a dead man' also provoked, as in his *Review*, serious argument as well as mischievous satire.[6] Passage 3.7 is representative of this.

From *Predictions Concerning the Raising the Dead Body of Mr. Thomas Emes,* 3.1 *Commonly Call'd Doctor Emes, Late of Old-Street-Square, in the Parish of St. Giles, by Cripplegate, London: Who On or About the 4th Day of December, 1707, Was Taken with a Most Violent Head-Ach, or Meagrim, and Died on the 22nd Day of December 1707, and Was Buried on the 25th Day of the Same Month, Being Christmas-Day, in the Burying Place, in Bun-Hill-Fields, Near Moor-Fields.* (1707)

Tuesday December XXIII. *Being the Day after the Death of* Dr. Emes. *Spoken by* A.M.K., *a Child of Twelve Years old, in a Publick Assembly, under the Operation of the Spirit.*   J.N.

Oh my People! You think not what it is I am preparing for you; nor you are not able to think: You are not able to think what I am bringing to pass. Here are some, in this Place, doubtful whether all will come to pass as my Servants have spoken; because of one Thing. But do you think that Death can hinder? For, tho' my Servant dies, have I not said, I will raise the Dead, by the Hand of my Servant? And think you not I am able to perform my Word? But perhaps you think my Servants were in Errour, when they spoke that. But, I assure you, they were not. Therefore judge you no more of what I have spoken, by my Servants. For that, as you think impossible, shall come to pass. But let me alone; I will work my Will. It is Presumption in you, to meddle in my Matters. Not only this thing, but more marvellous things than This, shall come to pass in a little Time. I will bring to pass such as never have been yet. Yes, Yes; Your Eyes shall see it . . .

Thursday December XXV. *Upon which Day* Dr. Emes *was Buried. Spoken by* J.P. *in a Publick Assembly, under the Operation of the Spirit.*   J.N.R.

I'll give now undeniable Proof, that this is my Word: That these distracted Motions are caused by the Operation of my Spirit, in my Children. The Restoring of the Blind, the Healing of the Sick, the raising of the Dead shall decide it,

---

[6] *Review*, 5/33 (12 June 1708).

after some months being interred. Will not this do? Take heed, you that say, I shall believe, when I see this. Take heed I say, you simple ones: For if Faith, as thou confessest, be the Gift of God; thou knowest not whether I will give Faith then. No, no, I will not gratify the Humours of my Worms, in whose Destruction I can be glorified; and I will, if you will not accept of this Act of Grace, which is now proclaimed by the Mouths of my Servants. Therefore it is now that I call unto you. Come, come, come; come all you that would escape approaching Judgements; and enter into this Ark, which I have prepared for your Safety. Yes, I will raise the Dead. By the same Power, that I have raised *Jesus*, will I raise that Body now asleep; More fat, and more fair, than ever he has been: It shall not be known by his Friends, that he has fasted so many Months. So fat, so lovely shall he appear, that the Beholders shall fall in Love with him. Yes, the same Body, the same Face, tho' more lovely. For the Beams of my Glory shall overshadow that Earthly Tabernacle; So as that it shall be made glorious thereby. Come, my Children, I know you wait. [*Here he fell back in his Chair and cryed out*] Oh Lord! What? Would you that I say unto you! *By another, Lord.* [*He then fell backward to the Ground and lay silent.*]

Thereupon, A.M.K. *aforesaid, was instantly seized. and under the Operation of the Spirit, said*;

Rejoice greatly, O my Children, and be exceeding glad: For great is your Reward in Heaven. And be you assured, that all that I have spoken by my Servant, at this Time, and all other Times, shall come to pass. And if you knew me, you would believe me. By the Hand of my Servant *Lacy*, will I raise the Body of my Servant, that is now dead. But you must wait my Time: For I am not at your Wills; neither will I be. He, I say, he shall arise and fulfill his Testimony. Did I ever speak in vain? No, I assure you; *I* never did; nor I never will. You have sufficient Proof already, That is the Power of God. But there is none can deny this, that I am going to bring to pass. If he be dead and rotten, yet will I raise him, as I have spoken, to fulfill his Testimony. There is not one Tittle of what I have spoken shall pass away. I will do greater Things, than these. Yes, I will do such Things as never yet have been.

Sunday Decemb. XXVIII. J.P. *was for a long Time under violent Agitations, and labour'd greatly, with great Surgings in his Throat and Organs of Speech, almost as if he were choaking; and utter'd some Inarticulate Sounds.*

Did ye understand, my Children? You shall know more perfectly in a short Time. The Words were pronounced, even the Day, in which my Servant, *Emes* shall rise. Take this as a Mark. [*Here the Spirit mightily threw him upon the Floor: Where he lay stretched out as dead, without Motion or Breathing. After some Time, there came a trembling Motion into every Part of him at once; his Feet, Legs, Hands, Arms, and Shoulders: After which there appeared some Breathing; which grew still louder and stronger in him. After he had been in this Manner, for some Time, he said;*] The Operation of my Spirit upon his Body shall cause the Earth over him to be loosened. You shall not break the Ground; no, he shall rise without: In this Form. [*Here he raised up his Head, and his Body forward, into a sitting Posture.*] By thy Mouth will I command. [*Thus he directed to* J.L. *who sat by him.*] and thou shalt raise him. [*He outstretch'd out his Hand, and took hold of* J.L.'s *Hand and thereupon stood up upon his Feet.*] . . .

Sunday Decemb. XXV. *as* J.P. *and* J.C. *were passing accidentally by the Place where Dr. Emes was Buried;* J.P. *was seized with the Spirit, and then said.*

Thou my Servant who lies interr'd in this Place, shalt in a few Natural Months arise. My Child, thy Tongue shall declare the Positive Day: Be thou obedient, and I will exceedingly reward thee: But if thou refusest, I will break thy Neck with a Rod of Iron. Consider therefore and be wise . . .

December 29. J.C. *under the Operation of the Spirit, in an Assembly, spoke as followeth.*

In *English* thus.

My Children, in a few natural Months you shall see greater Miracles wrought, than I my self wrought upon *Lazarus*. When *I* raised *Lazarus*, he had been but Four Days in his Grave. I commanded that the Stone that lay upon it, should be taken away; But you, and the Inhabitants of this City, shall, in a few natural Months, see my faithful Servant, who has been buried, raised in the presence of Men: My Children, he shall come out of his Grave, without the Earth being taken away, that lies upon him. He shall come forth, in the presence of Men, and he shall unty his Shroud, in which he is now wrap'd. This shall not be in secret; no, but in publick. I do ask of you all, if you do believe that I am able to do this. Answer me, if you have no Murmurings in your Hearts. Answer sincerely. I am the Invincible, the great *Jehovah*, who speaks to you at this time; the Almighty; the King of Heaven and Earth. [*Then one in the Company answered, Lord I believe that it is more easy to thee to raise him (if there be Differences in the Degrees of thy Power) than it was, either to create Man at the first, or to go on to produce them, by the ordinary way.*] Thy Faith is great, I say unto thee; but all those who hear my Voice, have it not in so great Measure. Cause them to understand these Things, that they may give their answer, in their own Tongue. [*The aforesaid Discourse being then read in English,* J.P. *answer'd, Lord, I believe thou canst and wilt.*] My child, thou knowest the Time, and I will make thee to declare it in a few Days. [*Then* J.C. *continued.*] Those who will cry to me,

Thou King of Heaven and Earth, All Might is in thy Hand; Thou canst do all Things; we make no Doubt of it; they shall see it, in Truth. I do protest to you with an Oath, that if you answer me with Sincerity, your Eyes shall see these Things.

———————

3.2   From *The Mighty Miracle; or, The Wonder of Wonders at Windmill-Hill. Being the Invitation of John Lacy, Esq; and the Rest of the Inspired Prophets, to All Spectators, to Come on Tuesday Next, the 25th Day of This Instant May, Where, to their Exceeding Astonishment, They May (Without Any Prejudice to their Eye-Sight) Behold Dr. Emms Arise Out of his First Grave, and Dress Himself in his Usual Habit to All their View, and With a Loud Voice Relate Matters of Moment, Preaching a Miraculous Sermon, Giving a Strange Account of Past and Future Events; the Like Never Seen or Heard in England Before, Exceeding Any Wonder or Show that Ever Was Seen on Windmill-Hill at Any Holiday-Time. Licensed According to Order* (1708)

THE Town having been busied with Apprehension of Wars in the North, and the Affairs of State, having almost suffered our late Doctor *Emms* to be buried in Oblivion, as well as in his Grave near *Windmill-hill*; and so, by Consequence, he may rise alone, or, as we term it vulgarly, in Hugger-mugger, without any to witness the Wonder: But let me acquaint you, that, as such Miracles are not common, it is fit they should be proclaimed aloud by Fame's Trumpet; neither have all Men the Gift of raising the Dead, nor hath it been known for many Ages. Esquire *Lacy* has published a Relation of the Dealing God with his unworthy Servant, since the Time of his believing and professing himself inspired, which befell him, the First of *July*, 1707: His Agitations coming upon him without the Working of his Imagination, upon what he saw in others, and proceeding from a supernatural Cause, separate and distinct from himself, whereby his Arm, Leg and Head have been shaken, his Limb twitched, the Respiration of his Breath has, for sundry Days, beat various Tunes of a Drum, and his Voice has been so strong, clear, and harmonious, that his natural one could never furnish: He has been carried on his Knees several Times round a Room, swifter than he could have gone on his Feet. Sir *Richard Buckley* has been cured of an Hospital of Diseases by a Promise thereof made through his Mouth, under the Operation of the Spirit; and by the same Means a Man purblind has been cured, and a Woman of a Fever, Mr. *Preston* of a Carbuncle, and another of a deep Consumption. Therefore Esquire *Lacy*, with the rest of the inspired Prophets, gives Notice, for the Satisfaction of the Unbelieving, that, according to their former Prophecy (who cannot err) that, on the Twenty-fifth of *May*, they repair to *Bunhill Fields*, and there in that Burying-Place, commonly called *Tindal*'s Ground, about the Twelfth Hour of the Day, behold the wonderful Doctor fairly rise; and in two Minutes Time the Earth over his Coffin will crack, and spread from the Coffin, and he will instantly bounce out, and flip off his Shroud (which must be washed, and, with the Boards of his Coffin, be kept as Relicks, and doubtless perform Cures by their wonderful Operation) and there, in a Trice, he dresses himself in his other Apparel (which doubtless hath been kept for that Intent ever since he was interred) and then there he will relate astonishing Matters, to the Amazement of all that see or hear him.

Likewise, for the more convenient Accommodation of all Spectators, there will be very commodious Scaffolds erected throughout the Ground, and also without the Walls in the adjacent Fields, called *Bunhill-Fields*, exceeding high, during this great Performance. The like may never be seen in *England* hereafter: and, that you may acquaint your Children, and Grandchildren, if you have any, that you have seen this mighty Miracle, you are advised not to neglect this Opportunity since it is plainly evident, that, of all the Shows or Wonders that are usually seen on Holiday-time, this must bear the Bell; and there it is ordered to be published in all News, that the Country may come in; the like never performed before. It is also believed that Gingerbread, Oranges, and all such Goods exposed to publick Sale in Wheelbarrows, will doubtless get Trade there, at this vast Concourse; therefore, for the Benefit of poor People, I give them timely Notice, since it is a bad Wind that blows none no Profit. But, besides this admirable Wonder of this strange and particular manner of his Resurrection, he is to preach a Sermon, and, lest it should not be printed, you are invited to be Ear-witnesses thereof, as well as Eye-witnesses to see his Lips go, in the Pronunciation thereof; all which will be Matter of great Moment, filling you all with exceeding Amazement and great Astonishment; his Voice will be loud and audible, that all may hear him, and his Doctrine full of Knowledge; undoubtedly you will return home taught with profound Understanding. Which Miracle, if you chance to see or hear, you will not forget, and so by Consequence, for the Future, be endowed with sound Judgement, and most excellent Wisdom, most eloquent Expressions, and what not: Then neglect not this great and most beneficial Opportunity, but for that Time set all your Affairs aside: And take this Advice from Mr. *Lacy*, and the inspired Prophets, together with Mrs. *Mary* of *Turnmill-street*, a she Prophetess, and the young Woman who sells Penny-pyes, who, in Hopes of obtaining all your Company, remains Yours; not questioning but to give you all Content with this rare Show.[7]

---

[7] The pamphlet is to be found reprinted in *The Harleian Miscellany*, vol. vii (1746), 185–6.

3.3   From *Esquire Lacy's Reasons Why Doctor Emms Was Not Raised from the Dead, on the Twenty-fifth of May, According to the French Prophets Prediction* (1708)

WE are not unsensible of the harsh Censures and uncharitable Reflexions that are cast upon us and our Brethren, the Prophets, in not raising from the Dead our late spiritual Brother Dr. *Emms*, on the precise Time we foretold; therefore, to prevent, as much as in us lies, all further Clamour and unnatural Violence that may be occasioned thereby, we have thought fit to give our Reasons for this Omission, in the following order:

First, and principally, we were threatened with a popular Rage and Violence, which the Laws of God and Nature allows all Mankind to avoid, having been practised by good and holy Men in all Ages of the World, even our Saviour himself, *John* x. 39, &c. who further confirms this Truth, *Matt.* x. 33, by advising his Disciples, when they were persecuted in one City, to flee into another. And, if it was lawful for the Apostles and Christ himself to avoid the Fury of their wicked and unbelieving Adversaries, we hope no Man can reasonably blame us from deferring the Accomplishment of the said intended Miracle. *Jonah* prophesied the Destruction of *Nineveh* in forty Days, but it was deferred near forty Years, on their repentance.

Secondly, The secret Decrees of the prophetical Spirit are treasured up in the Fountain of Wisdom, and consequently past Man's finding out, especially by a rebellious and gainsaying People.

Thirdly, Raising the Dead, Restoring the Blind and Lame to their Sight and Limbs, are great Miracles, and only performed by Faith, Prayer and Fasting; but, where a rude, enraged, and revengeful Multitude is gathered together in Defiance of Heaven itself, all Acts of Devotion are obstructed, and even suspended till a more seasonable Time.

Fourthly, Though Prophetick Periods do not always take Place, according to the punctual Warnings of the agitated Spirit in the Child of Adoption, yet, like a great Conqueror, who sometimes meets with Difficulties and Miscarriages in his March, in due Time break through all Obstruction, for the more glorious Accomplishment of the Promises.

Fifthly, and *Lastly*, Had we been peaceably suffered to appear on the Day and Hour we predicted, it would then have been decided who were the Cheats and Impostors (Names we have been notoriously loaded with) but when open Rage, Mob, Fury, and even Death itself not only threatened, but looked us in the Face; such a Time, we are sure, was inconsistent for the Undertaking of any Thing that related to a publick Satisfaction; for, had the Miracle really been wrought in such a confused Medley of ungovernable Rabble, instead of being acknowledged as such, we had run the Hazard of being torn in Pieces, and perhaps occasioned a fatal and general Disorder among the People; for whose Sake, more than for the Fear of our own Lives, we prudently delayed attempting the said weighty Undertaking till a more favourable Opportunity; though we could freely have sacrificed our Lives for the Sake of Spiritual Truth, if such a Dispensation had been either necessary or convenient; but (considering the Madness of the Age, the Malice of the Mob, and the Rage of many Malecontents against the present Government, who, in all Probability, would have took the Advantage of such a Confusion, in order to have promoted their long-wished for Treasons and wicked Designs) we preferred the publick Peace and Safety of the Government before our own Interest and Reputation, which, however so much shaken in this Particular, shall never discourage us from being loyal and obedient to our Superiors, notwithstanding our being rendered obnoxious to them by spiteful and malicious Agents, who are always fishing in troubled Waters, to bring about their own notorious and pernicious Purposes, though, to the Scandal of themselves, and Ruin of their Christian Brethren, whom they have for no other Reason than being honester than themselves.

To conclude: Let Men of carnal Principles have what Sentiments they please of us, we are resolved to act as the Spirit of Peace and Love within us shall dictate and guide us, and as the supernatural Agitations of divine Inspiration shall enlighten our Understanding.[8]

From *The Prophets: An Heroic Poem. In Three Cantos Humbly Inscrib'd to the*   3.4
Illumin'd Assembly at Barbican (1708)

I have spoke to a Music-Master of my Acquaintance, to set me a Prophetical Warning to a new Division in *Semi-demi-semi-quavers*, an Improvement of Music unknown to the Ancients. If you cou'd recommend one of the Inspir'd with good Lungs, and a tuneable Voice, to run it over clean at the next Music meeting in *York-Buildings*, we shou'd put down *Clinch*, and the new *Italian*. But of this in another place.—To go on with the Description. The Vibrations of the Head in general I have taken notice of, but did not accurately enough observe, whether it was "Forwards and backwards, or from *before* to *behind*"; which being a material Difference, I wou'd not come to Particulars,   P. 105
for fear of being mistaken in a Circumstance of that Importance. But what I most regret, is, That I did not hit upon that beautiful Thought, of the "Horizontal

---

[8] This pamphlet is to be found ibid. 187–8.

P. 105   Motion, as a Dog turns his Head when he comes out of the Water",
'twou'd have run naturally into Blank Verse.

> *As when a Dog (of Spaniel Breed suppose)*
> *In watry Chace of Duck, or Drake, sore tir'd,*
> *Takes to the Bank, and shakes his streaming Ears*
> *With Horizontal Motion, scatt'ring round*
> *Favours Canine, in misty Dew dispens'd*
> *So—— ——*

The involuntary Motion of the Tongue, and Lips, I have the Vanity to think not unaptly express'd in my third Canto; yet I must own it might have been considerably improv'd from Your pat Similitude of "The Mouth of *Balaam*'s Ass".

P. 45   This was (to speak the fashionable Language) signally *a propos:* But pardon me if I don't think it so artful as that Judicious Insinuation of yours concerning the false Predictions of the Old Scripture Prophets;

P. 78, 79, &c.   the Instances are well chosen, and the Application easie. However, (letting that pass) you have done me a particular Favour in giving the World this publick Account of the Predictions concerning Dr. *Eme*'s Resur-

P. 87   rection, and the Judgements to fall on Unbelievers: for to tell you the Truth, (the printed Account being for private Reasons of State suppress'd) I was almost afraid of being suspected for a Broacher of new Doctrines: But your Authentic Testimony has set all right, and my five Months from the Day of his Death, are found exactly to agree with your Computation; so that the signal Day for confirming the Elect, and extirpating Infidels, must be the 25th of *May* and no other; tho' some, no ill Friends of yours, have already found you out an Hole to creep out at, in case of Non-performance of Prophecy. For (say they) 'tis plain from a Text in the New Testament, that Great Works can't be wrought in an Unfaithful Generation: And for the other Branch of the Prophecy, about Destruction, *&c.* That (by the Prayers of the Elect) may be deferr'd to another Opportunity. But for my part I must own, I am still of Opinion, that after

P. 87   your solemn Declaration of "This Prophecy's being decisive, and that You are forbidden to pray for God's Enemies": You won't

P. 88   think of coming off by an Evasion you are forestall'd in. Remember Old *Chaucer*.

> *I hold a Mouse's Wit not worth a Leke,*
> *That hath but one Hole to sterten to,*
> *And if that faile, then is all idoe.*

Not that I in the least question, but you are better provided, yet it must be a Comfort to you to have so many antecedent Proofs of the Truth of this Prediction, amongst which I reckon the Gift of Tongues not inconsiderable . . .

Much happier art Thou, immortal *Emes*,
Whose Faith the Faculties lost Fame redeems.
    He, when the dreadful Megrims rack'd his Brain,
Confiding in the Spirit brav'd the pain.
The Spirit bid him hope, but Art despair,
Art he contemns, and tempts the dangerous Air:
Yet was he for a time (to try his Faith)
Deliver'd over to the Power of Death.
"Five Months compleat, shall Darkness veil his Eyes,
Then, on the Day he dy'd that Day he shall arise".
                                        Proph. Warn.
    No Weapon shall there need to cleave his way
No Force to seperate the binding Clay.
The loosen'd Mold shall voluntary break
In crumbling Hillocks, thence like one awake
From a refreshing Slumber, shall the dead
Shake off his Sleep, and rear his awful Head:
Whilst from his shining Temples wide around
The circling Rays shall gild the sacred Ground.
        * * * * *   *Desunt multa.*

The French Prophets Confounded: or, the Dead Man's Speech to the Presump- 3.5
tious Miracle-workers. Deliver'd under the Similitude of a Dream (n.d.)

THE French Prophets *having run very much in my Mind for some Time past, I*
have frequently dreamt something concerning them: But what I dreamt a Night
or two ago being very material, and worthy Notice, (especially at this Juncture) I
concluded it could not be unacceptable if I made it publick; which, in short, is this,
(viz) *I dreamt I saw in a very handsome Room Sir* R— B— *and Mr.* J— L—
sitting at a Table together, and contriving how they should manage the miracu-
lous Operation of raising Dr. EMES *to Life; when, on a sudden, methoughts I saw*
Dr. EMES's *Ghost appear, looking dreadfully pale and ghastly, and moving slowly*
towards 'em, spake as follows:

O Ye Presumptuous Sinners! who under the Notion of Sanctity and Inspiration,
pretend to the Working of Miracles, to make the World believe you *True*
Prophets, when indeed there never was nor can be greater Impostors. I was one
of those Giddy-Brain'd Wretches tha[t] danc'd to your Pipes; and those that now

do, may for ever Curse the Musick: For let me assure you, however you deceive the People upon Earth, there is a just God, who will not be deceiv'd, and whose Rod is in his Hand to punish you according to your Deserts. Therefore have a care those Judgments do not suddenly overtake you, which you so boldly threaten others with, I am commanded to tell you, that your bold Attempt of raising me from the Grave to live amongst you again, is a very Rash, Presumptuous, Dangerous, and Fruitless Undertaking; for I shall not be permitted to arise from thence till the General Retribution of all Things, when both you and I shall be brought to answer for every thing we have done amiss; and then it is not saying, We were Mad, Lunatick, or Distracted, will excuse us, without the Abundant Mercy of God upon us. O you Sir *R— B—*, and you Mr. *J— L—*, venture not to approach my Tomb, nor vainly hope for my sudden Resurrection, upon your hard knocking, or loud calling; for you may be assur'd I shall not hear you, neither shall I arise. Your Faith is not strong enough to remove Mountains, nor have you Power to raise the Dead to Life; That Power is only to be given from Above, from whence your inspired Thoughts had no [birth] Your Inspiration is only from the Devil, and you may very well fear a severe Suffering under his Delusions. Therefore, Unsanctified Wretches! once more I command you not [t]o approach my Grave, lest, upon your presuming to raise me to Life, you instantly drop down dead. The People upon Earth may look upon this Warning, or Caution, I am permitted to give you, as a very great MIRACLE; and if you have Power to raise me to Life again, it will be a FAR GREATER. But once more, I say, Attempt it not; for you shall certainly be Disappointed in your Hopes and Expectations, and be put to the Utmost Shame and Confusion.

This said, the Ghost immediately vanish'd; and the Two [a]foresaid Gentlemen went away very much astonisht and concern'd, I presently awak'd, and was somewhat affrighted my self; but finding it was no other than a Dream, I soon compos'd my self; and reflecting upon the whole Matter, I cannot but think there is a great deal of Truth in what I imagin'd I heard deliver'd.

3.6 **From Thomas d'Urfey, *The Modern Prophets; or New Wit for a Husband* (1708)**

The Prophet's SONG, in the Second Act.

We Prophets of the Modern Race,
To hide Rebellious Evil,
Pretend we all Excel in Grace,

And fight against the Devil.
> *We range, we roam,*
> *We quake, we foam,*

We breed by Inspiration:
We own the Call, the Spirit moves,
And then the Chosen Sister proves
> *By frequent Agitation.*

Strange Miracles we ne'er unfold,
> We scorn to understand 'em:

Those shewn the Mob in Days of Old
> Provok'd, but did not mend 'em.
>> We cant in Tone,
>> We sigh, we groan,

Nor do our Gambols tire us;
> And tho' our Preaching be Hum-drum,
> And Writing senceless as Tom Thumb,
>> We still have Fools Admire us.

Squire. Prodigious! I'm ravish'd.

Ned. No, only fool'd, Uncle, that's all. Ha, ha, ha.   [*Aside.*

Lord. The little Imp acts it to the Life.

Betty. Let me look on thee [*Betty comes up to* Ned.] I saw last Night in
   Vision—Angels—Fairys, Captains, Corn-Cutters, proud Lords, and
   pertinacious Prophets—thee, amongst the rest. Touch me thou frail one.

Squire. The Fit continues: Be sure you let her have her Humour.

Betty. Any new Adventure, Captain. Look grave and speak softly—
                          [*To* Ned *changing Tone.*

Ned. None, my Dear; but about the Hundred Pound, the Wretch won't part
   with a Penny.

Betty. Let me alone, [*To* Ned *changing Tone to Agitation.*] thou shalt have a
   Call; follow and Eat—Come, Prince, support me. [*To* Squire.] Yes, my
   Child, I say once more thou shalt be a Prince, a mighty Prince, so mighty as
   not able to discern the Beginning nor the End of thy Dominion.
                          [*Speaks as in Agitation.*

Squire. Now what think ye, poor People?

Lord and *Ned.* We are your Highnesses most humble Servants.

Squire. 'Tis a clear case, you see, she has it in her.
                          [*Exeunt* Squire *and* Betty.

Ned. Here comes one of the Spectators, I'll ask what News do'st hear, my
   honest Friend, has any thing appear'd yet.

Enter Cobler.

Cobler. Appear'd, ha, ha, ha,—What have we got a Fool in Red here too? I am glad o'that, we *Coblers* are safe then Faith: No, no, Captain, I believe you may get into a Hole by having another touch with the *French* in *Flanders*—before any thing will come out of one in *Bunhill-fields*—appear—Ha, ha, ha, 'tis a mere Cheat by this cutting Knife.   [*Exit.*

Guiac. Senseless Rascal! 'twould affront Inspiration to be the occasion of having such a dull Ox as that—I tell you once more. Cousin, you may depend upon his coming, he'll be at Home about Two; and I have accordingly bespoke a Dinner.

Clora. Pray what, Cousin? that must needs be something very Nice, Warm and Restorative.

Guiac. No, Cousin, no Kickshaws, he never lik'd 'em, his Appetite was always most pleas'd with common Diet; and to humour it, I have provided a wholesom Dish of Neat's Feet and fry'd Onions.

Lord. Egh—the Devil take him for a Fancy—Humh! Gad, I believe, they are dressing on't already—for to my thinking I have the damn'd Funk in my Nostrils now.

Ned. Ha, ha,—the sweetness of the Air yonder amongst the Mob, I confess is somewhat annoy'd; the Breezes have something of *Thames-street* and the *Butcher-row* in them.

Guiac. Well, Madam *Fidelia*, I thought you had valu'd your Father's prophetick Truths more than this comes to; you shew small respect to his Miracles, if you go away so soon.

Fidel. I assure you, Mrs. *Guiacum*, I can prove that I value 'em profoundly, for I have laid a great Wager upon this; you had best contrive well to make it fall out right, for you don't know what I may lose if the Doctor does not rise.

Clora. Not your Maiden-head, I hope, my dear.   [*Aside.*

3.7 **From N. Spinckes, *The New Pretenders to Prophecy Re-examined: And their Pretences shewn again to be Groundless and False* (1710)**

But never since the World began was a more unquestionable Failure, as to the accomplishment of any Prediction, than in what has been foretold concerning the RAISING of Dr. EMES. As every one must needs be sensible, that shall give himself the trouble of reading the Account in the Appendix, drawn up by some of themselves, and designed for an irrefragable Testimony to the truth of their pretended Mission. Which though I reprinted formerly, I hope it will not be thought a superfluous Work to do it again, since the intent of doing it is only to make it yet more publick, that they received not these Intimations from the Divine Spirit, which both can, and always will be sure to make good, whatsoever it at any time condescends to promise.

In this Relation are Predictions in abundance, and blasphemously said to be *from the Mouth of the eternal God*, Predictions in the Life time of *Emes*, and after his Death, by divers Persons, both in *English* and in *French*, and repeated from time to time, Predictions, of the Day and Hour of his expected Resurrection, of the Person that was to raise him, and of the Room he was to be seen in by many when raised,

He was to be raised, *not in secret, but publickly*, not privately, but *in the presence of Men*, and *by the* SAME POWER THAT RAISED UP OUR LORD JESUS CHRIST. *After he was dead and rotten*, he was to rise, *to rise more fat and more fair than ever he had been, the same Body, the same Face*, only *more lovely and glorious, overshadowed with the Beams of the Divine Glory*; so as to *captivate the Affections of the Beholders*, and in *Purity* and perfect *Innocence*. And in a word, this Resurrection was to *be a greater Miracle, than that of our Lord, when he raised* Lazarus; *and those who would not believe without seeing were to be consumed.*

Was ever Miracle more expresly foretold than this; together with its Time and Circumstances? There was shewn also a Type of it in *J.C.* raised by the hand of *J.P.* [*Cavalier*, I take it to be by the hand of *Potter*] and terrible Judgments threatned to those that should discountenance the Belief of it, which were immediately to come upon them. And themselves were so full of it, that Sir *Richard Bulkeley*, in his *Impartial Account, &c.* declared himself to be satisfied that *it was decisive*, and that he would quit their Society if it were not fulfilled. As Mr. *Lacy* likewise gave his word in another case, Oct. 27, 1707.

* *That if within six Weeks, the mighty Power of God did not attest his Denunciations were from him, he would acknowledge his Delusion before all the World,*

After so express a Promise, it is very strange to me how he can satisfie himself, in not acknowledging his Delusion, when he very well knows, that not only that Prediction on which this Promise was made, has utterly failed him, but others together with it, and particularly all those relating to the Resurrection of *Emes*. Never was false Prophet more plainly detected to be so, than this Gentleman; and how he can yet persuade himself he has not been deluded, I cannot imagine, unless by supposing (which I am very loath to do) that it was a known and wilful Imposture. However, I am desirous to say all I can for him, and do therefore testifie in his behalf, that he now lives orderly and frequents his Parish Church; and though I have reason to believe he does secretly abet and encourage his former Companions, he does not publish any further *Warnings* or

Relations of God's Dealings, nor can I learn that he pretends to any new Revelations.

VII. What does he mean by saying that *the most and greatest of the* Baptist's Prophecies are not fulfilled? This Assertion needs some Explication. For my part, I take the most and greatest of them to relate to our Saviour's manifestation of himself, and what he was to do in the World. And if Sir *R.B.* could have found out any others, any *more and greater*, as he pretends, why has he not told us where the *Baptist* predicted these to come to pass in his own time; because if he did not, it would be no impeachment of his Veracity, that they were not fulfilled sooner than he foretold they would be.

So that upon the whole matter it must be confessed that Sir *R.B.* was sadly out, in appealing thus to the Prophets of old, since there is nothing in all he affirms concerning them, that is for his purpose, but a great deal that is directly against him.

However, he has another shift, but in truth a very odd one, whereby he attempts to save himself.

* *If I should ask these Men*, says he, *How know they that Mr.* Emes *was not raised at the time predicted? they must not own it to be a sufficient Answer (even if they had been then at the Burying-place) that they did not see him. For I have shewn, out of the Scriptures, that the Eyes of Unbelievers are holden; they are too dim to perceive a raised Body.*

Was ever such shuffling seen? Or can any thing be more unworthy of one that would be thought to come in the Name of the Most High, and by his Authority? First, this Resurrection is decisively foretold, and he must own himself deceived, if it follow not accordingly; then upon failure of it, it was not necessary. What, not when expresly appealed to, and the whole stress of the Cause laid upon it? Well, But if this *Salvo* fail, he has another still behind, and that is, that those to whom it was promised, could be no competent Witnesses of the truth of it; for their Eyes were so blinded, that they could not possibly discern whether he were raised or no. They might see the Ground undisturbed, and the Person appointed for the instrument of his Resurrection not to be at the place, and that there was no more appearance of the Body of Dr. *Emes*, than of the Man in the Moon; but this would be no proof with Sir *R.B.* that he did not rise notwithstanding, and in that same place, and at the very same time. But then I would desire to know whether this sort of Sophistry would have been thought to signifie any thing, in case there had really been a Resurrection. If it would, it had been in vain to appeal to a Miracle, which those that were present, and were to be Judges of it, could know nothing of. If it would not, it is very unfair, and unbecoming one that professeth to be acted on by the Spirit of God to urge it here.

4. AFTERMATH

Disputes about the Emes affair destroyed the unanimity of the French Prophets. Clearly some prophecies—and some prophets—were not to be trusted. From the first, Lacy had tried not to encourage all his followers to prophesy. Now it was harder than ever to tell what was truly divine inspiration, and what was merely enthusiasm or wishfulness. The final crisis for the group appears to have come when Lacy claimed that he had received divine instruction to leave his wife and co-habit with the 'Prophetess' Elizabeth Gray. Extract 4.1 is taken from a pamphlet that he published to justify himself. It is written in the form of a letter to a fellow Prophet, Thomas Dutton.

Lacy and Gray settled in Lancashire and had several children. Whilst Lacy continued to write, justifying past 'inspiration', their involvement with the Prophets was at an end, as was the popular appeal of the sect itself.

From *A Letter from John Lacy, to Thomas Dutton, being Reasons why the*   4.1
former left his Wife, and took E. Gray a Prophetess to his Bed (1711)

So then, if my Conscience in the sight of God acquits me, that for above 23 Years of the Matrimonial State, I have not once ever violated my Conjugal Vow, and that I am now no ways influenced by base and filthy Lusts, and that no secret displeasure towards my Wife has any part in this matter, but whatever misbehaviour hath been on her part, I for my part have forgiven it sincerely, even as I hope for true forgiveness for my many offences against God himself; this being the Case, as I have often declared, and do now appeal to the Righteous Judge, who will avenge it upon me, if it be not; then the Trial is wholly of a Spiritual Nature, and ought to be taken for a Case extraordinary; and as the Angelick or Superior Power, which brings it on me, is assuredly attested to me, to be the very same Spirit's Operation, that I have openly avowed for Divine, I am willing to submit the Matter, to the Decision of the same Spirit, which I believe to be in you and many more, as the Divine President over us; in this Occurence it is a very small matter to me, to be censured by Man's Judgment, and I ought not, if it were your Case, what now is mine, to determine by my personal Reasoning; in the meantime, till the thing be decided by the Spirit in other Prophets, what would you have me do, who am intirely perswaded in my own Mind, that it is the Spirit of God? The Word of the Lord, by *Samuel*, is positive, that Disobedience to an immediate Command (and the particular Command there, was as exceptionable by *Saul*, as this to me, if given) is no less a crime than Witchcraft (viz a voluntary compact with the Devil) and stubborn opposition to it, parallel with Idolatry, what do you think? Are Idolatry and Witchcraft small crimes? Are they not rather damnable, and such as incur assured everlasting Miseries? Would you have me then, for fear of Consequences among Men, run the risque of that irretrievable Experiment? No! put it to your own Conscience, and I know you would not . . .

I request your answer hereto, with Prayer, on my part, that God would please to reveal himself even in this matter to you, as I beg yours for me, your (at present) grieved, but ever in Duty, and by the Spirit bound to be,

> Sir,
> Your kindly Affectionate Brother in Christ,
> John Lacy

Since this Letter I have receiv'd, by diverse Ways of Divine Manifestation, Orders to do what is this Day done; the last of which Orders was by a supernatural outward Voice heard, that threaten'd me with *Eternal Destruction* and Hell-Fire if I disobey'd; whereto believing it the *Word of Him*, who hath Power to inflict the same, I could not but subject my self to the *Father of Spirits*, in firm Hope to live by Faith.

3

FAIR-GOERS AND REFORMERS: THE STRUGGLE FOR BARTHOLOMEW FAIR

AN important aspect of what has come to be known as the commercialization of culture in the eighteenth century was the emergence of new forms of recreation, especially in the towns, where venues such as coffee-houses, pleasure gardens, and assembly rooms began to attract a new public for leisure. At the same time, however, fairs and other traditional sites continued to function both as important providers of entertainment and as markets for goods and services. In the 1750s, according to the most comprehensive eighteenth-century survey, more than 3,000 fairs were being held annually in England and Wales.[1] The division between the newer and older forms of recreation was in any case not clear-cut. Although fairs may be styled as customary events, each one having a specific identity defined both by time (its fixed position in the calendar) and place (the piece of ground on which it was traditionally held), novelty was an important factor in their appeal. New fairs could be (and were) founded, while established fairs exploited the drawing power of new kinds of entertainment.

When Bartholomew Fair closed for the last time in 1855 an almost unbroken history of more than 700 years was brought to an end. The fair's origins were monastic and charitable. In 1123 the Priory of St Bartholomew, together with a hospital for the care of the poor, was founded in Smithfield, close to the site of a weekly cattle market. Ten years later the priory was granted the right by royal charter to hold an annual fair on 23–25 August (St Bartholomew's Day being 24 August). As was the case in other early fairs, the religious, commercial, and recreational functions of Bartholomew Fair were closely linked. Originally confined within the precincts of the priory, the fair developed into an important national market for cloth. Outside the precincts, on the ground of West Smithfield itself and in the cloisters, streets, alleys, and yards of inns which led into it, a larger and more diverse fair developed, offering a variety of goods and, espe-

---

[1] William Owen, *An Authentic Account of all the Fairs in England and Wales, as they have been Settled to be Held since the Alteration of the Stile* (1756).

cially, entertainments to fair-goers. This part of the fair—the Bartholomew Fair of Jonson's play and of many subsequent literary representations—eventually fell within the control of the City of London.

During the period covered by our selection the relations between the City and the fair became increasingly antagonistic. The City's responsibility for the fair was customarily signalled by a ceremony of proclamation which took the form of a procession led by the lord mayor and other City officers who made their way (originally on horseback but in the eighteenth century in a state coach) from the Mansion House, via Newgate, to Cloth Fair where the mayor proclaimed the fair open and announced the regulations to be enforced by the City marshals. These regulations commonly concerned the fair's duration and the nature of the activities which could be legitimately conducted there. Some time after 1660 the fair had been extended from its official three days to fourteen. Repeated attempts were made, with only limited success, to restrict the fair to its original term, until the 1750s when the adoption of the Gregorian calendar, which separated the fair from its saint's day and moved its proclamation to the month of September, seems to have effectively reinforced the City's efforts at reform (see Chapter 6). In seeking to regulate the kinds of business carried on at the fair, the City authorities made a distinction between the sale of merchandise (which they saw as an appropriate commercial activity) and the staging of popular entertainments (which they regarded with hostility on the grounds that they were likely to deprave and corrupt). 'I presume not to determine how far some Amusements and Diversions may be tolerated, to draw Concourse to the Fair, for the Profit of honest Wareshops', reflected one concerned observer, 'But, certainly, even This can be no Equivalent for such Pastimes, and Places, as make *Smithfield*, for That Season, a Congress of all Impiety, and the Wickedness of a Fortnight Sufficient (by modest Computation) to stock a Nation with Calamities, and Judgments, for an Age.'[2] At times, in the texts of these early eighteenth-century reformers, we can still detect the accents of Jonson's zealous Judge Overdo, condemning the fair's amusements as 'enormities' and occasions for lewdness, to which servants, apprentices, and young people in general are dangerously susceptible.

In considering what attracted people to the fair it is important to remember that, in the first half of the eighteenth century at least, the spectators were far from being exclusively plebeian. Even allowing for commercial exaggeration, the following advertisement suggests that fair-goers from a wide range of social ranks were thought likely to visit the attractions:

To the Nobility and Gentry, and to all who are Admirers of the Extraordinary Productions of Nature.

---

[2] *An Account of the Last Bartholomew-Fair, And the Late City Order for Regulating the Same. With Two Letters to a Citizen of London on that Occasion* (1702), 6.

There is to be seen in a commodious Apartment, at the Corner of Cow-Lane, facing the Sheep-Pens, West Smithfield, during the short time of Bartholomew Fair,

MARIA TERESIA,

the Amazing CORSICAN FAIRY, who has had the Honour of being shown three Times before their Majesties.

She was exhibited in Cockspur-Street, Hay-market, at two shillings and sixpence each Person; but that Persons of every Degree may have a Sight of so extraordinary a Curiosity, she will be shown to the Gentry at sixpence each, and to Working People, Servants, and Children, at Threepence, during this Fair.[3]

The responses of 'the Gentry' to such spectacles may well have been shaped by special conditions of viewing and, above all, by socially specific expectations and tastes. If Smithfield was in this way a socially variegated site it was also a strikingly gendered one. Fairs were sometimes celebrated as occasions for the temporary relaxation or even reversal of conventional gender roles. At Horn Fair, held annually at Charlton on St Luke's Day (18 October), these reversals seem almost to have been institutionalized. Defoe observed that at Horn Fair

The mob . . . take all kinds of liberties, and the women are especially impudent for that day; as if it was a day that justified the giving themselves a loose to all manner of indecency and immodesty, without any reproach, or without suffering the censure which such behaviour would deserve at another time.[4]

At Bartholomew Fair too women were unusually visible, not only as spectators and consumers but also as retailers of food, drink, and gifts for fair-goers and as performers in the temporary booths erected for plays, music, and rope-dancing. As many of our extracts show, the economic agency of the women who gathered at Bartholomew Fair is typically figured in the discourse of both misogynistic libertines and troubled reformers as a prelude or equivalent to prostitution.

In one sense, the unrivalled range of entertainments at Smithfield certainly did allow fair-goers a temporary release from everyday codes and restraints. The fair exposed them to the grotesque, carnal, and riotous other side of polite culture: to the conspicuous consumption of drink and meat (notably pork, for which the fair was especially famed), to gambling, to the clowning of mountebanks and the merry-andrews who assisted them, and to the erotically charged performances of the female rope-dancers. Surviving collections of handbills and newspaper advertisements above all highlight the strangeness of the spectacles on display.[5] There were freaks of nature:

---

[3] Henry Morley, *Memoirs of Bartholomew Fair* (1859; repr. 1973), 432.

[4] *A Tour through the Whole Island of Great Britain*, ed. Pat Rogers (Harmondsworth, 1971), 115. See also Ned Ward's extended account in *A Frolick to Horn-Fair. With a Walk from Cuckold's-Point Thro' Deptford and Greenwich* (1700), and John G. Smith, *History of Charlton: A Compilation of the Parish and its People*, 3 vols. (1984), iii. 409–29.

[5] These examples are selected from the antiquarian Daniel Lysons's *Collectanea* (British Library

At the *Flying-Horse* Inn in *Bartholomew-Close*, near the Corner of *Duck-lane* in *West Smithfield*,

Is to be seen a most strange and monstrous Living Milch Cow, having Five Horns, Five Legs, Six Feet, and a Cod like a Bull.

To be seen, without loss of Time, During the Time of Bartholomew-Fair, at the last House but one in Hosier-Lane, Smithfield,

A Surprising and wonderful young MERMAID, caught on the Acapulco Shore, after six Hours dangerous Pursuit, whereby three Men belonging to the Adventurous Privateer were dangerously wounded in endeavouring to take her.

and itinerant human prodigies and performers:

THE *Italian Female Sampson,*

WILL EXHIBIT HER HERCULEAN POWERS,

Opposite the Greyhound, West Smithfield, during this Fair, 1752.

By elevating a large anvil three or four feet from the ground, only with the hair of her head: she will permit a large anvil to be laid on her breast, and two men to beat pieces of metal thereon with large hammers: she will put her head on one chair and her feet on another, and will bear six large men from her stomach to her instep . . .

We are desir'd by Mr. Henry Blaker, the Giant, to inform the Publick, that he is returned from Bristol, and is now prepared to exhibit himself to all such as have Curiosity to see him, at the Swan Tavern on the Paved Stones, West-Smithfield.

Much of what troubled and exasperated the reformers could be summed up in the misshapen figures of posture-masters, such as the celebrated Joseph Clark, who performed regularly at the fair. Where polite taste disseminated an ideal economy of the body in manuals of deportment, Clark specialized in the grotesque manipulation of his limbs, facial contortions, and an extravagantly lascivious leer reminiscent of traditional portraits of Vice. The questioning of boundaries (high and low; nature and culture) which many have attributed to the fair is well captured in Lauron's pictures of Clark in his *Cryes of London* sequence, where monkey imitates man, and man imitates monkey.

Much of the material which follows comes from the first decade of the eighteenth century, when the struggle between the City and the fair was especially intense. The texts highlight some of the issues of interpretation and problems of method to which we have drawn attention in our general introduction. Bakhtin's theory of carnival and the counter-arguments developed by critics of his work raise questions of special relevance to the analysis of fairs and markets. Is the fascinated disgust voiced by observers of the fair from Pope to Wordsworth an acknowledgement, at some level, of kinship, as well as an expression of cultural difference? Can the commercial and festive functions of the fair be clearly distinguished, or is the very construction of such categories an expression of the

c. 103. k. 11) and from *A Collection of Advertisements, etc, relating to Bartholomew Fair* (British Library c. 70. h. 6 (2)).

3. Marcellus Lauron, *The Cryes of the City of London Drawne after the Life* (1711), plate 4: 'The Famous Dutch Woman'. By permission of the Syndics of Cambridge University Library

4. Marcellus Lauron, *The Cryes of the City of London Drawne after the Life* (1711), plate 6: 'Clark the English Posture Master'. By permission of the Syndics of Cambridge University Library

high culture's desire to demarcate and police the low? To what extent does the eighteenth-century history of the fair belong to a larger narrative of the withdrawal of polite participation and recognition from popular culture, as suggested by a commentator in *The Morning Herald* in 1787?

Fifty years ago—the Fair continued a fortnight—it now only lasts three days—it then had regular plays—with Booths for their performance . . . Now what a falling off appears . . . Formerly—a visit to Bartholomew Fair was a treat for a Maid of Honor— now not a Maid overburthened with honor will be seen at it—once the favorite lounge of our England's fairest nobility, it is now over-ran with the dregs of mobility—so much for Smithfield and its annual triumph—a custom more honoured in the breach—than the observance.

REFERENCES AND FURTHER READING

The single most important secondary source for the study of Bartholomew Fair is Henry Morley, *Memoirs of Bartholomew Fair* (1859; repr. 1973). For information about popular theatre, Sybil Rosenfeld, *The Theatre of the London Fairs in the Eighteenth Century* (Cambridge, 1960) is indispensable. Robert Malcolmson, *Popular Recreations in English Society, 1700–1850* (Cambridge, 1973), and Robert Altick, *The Shows of London* (Cambridge, Mass., 1978) are important accounts of the social history of fairs in the period. On the Reformation of Manners movement and its impact on Bartholomew Fair, see A. G. Craig, 'The Movement for the Reformation of Manners, 1688–1715', Ph.D. thesis (Edinburgh, 1980), esp. pp. 151–62; Robert B. Shoemaker, 'Reforming the City: The Reformation of Manners Campaign in London, 1690–1738', in Lee Davison *et al.* (eds.), *Stilling the Grumbling Hive: The Response to Social and Economic Problems in England, 1689–1750* (Stroud, 1992), 99–120; and Margaret R. Hunt, *The Middling Sort: Commerce, Gender, and the Family in England 1680–1780* (Berkeley, Calif., 1996), ch. 4. Pat Rogers, *Literature and Popular Culture in Eighteenth-Century England* (Brighton, 1985) is helpful on the responses of high culture to the fair (see esp. chs. 2 and 3). Mikhail Bakhtin, *Rabelais and his World* (Bloomington, Ind., 1984) is a hugely influential study of the relations between official culture and the folk culture of carnival and the market-place. A response to Bakhtin, and the most searching interpretation of the fair in the broader context of eighteenth-century culture, is Peter Stallybrass and Allon White, *The Politics and Poetics of Transgression* (1986), especially chapters 1 and 2.

1. OBSERVING THE FAIR

The *Morning Herald* was wholly justified in claiming that Bartholomew Fair had once been a place of genteel resort. Newspaper accounts record a number of occasions in the first half of the eighteenth century when members of the aristocracy, and even of the royal family, attended performances in the fair's theatrical booths. Playbills announced arrangements made for the particular convenience of 'persons of quality', enabling them to avoid the press of the crowd by driving their coaches into the specially illuminated yards of inns where the plays and entertainments were staged. Early eighteenth-century commentators often draw attention to a festive mingling of social ranks at Bartholomew Fair. Reporting 'from the Gun Music-Booth in Smithfield' in 1699, Tom Brown suggests that the fair has become more fashionable since the days of Ben Jonson, and observes that 'Certainly no place sets mankind more upon a level than Smithfield does. Lords and bellows-menders, beaux and flayers of dead horses, colonels and foot-soldiers, bawds and women of virtue, walk cheek-by-jowl in the cloisters, and jostle one another by candle-light, as familiarly as Nat. Lee's gods in *Oedipus* jostle one another in the dark.'[6]

But if the audience at the fair was socially inclusive during this period, different groups of fair-goers did not necessarily encounter its spectacles in the same way. Entrance prices to plays and exhibits were fixed according to a scale of charges based on rank and occupation, suggesting that there were separate arrangements for viewing. Some (no doubt the minority) of fair-goers thought of themselves as observers rather than participants, and of the pleasure-seeking crowd as a source of instruction or amusement. Much of the surviving writing about the fair conforms to this code of detached and often critical observation, where the fair as a whole is conceived of as a picture of human nature. In 1685 the diplomat and future president of the Royal Society Sir Robert Southwell wrote a letter of advice to his son, then in London with his tutor, urging him to prepare for a visit to Bartholomew Fair by first reading Jonson's play:

Take then with you the impressions of that play, and in addition thereunto, I should think it not amiss if you then got up into some high window, in order to survey the whole pit at once. I fancy then you will say—*Totus mundus agit histrionem*, and you wou'd note into how many various shapes humane nature throws itself, in order to buy cheap, and sell dear . . .[7]

Southwell's letter lays down strategies of observation which shape many later representations of the fair, where the identity of the reflective or satirical onlooker is defined in opposition to the hucksters, performers, and pleasure-seekers who congregate at Smithfield. Ned Ward (1.1), derided in the *Dunciad* as a vulgar Grub-Street scribbler, is no less anxious than Pope to distance himself from the great mass of fair-goers.

---

[6] *Amusements Serious and Comical and Other Works*, ed. Arthur L. Hayward (1927), 143.
[7] Morley, *Memoirs*, 289.

1.1   From Ned Ward, *The London Spy*, Part X 1st coll. edn. (1703)

We order'd the Coachman to set us down at the *Hospital-Gate*, near which we went into a convenient House to Smoak a Pipe, and over-look the Follies of the Innumerable Throng, whose Impatient Desires of seeing Merry *Andrew's* Grimaces, had led them Ancle-deep into Filth and Nastiness, Crowded as close as a Barrel of Figs, or Candles in a Tallow-Chandlers Basket, Sweating and Melting with the heat of their own Bodies; the unwholesome Fumes of whose uncleanly Hides, mix'd with the Odoriferous Effluvia's that arose from the Singeing of Pigs, and burnt Crackling of over-Roasted Pork, came so warm to our Nostrils, that had it not been for the use of the Fragrant Weed, *Tobacco*, we had been in danger of being Suffocated . . .

The first Objects, when we were Seated at the Window, that lay within our Observation, were the Quality of the Fair,[8] Strutting round their Balconies in their Tinsy Robes, and Golden Leather Buskins; expressing that Pride in their Buffoonery Stateliness, that I could reasonably believe they were as much Elevated with the Thoughts of their Fortnights Pageantry, as ever *Alexander* was with the Glories of a new Conquest; and look'd with as much Contempt from their *Slit-Deal-Thrones* upon the admiring Mobility, who were gazing in the Dirt at their Ostentatious Heroes, and their most Superbitical Doxies, who look'd as Awkwar'd and Ungainly in the Gorgeous Accouterments, as an Aldermans Lady in her Stiffen Body'd Gown upon a Festival. When they had taken a turn the length of their Gallery, to show the Gaping Crowd how Majestickly they could Tread, each Ascended to a Seat agreeable to the Dignity of their Dress, to show the Multitude how Imperiously they could Sit. Then came the Conjurer of the whole Company, Merry *Andrew*, I suppose as much admir'd by the rest for a Wit, as the finest Dress'd *Jilt* amongst 'em was by the Mob for a Beauty. As soon as he came to his stand, where he design'd to give the Spectators some Testimonies of his Ingenuity, the first thing he did, he gave a singular Instance of his Cleanliness, by blowing his Nose upon the People, who were mightily pleas'd, and Laugh'd heartily at the Jest. Then, after he had pick'd out from the whole *Dramatic* Assembly a Man of most admirable Acquirements in the Art of Tittle-Tattle, and fit to Confabulate with the Witty and Intelligible Mr. *Andrew*, he begins a Tale of a Tub,[9] which he Illustrates with abundance of Ugly Faces and Mimical Actions; for in that lay the chief of the Comedy, with which the Gazers seem'd most to be affected. Between these two, the Clod-skull'd *Audience* were Lugg'd by the Ears for an Hour; the Apes blundering over such a parcel of Insignificant Nonsense, that none but a True *English* unthinking Mob could

---

[8] Principal actors.   [9] A cock and bull story (*OED*).

have Laugh'd or taken Pleasure at any of their Empty Drollery, the Insipidness of which, occasion'd my Friend to think, that ever since the *Andrew* was Whipp'd for Singeing his Pig with Exchequer Notes, and Roasting him with Tallies, it has made St. *Bartholomew* Jesters afraid of being Witty, for fear of Disobliging the Goverment.[10] For, says he, this is the Dullest Stuff that ever was Spew'd amongst the Rabble, since Heaven made 'em Fools, or ever any such Cox-comb in a Blew-Doublet undertook to prove them so.

The Epilogue of Merry *Andrews* Farce, was, *Walk in, Gentlemen, and take your places whilst you may have 'em; the Candles are all Lighted, and we are just agoing to begin*: Thus, Screwing his Body into an ill-favour'd Posture agreeable to his Intellects, He struts along before the Glittering Train of Imaginary *Heroes*, and their *Water-Lane Beauties*, leading them to play the Fool within-side, in answer to his Performances without; whilst some that had Money went in, and those that had none, walkt off Equally Satisfied.

The outside of the Droll Booths being all Garnish'd with the like Foollerie, we found nothing further amongst 'em worth Repeating; and being seated in a place where nothing else was to be seen, we were forc'd to remove from our Quarters, and hazzard our *Carcases* amongst the Crowd, and our *Pockets* amongst the Nimbl-Finger'd Gentlemen of the Diving Mysterie, or else we should see nothing worth the pains we'd taken. Accordingly we paid our Reckoning, and button'd up our Pockets, as securely as a Citizen does his Shop-Windowes when his Family goes to Church; and so Launch'd our selves into the Tempestuous Multitude, amongst whom we were hurry'd along from the ground by a Stream of Rabble, into the middle of the Fair, in as little time as a forward *Beau* may make a *Fumbler*[11] a *Cuckold*.

From *Bartholomew Fair: An Heroi-Comical Poem* (1717)   1.2

> WHILE busy Mortals, with the worthless Crowd,
> For State-Preferments still exclaim aloud . . .
> I, poor *Plebeian*, ramble up and down,
> To form new Scenes, divert the thirsty Town:
> To comic Humour my weak Muse inclines;
> Ill-natur'd Satyr fondly she resigns:
> And *London*'s Mart I now a Visit pay;
> The various Sights with Pleasure I'll display;

[10] Apparently the jest ridiculed measures taken in the early 1690s, including the founding of the Bank of England in 1694, to achieve financial stability. See Morley, *Memoirs*, 341–4.

[11] A sexually impotent man.

Assist me, *Phoebus*, Ruler of the Day . . .
To *Smithfield*-Bars[12] I speedy makes my Way,
There to pursue each Sight without Delay.
Here greasy Cook, of monst'rous Size, you spy;
Here craving Stomachs cast a greedy Eye,
With keen Desire approach the turning Spit,
Where Veal, and Pork, and Beef, promiscuous meet,
Each other baste; and dainty Kitchin Grease
Froths up, and browns the delicate fav'rite Piece:
With greasy Knife is cut the bounded Meal
Of Beef or Mutton, or the coarser Veal;
With thicken'd Gravie's fill'd the dismal Plate,
Compos'd of Fat, and on the Table sat
By dirty *Molly*, or the greasier *Kate* . . .
Here deathless Actors their Portraitures show,
And grand Comedians stand in graceful Row.
Here *Pinkethman* and *Bullock*[13] dauntless sat;
In fam'd Grimace they fondly emulate.
A comic Droll here ev'ry Hour is shewn;
Here *Robin Hood* and *Little John* are known:
A City Rake a noble King appears;
His Tinsel Dress each gazing Clown reveres.
A Porter here is dress'd in sacred Gown,
And round his Arms the fine Lawn Sleeves are thrown.
With Paunch unwieldy, and distorted Back,
For strong Portmantle he calls out, alack.
A Queen is found amongst the Girls, that trace
The youthful Swains receive their kind Embrace;
For Cakes and Ale their Bodies they resign,
And Clap you nobly for a Glass of Wine.
With tawdry Dress the Royal Consort clad,
A Crown and Scepter for the Fair is made,
And Paint Inch-thick on her wan Cheeks is laid;
Adorning Ringlets on her Shoulders play,
And with her Charms the Monarch she could sway.
A *Little John* is seiz'd within the Crowd,

[12] The Bars denoted the limits of the City Liberties, those districts lying outside the boundaries of the City but subject to its control. Smithfield Bars lay at the northern edge of the main market-place.

[13] William Penkethman (or Pinkethman) (d. 1725), actor and showman; member of Drury Lane company and proprietor of the theatre at Greenwich. William Bullock, comic actor, especially at the Haymarket Theatre. For a comparison between the two performers see *Tatler*, 188 (22 June 1710).

To act on Stage he's not a little proud;
By Trade a Cut-purse, he'll not fail of Art,
He plays, by Instinct, his allotted Part.
These strolling Actors, with an awful Tread,
They fill the fond Spectators with a Dread.
Apprentice-Boys, and Chamber-Dam'sels neat,
Th'admiring Audience hourly here compleat.
Here some with Mirth dispel pernicious Cares,
And others deal in fair *Miranda*'s Wares;
While Bagpipe plays, and the harmonious Strum,
And Frying-Pan is us'd for Kettle-Drum.
The Play's applauded with judicious Skill,
And loud Huzza's the lofty Play-house fill;
Each one commends what suits his wanton Will.
Tho' dull the Scene, th'approving Throng they ring,
And clap aloud the *Exit* of the King . . .
   Now standing still there mighty Mobs appear;
A greasy Butcher now approaches near,
With Paunch o'er-siz'd, and with a broad-brimm'd Hat,
Down to his Waste his monst'rous wide Cravat,
With noted Whiskers and a Visage stern,
The gazing Crowd his Pow'r he would learn,
His Staff advanc'd, the *Constable* she shows,
And to a Female there he straitway goes.
He Notice had to Lewdness she's resign'd;
He forward rushes with a dauntless Mind.
This famous Speech he made then to the Fair,
With kimbo'd Arm, and magisterial Air:
'Tis you must know, that now I represent
The Prince, who me this civil Staff hath lent;
My Power, large, now dooms you to the Goal;
You there will cool your hot lascivious Tail.
Dare you, you fair presumptuous Maid, to deal
Without my Leave, from me your Crimes conceal?
Know ye that I, who have a Kingly Pow'r,
Can licence Vice, or punish ye full sore?
My just Decrees prepare now to obey,
You strait to *Bridewell*[14] shall with me away;

---

[14] A house of correction originally established on the site of Bridewell Palace, near Blackfriars; later a generic term for a prison.

Then fiercely dragg'd her, would no longer stay.
Fine dress'd, the Female she's by all admir'd,
Her Beauties soon the num'rous Mob had fir'd.
They view'd around, and then resolv'd to try
To make a Rescue, lawful Pow'r defy.
Authority aloud commands the Peace,
The Mob persist, they'll no Pretensions cease;
They fell the *Staff*, the lovely Female take;
But 'mongst themselves they then a Squabble make,
And fierce *Bellona* made the Fair to shake.
Now broken Heads abundantly appear'd,
And gorey Blood the *Sundays* Cloths besmear'd;
Each strikes his Neighbour, but he knows not why,
And in Confusion some aloud do cry.
They treat each other with a sad Disdain,
The Oaken Cudgels broken are in Twain,
And many lay as if they had been slain.
This Battel fought, who should enjoy the Fair,
One unconcern'd possesses her with Care;
She's carry'd off, whilst they their Madness share . . .
   All Things now view'd, near *Bedlam* I repair'd,
From *Lunaticks* I no great Outcry heard;
Serene the Place, no dreaded Noise was there;
Not half so mad were they, as in the Fair.
Now Home I came, my Cause asham'd to own,
But long reflected on the vicious Town.

2. THE THEATRE IN THE FAIR

The introduction of new kinds of theatre at Smithfield during the closing
years of the seventeenth century is evidence of the fair's capacity for change.
Fair-goers were entertained by drolls and farces staged in wooden booths
specially erected for the occasion, usually in the yards of inns. The plays,
lasting for about an hour and performed several times a day, were based on
chapbook and ballad stories, biblical narratives, and famous episodes from
English history, or were adapted for the Smithfield audience from existing
pieces in the dramatic repertory. In 1698 a company from one of the patent

theatres (those licensed by royal authority) first appeared at Bartholomew Fair, taking the opportunity to earn profits of up to eighty pounds a night, according to one contemporary estimate,[15] during the otherwise theatrically dormant summer months. For Augustan satirists such as Pope, who in the *Dunciad* ridicules the City of London poet Elkanah Settle for his appearances in the Smithfield drolls, this accommodation between the supposedly high and low cultural spheres was symptomatic of a broader cultural crisis: living proof that, absurdly (as he thought), the Smithfield Muses had indeed reached the ears of kings.

Little is known about most of the drolls performed at Smithfield and the other London fairs, but the texts of a few were printed for sale at the booths. *Wat Tyler and Jack Straw*, excerpted below, had a special relevance for Smithfield since its climactic action—the fatal stabbing of the rebellious Tyler by William Walworth, lord mayor of London, in 1381—had taken place there. Exploiting this connection, the company apparently borrowed the surviving weapon for use in the production and concluded the entertainment with a re-enactment of the Lord Mayor's Day procession.[16] Officially, then, the play celebrates the triumph of the City's authority over the rebellious mob but, as Stallybrass and White put it in another context, 'there was never a guarantee that the "low" spectator would not find his or her radical identity in the "low" spectacle of the fair'.[17] In *Wat Tyler* the choric Mob's delighted assumption of the highest offices of state (in itself a kind of ritual of inversion) may have struck a positive chord with plebeian fairgoers.[18] The same may be said of the play's use of such slogans as 'Wat Tyler and Liberty' and 'Dam Work and Taxes'. Three years after *Wat Tyler* was first presented a ballad attacking Sir Robert Walpole's administration made a pointed reference to the incident said to have incited Tyler's rebellion, and warned that Walpole's notorious excise scheme might ignite a similar revolt.[19]

---

[15] *Smithfield Groans: Or, An Humble REMONSTRANCE TO THE Magistrates of LONDON, Concerning the horrid Wickedness committed and Conniv'd at, in Bartholomew-Fair, in open Defiance of the Laws of the Land, and the Express Order of the Right Honourable the Lord Mayor, and the Court of Aldermen* (1707), 2.

[16] Sybil Rosenfeld, *The Theatre of the London Fairs in the Eighteenth Century* (Cambridge, 1960), 34.

[17] Peter Stallybrass and Allon White, *The Politics and Poetics of Transgression* (1986), 43.

[18] One of the traditional Lords of Misrule who appeared during Christmas festivities at the sixteenth-century Inns of Court was known as 'Jack Straw'. See Ronald Hutton, *The Rise and Fall of Merry England* (Oxford, 1994), 9.

[19] *Political Ballads Illustrating the Administration of Sir Robert Walpole*, ed. Milton Percival (Oxford, 1916), 65.

2.1   From *Wat Tyler and Jack Straw; Or, The Mob Reformers. A Dramatick Entertainment. As it is Perform'd at Pinkethman's and Giffard's Great Theatrical Booth in Bartholomew Fair*[20] (1730)

ACT I. SCENE I.

SCENE, *KENT.*

Enter Wat Tyler *and* Mob.

MOB.

Huzzah! Huzzah! *Wat Tyler* and Liberty!

Tyl. Friends, hear me speak; nor let your smoaky Brains hurry you on to do you know not what: Is it sufficient that I lead you on, thro' Hedges, Bogs, thro' Woods and shaking Quagmires? Or will you let your Reasons cooly judge, and hear me tell, what you must fear and hope?

1 Mob. Ay, ay, let us hear a little Reason,—I love Reason, like Money, because they are both Rarities to me.

2 Mob. What a bold Voice the noble *Wat* has!

3 Mob. How fine a Face for a Conspirator!

4 Mob. Let us hear him—let us hear him—Peace.

Wat. Wou'd you, *Slice*, kill an Ox before you knew his Price? Or you, *Scythe*, mow a Field e'er you were told your Wages? Wou'd you, *Slash*, drive a Coach without your Hire? Or, *Grubby Squeeze*, lend Money not to gain by't?—Certainly no—then hear, my hearty Lads, the great Reward our Enterprize prepares—*Slice* on a Bench shall reverendly sit, and he who butcher'd Oxen, butcher Men—Exalted *Scythe* a Lawyer shall commence, and mow Estates instead of Meadows—*Slash* loudly crack the Politician's Whip, and lash the bounding Steeds of State—while the projecting Head of *Grubby Squeeze*, with some new taking Bubble shall be fraught—a *Mississippi*, or a new *South Sea.*[21]

1 Mob. Huzzah! long live *Wat* the first—

2 Mob. *Tyler* the great!

3 Mob. The Prince of popular Princes!

4 Mob. The mighty Head of us, the Quarters of Rebellion!

Tyl. You all then swear to follow and pursue these Heels and Feet, that have resolv'd to kick the Tyrant *Dick*, and lay him sprawling down?

All. We do, we do—

1 Mob. By the Cleaver of Justice.

---

[20]   William Penkethman, Jr; William Giffard, actor at Goodman's Fields Theatre.

[21]   Refers to the financial panic of 1720–1 caused by the collapse of the speculative Mississippi and South Seas companies.

2 Mob. By the Sickle of the Law.

3 Mob. By the Axle-Tree of State.

4 Mob. And by the Bags in the Treasury.

All. We swear to follow till our Heads are broke—huzzah! huzzah!—

Tyl. O glorious Men! that I cou'd hug ye all,
   And make you ride upon my panting Heart—
   But Hugs are nothing—Action must decide
   The mighty Strife—To *London* now, my Boys—
   Swift as the cleaving Pidgeon cuts the Sky,
   On the proud Wings of great Revenge I fly;
   Tyrant sit fast, or you may chance to know,
   The mighty Kick of *Watty Tyler*'s Toe.

                              [*Exeunt,* Mob *shouting . . .*

ACT II. SCENE I.

   SCENE *London.*

Enter Tyler, Pease-stack, *and* Mob.

Tyl. HOLD, honest Friends; since the last Pint of Brandy, I find my Senses overcome a little—Bring us a Chair—one with two Elbows, quick—A little Sleep
   I fancy may do me Service. In the mean time do thou, my faithful *Pease-stack*,
   High-Chancellor of *England* (so we call thee from this Time forth) Harrangue
   the Populace, and tell 'em what I mean while I'm asleep. You four, unsheath
   your Cutlashes, and guard me.
      [*Sits down to sleep in the Chair; four of the Mob guard him with their
           Swords drawn, two before, and two behind.*]

1 Mob. No Noise while his Majesty sleeps.

4 Mob. He's fast already; he snoars like the Lions in the Tower.

2 Mob. He drinks rarely, almost as well as he fights.

3 Mob. By the Mass! I am almost gone too.—I believe I must call for another
   Chair—but hold, I fancy the Ground may serve me this time; I am not got into
   the Coach-box of State yet.

Pease. Friends and Companions—

1 Mob. Peace, hear his Highness's Chancellorship.

Pease. That you may imagine, Friends, that what you are about to undertake
   does not as well want the Cloak of Religion, as of Justice, give me leave to tell
   you, That I have upon this Occasion turn'd over the Scripture; and tho' it
   does not encourage us (that I can find) to undertake this Rebellion, yet this I
   am positively assur'd of, that it does not say one Word against it: And you must
   be inform'd, Countrymen, that as Silence in a Maiden is a sure Token of her
   Consent, so not expressly forbidding our Enterprize in the Scripture, is a
   certain Sign of its approving it—And—

2 Mob. How like an Angel he argues!—Did you hear that, Neighbours? We have the Scripture on our Side as well as *Wat Tyler*. O, he's a rare Man!

1 Mob. Ay, and I'll warrant him a Wag too, *Scythe*, for did not you hear him talk about the Maiden and Consent? Ah,—

Pease. Will you indulge me, Friends, a Moment longer?

3 Mob. Peace, there!

4 Mob. Silence ho!

Pease. 'Tis true, indeed, I in some Places find Obedience very strenuously recommended to the Subject—

3 Mob. Ay! do you so?

1 Mob. Hold, hold Neighbour, I warrant you he'll bring all off again.

Pease. I say, the Subjects Duty to their Kings is thus strongly urg'd; but then I ask, What King? I'm sure it does not mention *Richard.*—But still to strengthen it—*England* is not once mentioned in the whole Bible.

1 Mob. There's for you, Man; Did not I tell you what he cou'd do? Why, I myself was a little puzzled about Obedience, and all that; but you see he has clear'd it all up again. Ah! I told you what he cou'd do—A meer Dab!—

2 Mob. But please your Eminence, my good Lord Chancellor, will you give me leave to ask my Question?

Pease. Freely, honest Fellow.

2 Mob. Thank you, forsooth—I grant your Excelcellence, there is not one Word of *England* mention'd in the Bible; but I am sure that in the latter End of the first Side of my Bible at home, I read—*London, printed by*—

3 Mob. Ay, so there is, I'll swear.

Pease. Hold, Countrymen, are you such Fools, such Asses? Why, I imagin'd you were Men of Sense; as such I spoke to you.—Cou'd you be so stupid as not to know that it was only Printed here in *London*?

2 Mob. Faith Neighbour, that's true, that was a damnable Blunder indeed. Dear, mighty Sir, I ask you Pardon on my Knees.

3 Mob. Ay, ay, dear Sir, we ask your Pardon, and are satisfy'd; we are thoroughly convinc'd that we have You, Religion, a good Conscience, and *Wat Tyler* on our Side.

Pease. Rise, Countrymen, and hear me yet a little farther:—To answer all Objections, and come directly to the Point—Who is there here that does not love a pretty Wench? Who wou'd refuse a glorious Pint of *Gin*? Or insolently turn his churlish Back on Beef and Pudding?

All Mob. None, my Lord, none.

Pease. Wou'd any here ev'n wish his Wife to stay, altho' the Devil pull'd her from him? Does any here love Work or Taxes?

All Mob. No, no, Dam Work and Taxes!

Pease. If there be any such as these, I heartily beg Pardon, and wou'd by all means advise 'em to return to their original Dunghil and Plough; and not incorporate with growing Spirits, that love Liberty and hate Oppression.— Liberty, my Boys!—Oh, what a Sound it has! Will it not be delicious, when not a Lad here who likes a Countess, or first Dutchess, but may enjoy her before Night, and she think herself honour'd by the Embrace!

All Mob. Huzzah! Huzzah! Liberty and a Countess!

Pease. Then let us resolutely throw down Nobility and Women at once, and magnanimously lift up Ourselves and Petticoats afterwards; to the Accomplishment of which, I throw in my hearty Huzzah, and expect every Body that likes the Cause to follow me.

All Mob. Huzzah! Huzzah! Huzzah!

[*Trumpets and Drums sound within. Exit* Pease-stack.

Tyler *starts from his Sleep, and draws his Sword.*

Tyl Saddle my Sorrel Nag.—Where, where is *Richard?*
     See how the Coward trembles!—Ha! have at thee—
     'Twas a fair Trip: How his Heels kick the Air!
     Pluck me his Crown off.—O, I want some Drink!

1 Mob. How wild the Brandy and the Nap have made him!

2 Mob. Yet warring in his Liquor!

Tyl. Fill me that Cistern there—some *Burgundy*—
     Bring me the Tun upon the Table, Drawer;
     Let me drink deep.—Alas! what am I saying?
                              [*Trumpets again.*
     What warlike Sound is that?

Enter Pease-stack

Pease. The great *Jack Straw*
     Salutes your Majesty, and comes to join
     His fair Ten Thousand to augment your Force,
     And seat the mighty *Tyler* on the Throne.

Tyl. Ha! by my glowing Hopes he's greatly welcome!

Enter Jack Straw *attended, embraces* Tyler.

     Welcome, thou dearest Partner of my Breast,
     Welcome as Sugar to a crying Child,
     Welcome as *Gin* to Oyster-bawling *Moll*;
     To Whores a Cully, or a Writ to Bailifs.

Straw. O let me hold my Gratitude and Speech;
     For shou'd I once begin to speak, my Tongue
     Wou'd tire and deaf thy overloaded Ear
     With an eternal Crack of Thanks and Praises.

Tyl. Excellent *Jack*! O let me hug thee to me!
 Dost thou forget when in the Wilds of *Kent*
 We chas'd the trigging Hare thro' all her Mazes;
 When those swift Feet, and eke also when mine
 O'ertop'd the Ditches, mill'd along the Plains,
 And almost robb'd the Grey-hounds of their Prey.
Straw. O glorious Time! and when in milder Play
 We struck the well-stitch'd Leather o'er the Field
 In artful Cricket, how the Maids wou'd sigh!
 So fast wou'd sigh,—'till they cou'd sigh no more.
Tyl. My *Jacky* still! Yes, 'tis my dearest Friend;
 And, by my Sword! we'll see far better Times:
 See how our Men in many loud Huzzahs
 Salute and court us to be Great and Royal:
 Fate pulls the Strings of this enormous Fiddle,—
 This ill-tun'd City.—Hark! the Base the Treble cracks,
 And we, my Friend, are destin'd to new-string her.
Straw. Still what thou wer't!—what *Watty Tyler* shou'd be!
 But still there wants to crown my Happiness,
 Light of the Moon, and fairer than the Lamps,
 My dearest *Suky*—O, I see not her!—
 Whiter than new-peel'd Turnips is her Skin,
 Her Breath far sweeter than the Smell of *Gin*:
 Her Eyes—
Tyl. Pr'ythee, *Jack*, spare your Raptures now.
 Thou shalt have her, my Lad; thou shalt eat her too as well as the Turnips, if
 you please. She's coming, my Lad; each Instant I expect her here, with my
 dear *Juggy*, and my old Mamma.
Straw. O happy *Straw*!   [*Trumpets sound.*
Tyl. Why sounds that Trumpet?
Pease. From *Richard*, Sir,
 A Message to your Majesty.
Tyl. Let the Fellow in.

         Enter Sir Robert Knolles

 Well, what with us, Sir?
Sir Rob. Thus from his Majesty I come to speak—
 Richard the Second, King of *England*:
 He wills to know why you assemble thus?
 Wherefore these Riots, and this wild Disturbance?
 If you complain of Wrongs and Injuries,

Why do you not address him calmly then?
Humble Petitions wou'd become you better,
And Justice sooner lean her Ear to Prayer,
Than Threats—so says my Royal Master—
He likewise wills you to dismiss your Train,
And each betake him to his sev'ral State,
Lest he account you Rebels, and proceed
With utmost Rigour of the Laws against you.

Tyl. How dare thy Master send—or thou convey,
A Message of such Insolence and Arrogance?
Is it because he once was call'd a King?
And that thou wear'st a Harness there of Lace?
Hence to thy saucy Master back—and tell him,
My Will is all the Answer I return,
For what I have, or what I yet shall do—
Tell him but this—the People are abus'd—
Wat Tyler is their Friend, and will redress 'em.

1 Mob. Ay, ay, *Wat Tyler* is our Friend, and so is the Bible—tell him that—do,
Fool—

Straw. Thinks he, because he from his Infancy
Plaid with a Globe, as I have done at Tennis:
Thinks he to crap our Liberties away,
Like Horses Tails—and with enormous Paw
To knock us down like Nine-pins?

Tyl. Well said, *Jack.*—

Sir Rob. Hear, ye mistaken Ideots—

Tyl. Hold, no more—if you regard your Bones, or Life, not one word more—this
is our Answer, and so bear it to him—but make good haste, or we'll be there
before you.   [*Exit Sir* Robert.

2 Mob. Huzzah! *Wat Tyler* and Liberty! Huzzah!

3 Mob. Lead us on, noble *Wat Tyler*, lead us on.

1 Mob. We'll burn the Palace, fire the City.

4 Mob. Huzzah! *Wat Tyler*, and *Jack Straw*—Huzzah!

Pease. We'll rifle Matrons and deflower Virgins—burn the old Bankers, Tally-
men,[22] and Usurers, and make Bank Notes as plenty as Bad Poetry—

1 Mob. Or stinking Meat in the Dog-days. Huzzah!

Enter on the other side young Walworth *with a Party.*

---

[22] Suppliers of goods on credit. M. Dorothy George, *London Life in the Eighteenth Century* (Harmondsworth, 1966), cites early eighteenth-century attacks on them for ruthlessly exploiting the poor
(p. 299).

Wal. Thanks, gentle Heav'n, see where th'Occasion offers,
　At once to serve my Loyalty and Love:
　I cannot doubt th'Event—the mighty Pow'r,
　That still presides o'er Innocence and Virtue,
　Will guide my Arm to reach the Rebel's Heart:—
　Fall on, my Friends—
　Serve your great King, and free your Country
　　　　　　　　　　　[Falls on Tyler's *Party.*
Tyl. Ha! On my Lads! and prove whose Blows are hardest.
[Several of Walworth's *Party are kill'd, and he taken Prisoner.]*
Wal. Unhappy Fate!—what are thou, Providence?—
　But let me suffer only, and 'tis well.
Tyl. So, so, Loyal Sir, we shall tame you, I believe—
　Why, what has all this Bustle of yours purchas'd?
Straw. Only a Halter—but harkee *Wat*—this Fellow dies immediately.—
Tyl. Right, to terrify the rest, and shew 'em with what Rigour we shall treat those
　that dare resist—string him, my Lads.—
1 Mob. You must Morrice indeed, Friend.
2 Mob. You shall have a fine easy Swing-swang.[23]—
3 Mob. I believe you never danc'd between Heav'n and Earth before.
4 Mob. You need not pray, Sir; the Loyalty of the Action has prepar'd you for
　going up Stairs—Come Sir—　　　*[Offers a Rope.*
Wal. Then do it, Slaves—
　Mercy were Murder from such Brutes as you.
[As they are putting the Rope about his Neck.]

Enter Mrs. Tyler, Goody, *and* Suky.

Straw. Ha! my dear *Suky*, do I dream or not?
Suky. No, Sir, I think that you are broad awake.
Tyl. My *Juggy*, oh!—Truce, Ministers of Death,
　Turn not the Stomachs of my Wife and Mother
　With the distorted Visage of that Traytor—
　He shan't die yet.—Your Blessing, good Mamma.
　　　　　　　　　　　[Kneels to Goody.
Straw. What shall I say to thee for all this Goodness?
　Tho' I never told thee so, I long have lov'd:—
　To find thee thus, thus ripe as bursting Cherries,
　Ready to drop their Sweetness in my Mouth—
　Is Joy so great—I know not how to bear it.
Suky. What shall I say to him, Mamma?

---

[23] *Morrice* and *swing-swang*: cant terms for execution by hanging.

Mrs. Tyl. Tell him 'tis very well, and you are satisfy'd.

Suky. 'Tis very well, and I am satisfy'd—

Tyl. Subjects, behold the Consort of our Bed—

   Juggy, salute our People with a Nod:—

   Suky, come hither—tip me your Fist, you Jade—

   Take her, *Jack Straw*, and with her half my Pow'r—

   Now let the Trumpet sound its sprightly Note,

   And three Huzzahs denote our Peoples Joy.

1 Mob. Long live King *Wat*, and Queen *Juggy*.

All. Long live, &c.

1 Mob. Long live Prince *Straw*, and Princess *Suky*.

All. Long live, &c.—Huzzah—

Tyl. Thanks, gallant Lads: now to our Warlike Enterprize.

   All draw their Swords, and follow where I lead—

   So, if we believe what lying Writers tell,

   When *Jove* was tir'd with Scolding and with Love,

   From *Juno*'s Arms he took his furious Way,

   Threw down what Mountains in his Passage lay,

   And dash'd th'aspiring Giants into Clay.   [*Exeunt.*

3. REGULATING THE FAIR

Like other fairs, Bartholomew Fair was regulated internally by a Court of Piepowders which had jurisdiction over commercial disputes during the three days when the fair was officially open for business. In the early 1690s pressure was brought to bear on the City authorities to impose more stringent and far-reaching controls on the fair's activities. This initiative was closely associated with the campaign for the Reformation of Manners which has been seen as part of a larger movement for the reform of popular culture.[24] Founded at the instigation of a group of City gentlemen, and enjoying the active support of the joint monarchy of William and Mary, the first societies for the reformation of manners campaigned vigorously in London (where thirty-two separate societies were active by 1698) until the movement finally petered out in the 1730s. The reformers were particularly concerned to punish offences against religion (blasphemy, swearing, and Sabbath-breaking, for example) and crimes of lewdness (especially prostitution). Their most controversial policy was to encourage right-minded citizens to

---

[24] See Peter Burke, *Popular Culture in Early Modern Europe*, rev. edn. (Aldershot, 1994), 207–43.

'go out into the streets and markets, and public places on purpose, and to observe the people's behaviour there, and of such offences as they observed to be committed . . . to give information to some justice of the peace at their next leisure'.[25] The conduct of such informers and of the parish constables who carried out arrests was frequently denounced as incompetent, hypocritical, or financially motivated.

In view of Bartholomew Fair's reputation for corrupting the morals of servants and apprentices, it is not surprising that it should have drawn the reformers' fire. A cluster of late seventeenth- and early eighteenth-century texts clearly reflects the reformers' programme and their efforts to exploit their connections with lord mayors such as Sir Richard Levett, who sympathized with their aims (3.1). The attempts they inspired to limit the duration of fairs such as Smithfield and to suppress drolls and other entertainments there sometimes met with violent resistance such as the murder of a constable while executing his duties at May Fair in 1702.[26] Other forms of opposition included printed satires and mock petitions which questioned the motives of the authorities and parodied the official discourse of reform (3.2 and 3.4).

3.1   Order of the Court of the Common Council (June 1700)

Levett   Mayor

THE King's most Excellent Majesty, and His late Religious and Gracious Queen, as also the Lords and Commons Assembled in Parliament, having frequently express'd their great Sense of the deplorable Increase of Prophaneness, Vice and Debauchery in this Kingdom, and their earnest Zeal and Desires of Reformation, and Prevention thereof for the future: And His said Majesty having by His Royal Proclamation[27] Commanded and Required all His Magistrates and Ministers of Justice, to put the Laws in full and due Execution against such Offenders. This Court, as well in Obedience thereunto, as out of their own hearty Desire to promote Reformation in the Premises, to the Honour of Almighty God, of the King, and of this City, and the good Government thereof, having taken into their serious Consideration the great Prophaneness, Vice and Debauchery too frequently used and practised in *Bartholomew-Fair*; And to prevent the same for the future, Do hereby strictly Charge and Command all

---

[25]   A. G. Craig, 'The Movement for the Reformation of Manners 1688–1715', Ph.D. thesis (Edinburgh, 1980), 31, citing Edward Stephens, *The Beginning and Progress of a Needful and Hopeful Reformation in England* (1691), 9–10.

[26]   Craig, 'Movement for the Reformation of Manners', 158.

[27]   *A Proclamation, For Preventing and Punishing Immorality and Prophaneness*, 24 Feb. 1697/8.

Persons concerned in the said Fair, and in the Sheds and Booths to be erected and built therein or Places adjacent, that they do not Let, Set, Hire or Use any Booth, Shed, Stall, or other Erection whatsoever, to be used or imployed for Interludes, Stage-plays, Comedies, Gaming-places, Lotteries, disorderly Musick-meetings, or other Occasions or Opportunities for Inticing, Assembling or Congregating idle, loose, vicious and debauched People together, under Colour and Pretence of innocent Diversion and Recreation; But that all Booths, Sheds, Stalls, Shops, and other Erections during the said Fair, to be had and made, shall be used, exercised and imployed for Merchandizes, Trade and Commerce, according to the good Intents and Purposes designed in the Granting, Erecting and Establishing the said Fair. And all Persons are hereby Required to take notice hereof, and yield Obedience hereunto, as they will answer the contrary thereof at their Perils.

Goodfellow.

Printed by *Samuel Roycroft*, Printer to the Honourable City of *London*. 1700

**From *A Pacquet from Will's: Or a New Collection of Original Letters on Several* 3.2
Subjects (1701)**

A Letter from an Actress of the Play-House, to a Stroler in the Country, concerning Reformation of Manners, and the Suppressing of Drolls in Bartholomew-
Fair.

My dear Harlikin,

I was in great Hopes we should have once more met, according to our old Custom, at the grand Revels at St. *Bartholomew*, to have solac'd our selves over a fat Pig and a Bottle, and have Droll'd upon the past Hardships of a long Vacation;[28] but the Master-Bee of the great Hive,[29] the City, to please the peevish Wasps, and zealous Horn-heads of the Canting Crew, has buzz'd about an Order, There shall be no Fair, to the Frustration of our Hopes, and Disappointment of our Creditors, that the Tally-Men walk about biting their Thumbs, like a broken Gamester at an Ord'nary: And our adjacent Cooks and Ale-house-keepers, have so alter'd their Countenances, that they look upon us Players with as evil an Aspect, as a rich Citizen does upon a poor Relation, or an uncharitable Usurer upon an insolvent Debtor.

But notwithstanding the fabulous Reports of totally Abolishing the Fair, the great Design was concluded in Prejudice chiefly to our Quality or Function; and

---

[28] i.e. when the patent theatres were closed.   [29] The lord mayor.

enquiring into the Reasons of this our terrible Persecution, I found the following Charge had been exhibited against us:

The Principal Causes of the Wickedness of the Age, say, the Reforming
Zealots, are prophane Drolls, wherein they us'd to ridicule the Grandure of the
City, in Contempt of the wise Magistrates thereof, and make a Lord-Mayor (as in
the Renown'd Play of *Whittington*,) beholding to so mean a Creature, as a Tabby
Cat, because she was a good Mouser, for his Riches and his Mayoralty; and are
so very insolent in the face of the City, as to hire a Paunch-gutted Porter, for half
a Crown a Day, to represent an Alderman in a Scarlet Gown, when a Lean-ribb'd
Scoundrel, for Mimicking a Fool in a Blew Jacket, shall have Forty Shillings;
which indeed (say they) are insufferable Indignities to be put on the Worthy
Magistrates of *England*'s Fam'd Metropolis: Further, charging us with teaching
upon our Stages, the wicked Mystery of Intriguing, Instructing their Wives, by
our Plots, to be too cunning for their Husbands; and their tractable pretty
Daughters, to be too witty for their Parents: Alledging, That had not the Drolls
been timely suppress'd thro' the Piety and Wisdom (tho' some say Interest) of
Domine Oroonoko,[30] they would have suffered under the frightful Apprehen-
sions of Cuckoldom over-running the City, as bad as Schism has done the
Church; and that their Wives, in a little time, would have thought Liberty of Conscience as good a Plea for withdrawing their Love from their Lawful Husbands,
and transferring it to their Gallants, as a double-refin'd Christian does for
renouncing the Lawful Church, and betaking himself to a New Religion: So that,
from these Considerations, we are depriv'd of our ancient Priviledge, and are
decreed to suffice Nature with Potatoes and Small Beer, during the merry Season
of the Fair, in which we us'd to indulge our Appetites with the palatable Dainties
of Pig and Pork, and wash away the Remembrance of our past Poverty, with the
Delights of the Bottle . . .

A Work of such Difficulty as the Reformation of a lewd Age, is an Undertaking of such great Importance that it can move but slowly: and truly so it does, for
it makes its Progression by such imperceptible Degrees, that all the Good they
have been doing for this many Years, is as yet to none but themselves discern-
able. But however, they think it no small Step towards the good End of their great
Design, to remove those two Evils, from the Fair, the Drolls and the Musick-
houses, which has depriv'd some that were honest, of a justifiable Livelihood,
and has occasion'd those that were bad, to become ten times worse; but yet
notwithstanding their great Zeal, to the Reformation of Manners, and Suppress-

---

[30] Presumably a reference to the playwright Thomas Southerne, whose tragedy *Oroonoko* was first
staged in 1696. In Defoe's *More Reformation* (1703) Southerne is the likely target of a passage ridiculing
'the new Reformer' (R. Jordan and H. Love (eds.), *The Works of Thomas Southerne*, 2 vols. (Oxford,
1988), i. xxvi). In *Reformation of Manners* (1702) Defoe specifically censures measures taken against
Bartholomew Fair (ll. 294–8).

ing of Indecencies, for some Reasons best known to themselves, they have suffer'd the Dancers of the Ropes, to stir up Concupiscence in Youth, by showing at once, both their Ar——s and their Activity: but 'tis thought, a way will be found by the next Season, to make 'em dance in a modester Dress, or put larger Pockets in their Diminutive Trunks, which the Reformers, when they see fit, will teach 'em to know the Use of . . .

POSTSCRIPT

How strangely pious is our Nation grown,
Such a Reforming Age sure ne're was known;
The Leacher of the Peace, who loves the Fact,[31]
Will punish what he can't forbear to act;
And oft commits the Miss of publick Trade
To *Bridewell*, whom he wishes in his Bed.
Nay, Poets too, like Magistrates reprove,
And scourge that Vice the most, which most they love.

The common Scoundrel so reform'd is grown,
He persecutes the Lady of the Town,
And lives on her poor Drudg'ry, not his own.
Forsakes the Rog'ries he was us'd to play,
That brought his Neck in danger ev'ry day.
Now turns Informer, gets a painted Staff,
And by betraying others, lives more safe.

But above all in this low'r World accurst,
We Play'rs sure are persecuted worst,
Whose very Bills are under such Disgrace,
My Lord-May'r pulls 'em down, whilst Dr. *Case*[32]
Struts on Church-walls, and Pocky Bills take place,
'Tis strange such vile Profaneness (but 'tis true)
In these good times escapes the Clergy's view;
When our poor Poets for such slender Evils,
As Gad and Fac[33] were maul'd like any Devils.
The *Hockley*[34] rough Game range the City thro',
Disperse their Bills amongst the crop-ear'd Crew.
Which shows his Majesty's Servants, we his Play'rs
By horn-headed Cits, and their more pious May'rs,

---

[31] Crime.

[32] A quack physician specializing in venereal disease; satirized by Samuel Garth in *The Dispensary* (1699), canto 3, 184.

[33] i.e. God and Faith. Profane swearing was one of the reformers' main targets.

[34] Hockley in the Hole, site of a famous bear garden.

Are less respected than his Majesty's Bears.
But that which grieves us starving Sinners most,
Is the great Benefit o'th' Fair we've lost
Which kept us all in decent Reparation,
And gave us Credit thro' the long Vacation.
But now they've put down Drolls, our Cooks seem shie,
And every Ale-house Scoundrel looks awry,
If we ask either mercenary Sot,
To trust us with a Dinner, or a Pot;
Good Heavens assist us in this vacant time,
When honest means to live are made a Crime.
And for the future give us Preservation,
From these severe Effects of Reformation.

3.3 From *Reasons Formerly Published for the Punctual Limiting of Bartholomew Fair . . . Now Reprinted with Additions, to Prevent a Design Set on Foot to Procure an Establishment of the Said Fair for Fourteen Days* (1711)

To the Right Honourable the Lord-Mayor, Aldermen, *and* Commons *of the* City *of* London *in* Common Council *assembled. The humble* Petition *of divers Citizens and Inhabitants in and near* West-Smithfield, *sheweth.*

THAT this Honourable *City* hath an undoubted Right to hold and keep a publick *Fair* in *West-Smithfield*, for the Sale of all Manner of *Cattle*, *Wares*, and *Merchandise*.

That by Length of Time and Depravity of Manners, the lawful Use and Benefit thereof, is of late wholly lost, and the same is become a meer *riotous* and *tumultuous* Assembly of the worst of People of both Sexes; by Reason whereof, many great Mischiefs and Disorders have been committed, to the high Dishonour of Almighty GOD, and the good Government of this City.

That the said *Fair*, as it is now used, is become a great Enticement to the Youth of this *City*, in the seeing of *Shews*, *Raffling*, and other *extravagant* and *lewd Courses*, whereby they are led to unlawful means of getting Money, to the Loss of their Masters and Friends, and at length to their own Ruin.

That your *Petitioners* are, by reason of the said Disorders, very much prejudiced and hinder'd in their lawful Callings and Imployments, and in their passing to and from their Habitations, and are in continual Fear of Mischief to their Persons and Estates, and in great Danger of *Fire*, by the Building of many great *Booths* and *Sheds*. And that these Evils and Dangers are very much encreased by the extravagant and unlawful *Length of Time*, to which the said *Fair* has of late Years been *protracted*.

That your *Petitioners* being inform'd, that this *Honourable Court* hath lately made an Order for *restraining* the Time of holding the said *Fair* for *Three Days*, according to the *first Institution* thereof; Your *Petitioners* did well hope, that the Mischiefs abovementioned would be thereby in a great Measure prevented.

That your *Petitioners* have heard, that some Persons are making their Efforts to get the said good *Order* repealed, upon Pretence that the Revenues of St. *Bartholomew's Hospital* would be prejudiced thereby.

That your *Petitioners* would be very far from obstructing any lawful Means for promoting the Benefit of the said *Hospital*, but they humbly conceive, that in this Case it would be to make Almighty GOD the Patron and Protector of the Wickedness and Disorders that are occasioned by the said *Fair*.

Your Petitioners do therefore most humbly pray, that this Honourable Court will confirm the said Order, and give Directions for the strict Observation thereof.

And your Petitioners shall ever pray, &c.

FINIS.

The Pigs Petition Against Bartholomew-Fair; With Their Humble Thanks to those Unworthy Preservers of So Much Innocent Blood (1712?)   3.4

Humbly Inscrib'd to the Illustrious C[ommo]n C[ounci]l.

> MAY't please your Wors—ps, craving your Permission,
> We *Humble Pigs* present our poor Petition,
> Beseeching you'd regard our woful Case,
> And save us from those *Black* and *Murd'ring Days*,[35]
> That *Fair* St. *Barthol'mew*, as People call it,
> May never relish with a Godly Palate.
> Suppress, we humbly pray, that hated Name,
> (For not a Pig on's can endure the same.)
> Such Havock has been made for many Years,
> The very Sound grows dreadful to our Ears:
> No *Shrovetide-Cock* can dread a Cat-stick more,[36]
> Than we that *Murd'ring Time* that sluic'd our Gore,

---

[35] Smithfield was a traditional site of executions. Forty-three Protestants were martyred there during the reign of Mary I.

[36] Killing tethered cocks by throwing sticks at them was a Shrovetide custom.

Where Thousands of us daily paid our Lives,
A Prey to *Suburb* trulls, and *Carmens Wives.*
Th'Inhumane Streams that have been Yearly spilt,
Let *Smithfield Cooks* be Witness of the Guilt,
And let 'em in due Time their Crimes attone
(Lest they feel hotter Fires than their own.)
Scarce were we farrow'd but were snatch'd away,
And to the reeking Knife were made a Prey;
While Hungry *Rabble* daily did confound
The fattest Pigs for almost Ten Miles round,
That sure those *Corm'rants* did design our Ends,
But you, we humbly thank ye, stood our Friends.

Go on then, finish what you have begun,
And crush those Vipers, every Mother's Son.
Let *Puppets*, *Drolls*, and *Tumblers*, Reign no more,
Nor Pigs be slaughter'd there, as heretofore.
Where *Satan* Yearly enter'd in the Rout,
Oh stop the *Cranneys* now to keep them out!
So may you be Renown'd for doing Good,
And saving Deluges of Harmless Blood.
Ev'n we poor Creatures must your Praises squeak,
(For now's the Time if ever Pigs may speak:)
More Fam'd than e'er *Hogsnorton*, be the *Time*,
When Pigs, instead of *Organs*, squeak'd in *Rhime*.

Oh may your Days be Lasting and Renown'd,
And with such worthy Actions daily Crown'd.
When *Christmas* comes may he that gives ye Meat,
Bless the *Plumb-Porridge* that ye Yearly Eat.
May Droves of *fatted Hogs* your Tables wait,
Serv'd up by Turns in each well-relish'd Cate;
Whence various Dishes gracefully may rise,
And be your Sauces season'd well with Spice.
May *Gammons* first against your *Sherry's* Arm,
And *Loins* and *Flitches* round your Larders swarm.
May *Collard-Brawn* its *Rosemary* disclose,
Nor *Mustard* ever bite you by the Nose.
For ever may *Pork Griskins* have Applause,
And all your *Spare-ribs* float with *Apple* Sauce
Hams with your *Chickens*, with your *Turkeys*, *Chines*,
To give a Relish to your choicest Wines.

May your *Black Puddings* and your *White Ones* please,
And strung be all your *Fowls* with *Sausages*.
May *Larded Turkeys* fat in Clouds arise,
And blest be both your *Pork*, and *Christmas Pies*.
Never may *Harslets* fail you, cold or hot,
Nor quite be honest *Pork* and *Pease* forgot.
May you ne'er know the want of *Chitterlins*,
Nor *Bacon* ever fail you to your *Beans*.
Be this your Fare, and when the Season comes,
May your *Pig-Sauce* be ever full of *Plumbs*.
May *Collard-Pig* the cleanly *Side-board* Grace,
And *Pettitoes* for ever find a Place.[37]

This is the Sum of what we have to say,
While every Year, on that once *Fatal Day*,
A Thousand *fatted Pigs* their Throats shall pay;

And we in Duty Bound, shall ever pray.

FINIS

Lady Holland's Mob

3.5

'Lady Holland's mob' was the name of an unruly crowd which assembled at
the Hand and Shears tavern (where the Court of Piepowders traditionally
convened) on the eve of the formal opening of the fair. The origins and
customs of the mob are obscure, but it appears from surviving descriptions
that it parodied the official administration of the fair, travestying the mayoral
ceremony of proclamation (and thereby contesting the City's authority over
the fair), before spilling out into the streets of Smithfield and neighbouring
districts where householders were ritually disturbed and insulted. Morley
describes the mob as 'an institution of the Fair', but if its disorder was in some
sense institutionalized, it does not always appear to have been effectively contained. What little we know about the mob suggests that, as in other traditions of licensed misrule, there was always an element of unpredictability in
its conduct.

Reports in the newspapers indicate that Lady Holland's mob was particularly active in September 1802, when Charles Lamb guided Wordsworth

[37] *Collard*: pig's meat 'boiled, cut into small pieces and pressed into the shape of a roll' (*OED*);
Griskin: 'The lean part of the loin of a bacon pig' (*OED*); *Harslet*: 'A piece of meat to be roasted, *esp.*
part of the entrails of a hog' (*OED*); *Pettitoes*: pig's trotters.

through Smithfield: a visit which inspired the most famous of the many antagonistic descriptions of Bartholomew Fair (*The Prelude*, VII. 648–94).

From William Hone, *The Every-Day Book, or Everlasting Calendar of Popular Amusements, Sports, Pastimes, Ceremonies, Manners, Customs, and Events* (1826–7)

On the night before the day whereon the lord mayor proclaims the Fair, a riotous assemblage of persons heretofore disturbed Smithfield and its environs, under the denomination of 'Lady Holland's mob'. This multitude, composed of the most degraded characters of the metropolis, was accustomed to knock at the doors and ring the bells, with loud shouting and vociferation; and they often committed great outrages on persons and property. The year 1822, was the last year wherein they appeared in any alarming force, and then the inmates of the houses they assailed, or before which they paraded, were aroused and kept in terror by their violence. In Skinner-street, especially, they rioted undisturbed until between three and four in the morning: at one period that morning their number was not less than five thousand, but it varied as parties went off, or came in, to and from the assault of other places. Their force was so overwhelming, that the patrol and watchmen feared to interfere, and the riot continued till they had exhausted their fury.

It has been supposed that this mob first arose, and has been continued, in celebration of a verdict obtained by a Mr. Holland, which freed the Fair from toll; but this is erroneous. 'Lady Holland's mob' may be traced so far back as the times of the commonwealth, when the ruling powers made considerable efforts to suppress the Fair altogether; and when, without going into particulars to corroborate the conjecture, it may be presumed that the populace determined to support what they called their 'charter', under the colour of the 'Holland' interest, in opposition to the civic authorities. The scene of uproar always commenced in Cloth-fair, and the present existence of an annual custom there, throws some light on the matter. At 'the Hand and Shears,' a public-house in that place, it is the usage, at this time, for tailors to assemble the night before the Fair is proclaimed by the lord mayor. They appoint a chairman, and exactly as the clock strikes twelve, he and his companions, each with a pair of shears in his hand, leave the house, and, in the open street of Cloth-fair, the chairman makes a speech and proclaims 'Bartholomew Fair.' As soon as he concludes, every tailor holds up and snaps his shears with a shout, and they retire, shears in hand, snapping and shouting, to the 'Hand and Shears', from whence they came forth; but the mob, who await without, to witness the ceremony, immediately upon its being ended, run out into Smithfield, and being joined by others there shout again. This second assemblage and shouting is called 'the mob proclaiming the Fair;' and so begins the annual mob, called 'Lady Holland's mob.' Since 1822, the great body have confined their noise to Smithfield itself, and their number and disorder annually decrease.

4

ALMANACS: ASTROLOGY
AND POPULAR PROTESTANTISM

BY one crude definition, almanacs unarguably constitute a significant part of popular culture in the eighteenth century: they were consistently the best-selling publications of the period. Their popularity was such that they naturally claim a place in this book. At the end of the seventeenth century, over 400,000 almanacs were being sold annually under the monopoly of the Stationers' Company. No other printed matter could compete with these sales figures. Successful individual almanacs like those of Gadbury and Partridge had print runs of some 20,000. Through the first half of the eighteenth century, overall sales figures remained at about this level, although they were less evenly distributed between different titles; Moore's *Vox Stellarum* became the dominant almanac, and by the 1760s had ten times the sales of its nearest rival. Simply put, what these numbers mean—given multiple readership and the possibility that some parts of almanacs might be read to those who were not fully literate—is that a large proportion of the population will have used almanacs and been open to their shaping influences.

All the evidence is that almanacs appealed to an extraordinary range of readers. References in the period to the appeal of these publications to 'the vulgar' should probably be taken in the same way as disparaging remarks about the appeal of novels to a 'low' readership. We know that, in the latter case, a literary and moral judgement—rather than a sociological observation—is usually being made. As Bernard Capp, the foremost historian of almanacs, observes, the very existence in libraries of significant numbers of almanacs from this period is evidence of propertied readers. 'Most surviving copies originally belonged to the gentry or professional men; although the great majority of buyers were yeomen, husbandmen and artisans . . . their purchases have long since perished.'[1] Often the copies that have been preserved in libraries include the handwritten annotations of evidently educated owners. For some of these, almanacs doubled as diaries recording personally important dates and memoranda.

[1] Bernard Capp, *Astrology and the Popular Press: English Almanacs 1500–1800* (1979), 60.

In whatever ways almanacs varied, they always provided a calendar of each month of the coming year, with saints' days and important anniversaries marked out. Sometimes the choice of important dates would itself proclaim the character of the almanac. Opposite his calendar for January, for instance, the Tory almanac-maker George Parker printed,

> *King Charles I* Murther'd *Jan.* 30. 1649.
> *O. Dismal Day, the like ne'er seen before,*
> *For Charles our King, lied weltring in the Gore.*

Whig almanac-maker John Partridge, in contrast, printed the following alongside his calendar for May 1700:

May the 20 and 22 in 1685 Dr *Oats* was whipt for accusing the Papists with matter of Truth: It was a barbarous Punishment, but too much like the Papists.

Both these were included amongst the respective almanacs' 'Observations' for a given month. 'Observations' were, for the most part, predictions for that month. They were provided by all almanacs with an astrological bent—which means the most successful ones in the early part of the eighteenth century. They might refer to political events, or merely to the weather, and would typically be printed alongside the calendar for a particular month. Other common elements in almanacs were chronologies of important historical events and of the reigns of English monarchs, tables of eclipses and other astronomical events, often elaborate astrological summaries of the positions of the important planets and constellations for the four seasons of the year, horticultural and agricultural advice, gazetteer-like information about the country and its counties and towns, the dates and places of coming fairs and markets, and material of specific local interest (almanacs aimed at Londoners, for instance, might have tide tables for the Thames).

The most renowned, and one of the most successful, of eighteenth-century almanac-makers, John Partridge, is now best known through Jonathan Swift's destructive parody of his 'predictions', and this is sometimes taken to exemplify a growing disdain amongst the educated for popular astrology. We should notice, however, that Swift's spoofs relied on witty readers being able to recognize the very detail of what he was parodying. In one sense, then, Swift's so-called *Bickerstaff Papers* (1708–9) are further testimony to the popularity of almanacs across the social spectrum. This might tell us of one useful way of thinking about popular culture in at least the early eighteenth century: not in terms of its putatively lower-class readership (though there clearly was such a readership for almanacs), but rather of its status as non-polite reading for even the politest. Linda Colley's characterization of early eighteenth-century almanacs as 'the contemporary equivalent of the tabloid press, both in tone and popularity' is perhaps too cheerfully anachronistic, but there is certainly evidence that those who were educated continued to be intrigued by the 'prophetic' almanacs that were supposedly 'low' reading.[2]

Swift fixed on Partridge's astrological predictions as matter ripe for ridicule. It has been argued, most influentially by Keith Thomas in *Religion and the Decline of Magic*, that the last decades of the seventeenth century saw a drastic decline in the status of astrology amongst the educated. Although, as a fact of intellectual history, this seems undeniable, almanacs themselves provide evidence that astrological interest remained alive in the eighteenth century. Patrick Curry has argued that the popular appeal of astrology amongst the uneducated remained undiminished, and indeed that it was only ' "high" or cosmological-philosophical astrology' that withered.[3] It is true that some almanacs avowedly aiming at a higher class of readership specifically excluded astrology. Particularly noteworthy is *The Ladies Diary: or, the Woman's Almanack*, whose subtitle advertised 'many Delightful and Entertaining Particulars, peculiarly adapted for the Use and Diversion of the FAIR-SEX'. A characteristic preface from this publication (in the 1716 edition) talks of 'the Contempt with which a Writer of Almanacks is look'd upon' and of how, in *The Ladies Diary*, 'the Design is different from all our Annual Writers, being intended to promote some Parts of Mathematical Learning amongst the Female Sex'. Most almanacs, however, continued to vaunt their prophecies, even if these were usually very generalized. Curry notes that the most successful, *Vox Stellarum*, was also 'the most overtly astrological and prophetic almanac of them all'.[4]

It is true that judicial astrology, involving the making of precise predictions about specific individuals, was widely ridiculed (though we can also see from Section 2 of this chapter that jobbing astrologers continued to advertise their expertise in precisely such fortune-telling). It is also true that it was important to the astrological almanacs that their prophecies be made compatible with Christian doctrine (if only by the repeated assertion that they were so). Neither of these considerations stood in the way of the business of prophesying about—one might say, on behalf of—the nation. Indeed, it was a sense of the nation—of its future and of its past—that almanacs insistently communicated. Even the miscellaneous information that they contained, whether geographical or pragmatically economic, often spoke for some idea of national belonging. The emphasis of this chapter is, in the end, on nationhood, and on the different versions of patriotism and religious orthodoxy that went with it. This means thinking of almanacs through their political allegiances and aspirations.

The role of politics in the composition and distribution of almanacs carries through from the seventeenth century into many of the examples in this chapter. Two of the disputants in several of the extracts that follow, the almanac-makers John Partridge and George Parker, had first come to rhetorical blows over the Exclusion Crisis of the early 1680s, and were still trading invective almost thirty years later. Anyone interested in the politics of almanacs, and in particular of astrology, in the seventeenth century has excellent guides in the work of Capp and Thomas. It needs to be acknowledged, however, that the place taken by almanacs in the eighteenth century has been insufficiently studied. Perhaps we still have little idea of what influence the pronouncements of Moore, Gadbury, and their ilk had on popular feeling. It is easy to be deflected by the widespread educated disdain for the prophetic pretensions of these publications, but Colley is surely right to suggest that their rhetoric exemplifies the tenor of popular patriotism (and popular prejudice) in at least the early part of the century.

Different almanacs, of course, had markedly different personalities, despite— or perhaps because of—the similarity of much of their contents. Many almanacs were strongly associated with their particular compilers, an association that usually lasted well beyond the death of the individual under whose name a certain almanac was published. The most famous example of this is *Moore's Almanack*, officially entitled *Vox Stellarum* in the eighteenth century, which lived on into the twentieth century even though its originator, Francis Moore, died in 1714. It will be seen from some of the extracts given below from 1716 and 1717 that life after death was the rule for successful almanac-makers. After John Partridge's death in 1715, his *Merlinus Liberatus* for 1717 gave this prefatory reassurance to prospective purchasers:

Dr. Partridge, for your Service, and the Publick Good of his Country, having with much Labour and great Industry calculated *Ephemerides* for several Years to come:

This is to Certify all those who shall buy this Almanack, That it is Printed from a Transcribed Copy, written with the Doctor's own Hand.

The preface was addressed 'To the Protestant Reader', in effect declaring that the almanac would retain the strongly pro-Hanoverian and anti-Catholic enthusiasms of its inventor. Indeed, the personality of an almanac was often a matter of ideology (clearly represented in the animosity between Partridge and George Parker, exemplified in Section 1 of this chapter).

Rivalry between different almanacs was also commercial and sometimes one suspects that political and religious conflicts were heightened in order to produce commercially differentiated products. The almanac trade was a peculiar one given that it took place under the monopoly of the Stationers' Company. In 1603 the company had received a Royal Grant of the privilege of producing, and enjoying the profits from, psalters and psalms, primers (i.e. elementary schoolbooks), almanacs, and 'prognostications'. Anyone infringing this monopoly would be fined and would forfeit all copies of the offending edition. These publications became known as 'the English Stock'; members of the company could buy shares in this stock and share its profits, which were considerable. Shares in the English Stock in the mid-eighteenth century were paying the exceptionally high interest rate of 12.5 per cent. Almanacs had to be licensed by the Stationers' Company, which jealously guarded its privilege and was always looking to weed out illicit publications. As we will see below, those almanac-makers who fell out with the company found their trade threatened.

The interests of the Stationers' Company were primarily commercial, though it did also enforce some ideological conformity. Even after the licensing laws lapsed in 1694, the company continued to submit publications for episcopal approval. Capp notes that offending material was sometimes censored.[5] Almanacs traded in visions of the nation's religious destiny, and it is not therefore surprising that their contents were able to cause offence to Church authorities. The more 'prophetic' purported to provide, in effect, summaries of the workings of providence in the nation's history. For though the emphasis of almanacs seems to be on the future, they were in fact always looking backwards. The more astrologically inclined are full of 'prognostications', and even those that avoid prophecy provide maps of forthcoming events: eclipses, tides, feast-days, fairs, and markets. Yet these 'ephemerides' were also ways of making sense of the past, and particularly the recent past. Colley has argued that 'almanacs constituted the only history lessons the majority of Britons received'.[6] Certainly they look forward only by giving shape to what has gone before.

For this reason, Section 3 of this chapter takes extracts from almanacs published in the two uneasy years after the death of Queen Anne in 1714, and the Jacobite Rebellion of 1715. In this period the fate of the nation really did seem uncertain, and it is interesting to catch the ways in which almanacs reflected this. Sections 1 and 2 provide, in effect, some background to these case-studies. Samples from almanacs in other years would have shown many of the same characteristics, though patriotic feeling is intensified in the years that have been chosen. The almanac-maker had every reason to want to tap this feeling.

REFERENCES AND FURTHER READING

Particularly rich collections of eighteenth-century almanacs are held by the British and Bodleian libraries. The latter has a catalogue dedicated to its early almanac holdings. The indispensable history of English almanacs is Bernard Capp, *Astrology and the*

---

[5] See Capp, *Astrology and the Popular Press*, 240.
[6] Colley, *Britons*, 22.

Popular Press: English Almanacs 1500–1800 (1979). Maureen Perkins, *Visions of the Future: Almanacs, Time, and Cultural Change 1775–1870* (Oxford, 1996) deals with their later history. A helpful account of the status of astrology in the period is Patrick Curry, *Prophecy and Power: Astrology in Early Modern England* (Cambridge, 1989). This extends, but also challenges, the discussion of almanacs and astrology in the late seventeenth century in Keith Thomas's *Religion and the Decline of Magic: Studies in Popular Beliefs in Sixteenth and Seventeenth Century England* (1971), esp. chs. 10 and 11. Populist Protestantism, in which almanacs played a part, is discussed in the opening chapter of Linda Colley, *Britons: Forging the Nation 1707–1837* (New Haven, Conn., 1992). Details about the role of the Stationers' Company in the almanac trade can be found in Cyprian Blagden, *The Stationers' Company: A History, 1403–1959* (1960). Also helpful, though mainly for the later eighteenth century, are the same author's 'Thomas Carnan and the Almanack Monopoly', *Studies in Bibliography*, 14 (1961), and Robin Myers, 'George Hawkins (1705–1780): Bookseller and Treasurer of the English Stock of the Stationers' Company', in Robin Myers and Michael Harris (eds.), *The Stationers' Company and the Book Trade 1550–1990* (Winchester, 1997). John Brewer, *The Pleasures of the Imagination: English Culture in the Eighteenth Century* (1997), ch. 3, discusses the powers of the Stationers' Company and the profitability of the English Stock. For the sales of almanacs in the latter seventeenth century see Cyprian Blagden, 'The Distribution of Almanacks in the Second Half of the Seventeenth Century', *Studies in Bibliography*, 11 (1958); both Capp and Curry attempt to quantify eighteenth-century sales. An interesting supplement to our knowledge of George Parker is provided by Adrian Johns, *The Nature of the Book: Print and Knowledge in the Making* (Chicago, 1998), which details his conflict with astronomer John Flamsteed.

1. QUARRELLING ALMANACS

The most extreme of the antagonisms between almanac-makers was that between George Parker and John Partridge. One would have to reach well back into the seventeenth century to trace its roots, and so our selection must intervene in the middle of a long altercation. In his 1699 almanac (**1.1**) Parker is characteristically replying to what Partridge has already published. George Parker was the most Tory of the almanac-compilers, with strong Jacobite sympathies. A physician who made and sold his own medicines, he was banned by the Stationers' Company from publishing almanacs for the first decade of the eighteenth century because of the Jacobite tendencies of his publications. He continued, however, to publish his *Ephemeris*, contending that, not containing a calendar, it was not truly an almanac. (His quarrel with the Stationers' Company is referred to in **1.5**). Partridge was a vituperative Whig who himself fell out with the Stationers' Company over the size of the fee that the company should pay him. As a result, he was banned from publishing his almanac between 1710 and 1713. His was probably the most popular of almanacs in the early eighteenth century, and the company was eventually to strike a deal with him. John Gadbury, whom Partridge is accused of abusing, was also a Tory, though a good deal more reticent about expressing his sympathies. In his almanac for 1692, Partridge had accused Gadbury of debauching another man's wife and arranging for the murder of her husband.

In 1.1 Parker attacks Partridge for his ignorance of geometry and astronomy, but goes on to recall his fleeing the country on the accession of James II, and to find him guilty of involvement in both the Rye House Plot to assassinate Charles II and Monmouth's rebellion against James II. The second part of Parker's rejoinder to Partridge savours of the true animosity of this relationship, as Parker replies furiously to accusations of mistreating his wife. The next set of extracts (1.2) is taken from Partridge's almanac of the following year. Its very title-page gives a flavour of its animus, dating the almanac, in large lettering, to the tenth year of 'our Deliverance from Popery and Arbitrary Government: But the Fourth from the Horrid Popish JACO-BITE-PLOT'. It everywhere breathes angry partisanship and anti-Catholicism, sweeping up Parker and other Tory astrologers in its denunciations of papist plotters. We give its grandiloquent rhyming introduction (which celebrates William of Orange's God-like routing of his enemies), a specimen of Partridge's response to the accusation of mathematical incompetence (which accuses Parker of having lifted his tables of planetary motions from the Tory astrologer John Merrifield), an example of the rhymes and observations accompanying the calendar for one month, and a brief extract from his long and quarrelsome concluding self-justification, where he vaunts his own principles over those of other astrologers (all of them, naturally, political foes).

The quarrel between the two men came to court in 1700, as reported in the *Post-Boy* in May that year (1.3). Partridge went to law to seek redress for the 'abuse' heaped on him in Parker's *Ephemeris*. The case was almost instantly incorporated into the last monthly part of Ned Ward's *The London Spy* (1.4) which took great delight in mocking the pretensions of the two quacks, and conjured an image of the court crowded with all the fortune-tellers in town. In the event, Partridge won his case, apparently receiving £5 in compensation from Parker. In his almanac for 1701 (1.5), which was composed towards the end of 1700, Parker grumpily and self-righteously withdrew from the fight, but also vented some of his spleen against both Partridge and the Stationers' Company. Soon, however, he was roused again, and pursuing his guerrilla war against Whig almanac-makers, this time singling out John Wing (1.6).

From George Parker, *An Ephemeris of the Cœlestial Motions for 1699*   1.1

It would be a grand absurdity in me to undertake by my own hand to build some noble Structure or other Edifice from the ground; and at the same [time], at the sight of a Hand-saw, or a Hatchet, &c. to admire at those Implements, and wonder to what use and purpose they are design'd for. This is the Case of *John Partridge*, for demand of him the several uses of the Logarithms, Sines, and Tangents, he's silent; or the Solution of a plain Triangle, tho' but lately at the Coffee-house a learning of it, yet he is as mute as a Mouse; Or what denomination the Circles of the Sphere shall have upon any certain Division of the same, than he's Planet-struck. Or if a certain Circle be given, and it be demanded where its Pole will fall; then he's in Amase, and has Senses quite bewildred: And all this is palpable from his own Works, and in a great measure, from that wooden Discourse, in his Division of the Twelve Houses, and Scheme of the Moon's way, in his defective Book lately Published. O rare Doctor, this is he, that for Ignorance may vye with any Man; and yet has the Confidence to think by his Noise, to pass for the Bell-w[e]ther of the Flock . . .

But it is no wonder he should be so malicious against me on so small Occasion, if the Temper and the Principles of the Fellow be considered; for he is by Nature Letigious, and Quarrelsome, 'tis as Nurtural to him as Milk to a Calf, as is manifest in these Particulars.

   1. Not long since, for several years successively, was he in a most grievous manner abusing and villifying Mr *Gadbury*, the very Person that first learnt him Art, and taught him how to get his Bread; yet the Person must not go scot-free, but must be the Subject of his Raillery.

   2. Having worried himself at Mr *Gadbury*, and raised all the Dust he could there, his next work was fall upon Mr *Coley*, a Person of a quiet and peaceful Disposition, abusing him also, and giving him hard Provocation, with scurrilous Epethites.

   3. When this is over, and [he] knows not what to say further, then he ranges all the Town over, like an ill-natur'd Dog, Snapping, and Snarling at every one he meets, to see who he can fasten on, viz. He in *Moorfields*, the fuddy fac'd Conjurer, as he terms him; He in *Fleet-Street*; He at *Westminster*; She at *So-hoe*; but above all for Impudence, He in *Whitecross-Street*. Now, what does the Fellow think; Does he imagine himself Licensed, or Tollerated by *Pluto* the God of Hell, to Abuse all Ma[n]kind whatever, without controul? If so, he's certainly mistaken . . .

However for a Man to be forc'd to fly for shelter and save his neck, for high Treason, as *J. Partridge* did, is a prodigious Crime indeed, it is that, that is

Obnoxious to all men whatever, to be in a design to Spill the blood or destroy the life of any person, is a most abominable thing: But if it be a King, the higher the Person the more notorious and Barbarous the Crime, because the Sacred Scriptures expressly forbid it, saying; Touch not my annointed, do my Prophets no harm; moreover there is a vast difference between absconding for debt and absconding for *Treason* in the intentional part or first beginning, if nothing else was to be objected, for a Man may project and design well, yet miss of Success to Crown his work; But is it otherwise in the Traytor, for there he's altogether active; no danger attends any man that way but by doing, or promising to do, by Joyning in the Confederacy, and this is the Case of my Antagonist, that bold villain *Partridge*; and because my Reader may not think I put too hard upon him, I will transcribe the Depositions made against him on Oath, as I find it in *Folio* Historical of the Rye-house Plot, printed by Order of *K. Charles* the Second; and since he request to have it yearly printed, it is done accordingly, that it may be a perpetual Brand of infamy upon him and his memory for ever . . .

So likewise for a further testimony of his Ignorance and Audacious Boldness this fellow . . . was the State Astrologer to the Fanatical Crew, And in Order to Engage and Animate the then *Duke of Monmouth* to take part with them in their Hellish designs, this very Quack takes upon him to Calculate that most unhappy and unfortunate Peer's Nativity, and therein by his flattering and false principles in Astrology, imposes upon that noble, but easy tempered Duke, and by his pretended Skill in the said Art, Causes him to believe that in a little time he should be in possession of the English Diadem, when on the Contrary this unhappy and misled Peer's Hileg [*sic*] was never Expiring for in two years afterwards, he being attainted of his Treason, made his *Exit* on *Towerhill*, and that Head who was predicted to wear the Imperial Crown of three Kingdoms, on the Contrary fell into the hands of a Miscreant.

Now it is possible that any person whatever, that shall for the future be so Credulous as to believe any of his Idle and impertinent prognosticks, if so, let them go on and welcome, 'tis pity they should be stop'd in their Carreer . . .

J. Partridge's Scurrilous Reflections in his Almanack for the Year 1699, Answered.

Of all the knavish Blood-thirsty Villains that is to be found, it will be difficult to find one to parallel *J. Partridge*, for he makes it no matter of consequence to be brewing his hands in the Blood of Men, as appears by the foregoing Depositions: And of lesser moment to be ruining a Man's Reputation, which is a sort of Murther too: for if by that means a person be deprived of an honest Method of getting his bread, he must inevitably Starve. And this he has and does endeavour, by all the ways and stratagems he can Invent, to bring me to, (as appears by his Almanack for this year,) and this without any provocation, except what is before related . . .

So likewise for the Report of Keeping Whores under her Nose, that was as common as the Poyson, yet never could prove any such thing upon me; and all the Servants were deem'd Whores, whenever they refused to comply with her in Conveying Goods out of the House; and indeed once she reported one to be with Child by me, so that I was obliged to Request her to tarry longer than she would have done, to Convince those that were too Credulous, and imposed upon by her.

For Locking of her up, that I own, for what is matter of Fact, I'll not deny; but it will be necessary to enquire into the Cause, for every Action is good or bad, as Circumstances stand. For dealing in Gloves, and having serv'd a Funeral with about 8 l. worth, the Funeral Tickets were convey'd away by my Wife, so that the Money could not be received, and these Gloves were not paid for to the Maker, who earnestly demanded the Money of me; upon this, I demanded what was become of the Tickets: And much Entreaty was used tho' in vain, for she absolutely refused to acquaint me; upon this, I told her, she should never go out of that Room till I had them (we being then in Bed together,) and at four days end, they came home by Penny Post, and then I discharged my Prisoner. But where they were, I know not, to this Day. This is matter Fact, without mincing of it, and do not think I cannot be thought a servere Jaylor, for I eat, drank, and lay with my Prisoner all the while. And am so far from thinking I was in the wrong, that if the same Occasion offer'd it self, I should do the like again. And I think there is few Men but that would do the same, if they were yoaked to a Woman that used all Tricks and stratagems to bring a Man to Prison as my Wife did.

John Partridge, *Merlinus Liberatus for 1699* (1700)   1.2

INTRODUCTION

> When God's full time for Punishment is come,
> And man on man must execute that Doom,
> Th' Eternal Throne hath pre-ordain'd the way,
> And ev'ry Passive Agent must obey,
> Whole Mines of Matter flow from diff'rent parts;
> From Earth and Air, malicious Brains and Hearts.

Some Haughty Nimrod arm'd with Fraud and Lust,
In whom no man Confides, nor none can Trust.
With Crimes, Tongue-Treachery and Murder cloy'd,
And when his Potions miss, the Sword is imploy'd.
Sometimes a Kingdom's sick, sometimes a Crown,
Sometimes a Tyrant takes what's not his own,
Sometimes 'tis Faith, sometimes a Fury rules
Sometimes a Tyrant, or the Murmuring fools.
Monstrous Designs, when Heaven struck, retreat;
Small things impower'd to destroy the great,
Thus something always (sometimes from afar)
Is Matter, Cause, or Product for a War;
Those to destroy, and be destroy'd are both,
With matter fill'd, fit for the Day of Wrath.
Thus t'was of late when you the Cut-throats fear'd,
In loud Effects God's Presence thus appear'd;
One Great in merit (few I think before
So much of Virtu, and true Courage bore).
Stept forth to stop the Storm that rose apace
With dreadful Torrents and Fury in its Face
By Heaven arm'd. Go said the Sacred word,
And let our Foes feel this thy pow'rful Sword.
In vain his Enemies disdain'd this Rod;
They led by Lies, he by the Arm of God
No man more brave; Brave to the last degree,
His Cut-throat Foes can't this great Truth deny.
He rescu'd us by Courage, Toil and Care,
At first from Slav'ry, now again from War.
'Tis Brave and Great, and shows Heaven has design'd
Still greater things for his immortal mind
When from the War, he the night Tidings brings,
(A thing not us'd of late by British Kings)
His Subjects wisht to see him, Hope and Pray,
Freely Rejoyce, and willingly Obey . . .

The principal Reason that moved our Author to this good Work, was his observing that Abuse put upon the World last Year, and call'd, An Ephemeris, and said to be done de Novo from the Caroline Tables, when indeed it was de Novo from Merifield's Ephemeris only, and perhaps something worse. And such another, by the same hand, we are like to have put upon us again this Year, with the same Terms and Errors; but Caveat Emptor . . .

August hath XXXI Days.

> Flatter your selves no more, 'tis all deceit,
> The Great Millennium will not enter yet:
> Your Eyes shall see, before that Work's begun,
> The Turk destroy'd and, quickly after, Rome;
> But Rome will yet some years (in this I'm bold)
> 'Gainst God and Truth her Pride and Power hold
>
> So have I seen these Spiritual Juglers play
> Their Tricks, to make unthinking Sons obey.
> Here Jack and Tom! What's this? What is't? 'Tis Bread:
> Hocus, Pocus, Presto; now it's a God.
> This is fine Priest Craft, and perhaps you'l guess
> The Sot can make his Maker, nothing less.

Monthly Observations.

We English have two sorts of People among us; one of them grumble without cause, and the other hope without ground; and how to cure them is a work too hard for me. The fore part of this Month gives us but little fresh Intelligence, but what was the effect of the last Month.

But the latter part of this and the former part of the next will furnish us with many a lamentable Story, and therefore pray observe; for about this time you will hear of more Duals, Murders, Inhuman Cruelties, Self-Murders, and unhappy Accidents of Death and Mortality, than at any one time in this whole Year beside: Ill news from Ireland that sounds to the same purpose, and I hope a just Punishment will follow them as their due . . .

And now to any man that doth deny these Aphorisms, I do challenge him to prove his own, and disprove my Doctrine by Experiments in print; and I will vindicate my Master Ptolomy not only in these, but the rest of his Aphorisitical Doctrine on Nativities. I do also here again renew my Challenge to Gadbury and Coley, if they dare accept it, to print half a dozen Nativities, or more, and give Judgment on them according to their Principles; and I will print the same, and give Judgment according to mine, and then the World will be able to Judge who is in the right: and in so doing we shall by degrees bring this Debate to an Issue. And let them take notice I Challenge them to do it.

The Post-Boy (7–9 May 1700)   1.3

This week commences a Tryal at Guild-Hall, between Partridge, the Almanack-maker, and Parker, the Astrologer; the first is Plaintiff: He brings an Action of a

1000 l. against the other, for Printing in his Ephemeris this Year, That He's a Rebel in his Principles; An Enemy to the Monarchy; Ungrateful to his Friend; A Scoundrel in his Conversation; A Malignant in his Writings; A Lyer in his Almanack; And a Fool of an Astrologer. Tho' they are great Men in the way of Predictions, they can't tell how the Cause will go. We hear the polite Gipsies, alias Judicial Fortune-tellers, lay great Wagers on both sides.

1.4   From *The London Spy* (May 1700)

The Town having receiv'd Notice, by an Advertisement in the Post-Boy, of a great Cause to be try'd on the following Wednesday, at the Kings-Bench Bar at Guild-Hall, between one of St Hugh's False Prophets, who can foretel more in an Hour than will prove true in an Age, Plaintiff; and a famous Student in the Coelestial Sciences, most highly Learn'd in the Language of the Stars, Defendant; the former having Secundum Artem, pursuant to the Old Custom of Almanack-makers, most closely Attack'd the latter about several profound Points in the Mystery of Astrology, in which many Fools put more Faith, than they do in the Twelve Articles: And Wisely knowing a Volley of Scurrility, where Scoundrels are to be Judges of the Battel, would do more Execution against a rising Competitor, and Wound the Reputation of such an Adversary far Deeper than the Dint of Argument, drawn from the Rules of Art, assisted by sound Reason, Reason thought it therefore his safest method to stuff his Almanacks as full of hard Calumny and Ill-Words, as the Art is full of Fallacy and Lying ones; accordingly began the Quarrel in Publick, in as pretty, sweet, obliging Language as ever Billingsgate Tirmagant bestow'd in Anger upon a provoking Sitter, in the Turbulent Times of Herrings, Sprats or Mackarel-Season, as if Sense and Manners were incongruous with Star-Fumbling; and Railing and Lying were the Two supporters of Astrology . . .

The Day being Appointed for Tryal, amongst the rest of the Fools, my curiosity must needs lead me to hear the matter determin'd: When I came into the Hall, all the Fortune-telling Wise-Acres in the Town both Male and Female, were drawn in a cluster from all the By-Allies in Morefields, White-Chappel, Salisbury Court, Water-Lane, Fleetstreet, and Westminster, who, I perceive, notwithstanding their Skill in Conjuration by which they pretended to tell Fools their Fortune, and help the Credulous Ignorant to Lost Spoons, Thimbles, and Bodkins, yet could not by their Art foresee which of the two contending Planet-Peepers were most likely to obtain the Victory . . .

In half an Hours time from the beginning of the Debate, the Business without much trouble was brought to a Determination: The Plaintiff, however his Stars favour'd him, obtaining a Verdict, the Compassionate Jury, not knowing but some time or other it may be their own Case, gave him Five Pound damage for the great Abuses he had very Honestly deserv'd by just Provocation.

The decision of this Controversie prov'd very unlucky to both Enemies, for they were neither of them well satisfied with the Justice done to both Parties, the Plaintiff being very angry his damage was no more, and the Defendant very much displeas'd they had given him so much; so that the Jury would have had a very hard Task to have pleas'd both, since they were so unfortunate in their Concurrence they could content neither.

> When Conjurers their Purses draw,
> And like two Blockheads go to Law;
> They show by such Expensive Wars,
> There's little Wisdom in the Stars;
> And that they Act, who know the Heavens,
> Like us, by Sixes, and by Sevens;
> For if one Wizard had foreseen,
> The other should the Battle win,
> He'd cry'd Peccavi, and not come
> Before a Judge to know his Doom;
> I think from thence the World may see,
> They know by th' Stars no more than we.

From George Parker, *A Double Ephemeris. For the Year 1701*   1.5

Reader,

It is prop'sble some Persons may expect in the ensuing Pages, a farther Prosecution of my last Years Discourse against my inveterate Enemy. Others, perhaps may deem me some fantastical Maggot, for changing so often the Form and Method of my Annual Book. At the same time, a third Sort may expect my Calculations of the Planets Places, should be performed from the New Tables in Scientia Stellarum; having formerly declared that I was not merely Wedded in Opinion to any Author, but should be ready to reject the Caroline Tables, and Embrace better whenever they Appear'd. To all which, I think proper to speak a Word or two.

To the first, my Antagonist has declared positively, for the future he will be Silent and Meddle no more; I wish he keeps his Word, and that he had always been of this Mind, then I should have done the same, for I assure him, if my Reputation (which I Value as Gold) had not been scurrilously attack'd, he had never been interrupted by me. To Oppose him, or any other in point of Art, I do not Conceive is a Crime, especially if it tend for the Information of others; he may do the same, and this may be done without Gall or implacable Malice; and if I was a little too Tart with him in my Reply, it was only to meet him in his own way. Peace is a Jewel I highly Prize, yet am not willing to purchase it at too dear a Rate. Therefore, if at any time he found the Trumpet of Discord to Contrive my Ruin, he must expect me as ready to Engage him as ever, either as the same Weapons over again (my Ammunition being not half spent) or any other he thinks fit.

For the second, it is not Choice but Necessity, that Obliges an Alteration, for it seems my Antagonist, notwithstanding his Word, as above, is not able to leave his old Habit, and is the only Active Person to inflame the Company of Stationers against my Book, to prevent its Printing, which is the Cause of its being so late this year ere it be Published. And so also ready to Swear my last Contains a Calendar (which I must not meddle with) tho' it wants the proper Furniture thereof, viz. Never a Dominical Letter, neither is the Calends incerted therein.

1.6   From George Parker, *A Double Ephemeris for the Year of Our Lord 1703*

A necessary Reply to John Wing's base Reflections on this Author, with a further Detection of his notorious Errors, and disingenious Quotations.

Mr Wing, whether induced by an innate propensity to Reviling, or agitated thereto by my malicious and implacable Enemy J. Partridge, in conjunction with that Man-setter, the nocturnal Guardian to a Deal-Yard, F. Moore of Lambeth, and thereby become their Tool, I shall leave to his own Determination: Tho' I am of Opinion, and that on good Reasons too, there is a mixture of his own baseness in the Composition.

An Incendiary or Eves-Dropper, is a most despicable Creature, and obnoxious to all human Societies, being the bane of all Felicity, the very pest of Concord and Harmony; for where he finds footing he changes the Scene, and in the room of Peace brings Discord and Confusion.

The last of which John Wing has been too sedulous in promoting; if he denies it, I demand what business he had with my Heifer, or Domestick Affairs? 'Tis foreign to what he pretends to be disgusted at; therefore the part of a busie, troublesom Person, a sorry Fellow, and betokens little Wit or Discretion to meddle therein, and I doubt not but the Person chiefly concerned in that unhappy Matter, is sufficiently sensible of their Error e're this time; but whether so or not, 'tis no business of John Wing's, nor has the least relation to the matter in hand.

This part the Infamous P—dge has been acting already to his shame, and to whom I have given a full answer in my Ephemeris for 1699, therefore count it needless to repeat here; and as I was obliged to dissect and openly expose the inside of that empty Goliath, so being again provoked to use my Pen for my own Justification, is the occasion of what follows; and am so far from thinking that this Antagonists borrowing half a dozen lines from his envious Crony J. P—dge, Flagitiosies Mercurius, &c. will be a sufficient answer to what is here objected against him: That if he quote all the rest of the scurrilous Pamphlet, it will not do it. And if this Caviller, who has so violently without any reason attack'd me, goes home by weeping Cross, meeting Disgrace instead of Applause, let him take it for his pains.

2. ASTROLOGY ADVERTISED AND ATTACKED

The trade in astrology was clearly open to mockery in the early eighteenth century, not least because of its frequently earnest intellectual pretensions. A specimen of such mockery is the short-lived periodical *The Jesting Astrologer* (2.1), apparently written in large part by Thomas Brown and Ned Ward. Evidently Swift was perfecting in his *Bickerstaff Papers* an established vein of satire. Such satire, of course, would have had no purchase if astrology had not been a thriving trade, and 2.2 is an advertisement, probably from about 1720 (see 2.4), for the skills of one living off that trade. These are the kinds of claim parodied by Tom Brown in his *Comical View* (2.3), in a passage that derives from his contributions to *The Jesting Astrologer*. His mock-predictions are all of eminently predictable events in the ordinary life of London. The newspaper article (2.4) is given as another specimen of hostility to the popular purveying of prophecy in the period. The advertisement that follows (2.5) probably dates from nearly the same time as 2.4; the two are placed together in the scrapbook (or *Collectanea*) of the nineteenth-century antiquarian Daniel Lysons.

The Jesting Astrologer, or The Merry Observation (24 February–3, March 1701)   2.1

Gentlemen,
It's as natural for we Star-gazers, to give ourselves a little Light into the dark mistery of Physick, as 'tis for a Dancing-master to scrape upon the Violin, or a Noble Man's House-

keeper to understand Pickling and Preserving; and the only Reason I conceive, why Astrologers have so great a Propensity to the Knowledge of Medicine, is that our Ptolemean Fraternity very wisely consider, that the Title of Doctor, is more Reputable than that of Conjurer; for by one or the other, we are most commonly distinguish'd. I have therefore, like a cunning Angler, thought it my best Way to bait two Hooks, the one to catch sick Fools, who want Health more than Wealth, and the other to allure such dissatisfied Wise-akers, who fling away their Money, to know that which no Body can tell 'em: Professing thus both Physick and Astrology, as I was, the other Day, sitting in my Study, tumbling over some old musty Receipes, that were left me by my Grand-mother, a Female Patient, Mask'd, wrapt up in Velvet-hood and Scarf, came and Thump'd at my Door, with as much Authority, as a Poor Cuckold at Midnight, knocking for a Midwife at the Sign of the Cradle; my Man steping to the Door, with an audable Voice, she enquired for the Doctor; upon which I went down Stairs, and examined her Business, who in plain Words, told me, she was Clap'd, and ask'd me for what Mony I'd undertake to Cure her; I told her, five Pounds; Confound you, says she, for an old groping Fumbler, I have been a Trader in this Town, almost this twenty Years, and never gave above a Guinea in my Life. Indeed, Madam, said I, I cannot undertake the Cure for so inconsiderable a Sum. Well, says she, I'll defer Physicking a little, and Kiss on for a Fortnight or three Weeks longer, for the Benefit of your Profession; and if you wont undertake me then for the Mony I have offer'd, you are the most ungrateful old Tuzzy-wuzzy-mender, that ever handled Surringe; and away she trip'd, without another Word, as nimbly out of my Doors, as a Town Lady early in the Morning, out of a Temple Stair-case; after which I retir'd to my Study, and by the help of the Stars, compos'd the following Predictions.

The Beards of Coffee-house Politicians will Wag mightily, during this Sessions of *Parliament*; and every flying Gull, and foolish Imposition, inserted in the Newspapers, will go down as glib, with the Sipers of Ninny-broth, as a *White-Fryers* Falsity, publish'd by a sham Authority, does oftentimes with the too credulous Multitude.

Great talk of strange Plots will addle the Noddles of the Publick, and those who are silly enough to believe the Reports of ill Designs, without good Grounds for it, tho' they are much more safe, are but very little wiser, than those who are drawn into the Project, to be made a hanging Testimony to convince the World of the Truth thereof; who are apt, in such Cases, to be better confirm'd by a dying Convict, than a living Evidence.

It will be hard for a poor Man to be thought a good Man, or a rich Man an ill Man, in this Age; whilst Men shall be esteem'd Honest for their Wealth, much rather than their Vertues; and as for *Epictetus* or *Seneca*'s Morals, they are much talk'd of amongst Schollars, but not half so much practis'd as *Machiavil*'s Politicks amongst Courtiers; so that I fear in a little time, the World will be of an Opinion, that Religion and Interest, Riches and Honesty, Greatness and Goodness, and Poverty and Knavery are as inseparable Companions, as Pride and Beauty in a Woman, or the Words Popery and Slavery in a true Protestant Address.

A Broadside Advertisement (n.d.)   2.2

A Licensed Astrologer and Physician

In Cripplegate Parish in Whitecross-street, almost at the farther End, near Old Street, (turning in at the sight of the Black-Croe in Goat-Alley streight forwards down three steps, at the sign of the Globe) liveth one of above Thirty years Experience, and hath been Counsellor to Counsellors of several Kingdoms; who resolveth these Questions Following:

Life Happy or Unhappy? If Rich, by What means attain it, and when? What matter of Person one shall Marry? If Marry the Party Desired, and the time When? What Part of the City or Country is best to live in? A Ship at Sea if safe or not? If fast when Return? If a Woman be with Child with Male or Female, and whether deliver'd by Night or Day? Sickness, the Duration, and whether end in Life or Death? Suits at Law, who shall overcome and when? With all Lawful Questions, that depend on that most Noble Art of CHRISTIAN ASTROLOGY.

Likewise, he telleth the Meaning of all Magical Panticles, Sigils, Charms and Lamens, and hath a Glass, and helpeth to further Marriages.

He likewise hath attained to the Green, Golden & Black Dragon, known to none but Magicians & Hermetick Philosophers; and will prove he hath the true and perfect Seed & Blossom of the Female Fern, all for Physicians uses. And can tell concerning every serious Person, what their Business is on every Radical Figure, before they speak one Word; secondly, what is past in most of their life, what is present and what is to come; where that they have Moles, what colour they are, and what is the meaning of them, &c.

He hath a secret in Art, far beyond the reach or Knowledge of common Persons.

He is to be spoken with any day of the Week, from 7 of the Clock in the Morning, till Noon; and from 2 in the Afternoon, till 7 at Night.

2.3 From Tom Brown, *A Comical View of the Transactions That Will Happen in the Cities of London and Westminster* (1705)

Gentlemen,

Whereas the Town has been Banter'd near two Months with a Sham Account of the Weather, pretended to be taken from Barometers, Thermometers, Hygroscopes, Telescopes, and such Heathenish Instruments; by which means, several of her Majesty's good Subjects have put on their Prize Coats, expecting it should Rain, when it has been Fair; and wore their best Cloaths, thinking it would be Fair, when it has rain'd to the no little Detriment and Prejudice of the aforesaid Cloaths and Persons: And likewise, whereas the Planets that have regulated the Almanacks for about two thousand Years, have been most wickedly slander'd by a late Author, as if they had no influence at all upon the Weather, the Publisher of this Paper has been Perswaded by his Friends to print these his infallible Predictions, gather'd from the Experience of thirty Years and Upwards; and will warrant them to be true, tho' he never travell'd Abroad, nor pretends to be the Seventh Son of a Seventh Son, nor calls himself the Unborn Doctor, nor has the Seed of the Female Fern, the Green and Red Dragon, or any of the like Secrets.

Wednesday 16.] Cloudy Foggy Weather at Garraway's and Jonathan's and most Coffee-houses, at and about Twelve. Crowds of People gather at the Change by One, disperse by Three. Afternoon noisie and Bloody at her Majesty's Bear-Garden in Hockley-in-the-hole. Night Sober with broken Captains and others, that have neither Credit nor Money. If Rainy, few Night-walkers in Cheapside and Fleet-Street. This week's Transactions censur'd by the Virtuosoes at Child's from Morning till Night.

Thursday 17.] Coffee and Water-gruel to be had at the Rainbow and Nando's at Four. Hot Furmety at Fleet-bridge by Seven. Justice to be had at Doctors-Commons when People can get it. A Lecture at Pinners-Hall at Ten. Excellent Pease-porridge and Tripe in Baldwin's Gardens at Twelve. At Night much Fornication all over Covent-Garden, and five Miles round it. A Constable and two Watch-men Kill'd or near being Kill'd in Westminster; whether by a Lord or a Lord's Footman, the Planets don't determine.

Friday 18.] Plenty of Cuckold trudging from all parts of the City towards Horn Fair by Eight. Damsels Whipt for their good Nature at Bridewell about Ten. Several People put in fear of their Lives by their God-fathers at the Old Baily at Eleven. Great Destruction of Herrings at One. Much Swearing at Three among the horse-coursers in Smithfield; if the Oaths were Register'd as well as the

Horses, good Lord, what a Volume 'twould make! Several Tails turn'd up at Paul's School, Merchant-Taylors, &c. for their Repetitions. Night very Drunk, as the two former.

Saturday 19.] Twenty Butchers Wives in Leaden-Hall and Newgate Markets overtaken with Sherry and Sugar by Eight in the Morning. Shopkeepers walk out at Nine to count the Trees in More-fields, and to avoid Duns. Peoples Houses clean'd in the Afternoon, but their Consciences we don't know when. Jews fornicate away the Sabbath in Drury-Lane and Wild-Street. Evening pretty Sober.

Sunday 20.] Great Jangling of Bells all over the City from Eight to Nine. Psalms murder'd in most Parishes about Ten. Abundance of Doctrines and Uses in the Meetings, and no Application. Vast Consumption of Roast-Beef and Pudding at One. Afternoon sleepy in most Churches. Store of Handkerchiefs stolen in Paul's at Three. Informers busy all day long. Night not so Sober as might be wish'd.

Monday 21.] Whores turn'd out of the Temple, Gray's-Inn, &c. by Six. Catch-poles up early to seize their Prey against the first Day of Term. Journey-men Taylors, Shoe-makers, and 'Prentices Heads ake with what they had been doing the Day before. Tradesmen begin the Week with Cheating as soon as they open Shop. If Fair, the Park, full of Women at Noon, some Vertuous, and some other-wise. Great shaking of the Elbow at Will's &c. about Ten. Two Porters fall out at Putt in a Cellar in the Strand at Twelve precisely.

Tuesday 22.] Wind, whether E. W. N. or S. no matter, but in one Corner or other of the Compass most certain: If high, the Beaus advised to be merciful to their long Periwigs. Mullins and Pepper rife at the East India House at Twelve. Cali-coes fall before Two. Coach'd Masques calling at the Chocolate-houses between Eight and Nine. Bastards begot, and Cuckolds made this Week numberless.

Advertisement to Ladies

Women, whether with Child or no? Children, whether Male or Female? Young Maidens, whether they will have their Sweet-hearts, or no? and Lovers, whether Able and Constant? The Critical Minute of the Day to Marry in. What is the best Hour for Procreation? Husbands, whether long liv'd or no? The second Match, whether happy or Unhappy? What part of the Town best for a Sempstress to thrive in? What the most fortunate Signs for a Shopkeeper, and under what Planet to be set up? With other like Questions, fully and satisfactorily Resolved by me Silvester Partridge, Student in Physick and Astrology, near the Gun, in Moorfields . . .

From Octob. 22 to Octob. 29. Friday 25. Mr Ordinary visits his melancholy Flock at Newgate by Eight. Doleful Procession up Holborn-hill about Eleven. Men handsome and proper, that were never thought so before, which is some Comfort however. Arrive at the fatal Place at Twelve. Burn Brandy, Women, and Sabbath-breaking repented of. Some few Penitential Drops fall under the Gallows. Sheriff's Men, Parson, Pick-pockets, Criminals, all very busie. The last concluding peremptory Psalm struck up. Show over by one.

Advertisement to Ladies

The best time to Cut Hair. How Moles and Dreams to be interpreted. When most proper to Bleed. Under what Aspect of the Moon, best to draw Teeth, and cut Corns. Pairing of Nails, on what Days unlucky. What the kindest Sign to Graft or inoculate in; to open Bee-hives, and kill Swine. How to get Twins. And how many Hours boiling my Lady Kent's Pudding requires: with other notable Questions, fully and faithfully Resolved, by me Silvester Partridge, Student in Physick and Astrology, near the Gun in Moor-fields.

Of whom likewise may be had, at reasonable Rates, Trusses, Antidotes, Love-Powders, Washes for Freckles, Plumpers, Glass-Eyes, False Calves and Noses, Ivory Jaws, Stiptic Drops to Contract the Parts. A new Receipt to turn Red Hair into Black: As likewise, the Famous Annulus Anti-cornutus, or a Ring to prevent Cuckoldom, very useful for all married Persons: 'Tis a Hair Ring, of a bright beautiful Red within, and is of that wonderful Efficacy and Vertue, that so long as a Man keeps it on his Finger, he may defie all the Devils in Hell, nay, what's more, the Wife of his Bosom to Cuckold him, tho' she has never so great a Mind to it . . .

But what I value my self upon, and indeed I defie any Doctor within the Bills of Mortality, (you see I circumscribe them, Gentlemen, within their own Dominions) to do the like, I have so improved the ancient and laudable Art of Ouromanteia, or Ouroscopy, that is to say, of Prognosticating all future Contingents by Urine, that the like was never heard of in Europe. I know that several Block-heads pretend to tell a Man the present State of his Body, by seeing his Urine, (and what Fool by the Broth cannot make a shift to guess at what Meat is in the Pot;) but I have carried my Disquisitions much farther: As for Instance, Let an Attorney bring me his Water, and I will tell him how his Client's Cause will go in Westminster-hall, a[n]d whether any of his Adversary's Witnesses are likely to Perjure themselves. Let a young Maiden shew me but a Thimble-full of her Urine, and I will resolve her when she shall be married, how many children she shall have, and what thei[r] respective Fortunes shall be. This, Gentlemen, may suffice at present, to let you see I can do somewhat more than my Brethren. Next Wednesday I shall address my self to the Ladies.

London Journal (4 July 1724)   2.4

One Susannah Howard, a pretended Fortune-Teller, was last Week Committed
to Bridewell, for defrauding a young married Woman of Ten Shilling, on
Pretence of helping her to threescore broad Pieces of Gold, and a Box of
Plate, which was to be her Luck only to find out, by the Assistance of the
said cunning Woman's Art. Several Persons appeared before the Justice, whom
she had imposed on in like manner; but such was her Misfortune, that she could
not tell her own Fate, whether she should be sent to Newgate, or the House of
Correction: In a Word, she was every Way as ignorant as Dr. F——, who in his
Bills, tells the Town, That he has been Counsellor to the Counsellor of several
Kings and Princes, and is arriv'd to the Knowledge of the Green, Black and
Golden Dragons, known to none but Magicians and Hermetick Philosophers
&c.

Advertisement, undated (*c.*1724?)   2.5

At Mr. Cannon's, a Smith, next door but one to the Bakers in Maypole Alley,
by Stanhope-Street, Clare Market, may be spoke with, One who through
many years study and experience has attained exquisite knowledge in astrology,
philosophy, and metaphysicks (the highest part of which treats of God, spirits,
&c.) and is thereby capable of resolving all manner of reasonable Questions
relating to humane Life, past, present, and to come, with the utmost exactness
and certainty, to the surprise of the most curious and judicious. Therefore whatever your doubts, griefs or troubles be, there you may depend on (most just
usage, and having your secrets kept, and) receiving most effectual advice and
counsel, without flattery, or those doubtful ways of expression wherewith others
(who only are pretenders to these sublime arts) amuse and deceive people. Also
there you may know the genuine signification of any dream, and have any nativity judiciously calculated. Those who are indisposed either in mind or body
(altho' the mischief be supposed to be done by philter, charm, spell, hag, witch,
evil spirit, &c.) may receive such help under GOD as will totally remove it. Also
there is sold a precious water, very effectual in dimness, pains, bloodshot, and
most diseases in the eyes, and a toothpowder, with a present remedy for the
toothach.

N.B. Go directly up One pair of stairs to the door facing you, and ask for the
person who sells the tooth-powder.

3. AFTER THE JACOBITE REBELLION

As explained in the introduction to this chapter, passages in this section have been taken from almanacs composed during a period of considerable political—indeed dynastic—uncertainty. Typically, like 3.1, they express and exploit this uncertainty, whilst usually trying to suggest that, providentially, Britain would survive any turmoil. Those almanacs, like Coley's (3.2 and 3.3), which were least enthusiastic about the Hanoverian accession, limited themselves to colourlessly patriotic hopes and predictions. Others, like the *Vox Stellarum* (continued in Moore's name after his death) and *Merlinus Liberatus* (similarly continued after the death of its originator, Partridge), were militantly Protestant and Hanoverian, and were quite happy to refer to the failed Jacobite rebellion of 1715 (see 3.4 and 3.5). For good measure, the latter also carried a 'Kalendar, of the Cruelties of the Papists to PROTESTANTS' to recall for its readers the persecutions that justified its ideological enthusiasm. Wing's almanac also felt it necessary to appeal to Protestant patriotism (3.6), while George Parker, especially in his chronologies, continued to remind readers of the excesses of republicans and Whigs (3.7). His fury against Whiggish almanacs was undimmed by the years. As revealed in Adrian Johns's *The Nature of the Book* (pp. 544–6), the person whom Parker attacks by the name of 'Fielden' in this extract is John Flamsteed the first Astronomer Royal ('Fielden' having been Flamsteed's pseudonym when he had, abortively, attempted to launch an almanac). The chapter ends with a more representative example from the period, taken from Gadbury's almanac (3.8), which combines generalized political prognostication with dietary, medical, and horticultural advice.

3.1   **From William Andrews, *Great News from the Stars or, an Ephemeris for the Year 1716***

January's Observations

Many have been the Disturbances and Misfortunes of War of late in several Parts of Europe, and what is yet to come will not be conceal'd long: Some Kingdom stands at present but upon a tottering Bottom, tho' we of Great Britain (at present) seem to be free from such slavish Fears, for the present Position of the Heavenly Bodies, seem much more to befriend us than fright us, in this Month of January; tho' some deep Consultations, in some remote Countries, of an unhappy Consequence seem to be on foot about the latter end hereof.

Let it be remembered what the fiery Zeal of the Idumæans came to, when (upon a groundless Bottom) they went to assist the Zealous at the City and Temple of Jerusalem, which proved their inevitable Ruin, and of that glorious City and Temple, and also the utter Extirpation of the Jews by the Hands of the Romans in the Time of the Emperor Vespasian.

It were indeed heartily to be wish'd, that the noise of War might cease in all Places, but more especially among Christians, it would be much better for those that occasion'd it, and seem still to be in the wrong of it, to take a Noble Philosophers Advice, viz. The best way to keep out wicked Thoughts, is to be always employed upon good Ones . . .

Astral Observations, 1716, Summer Quarter

. . . All or most of the Transactions of Europe will be visible so far that the World may see who and who's together, about the latter end of June or beginning of July, we shall have News from several Parts, but not all to be rely'd on, for Mercury is in the Dignities of the Moon, yet being so near Mars is a Testimony our News will be variously reported, tho' presently after we shall with more certainty hear of some remarkable turns and exploits, and many great Counsellours of State are deeply concern'd, to bring to pass what may best suit their turns, but 'tis to little purpose, for the Conjunction of the Sun and Mars is not for the ending of Controversies, it rather sets turbulent Spirits to Work, and maketh the Breach yet wider amongst those Grandees, where they have for some time been Plotting and Contriving the ruin of one another, and the envious Planet Saturn is Square to the Sun and Mars from Cardinal Signs, makes things of this nature still further out of Order, and if not the occasion of a new War breaking out, it foments further differences in several parts of the World, as well by Sea as by Land, tho' we here in England are (and so likely to continue) in a flourishing and prosperous condition, notwithstanding those that the contrary, and let us all pray to God it may so long continue, and to give us thankful Hearts for the same . . .

From Henry Coley, *Merlinus Anglicus Junior: or, the Starry Messenger For the Year of our Redemption, 1716*   3.2

Observations

March, 1716. This Month is usher'd in with a Conjunction of Mars and Venus in Aires, which either brings welcome News to this Kingdom, or that we are happy in our National Affairs, and that those great and valuable Blessings of Peace and Plenty, are by the Mercy and Goodness of God still continued to us, not but that there will be in some kind or other some disorderly Practices discovered, but let them have a care, Saturn is in Libra still, and in opposition to the Sun in Aires, Justice not only follows but overtakes them.

God preserve us from all Contagious Diseases this ensuing part of the Year.

> Let's make our Peace,
>   with that correcting Hand
> Who at each Moment,
>   can our lives command . . .

October 1716. There is in all probability like to be great Alteration in Mundane Affairs in this and the succeeding Month; the face of the Heavens seems very much for Peace, Unity, and Concord among the European Princes, and, I heartily wish too, that the just Principles of the Primitive Christian Religion were but truly and conscientiously practis'd, then would the Wars cease in all or most part of Christiandom. Men in all Parts, in religious Orders, are had in great Estimation, and the Common People receive further Satisfaction, in respect the prospect of the Times seems more favourable and satisfactory to them.

> We need not fear
> October's good Conclusion,
> If freed we are
> from faction and Confusion.

3.3   Henry Coley, *Merlinus Anglicus Junior: or, the Starry Messenger for the Year of Our Redemption, 1717*

> King GEORGE is lately plac'd upon His Throne,
>   And with his Parliament agree as One;
> There may both Peace and Unity long Reign
>   In loyal Hearts, and always there remain,
> Free from Discension, Feuds, and Evil Actions,
>   Plots, and Conspiracies, and Knavish Factions

January 1717: Observations.

Tempora Mutantur. Many dangerous and troublesome Transactions hath England laboured under for many Years past, but the Storm is well nigh over, yet some Difficulties still daily are among us both in Church and State affairs; Saturn about the middle of the month becomes stationery to Retrogradation, and

Jupiter still Retrograde in Gemini, and in Trine to each other, and the Sun in Trine to them both, which we may reasonably hope is in order to qualify some active and turbulent Spirits in some parts of Europe; these are things of Consequence debated about this time in several Princes Courts, but little at present concluded on, tho great things appear before the Years end. God preserve us from both Domestick and Forreign Enemies, and keep us in Peace and good order at all times.

From *Vox Stellarum; Being an Almanack for the Year of Human Redemption* 3.4 *1717*

The Introduction

> . . . With Mercy cloath'd, GEORGE wou'd not Thunder wear,
> He craves his Peoples Love more than their Fear:
> His pious Ancestors their Blood did spend
> For our Religion, which He does defend;
> Bravely for which He draws his conqu'ring Sword,
> Which to secure we have his Royal Word.
> At Home ungrateful Britains are in Arms.
> Ah! foolish Men, who can your grief express?
> Refusing madly thus your Happiness!
> Slighting those Charms, which all the World does bind!
> Spurning at GEORGE the Darling of Mankind!
> O! tell it not in Gath, nor Askelon,
> What English Protestants would now have done!
> Dethrone their KING, and try'd their fatal Chance,
> For a Popish Fool disciplin'd in France!
> So Indians Trifles chuse, and simple things,
> For all those Treasures which the Merchant brings:
> They blow the Trumpet of unnat'ral War,
> Brandish their Sword, and burnish Arms for Mars:
> Like Necromancers, as the People say,
> They've rais'd the Devil, which they cannot lay.
> Only our Glorious KING these Wounds can heal,
> Our strength lies not in glittering Arms and Steel;
> No; 'tis His Wisdom, and His wondrous Art
> To Govern Men and Captivate the Heart,
> Which Providence will use to still these Jars,
> And put an End to these Land-wasting Wars . . .

February 1717

Astrological Observations. Violent Spirits of different Perswasions appear, and about this Time fully discover their Designs; the Square of Mars and the Sun, and of Mars to Mercury, seems to indicate all this, and more to the same purpose; and if I may use Plain Dealing, it is not what they so much contend for that causes such Differences and Distractions (not only here, but in divers Foreign Countries) but for some more sinister and indirect Ends, though at present all seems plausible, and to be carried on with both Judgment and Prudence; but a Snake in the Grass is not easily discovered, except it move. The Trine of Saturn and Jupiter to Venus, disperses some Fears and Jealousies amongst us, and especially befriends our Metropolis London.

3.5   From *Merlinus Liberatus for 1717*

The Prologue

> How long shall Britain in divided State,
> Hang in the Balance of a doubtful Fate?
> Shall hateful Jars, and bloody Discord reign,
> Unless High-Church shall rule Britannia's Main?
> Shall the Word Church be still the specious Bait,
> For crafty Villains to destroy the State?
> How long with Rebels will ye Tories side,
> And as Occasion serves, our Land divide?
> Will ye to France give up your martial Realm,
> And tamely let their Pilots steer the Helm?
> Shall wild Dissention spread its baneful Seed,
> Will no brave Theseus on the Monster tread,
> And crush to Atoms its aspiring Head?
> For Shame, your base Unchristian Feuds decline,
> And swallow not that Gudgeon, French Design.
> You are the Men that cause all Discontent,
> Railing at Low Church, you the heats foment;
> Crying, that Millions for their Cause were paid,
> Yet still forget the Plot your dear selves laid;
> You Thirteen Millions rais'd in Two Years Space,
> For France's Service, Perkin and his Race:
> The Difference 'twixt both, is clearly seen;
> Their's kept them out, your's strove to let them in.

As Bully, you for Romish Church do Rant,
And make a Noise for Pageantry and Cant;
Whilst Clemency and Peace, its purest Springs,
Are by ye laid aside, as useless Things:
With half a Look your Actions we descry,
Too deeply ting'd in Fraud and Villany.
Speak plain the Cause of all your loud Complaints,
(Tho' you are too well known to pass for Saints,)
Delude the World no more; but say, 'Tis your Defender,
Your poor Impostor, Warming pan Pretender;
To Britain's Mighty Throne, you wou'd advance
By Papal Power, tack'd with that of France.
This, Tories, is your Aim; but learn to Fear!
Whilst we, Bold Britons, G E O R G E ' s Name revere;
Whilst Sacred are the Ties of Publick Good,
And Protestants owe him their dearest Blood;
The British Crown secure from spurious Race,
Illustrious Hanover alone shall grace.

January hath XXXI Days.

Rouze, Protestant Muse, tell what the Stars relate;
How, when & where, they will dispense their Fate;
How England thrives, how her Affaires go on;
What will by Perkin and the Pope be done;
Who will be Priest-rid, and believe the Threats
Of Purgatory, and such pious Cheats.

February hath XXVIII Days.

Rouze, Protestants, the Year of Wonder's gone,
Great GEORGE is now establish'd on the Throne;
A Mighty Prince, by God for us prepar'd,
Us to preserve from Dangers greatly fear'd;
From Popery the Devil's great Master Fear,
Where Men are Slaves, and Priests their Gods do eat . . .

Kalendar, of the Cruelties of the Papists to PROTESTANTS.

July. Altho the Weather in this month was hot, yet the Persecution of poor Protestants by the Papists was much hotter, as you may see by following List of Martyrs who underwent fiery Trials, because they would not turn Papists, and renounce the Protestant Religion, the Names of Some of them were John Frith, Anth. Person, Robt. Testwood, H. Filmoore, John Badford, Preacher, John Leate, John Pelly, Will Ming, Minister; Rich, Hook, John Bloud Preacher; John

Frank, Hum. Middleton, Nich. Shetterden, Wil. Dighel, Der. Carver, Rutter Crauches, and Per. Malfey; her Daughter, the said Peratine was big with Child, they would not repreive her 'till delivered, but burnt her & her Child, the Child with the violence of the Flames burst out of her Womb, and was thrown into the Flames again, by those bloody Persecutors: The same Cruelty was by them executed upon Jo. Foreman, Sam. Miller, and Eliz. Cooper . . .

Astrological Observations, on the Four Quarters of the Year 1717: Together with the Eclipses of the Sun and Moon

. . . Nothing is more manifest to those who are but moderately skill'd in Astronomy and have made any Progress in History, [than] that those Years, wherein Saturn in an Astrological Sense had Dominion, have proved none of the kindest to mankind, in those Countries signified by the Signs he afflicted: Look back into Astronomical and Civil History, and you will find what followed such Positions and Transits in the Years 1628 and 1629, 1656 and 1657, 1685 and 1686: That Jealousies, Fears, Murmurings Factions, &c. Dangers and Troubles, in and about Religion, then troubled the Government and People in those Countries; which he afflicted by Position or Aspect. See what Designs were then continued, hatch'd and set on foot against the Protestant Religion: How Factions and Insurrections sometimes prevailed; how the People suffered at other times by Sickness. Loss of their Substance by the Plagues amongst Horses at one time, death of Cattle at another time, and Dearth of Wheat at another; and many other Misfortunes. If like Causes produce like Effects, or like Signs have like Significations, you may conclude that those Countries signified by Libra, and the opposite and Quadrangular Points, will be sensible of some, if not all the like Effects. If so, Germany, Sweden, Denmark, Venice, Holland, part of France, and Scotland; Italy and Turkey, the cities of Naples, Florence, Lisbon, Antwerp, Milan, Gaunt, Oxford, &c. will labour under some of those Misfortunes.

3.6 *Olympia Domata; or, an Almanack for the Year of our Lord God 1717*

Dame Flora in bright Order doth appear,
To welcome in the Spring, and the rest o'th' Year;
In which, both Peace and Plenty we enjoy,
Yet there are some that would all this destroy.
Tho' most wish well, and doth all for the best,
But restless Spirits that ne'er will be at rest.
Now, What doth all this mean, but Discontent

Against our Glorious King and Government?
Mauger be Malice of such pretty Tools,
Who act like Knaves, and then appear like Fools.
Thus are we like to be at Peace and rest,
Since Justice hath to such her self addrest:
And should we all be better understood,
To study and promote each others Good;
None need to fear the Frowns of Britain's Foes,
Nor none that would her Happiness oppose.
May such encourag'd be, that's just and true
To God, their King, and to their Country too.

From *Parker's Ephemeris for the Year of our Lord 1717*   3.7

May 29th 1630 and 1660.

King Charles II. Our late Lord,
The 29th Born and Restor'd:
A Prince in each part so Compleat,
As might Entitle him Charles the Great
Whose soul no doubt is now at Rest,
With his dear Father Charles the Blest.

. . . Since Good King Charles resign'd his Royal Head	70
Since Vertue, Truth and Justice all lay dead	70
. . . Since th' infernal Rye-House Plost was detected	34
Since Booths and Taverns were on the Thames erected	33
Since the fam'd Oats for Perjury was strip'd of's priestly	
Habit, and thro, London whip'd	32
Since James the Second did the throne ascend	32
Since Monmouth's Rebellion had a final end	32
Since the Seven Bishops to the Tower were sent	29
Since the Lord Jefferies thither also went	29
Since the Prince of Orange landed at Torbay	29
Since the late King James to France did make his way	29 . . .

What have I done, to incur the Malice or ill will of any of my Brother Almanack Makers, one or another of 'em, will be ever and anon Guilty of those inhumanities and Baseness towards me, endeavouring thereby as much as in them lyes, to make me Obnoctious to the World, especially to Men of Honours and

Integrity, I know not. Sure I am, No real cause has been given at any time, to any One of them, to treat me unhandsomely. And as those Johannidians, J. Partridge, and his second J. Wing, who some years since for their Insolent and Brutish Usage of me, went off by Weeping Cross, and met with shame, and disgrace instead of Commendation: so I dont doubt at this time, but that Johannidian Fielden, an Author, who (some years since) presented the Copy of an Almanack to the Company of Stationers, will meet his Just reward and become the Contempt and Derision of all Honest Men: For if Sincerity and Truth speaking be Commendable Qualities, and as such, ought to be Valued and Propagated among Men; Then Backbiters and Slanderers must of course become Obnoxious Persons in all Civil Communities. And if this detestable Calumniator here, concerned, shall be found to be one that has assum'd the Sacred Robe which all Men have (or at least shou'd have) a Venerable esteem of, as being devoted to the Service of the Omnipotent CREATOR, for the Reproof and Instruction of those over whom God has placed him, and from whose Lips according to St. Paul's charge to Timothy, nothing ought to appear but Truth and Soberness of speech, Conformable to the Character of his Patron Our Lord Jesus Christ, whose cloth he has taken upon him to ware, Therefore not Peevish, or Malicious, not given to lying and rending his indignation by inventing Monstrous False Tales, and then report them for Truth. Such doings as these becomes one that has taken upon him that Sacred Function. Yet so it is, Johannidian Fielden has Falsly and Maliciously rended his spleen against me, and reported a Story for truth, which he knows nothing of, or indeed has any real Grounds for so doing. Viz that I am become a Papist, which Malicious invective, None but Lucifer the Father of Lies, could ever infuse into his Noddle.

3.8 John Gadbury, *Ephemeris . . . for the Year of our Lord, 1717*

The Sun is wholly Ruler of the Ascendant 'tis true, being in a quadrat Ray with the Moon, 'tis to be predicted some unhappy Jealousies and Fears may possess the Minds of the common People, and render them very uneasy; that many scandalous Pamphlets will be spread abroad at about this Season, to disturb the Peace and Tranquility of the Commonwealth by discontented factious Spirits, who (at one time or another) assuredly expect, that the [?] of Justice will certainly overtake them, and they will receive a due Reward according to their Deserts.

The Position of Jupiter in the eleventh House, and the Moon be in another Sign, yet they being virtually [?] therein, doth portend some Felicity; and good reason there is to hope that these Evils may be much mitigated, especially in those Countries and Cities that are under the presence of the Sign Gemini, of which London is particularly one, and some other Places in the Western parts of the Kingdom 'tis very likely will partake of the Benefits of Peaceable Position, to which Felicity, Let all say Amen. Saturn is Lord of the Sixth House, and he is posited in [?], from whence the Diseases that are most predominant this Quarter, will be such as arise from Wind and Cholick in the Bowels, and Putrefaction of the Blood. In the [?]th of March use such Meats or Medicines which purge and sweeten the Blood; in April you may bathe and purge the stomach by Potion, or otherwise: Now you may freely enter into a Course of Physick for any Disease, but drink moderately, because 'tis more dangerous now than at any other Season of the Year, and forbear as much as may be all salt. In May you may take gentle Physick to purge the [?] or Blood upon occasion. Now 'tis wholsom to drink [?] Ale, for it cools the Body and sweetens the Blood, but not Wines (especially to excess) and all such Meats as of a hot Quality. Thus much for the Spring Quarter, so I conclude with this short piece of Poetry.

> Earth so hard, so parch'd with Cold, but now
> Smiles on us with a soft and silken Brow.
> Streets that were o'erspread with Dirt and Mire,
> Put on a Sunday's Dress, a cleaner Tire:
> Trees don't shrowd their naked Heads with Snow;
> Robes of Green they now themselves do show:
> The Nightingale (that Prologue of the Spring)
> With Sweeter Notes, and pleasant Tunes doth sing:
> The Fields are painted o'er with Golden Flowers,
> And the Heavens melt into Balmy Showers:
> The Hills are Gilded with the Morning Sun,
> As Nights grow short, the Day is soon begun.
> Adieu (chill Winter!) joyfully adieu!
> The pleasant Spring's a Paradise to you.

November, 1717.

Observations.

1. Days are shorten'd of hon. 36 min.
   The day is 8 h. 50 m. Long:
6. The 7 Stars south about midnight.
9. The Sun rises S. E. By E. And sets S. W. By W.

The Configuration between Jupiter and Mercury, the one posited in a fixed Sign, the other in Scorpio, a prevaricating one, ushers in a great deal of Fraud and Corruption: much Contention and Division appears among parties, whereby no small number of Lies and Stories are spread and industriously reported, to render the other Party contemptible. And as Lying seems to be the chief Basis on which this Mischief depends, our Reverend Clergy will be sharers also in the malignity of it, from the Furiosa Zealots of the Age, whose crablanthorn Countenances bespeak them the sons of Belial.

5

CRIME: THE FORTUNES OF JACK SHEPPARD

THROUGHOUT eighteenth-century literature, we keep glimpsing the lives and exploits of criminals. In some works—several of Defoe's novels, Gay's *The Beggar's Opera*, Fielding's *Jonathan Wild*—criminals are actually the protagonists. In these cases we are often invited to see their crimes as mirroring the misdeeds of their social superiors. In other works, especially in many novels, we are aware of the constant proximity of the world of the criminal; indeed, we are commonly taken, by Defoe, Fielding, Goldsmith, or Smollett, behind the gates of the prison itself. Such a literary preoccupation tells us more than that crime was in this period, as it ever is, an issue of widespread social concern. It also reveals something of how crime could be thought to be—sometimes worryingly, sometimes comically—close to the experiences of polite readers. This might be because the activities of criminals could be seen as the distorted consequence of an increasingly commercial society. Some of the kinds of adventurer widely mythologized in the first half of the century, highwaymen and pirates for instance, could be thought of as opportunists in an age of economic individualism. It might also be because writers were conscious of the sheer popularity and ubiquity of criminal tales. The true stories and confessions of criminals constituted, as it were, an underworld of exciting or terrible narratives, upon which any writer could draw.

The suspect allure of criminal tales is exemplified in a passage from James Boswell's *London Journal* for 4 May 1763. Explaining his curiosity to witness 'the melancholy spectacle of the executions' at Tyburn, he confesses that 'In my younger years I had read in the *Lives of the Convicts* so much about Tyburn that I had a sort of horrid eagerness to be there.'[1] Boswell could here be referring to any number of collections of such 'Lives' published during the eighteenth century. A selection like this one cannot represent the sheer bulk and range (and sometimes repetitiousness) of accounts of criminals in the period. Any reader

---

[1] *Boswell's London Journal 1762–1763*, ed. Frederick A. Pottle (1950), 252.

wishing for an overview, and a substantial bibliography of sources, might turn to Lincoln Faller's *Turned to Account* (Cambridge, 1987). However, in looking at the case of the notorious burglar and 'prison-breaker' Jack Sheppard, it is hoped that we can see a sample of the ways in which criminal exploits were narrated and marketed in at least the earlier part of the eighteenth century. Sheppard has been chosen because his story genuinely seems to have seized London for several months in 1724; his final court hearing and then his execution were accompanied by crowds whose size amazed eyewitnesses. His case is also interesting—to us, and to his contemporaries—because of his connections with perhaps the century's most famous villain, in fact and in literature, Jonathan Wild, the 'thief-taker general'. Wild made his living 'recovering' stolen goods, for whose theft he was often himself responsible, and by selling wanted criminals to the authorities. Sheppard was an associate of Wild, and was betrayed to the authorities by him. Unlike Wild, he had an almost heroic status, conferred largely because of his audacious escapes from captivity. The fact that he was doomed by the double-dealing of a man who became a byword for sophisticated perfidy attracted, especially posthumously, yet more sympathy.

We do not have to go as far as Peter Linebaugh who, in *The London Hanged*, depicts Sheppard as a proletarian anti-hero whose 'dazzling feats' provided 'an example of resourcefulness and freedom to the London weavers and labouring poor'.[2] Linebaugh takes it that Sheppard's fame, preserved in 'an "other history" of histories, pantomime and song', was a consequence of his background as well as his exploits.[3] He was an 'idle apprentice' who had lived in the workhouse—a rebel against the order of things. Posthumous accounts certainly emphasized Sheppard's fall from the grace of his apprenticeship as a carpenter: as one puts it, he 'had a ready and ingenious Hand' and 'the Character of a very sober and orderly Boy'.[4] He would never have attracted attention, however, if it had not been for his increasingly audacious escapes from custody. In order to make these escapes, it was presumed that he misapplied some of the skills that he had learned as an apprentice.

The story of the last months of Sheppard's life is told in the newspaper extracts that make up Section 1 of this chapter. In his early twenties he had taken to burglary, in the company of his brother Thomas and others. He was first arrested in spring 1724 and imprisoned in St Giles's Roundhouse, but escaped. He was recaptured and put in New Prison in Clerkenwell, together with his common-law wife Elizabeth Lyon, known as 'Edgworth Bess'. Breaking through

[2] Peter Linebaugh, *The London Hanged: Crime and Civil Society in the Eighteenth Century* (Harmondsworth, 1991), 14.   [3] Ibid. 8.

[4] *The History of the Remarkable Life of John Sheppard*, in *The Fortunate Mistress Vol. II. John Sheppard, &c.*, The Shakespeare Head Edition of the Novels and Selected Writings of Daniel Defoe. (Oxford, 1928), 167.

the wall of his cell with tools smuggled in to the prison, he escaped again on 25 May, with Bess. He teamed up with Joseph Blake, alias 'Blueskin', who was also an associate of Jonathan Wild. Together they broke into the shop of Mr Kneebone, a draper on the Strand for whom Sheppard's mother had once worked. Kneebone went to Wild, who discovered Sheppard's whereabouts and arranged for his arrest. Sheppard was imprisoned in Newgate and convicted. While awaiting execution, which was to have taken place on 4 September 1724, he escaped yet again, on 31 August 1724, cutting through a bar in his cell door and walking out of the prison shrouded in a cloak. He was rearrested ten days later in Finchley, north of London; one of his peculiarities seems to have been his carelessness of concealment once at large. He was returned to Newgate, where he was loaded with fetters and chained to the floor of the most impregnable room in the prison, the 'Castle'. Yet, incredibly, on the morning of 16 October, the turnkeys found that he had escaped once more, breaking through six locked doors and climbing from the prison tower onto the roof of building adjoining Newgate.

This, his most brilliant escape, was his last. He was arrested for a final time some ten days later, in a Drury Lane gin shop, presented for identification by the King's Bench court at Westminster Hall, and, the next week, on 16 November 1724, taken from Newgate to Tyburn and hanged. By the time of his final arrest he had been made famous through newspaper reports. Many of the newspapers of the early eighteenth century, in the provinces as well as in London, were preoccupied by the exploits of criminals. Amongst their human-interest stories—tales of everyday disasters and domestic tragedies—crime is the dominant source of narratives: crimes perpetrated, criminals caught and tried, the names and bare details of persons convicted and punished. Usually the stories of criminals found in newspapers were soon ended because the criminals, once identified, were swiftly despatched. By escaping so often, Sheppard delayed his fate and became famous while he was yet alive. The first of the sections below tracks the growth of his popular fame up to his execution.

Our latterday sense of Sheppard's contemporary fame has been complicated by Daniel Defoe's supposed involvement in the telling and retelling of his story. This involvement was 'discovered' by William Lee in the mid-nineteenth century. In his *Daniel Defoe: His Life and Newly Discovered Writings* Lee argued that, from 1720, Defoe had worked for John Applebee, the main London publisher of criminal lives. He had become convinced that Defoe wrote the lead articles in Applebee's *Original Weekly Journal*, more commonly called *Applebee's Journal*, and that these included all the reports on the exploits of Sheppard. He therefore supposed that Defoe was the author of two anonymous accounts published by Applebee: *The History of the Remarkable Life of John Sheppard* (which appeared on 19 October 1724, after his most audacious escape but before his recapture) and *A Narrative of All the Robberies, Escapes, &c. of John Sheppard* (published on 17 November 1724, the day after his execution). These two accounts have subsequently been included in editions of Defoe's writings and, because they are therefore widely available, are not excerpted in this chapter. It must be recognized that there is little in the way of evidence for Defoe's association with Applebee, and that Lee's attributions, accepted by later biographers, have in recent years been strongly contested.[5]

Lee was convinced that Defoe visited Newgate on Applebee's behalf after Sheppard's first escape from there and wrote a report for *Applebee's Journal*.[6] He cited a contemporary report that Sheppard handed over his own account of his exploits at Tyburn (see 1.7) and inferred that Defoe was not only the recipient, but also the author, having ghost-written *A Narrative of All the Robberies, Escapes, &c. of John Sheppard* with Sheppard's agreement.[7] Perhaps we will never know whether Defoe was involved or not. We can, however, catch sight in all this of the importance of John Applebee in the popularizing of Sheppard's story, and of criminal lives more generally. Applebee's role is implicit in the passages we have given from his *Journal*: it is further reflected in the third section of this chapter, in which we try to show something of the context in which Sheppard's story was told and retold. To spend any time with the newspaper reports, pamphlets, and anthologies of criminal lives and 'confessions' published in the first half of the eighteenth century is to keep coming across Applebee, not only as the chief producer of this popular literature, but also as the man widely acknowledged to be its chief producer. 'Mr. Applebee takes care to purchase from all our dying Criminals the private *Memoirs* of their Lives and *Conversations*', wrote Eustace Budgell in 1733. 'Whenever the case or Behaviour of a condemned Criminal has something in it extraordinary, we shall consult this ingenious Biographer for the most exact and authentick Account of it.'[8]

Applebee published a variety of other criminal lives and confessions, sometimes in collaboration with fellow booksellers. Judged by the number of editions, *A Narrative of All the Robberies, Escapes, &c. of John Sheppard*, reprinted six times during 1724, was the most successful of all these. No doubt this was because it had claims to be Sheppard's own account, dramatically deposited with Applebee just before he was killed. During the 1720s Applebee produced at least ten other criminal biographies, usually pamphlets less than fifty pages

---

[5] See P. N. Furbank and W. R. Owens, 'The Myth of Defoe as "Applebee's Man" ', *Review of English Studies*, 48 (1997), 198–204. See also the same authors' *Defoe De-Attributions* (1994), especially pp. 136–40.

[6] William Lee, *Daniel Defoe: His Life and Newly Discovered Writings*, 3 vols. (1869), i. 384.

[7] Ibid. 387.

[8] In *The Bee* (Feb. 1733), cited in Michael Shugrue, 'Applebee's Original Weekly Journal: An Index to Eighteenth-Century Taste', *The Newberry Library Bulletin*, 6/4 (Mar. 1964), 111–12.

long. During the 1730s he produced more criminal lives and 'confessions', as well as his first anthology of criminal biographies, *The Lives of the Most Remarkable Criminals, who have been Condemn'd and Executed . . . From the Year 1720, to the Present Time*. This included 'The Life of the famous JOHN SHEPHERD, Foot-Pad, House-breaker, and Prison-breaker', who was characterized as one of 'the Prodigies of ingenious Wickedness and artful Mischief, which have surprized the World in our time'.[9] It added to the story a good deal of detail about Sheppard's supposedly stormy relationship with Edgworth Bess, and his further corruption by his next doxy, '*Mrs. Maggott*, a woman some-what less boisterous in her Temper, but full as wicked'.[10] As well as producing such vividly embroidered criminal tales, Applebee collaborated with several other booksellers in the production of a series of accounts of 'state trials'. More significantly, in 1718 he had begun printing the 'confessions' of condemned criminals transcribed by the Ordinary (i.e. chaplain) of Newgate, and these remained his staple until the 1740s. The first one that he published was by Ordinary Paul Lorrain; there followed a series of these accounts by Lorrain's successor Thomas Purney (Lorrain died in 1719). There were at least thirty-nine such texts between 1720 and 1725. Purney, however, was ill in the period leading up to Sheppard's execution, and there is therefore no such Ordinary's version of his 'confessions'. A parson named Wagstaff was acting as Purney's deputy for much of the time Sheppard was in prison, and is often mentioned as an authority in accounts of his confinement.

These accounts by the Ordinary of Newgate were the most renowned, and probably most influential, versions of the lives of criminals that were cheaply available to readers of the period. Published in the wake of each batch of hangings at Tyburn, they purportedly provided 'the Behaviour, Confessions, and Last Speeches' (as the title usually put it) of recently executed 'Malefactors'. The Ordinary would supplement his meagre stipend (no more than £35 per annum, plus a house in Newgate Street) with these popular accounts, which would then often be cited in newspapers and other publications. We might recall the sardonic references in Defoe's *Moll Flanders* to the Ordinary of Newgate's interest in condemned felons' stories: 'all his Divinity ran upon Confessing my Crime, as he call'd it (tho' he knew not what I was in for) making a full Discovery, and the like, without which he told me God would never forgive me'.[11] By Moll's account, the Ordinary is usually drunk by noon. Examples from the Ordinary's texts are given at 3.1 and 3.2. These are designed to be salutary, and, it should be said, often to emphasize the chastening effects of the Ordinary's pious exhortations to the condemned criminal. Accounts always end with

---

[9] *The Lives of the Most Remarkable Criminals*, 2 vols. (1732), i. 371.   [10] Ibid. 374.
[11] *Moll Flanders*, ed. G. A. Starr (1971; repr. Oxford, 1990), 277.

descriptions of the criminals' behaviour and speech when they come to the scaffold at Tyburn. These usually involve prayers and warnings to the spectators to learn terrible lessons from their examples. They also often involve confessing to other crimes.

Unsurprisingly, Applebee's publications were full of cross-references to and advertisements for each other. So in the Ordinary of Newgate's accounts there are signs of Applebee's other publications in the field: one account, for instance, includes a note that 'There being such a variety of uncommon facts, in the Life of the two before-mention'd Malefactors', and the Ordinary 'being confin'd to so small a Compass', curious readers are referred to 'Applebee's Weekly Journal, of Saturday next, where they may depend on an impartial Account'.[12] At the end of other Ordinary's accounts he advertises some of his other lives of criminals. Equally, he, and his writers, keep recycling material. A narrative would often appear first in *Applebee's Journal* and then in a longer pamphlet form. Columns from *Applebee's Journal* were, without acknowledgement, the basis for *The History of the Remarkable Life of John Sheppard*, so often attributed to Defoe. Parts of this biography were indeed taken verbatim from Applebee's newspaper. Applebee's contractual arrangement with the Ordinary of Newgate naturally gave his versions a tang of the authenticity that was the promise in all his advertisements and title-pages. If Sheppard is an exemplary protagonist of the criminal tales of the period, Applebee deserves his place in this anthology as the most important purveyor of those tales.

REFERENCES AND FURTHER READING

A good short account of Sheppard's life is given in Gerald Howson, *Thief-Taker General: The Rise and Fall of Jonathan Wild* (1970), ch. 20, which is a readable introduction to crime and punishment in the period. Also useful is Peter Linebaugh, *The London Hanged: Crime and Civil Society in the Eighteenth Century* (Harmondsworth, 1991), and Horace Bleackley and S. M. Ellis, *Jack Sheppard* (Edinburgh, 1933). The most thorough account of 'true stories' of criminals in the period is Lincoln Faller, *Turned to Account: The Forms and Functions of Criminal Biography in Late Seventeenth and Early Eighteenth-Century England* (Cambridge, 1987). For the activities of the Ordinary of Newgate, see the same author's 'In Contrast to Defoe: The Rev. Paul Lorrain, Historian of Crime', *Huntington Library Quarterly*, 60 (1976), 139–66, and Peter Linebaugh, 'The Ordinary of Newgate and his *Account*', in *Crime in England, 1550–1800*, ed. J. S. Cockburn (Princeton, NJ, 1977). Most of what is known about John Applebee is to be found in Michael Shugrue, 'Applebee's Original Weekly Journal: An

---

[12] James Guthrie, *The Ordinary of Newgate his Account, of the Behaviour, Confession, and Last Dying Words of the Five Malefactors, Who Were Executed at Tyburn on Tuesday the 12th, of this Instant May, 1730* (1730), 4.

Index to Eighteenth-Century Taste', *The Newberry Library Bulletin*, 6/4 (1964), 108–21. Doubts about Defoe's involvement with Applebee are expressed in P. N. Furbank and W. R. Owens, 'The Myth of Defoe as "Applebee's Man"', *Review of English Studies*, 48 (May 1997), 198–204.

1. SHEPPARD'S EXPLOITS

The earliest mention of Sheppard in print seems to be a paragraph in *Applebee's Journal* for 1 August 1724:

Shepheard, the notorious House-breaker, who lately escaped from New-Prison, and was retaken by Jonathan Wilde and committed to Newgate, attempted to escape also from that Gaol a Day or two ago, several Saws and Instruments proper for such a Design being found about his Bed; he is since confined in an Apartment call'd the Stone Room, kept close, and sufficiently loaded with Irons, to prevent his Designs for the future.

Soon the story was taken up by other newspapers (see **1.1**). By the time of Sheppard's trial on 13 August 1724, he was already a minor celebrity. The outcome of the trial was reported in *The London Journal*, in its regular column of London news, on 29 August 1724:

'Tis said, that Joseph Ward, Anthony Upton, and John Shephard, 3 of the Malefactors condemn'd at the late Sessions at the Old Baily, are order'd for Execution the 4th of September next; and that Robert Colethorpe, Stephen Fowles and Frances Sands are reprieved, in order for transportation.

The Original London Post for 17 August 1724 reported the conviction and sentencing to death at the Old Bailey of 'John Shepher for Burglary, along with Joseph Ward, Anthony Upton, Robert Colethorpe, Frances Sands and Stephen Fowles'. A summary of the trials of all of these appeared in the issue of 24 August 1724. A summary of Sheppard's trial alone appeared in the issue of 26 August 1724 (**1.2**).

Soon Sheppard was at large again. His first escape from Newgate was reported widely in the London newspapers, and was described most fully in *Applebee's Journal* (**1.4**). The report in *The London Journal*, published on the same day, is given for comparison (**1.3**). Both newspapers, which were rival weeklies, printed news of his capture in Finchley on the same day. *The London Journal* reported that he had 'been at his old Trade, for Two Silver Watches were found on him'. *Applebee's Journal* included Sheppard's denial that 'he ever was Married to the Woman who assisted him' in his escape (Edgworth Bess) and his declaration that 'he found her a common Strumpet in Drury Lane, and that she hath been the Cause of all his Misfortunes and

Misery'. The next week both papers reported that, in Newgate, he had confessed to a series of robberies, and also that, rather belying the penitence that
he had been professing, the keepers had found 'a small File concealed in a
Bible, which was lent him for his Preparations' (*London Journal*, 19
September 1724) and 'two Files, a Chisel, and a Hammer, hid in the bottom
of a matted Chair' (*Applebee's Journal*, 19 September 1724). Clearly he was
indefatigable.

On 10 October both papers reported that Blueskin had been charged with
the burglary of Mr Kneebone's shop. 'On Saturday last, one Joseph Blake,
alias Blueskin, was committed to Newgate. He stands charged with being
concern'd with the notorious malefactor Shepherd, in some Robberies'
(*London Journal*, 10 October 1724). Blueskin had himself (perhaps at Wild's
behest) helped convict fellow thieves. 'This Blueskin was himself formerly
an Evidence, against Junks, alias Levee, Flood, and Oakey, who were Executed at Tyburn for robbing the Honourable William Yonge, Esq. and
Colonel Cope, near Hampstead' (*Applebee's Journal*, 10 October 1724). A
week later came the reports of Sheppard's great escape. *Applebee's Journal*
told its readers that 'he broke through Six Strong Rooms, where People had
formerly been confined, but had not of late been in Use, got up to the top of
the Gaol, then descended from thence by two Blankets tied together' (*Applebee's Journal*, 17 October 1724). Its rival paper reported the attempt by Blueskin, who was waiting for trial, to cut Jonathan Wild's throat in the Bail Dock
at the Old Bailey Sessions House, which Wild had incautiously entered. It
then added hurriedly, 'Yesterday Morning early, Sheppard made his Escape
again out of Newgate' (*London Journal*, 17 October 1724). Not until a week
later was it able to give the details (1.5), adding in the same issue the news
that Blueskin '(who attempted to cut Jonathan Wild's Throat)' had been sentenced to death for 'Felony and Burglary'.

The mischievous delight that some might have taken in Sheppard's
exploits is evident in a mocking piece from *The Weekly Journal*, a 'letter'
from Sheppard to the hangman (Jack Ketch, its addressee, was a famous
seventeenth-century executioner whose name became a pseudonym for any
hangman), published a fortnight after Sheppard's escape (1.6). It also
demonstrates the clash of registers that characterizes some writing on crime
at this time: it is supposed amusing that Sheppard might dispute in Latin
phrases and have an elevated idea of himself. A week after this appeared, the
papers were reporting his arrest in a gin shop, scarcely lying low, but dressed,
according to *The London Journal* of 7 November, in 'a handsome Suit of
Black, with a Diamond Ring and a Cornelian Ring on his Finger, and a fine
Light Tye Peruke'. A few days later he was taken to Westminster Hall to the
court of King's Bench and ordered for execution. 'He was remanded back to
Newgate, thro' the most numerous Crowds of People that ever were seen in
London; and Westminster Hall has not been so Crowded in the Memory of
Man. A Constable who attended, had his Leg broke; and many other Persons

were hurt and wounded at Westminster Hall Gate' (*Applebee's Journal*, 14 November 1724).

The next week Sheppard's execution, on 16 November, was widely reported. *Applebee's Journal* for 21 November described how, as he travelled from Newgate to Tyburn, 'The Crowd of Spectators all the Way was prodigiously great'. *The Weekly Journal: or, British Gazeteer*, more commonly known as *Read's Journal*, included in its account the detail of Sheppard handing 'a Paper' to someone even as he mounted the scaffold (see 1.7). Recognizing that Sheppard was already passing into myth, it also gave up a third of the paper to an 'Abridgement of the Life, Robberies, Escapes, and Death, of John Sheppard'. *Mist's Journal* of the same day (see 1.8) provided a more detailed account, not only of Sheppard's death, but of the crowd disturbances that followed. These were confirmed by other newspapers of the time (see *The Post-Man*, 17–19 November, and *The Post-Boy*, 17–19 November). The sense of Sheppard already becoming a semi-fictional character is caught in the issue of *Applebee's Journal* that reported his execution. Happy to match the jocular with the terrible, it also carried a 'letter' from one 'Betty Blueskin', supposed niece of Moll Flanders, telling of her life of crime, and her passion for Jack Sheppard. Had they made a match, 'what a clever Couple should we have been', she exclaims, and laments the fate of 'poor dexterous *Jack*'. *The London Journal* combined the two tones of gravity and jocularity in a single item (1.9), with which the section ends; it begins with a description of Sheppard's arrival at Tyburn's 'fatal tree' and concludes with a kind of advertisement for a forthcoming theatrical entertainment based on Sheppard's exploits.

The Original London Post. Or, Heathcote's Intelligence (3 August 1724)   1.1

Whereas one John Shepperd the notorious House-breaker, with his Wife, who is commonly called, and most known as Edger Bess, were committed to New-prison by Geo. Walher, Esq.; for several Burglaries and Felonies; and some of his Companions abroad having privately conveyed to the Hands of the said Shepperd, a Watch Spring Saw, with which he saw'd the Irons off his Legs, as likewise the Iron Bars of the Window, by which Means they made their escape; but by the Diligence of the Keeper of the said Gaol; they were both retaken by the Famous Thief Taker, Jonathan Wyld and Quilt Arnold, they both being as famous for that Exercise as the other is notorious for his Calling; she being taken in Fleet Street, and he at an honest House within a Half a Country Mile of Rag Fair, and they being carry'd back to New Prison aforesaid, he was very handsomely Ironed and sheered for his Fault, and she Log'd for playing at Truant; Shepperd on a further

Examination since re-taken before Mr. Justice Blackerby, is committed to Newgate, there to spend the remaining part of his Life, waiting the call of the Sheriff, and the service his Friend Dick Arnold is to do for him; Edger Bess is hourly expected to follow, but she has the old Proverb, only this, that she must wait the Call of Merchant Forward. They being both notorious Persons, and the most fit in the World for the Gentleman they are recommended to, and then our Subjects may be a little more at rest than they are, if about our City and Suburbs thereto belonging.

1.2 *The Original London Post* (26 August 1724)

The Tryal of John Shepherd

John Shepherd, was indicted for breaking the House of William Kneebone, in the Night-time, and stealing 111 Yards of Woolen Cloth, the 12th of June last. The prosecutor deposed, That the Prisoner had some time since been his Servant, and when he went to Bed, the Time mentioned in the Indictment, about 11 a Clock at Night, he saw all the Doors and Windows fast; but was called up about 4 in the Morning, and found his House broke open, the Bar of a Cellar Window having been cut, and the Bolts of the Door that comes up Stairs drawn, and the Padlock wrenched off, and his Shutter in the Shop broken, and his Goods gone; whereupon, suspecting the Prisoner, he having committed ill Actions thereabouts before, he acquainted Jonathan Wild with it, and he procured him to be apprehended. Joseph Blake, alias Blueskins (lately Executed) and William Field were Accomplices with him in this Fact, and Field was an Evidence against him. The Fact being plainly proved upon him, he was found guilty.   Death.

1.3 *The London Journal* (5 September 1724)

Yesterday Two of the Three Criminals condemn'd last Sessions, and whom in our last we mention'd to be order'd for Execution, were executed at Tyburn, viz. Joseph Ward, for the Highway; and Anthony Upton, for Burglary. John Shepherd was in the Dead Warrant; but the Day it was brought to Newgate he found Means to make his Escape; for being provided with Saws and other Implements, he cut off one of the great Spikes over the Door of the condemn'd Hold, and being of a slender Body, got him self thro' into the Lodge, and from thence into the Street, and so escaped, being assisted by his Wife and another Woman. He went off in his Irons, (which were hid by a Night Gown) whilst several People were in the Lodge talking of his former Dexterity in breaking out of New-Prison some time ago. His Wife is since committed to the Compter, for assisting him in his Escape.

Applebee's Journal (5 September 1724)   1.4

The Escape of John Sheppard from the Condemn'd Hold in Newgate, on Monday last, was contrived as follows, viz. His Wife having furnished him with a Saw, File, &c., he proceeded to cut off one of the large Iron Barrels from his Links; and then, to prevent their Shackling, made them fast to one Leg, at the same time setting the other at perfect Liberty. He next cut an Iron Spike over the Door of about six Inches in Length, and one and a half square, his Tools being dipt in Oil; and his Wife with another Woman, pretending to be in close Conversation with him, he soon sawed it asunder, without being heard or suspected. The interval thus made, being capable of admitting his slender Body to pass thro', and assisted by the women, he instantly perfected his Liberty, and went out at the Lodge Door, together with them, in a Night-Gown, which concealed his Irons, at between Seven and Eight in the evening; the Turnkeys being at the other end of the Lodge at that Instant, concerting Measures for his Farther Security, as well on Account of his notable Escape not many Weeks before from New Prison, as his present Circumstances, being ordered for Death with them who were executed yesterday. The other Prisoners, having no Friends at Hand, and being withal too Corpulent to pass thro' the Breach; then called to the Turnkeys, and told them Sheppard was gone. He is about 22 Years of Age, by Trade a Joiner, and is suspected of having committed many more Burglaries, besides that of which he was convicted. He has a Brother named Thomas Sheppard, convicted in last July Sessions for Felony, and lies in Newgate for Transportation. It has since been known, that a Waterman's Boy plied him a Black Friers Stairs the same Night, and landed him at the Horse Ferry at Westminster, the Boy observing his irons under his Gown.

On Tuesday Night his Wife was committed to the Compter for assisting him in his Escape; having been apprehended and taken that Day by Mr. Jonathan Wild.

1.5   *The London Journal* (24 October 1724)

Sheppard's second and most astonishing Escape from Newgate, is what has been the Talk of almost all Companies for this Week past, and has induced several Gentlemen to go to that Prison to see in what manner the dextrous Rogue made his Way from so strait a Confinement to Liberty. The best Account given of him is, that he found Means to loosen the Staples to which he was chained down in the Castle, and getting rid of his Hand Cuffs by means of a crooked Nail, which he held in his Mouth, he unlock'd a great Horse Padlock that was fixed on his Irons; and then, with the help of an Iron Bar that he found in the Chimney, broke through a Wall (some have said nine Foot thick) into a strong Room, the Locks whereof had not been opened some Years, which he forced, as he did the Locks and Bolts of five more strong Rooms where People had been formerly confined. After this he got to the Top of the Gaol, and having torn, and tied the Slips of his Blankets together, descended to the Turner's House that joins to the Prison, which, finding means to enter, he passed through unheard, and so made an entire Escape. Great Care is taken to prevent any thing like this for the future; for the Condemned Hold is now barr'd up, so that those under Sentence of Death, have not the Liberty of coming down to the Gate in the Lodge to converse with their Friends as heretofore.

On Tuesday last a Debtor escaped from the King's Bench Prison in the following manner. Being provided with a Rope, to which he had fasten'd a Hook, he threw it to the Top of the Garden Wall (which is Twenty Foot high) where the Hook fixing (and having knotted the Rope to secure his Hold) he mounted as readily as even Sheppard himself could have done, and, descending on the other Side, got clear off.

1.6   *Read's Journal* (31 October 1724)

To Dr. *John Ketch*, at the Sign of the *Three Legg'd Stool*, near *Hyde-Park* Corner.

Dear Doctor,   *Thieving Lane, Oct.* 19, 1724

After excusing myself to the Reverend Ordinary, my good Friends the Keepers, and Mr. *Jonathan Wild*, I ought to make some Apology to you, for my withdrawing in so clandestine a Manner, and declining to put myself into your Hands. I have been told, you have affirm'd, you had a Right to me for a Patient; but pray, Sir, what Right? Not an hereditary one surely; I dare appeal to the Ordinary, if I am not a better Christian to violate That: I am sure you will not, nor dare

not say 'twas an indefeasible one; for every Body would laugh at such an Assertion; nay, I am bold to affirm, you had not so much as a legal one having neglected
to take out in due time a *Habeas Corpus*, with a Writ annex'd, *ad suspendend per
Coll*, and I appeal to you and all Mankind, whether I am blameable for taking
Advantage of such Neglect, in a Case where my All depended. You know that a
Dog that has been hang'd on a Crabb-tree, can never love Verjuice; and to tell
you the Truth, I have seen some of my Friends under your Hands, make such
wry Mouths, and awkward Wrigglings, as have put me out of Conceit with the
Operation, and have bred in me an Opinion, that (however expert you may be in
the *Cito* and *Tuto*) you have not attained to the *Jucunde* of your Art. Moreover,
I have a moral Aversion to *Hemp*, it being, as I am inform'd, an Herb of a suffo-
cating Quality; and to deal plain with you, I had rather take a Swing in ten
Fathom of Blanket, and venture my Neck four Stories high, than be suspended
in ten Foot of Cord, like a Meteor in the Air, to be gazed at by every Fool that
thinks it worth his while to make an Holiday. I hate hanging in Suspense for an
Hour together: To this I add, that I have naturally an Impediment in my Speech,
and should it so happen (as I know it has to many) that I should entirely lose that
Faculty in the operation, I doubt whether it be in your Power, or that of the whole
College, to recover it.

Next Day after my Retreat, a general Court of the whole Society assembled,
wherein I was unanimously chosen their President: This will put it in my Power
to make you some Amends for what you may have lost by me; and I doubt not,
but e'er the Year comes round, I shall send you many a Patient; and if my ill Fate
should oblige me to be cut for the Simples, I should put myself into your Hands,
as soon as any Man's of your Profession.

Give my Service to poor Jo. Blueskin: I am told he takes in great Dudgeon my
withdrawing in such a Manner; complains of Breach of Articles, by which (as he
says) we were oblig'd to *hang together*. I am sorry he is out of Humour; but pray
tell him he might have learn'd from a greater Man in the Trade than ever he or I
were, to distinguish between the *Spirit* and *Letter* of a Treaty: I defy him to say
I ever flinch'd from him in any felonious Attempt we undertook in Company, or
that ever I perform'd my Work by *Halves*, as he has lately done; besides, I am
advised by my Council learned in the Law, that if I should voluntarily submit to
be hang'd, and die in the Operation, I should become a *Felo de se*, and incur For-
feiture of my Goods and Chattels, which sure no reasonable Man can desire. I
make great Allowances for his being out of Humour when I consider his Circumstances; for I remember an Observation of a learned Doctor, made some
Time ago before a learned Body, *viz.* That when a Man receives Sentence of
Death, it is apt to make him very chagrine. After all, I wish him a safe Deliverance, and if that cannot be, a good Journey. And now, Sir, before I conclude, let
me conjure you not to harbour any ill Thought of me from what has happen'd

for 'tis very possible I may perhaps, when you least expect, convince you and all the World, that I am,

Yours, &c.

John Sheppard

1.7   *Read's Journal* (21 November 1724)

At the Place of Execution he behav'd very gravely, spoke very little, gave a Paper to a Friend, and after some small Time allow'd for Devotion, he was turn'd off, dying with much Difficulty, and with uncommon Pity from all the Spectators. The same Night his Body was bury'd in St. Martin's in the Fields, with a velvet Pall, and the Funeral Service perform'd, &c. a Detachment of the Prince's Guard attending the Corps, with their Bayonets fix'd on their Musquets to prevent the Violence of the Populace, who had been very tumultuous all Day, no farther Disorder happen'd.

1.8   *Mist's Journal* (21 November 1724)

He was attended to the Place of Execution by numerous Crowds of People. An Undertaker with a Hearse follow'd him to Tyburn, in order to bring back his Body, and to bury it in St. Sepulchre's Church-Yard, where a Grave was prepar'd; but the Mob having a Notion, that it was design'd to convey him to the Surgeons, carry'd off the Body upon their Shoulders, and brought it to the Barley-Mow, an Alehouse in Long-Acre; the Undertaker got off from them with great Difficulty. The Mob continuing in a riotous Manner in Long-Acre and Drury-Lane, several Justices of the Peace met together, and the Proclamation against Riots was read to disperse them; also a Detachment of Soldiers from the Prince's Guard, and from the Savoy, was sent thither to prevent Disturbance; and Orders being given to deliver him up to the Person that was to bury him, he was accordingly interr'd that Night in the burying Ground belonging to St. Martin's in the Fields, the Soldiers guarding it all the Way.

1.9   *The London Journal* (21 November 1724)

On Monday last the notorious House breaker, John Sheppard, was executed at Tyburn, pursuant to the Rule of Court of the King's Bench, Westminster: As he was an enterprizing Fellow, his Hand Cuffs were continued on him even to the Gallows. Never was there a greater Crowd assembled on any Occasion, than to see this Criminal; and however undaunted he might appear before, he was greatly shocked at the fatal Tree; and probably the more, in that to the last he had meditated an Escape; for, on his Entrance into the Cart, a naked Knife was found on him, with which, 'tis thought, he designed to have cut the Cords that tied him, or the fatal Noose, and so have thrown himself out, and taken refuge amongst the Mob. At Tyburn he declared he would confess no new Robbery except one, which he committed in Monmouth Street since his last Escape. If our Readers have recourse to our Paper of the 31st past, they will find the Particulars of that Robbery there, of which we mentioned Sheppard as the Person suspected.

So amazing have been the Actions of this Desperado, that, we hear, they have got the *Escapes* of John Sheppard, *or Harlequin in Newgate*, now in Rehearsal at the new Play House; Mr. Lun not doubting but to make as much of him as he has done of Dr. Faustus. The Person who plays *Sheppard*, it seems, went to see the *Original* in Newgate; who told him, *He should be glad to have it in his Power to play his own Part.*

2. SHEPPARD'S POSTHUMOUS FAME

Trumping competitors, Applebee published *A Narrative of All the Robberies, Escapes, &c. of John Sheppard* only a day after Sheppard's execution, making more plausible its claim that it was truly Sheppard's own story, told to contradict the 'various Pamphlets, Papers, and Pictures' which 'are gone abroad, most or all of them misrepresenting my Affairs'.[13] But Sheppard's story kept being retold. An extract from one of the earliest versions, *Authentic Memoirs of the Life and Surprising Adventures of John Sheppard*, is given below (2.1). As will be seen, the unknown writer ('G.E.') recognizes Applebee as his competitor. In fact, he elsewhere dismisses Applebee's *Narrative* as 'Spurious Copy' (p. 72). His dedication explicitly contests Applebee's '*Prior-Title* to your Favour and Affection' (p. vi). G.E. assures his readers that '*My Intelligence* is full as Genuine as *His*' (p. vi). 'I received all my *Instructions* from a Gentleman who was intimately acquainted with *Sheppard* in his Infancy, and has had an uninterrupted Correspondence with him during the whole Time of his Confinement.' The passage given below tells a story against Applebee before inventing a mock-diabolical final speech for the 'hero'.

A few months after Sheppard's hanging, the lord chancellor, Lord Macclesfield, was impeached for embezzlement. He had interviewed Sheppard

[13] In *The Fortunate Mistress Vol. II. John Sheppard, &c.*, 209.

at the Westminster Hall hearings (see above), and the undated broadside given in full at 2.2 must have been published while the coincidence—one criminal sitting in judgment on another—was still fresh. The same month as the execution, theatre-goers could enjoy *Harlequin Sheppard. A Night Scene in Grotesque Character*, by John Thurmond, the publication of which was being advertised in newspapers in early December 1724 (see, for instance, *Daily Courant*, 2 December 1724, and see this anthology, pp. 62–3). One advertisement proclaimed that it included 'New SCENES painted from the Real Places of Action: Also a SONG occasion'd by Blueskin's cutting Jonathan Wild's Throat, sung by Mr. Harper to the Tune of Packington's Pound' (*London Journal*, 5 December 1724). Its introduction provided yet another short life of Sheppard. A more intriguing Sheppard-based drama, for our purposes, was *The Quaker's Opera* of 1728. This was based on *The Prison-Breaker; or, the Adventures of John Sheppard. A Farce*, published in 1725. Though 'intended to be acted at the Theatre Royal in Lincoln's-Inn Fields', this comedy, much of which consists of argot-filled conversations between members of Sheppard's 'gang', was never staged. However, it was adapted for more popular staging as *The Quaker's Opera*. The title-page of the first edition of this specifies, 'As it is performed at Lee's and Harper's Great Theatrical Booth in Bartolomew Fair'. The most important change was the addition of a large number of songs, three of which are included in the scene given below (2.3). In these as well as the dialogue, it preserves *The Prison-Breaker*'s delight in slang.

After the immediate hum of interest in Sheppard that made these works possible had died away, his story continued to be told in the collections of criminal tales that appeared throughout the century. *The Tyburn Chronicle*, from which extract 2.4 is taken, was but one of these. This anthology made a virtue of its derivativeness: 'every thing worth our notice that has been heretofore printed, has been examined with care, and the essence of all the other books of this kind extracted for the embellishment of our own' (pp. v–vi). It gave 'The Trial of JOHN SHEPPARD for Burglaries; with a particular Account of his Life and Exploits' and included a purported transcript of a declamation by 'Mr. Wagstaff (the Ordinary's journeyman)' from his account of the last confessions of Joseph Ward and Anthony Upton (with whom Sheppard was to have been executed). Wagstaff, robbed of the 'confessions' of Sheppard that he would normally have published, warns against the danger to law-abiding citizens of 'this inhuman, barbarous thief, and house-breaker' (p. 94).

The Tyburn Chronicle repeated the story, first published in *Applebee's Journal*, 31 October 1724, that after his most daring escape Sheppard triumphed over his gaoler and shared the joke with Applebee himself. It gave the two supposed letters that Sheppard left with Applebee while on the run (the Mr Austin referred to was the keeper of Newgate prison). Also included in 2.4 is the anthology's account of Sheppard's plans to escape, even as the cart was taking him to the gallows. This account is immediately followed in the collection by 'The Trial of JOSEPH BLAKE, alias BLUESKIN, for Burglary; with an Account of his Life and Behaviour'.

From *Authentic Memoirs of the Life and Surprising Adventures of John*   2.1
Sheppard: Who Was Executed at Tyburn November the 16th, 1724 By Way of
Familiar Letters From a Gentleman in Town, to his Friend in the Country
(1724)

Mr. *App——by*, in Gratitude for the many good Services our *Hero* had done him, and as sole Executor to the Deceas'd, at his own Expence, hir'd a Mourning Hearse to attend the *Gallows*, in order to convey the Corps to some decent Place of Interment. But the Mob, misconstruing this good Intention of his Friend, and mistaking it for an *Antomical Preparation* of the Society of Surgeons, declar'd *Open War* against the *Charioteer*, fir'd their *Cannon* at him, loaded with Dirt and Stones, and obliged him to quit the Field with the Loss of his *Standard*.

This Day Mr. P——y has oblig'd the World with an Account of his most Learned and Judicious *Prepartory Sermon* on this Occasion, and the Behaviour of our Unfortunate Hero, before the *Finishing Stroke* was put to his Execution. But as he is perfectly silent as to his *Dying-Speech*, I presume, in reality, he made none. Yet as I have been writing a sort of a *Tragedy*, and divided it regularly into several *Acts* or *Letters*, I cannot be reconcil'd to his quitting the *Stage*, 'till, *Swan-like*, he sings his own *Requiem*. I shall, therefore, in Imitation of the greatest Poets of the age, close my *Play* with an imaginary *Speech*, and let him take his leave of the Spectators, like a Man, and like a *Hero*.

JOHN SHEPPARD'S Suppos'd SPEECH

> *Like Doctor* Faustus, *I my Pranks have play'd,*
> *(By Contract with his* Master *long since made)*
> *Like him liv'd Gay, and revell'd in Delight,*
> *Drank all the Day, and Whor'd the livelong Night.*
> *To raise my Name above all Rogues in Story,*
> *I've made Chains, Bolts, and Bars fly all before me:*
> *But, heark, the Dismal Sound! the Clock strikes One:*
> *The Charm is broke, and all my Strength is gone:*
> *The Dragon comes, I hear his Hideous Roar;*
> *Farewell, my Friends, for now poor* JACK's *no more.*

2.2 *An Epistle From Jack Sheppard to the Late L—d C—ll—r of E—d, Who When Sheppard was Try'd, Sent For Him to the Chancery Bar* (n.d.)

> Since your Curiosity led you so far
> As to send for me once to the Chancery Bar
> To shew what a couple of rascals we were,
> > Which no Body can deny.
>
> Excuse me the Freedom in writing to thee,
> For the World then allowed they never did see
> A Pair so well match'd as your Lordship and me,
> > Which, &c.
>
> At thy present Disgrace, my Lord never repine,
> For Fame rings of nothing, but thy Tricks, and mine,
> And our Names will alike in all History shine,
> > Which, &c.
>
> Tho' we two have made so much Noise upon Earth,
> Thy Fate would be now but a Subject of Mirth,
> Shou'd your Death be like mine, as we're equal in Birth,
> > Which, &c.
>
> Were your Vertues, and mine to be weigh'd in a Scale,
> I fear, honest *Tom*, that thine would prevail,
> For you broke through all Laws, while I only broke Jail,
> > Which, &c.
>
> Yet Something I hope to my Merit is due,
> Since there ne'er was so barefac'd a Bungler as you,
> And that I'm the more dext'rous Rogue of the two,
> > Which, &c.
>
> We who rob for our Living, if taken must die;
> Those who plunder poor Orphans, pray answer me why
> They deserve not the Rope more than *Blueskin* and I?
> > Which, &c.
>
> Tho' the Masters were Rascals, that you should swing for't
> Wou'd be damnable hard, for your Lordship in short
> Was no more than the *Jonathan Wilde* of the Court.
> > Which, &c.

Alike at the Helm you and *Jonathan* sit,
While your *Myrmidons* plunder, you seize what they get;
To save their own necks they must lie at your Feet.

> Which, &c.

But *Jonathan's* Politicks must be allow'd
Far better than thine; for he often has shew'd
Himself he could save, yet hang whom he wou'd.

> Which, &c.

But as thou, and thy Gang, must come in for a Rope,
The Honour of being the First that's truss'd up,
Is the principal Favour your Lordship can hope.

> Which no Body can deny.

From *The Quaker's Opera*, 4th edn. (Dublin, 1728)   2.3

ACT II. SCENE I

Coaxthief's *House*.
Wine, Ale, &c. on a Table
Shepard, Nymm, File, Hempseed *and Boy*; Coaxthief *waiting*.

AIR VIII

> *Shep. And when we come unto the Whit,*
> *Our Darbies to behold,*
> *Our Lodging is on the bare Ground,*
> *and we boue the Water Cold:*
> *But as I've lived to come out again,*
> *If the merry old* Roger *I meet,*
> *I'll tout his Muns, and I'll snable his Poll*
> *As he Pikes along the Street.*
> *At St.* Martin's, St. Gile's, *we shall have Burial still,*
> *And here the Bowman Prig stands Buff,*
> *And the Pimps have miss'd their Will.*
> [The three last lines repeated in Chorus.]

Omnes. O Brave *John Shepard.*
Nym. Well, this last Escape of yours was a Masterpiece; none but your self, my
  Blood, cou'd contrive or execute so well.
Hemp. Plague o' that Word Execute, it makes my Heart ake.

Shep. Well, but my Lads, don't let us sot away our Time here; there's Work to be done. I did not make my Escape for nothing. I was more concern'd during my Confinement for the laxy Life I lead, than the fear of Botts or Hanging; now I am at Liberty, let me not be Idle—Idleness is the Road to the Gallows—*File*, have you made any Discoveries lately, is there any House hereabouts worth robbing.

File. You know I only go to the sneaking Budge, I don't deal in Houses.

Shep. Ah, *File*, thou'll never make any Figure in Life if thou art so modest in thy Pretensions.

Nym. Sir, I have a young Lad here that is fir'd with the Love of your great Actions, who hast a vast Ambition to be your Servant.

Boy. Yes, Sir, I wou'd be Apprentice to you, to learn the Art and Mystery of Thieving.

Shep. Ours is not Trade, it is a Calling, Child; we never take Apprentices,—but you may be a Clerk.

Boy. Well, I hope I shall Clerk it as I ought then. But I don't desire you to trust me in any thing, 'til you find I have done something to deserve it.

Shep. That's a brave Lad—fine Spirit—'ll undertake whenever this Boy dies it will be for the good of the Publick. Where did you get this Livery, my Boy?

Boy. I won it of Lady's Foot-Boy at All-Fours, Sir.

Nym. Oh here comes our Intelligence *Bulk*.

Enter Bulk.

Bulk. Come, come, all's snug; let us be gone, I saw where they put the Goods; so I am sure there's no Body to squeak in the whole House. Where's the Boue? Master *Shepard*! Lud have Mercy upon me, who thought to see you here?

Shep. Ha, Old *Brawn* and *Chine*! how is it with thee?

Bulk. The better to see you, Master.

Shep. How are all the Bloods in the Market?

Bulk. All rug, all well, Master; they'll be glad to see you among 'em again.

Shep. I'll be there by and by, but we must mount first. I can't go among 'em but like a Gentleman, as I always appeared.

AIR IX. March in *Scipio*.

> *Poor Thieves are scorn'd the Universe around,*
> *Yet have their Friends and Parties when with Success they'r Crown'd.*
> *Wou'd you be great, my Friends, and fortunate? be Gay:*
> *Your Outside must shew Fairer than your cover'd Play.*
> *'Tis but to fix your Character, and get a Name,*
> *Then plunder whom you please, for all Mankind's your Game.*

Bulk. I hear *Jonathan* is abroad again, Mr. *Hempseed*.

Hemp. Damn the Prig, I don't value him a Louse. I know the worst if he does take me.

Bulk. Besides, the Bum who has the Writ against you, swears he'll nap you, unless you come down another Ounce.

Hemp. Well, am not I going in order to get some Money for him? These damn'd Rogues the Bailiffs, are for tearing a Man in Pieces I think—I rob and I rob, from Morning till Night, and from Night till Morning, and all to stop their Mouths; a parcel of Cut-throat Dogs.

Shep. But tell me, what Lay is this you're upon? for if I don't approve of it, (having better Adventure in my Eye) I'll not be concern'd with you.

Nym. A Ware-house of Cloaths, only—Well, what wou'd you propose for us to do? if yours is best, at that first.

Shep. Last time I broke out, I took a plaguy Fancy to a House on *Saffron-Hill*; 'tis a Lawyer's who has got damn'd deal of Money this Term; he's a *Welch* Attorney. You all know the Place; meet me there. I'll soon force my way into the House, you shall have nothing to do but to plunder and carry off; don't fail, for I am going thither directly.

AIR X. Jovial Beggar.

> *To plunder a Lawyer,*
> *Who lives by Debate,*
> *Undoing and Ruin,*
> *Let's hazard our Fate.*
> > *And a Milling we will go, &c.*
>
> *Whatever shall betide us*
> *From our attempt To-night,*
> *No Mortal can deride us*
> *If we Biter bite.*
> > *And a Milling we will go, &c.*   [Exeunt

From *The Tyburn Chronicle: or, Villainy Display'd in All Its Branches*, 4 vols.   2.4
(1768), vol. ii

He had not been many days at liberty, before he wrote the two following letters; and, dressing himself at night like a porter, went to Mr. Applebee's house in Black-Fryars, and left them with his maid servant.

Mr. Applebee,

This with my kind love to you, and pray give my kind love to Mr. Wagstaff, hoping these few lines will find you in good health, as I am at present; but I must own you are the loser for want of my Dying Speech. But to make up your loss, if you think this sheet worth your while, pray make the best of it. Though they do say that I am taken among the smugglers and put into Dover-Castle, yet I hope I am among smugglers still. So no more, but

Your Humble Servant,
John Sheppard.

And I desire you would be the postman to my last lodging, so farewell, now I quit the English shore.

Newgate Farewell.

Mr. Austin,

You was pleased to pass your jokes upon me, and did say you should not have been angry with me, had I took my leave of you; but now, pray keep your jokes to yourself, let them laugh that win: for now it is an equal chance, you to take me, or I to get away, but I own myself guilty of that ill manners; but excuse me, for my departure being private and necessary, spoiled the ceremony of bidding adieu. But I wish you as well as I am at present. But pray not be angry for the loss of your irons, had you not gave me them, I had not taken them away; but really I have left them behind me had convenience a served. So pray don't be angry.

> How Austin and Perry you did say,
> If ere the Sheppard got away,
> That in his room hang'd you'd be,
> Upon that fatal Tyburn tree.
>   But that rash way I pray forsake,
> Tho' Sheppard is so fortunate,
> I would have you with patience wait,
> Tell that again you do him take.
>   For you are large and heavy men,
> And two the weight what was of him;
> And if a way to that tree you take,
> Upon my word you'd make it shake:
> So farewel now, my leave I take.

And what's amiss done, you write, for my scholarship is but small.

This from you fortunate prisoner,
John Sheppard.

The fatal day arrived, but Jack had still some hopes of eluding justice. Somebody had furnished him with a penknife: this he put naked in his pocket, with the point upwards, and (as he told one whom he thought he could trust) his design was to lean forward in the cart, and cut asunder the cord that tied his hands together, and then, when he came near Little Turnstile, to throw himself over among the crowd, and run through the narrow passage, where the officers could not follow on horseback, but must be forced to dismount; and in the mean time doubted not, but, by the mob's assistance, he should make his escape.

It is probable that he pleased himself with these thoughts, when he said, 'I have now as great a satisfaction at heart, as if I was going to enjoy an estate of 200 l. a year;' though the Chaplain understood it in a different sense. But this hopeful scheme was discovered in the Press-Yard, in Newgate, just as he was going into the cart, though it was not prevented without some loss of blood; one Watson an officer, too incautiously examining Jack's pockets, unluckily cut his own fingers.

Sheppard had still another project in his head. He earnestly desired some of his acquaintance, that, after his body was cut down, they would, as soon as possible, put it into a warm bed, and try to let him blood; for he said, he believed if such care was taken, they might restore him to life.

At the place of execution he behaved himself very gravely, confessed in particular, that he robbed Mr. Phillips and Mrs. Cook, though, for want of full evidence, the jury had acquitted him of both; and declared, that when he and Blueskin robbed Mr. Kneebone, Will. Field was not with them.

He was hanged at Tyburn, on Monday, November 16, 1724, in the 23rd year of his age. He died with great difficulty, and much pitied by the mob. When he had hung about a quarter of an hour, he was cut down by a soldier, and delivered to his friends, who carried him to the Barley-Mow in Long Acre, and he was buried in the same evening in St. Martin's church-yard.

Perhaps there never was any felon in this kingdom, whose adventures have made so much noise as Sheppard's. He was for a considerable time the common subject of conversation. There were six or seven different histories of his life; and several copper-plates, representing the manner of his escapes out of the Condemned-hold, and the Castle in Newgate; besides other prints of his effigies.

3. JOHN APPLEBEE AND THE ORDINARY OF NEWGATE

To some, Sheppard was so closely associated with John Applebee as to seem his agent, or even invention. Anyone wishing to write about Sheppard seemed to have to wrest him from Applebee's control (see 2.1). In *Sheppard in Ægypt, or News from the Dead*, Sheppard, in the underworld, complains about the versions of his life sold by 'Female *Hawkers* or *News-Cryers*', with '*Halfpenny-Posts, Blueskins* and my own *Dying Speeches*, and several other *Grub-street* Papers tuckt up in their blue aprons' (p. 15). He also tells 'Mr. *App*—I am at this instant soliciting a Furlong for leave to step abroad for two or three Nights in the Quality of a Ghost or Hobgoblin', and that 'I shall be sure to give you previous Notice when this is to happen, that you may be ready to pop out first with it in your *Journal*, for I know that Priority is mightily contended for, and valued amongst you Intelligencers' (pp. 19–20). Applebee did live off crime, and, as we have seen, he also lived off his ability to produce rapidly the very latest criminal tales. Amongst these were the accounts of the Ordinary of Newgate, two samples of which are given in this section.

Despite his importance and his fame, Applebee remains an obscure, under-researched figure. He is not included in the *Dictionary of National Biography*. According to Henry R. Plomer's *Dictionary of the Printers and Booksellers Who Were at Work in England, Scotland and Ireland from 1668 to 1725* (1922), he was a 'printer and bookseller', specializing in 'pamphlets and Broadsides', first 'a little below Bridewell Bridge in Black-Fryers', then at 'Fleet Ditch': 'His printing was very bad, and his type worn and old' (p. 8). He later moved to Bolt Court, Fleet Street, and in 1748, presumably because of his involvement with printing material about crime and trials, he became printer to the Middlesex Court of Sessions. He died in 1750, his business being carried on by his widow Elizabeth. The first work bearing his name was a pamphlet concerning the so-called French Prophets, whose activities are the focus of Chapter 2 of this book. After he began printing and selling the Ordinary's accounts, crime dominated his output. We might see this as the context for his printing in 1738, 'for Ward and Chandler', the fourth edition of Defoe's *Colonel Jacque*, 'Written by the author of Robinson Crusoe', and with Defoe's name given at the end of the preface (it was the first edition of this novel since the third edition of 1724). Further editions followed in 1739 and 1747. In 1740 a version of *Roxana* was published with Elizabeth Applebee's imprint.

During the 1720s Applebee was publishing, on average, four or five of his Ordinary's accounts each year. 3.1 is an example from some six months after Sheppard's execution and includes the last moments of Sheppard's betrayer, Jonathan Wild. This is one of the last such accounts by Thomas Purney. Its brevity might be explained by the fact that Purney was gravely ill at the time. It is very poorly printed (thus, as indicated, some readings are uncertain) and contains much unsteady grammar and punctuation. The accounts produced by his successor James Guthrie were usually rather longer than Purney's, being printed in double, occasionally triple, column (priced 2*d*.). Commonly, the Ordinary's accounts are six pages long, headed by a woodcut depicting the malefactors caught between a bible-holding minister and a devil emerging with pitchfork from the flaming mouth of hell. They usually give an extended version of what the Ordinary has told the condemned men, with some illustrative passage from the Bible, followed by details of the crimes that each of the men (or occasionally women) has committed. The Ordinary also provides potted biographies, purportedly from the lips of the criminals. These invariably include a strain of explanation or exculpation, often to do with keeping the wrong company. Here, for example, is Humphrey Angier, executed at Tyburn on 9 September 1723: 'After this, being known to one *Duce* (who suffer'd at the last execution) he improv'd in a wrong way from his Conversation';[14] 'In the midst of this hurry of Vice, he said he resolved to repent, and not only to shake off all his old Acquaintance, but also to leave his Wife and his own House; and the better to do this, he again enlisted himself in the Guards.'[15] We often hear of one dragged into criminality against his better nature. This is not because the writer has or appeals to a liberal conscience. It is rather that the narrator must show crime to be deviant, and the criminal a person who can be separated from the crime (and therefore ministered to). It is this separation that makes the story worth telling (officially, at least). In a final confession, the convicted criminal admits everything and repudiates his crime.

So Joseph Middleton, executed with Angier, 'affirm'd, as he said before the Justice at his Commitment, that it was entirely Necessity that put him upon pursuing those Measures which must necessarily terminate in Misfortunes and Ruin'. He also had been led into crime—like many a condemned man, by a woman: 'He lamented his being acquainted with one E. Paret, and wish'd that he had never beheld her.'[16] Richard Whiting, executed on 6 November 1723 for robbing his master's house, 'said his Ruin was owing to bad Company, for having gotten Acquaintance with two *Irishmen*, who were with him in the Fact, they persuaded him to so wicked and ungrateful a part; he added, that he was two Nights without any sleep, considering whither he should prove faithless and treacherous to his Master and Benefactor or not'.[17] Thomas Burden, a sailor convicted of assault and robbery, felt uncomprehending disgust for his own actions: 'he had so much Virtue in him (for such he accounted it) as Devoutly and fervently to pray to God, and always with Tears did bewail his Sins, and resolve on a new Life: But after the Fights [i.e. naval battles] were over, the Devil was so powerful that he tempted him to deviate from his Resolutions, and to lead a careless Life'.[18]

---

[14] Thomas Purney, *The Ordinary of Newgate his Account, of the Behaviour, Confession, and Last Dying Words of Humphrey Angier, and Joseph Middleton* (1723), 3.

[15] Ibid. 5.   [16] Ibid. 6.

[17] Thomas Purney, *The Ordinary of Newgate his Account, of the Behaviour, Confession, and Last Dying Words of James White, Richard Whiting, and James Mackey* (1723), 5.

[18] Thomas Purney, *The Ordinary of Newgate his Account, of the Behaviour, Confession, and Last Dying Words of the Five Malefactors, Who Were Executed at Tyburn on Wednesday the 29th of April 1724* (1724), 2–3.

He could only blame 'the prophane Conversation of some Companions on Board the Ship'.

The details of the lives and deaths recorded by the Ordinary of Newgate can still speak vividly of the fates of particular individuals. Yet each 'life' proceeds by an established narrative pattern, as if each taught the same lesson. The didactic sense was strong, as were sensitivities to the accusation of the ill effects of the criminal tale. **3.2** is interesting in this respect because it includes Applebee's own advertisement of his unease at the notion that the criminal might become an anti-hero. The extracts are taken from the Ordinary's account of the last confessions of Stephen Barnham, one-time member of the same gang as 'Blueskin' Blake. As is often the case, the story that Barnham has 'confessed' follows a clear cautionary pattern.

3.1   Thomas Purney, *The Ordinary of Newgate his Account, of the Behaviour Confession and Last Dying Speeches of the Four Malefactors that Was Executed at Tyburn on Monday May the 24th 1725*

William Sperry, was indicted for assaulting Tho. Golding on the Highway, putting him in Fear, and taking from him a Coat val. 4 s, a pair of Breeches, Stockings, Shoes and Buckles, a Hat, a Rule, a pruning-Knife, and a penife, on the 20th of April last. he was also indicted for breaking and entering the House of Tho. Hilton, and taking from thence a wig val. 2 s two [?] 3s. a looking Glass 1 s and three ounces of Human Hair val 10s the Goods of Tho. Hilton on the 27th Apil in the night he was the 3 time indicted for breaking and entering the House of William Colbirg and taking thence three Wigs val 9 l and 15 Ounces of Human Hair val 21 l on the 27th of April last in the Night he was the 4th time indicted for breaking and entering the House of Mr. James Walker, and taken thence six pair of stocking val. 15 s on the 28th of April he said he was about 27 years of age he Confessed the first for wich he suffer'd i offen asked him if ever he had been guilty of any other Roberry besides that he was to suffer for, or wether he had Ever had [been?] guilty of Murder he Replyed he Blest the allmity god he never was gelty of the Later and Desiereth me to ask him no more abought any such things as Roberrys for i Could not for give him if he Discovered Ever so many.

Robert Sanford of S. Giles's in the Fields, was indicted for assaulting Peter Goutier on the Highway, putting him in fear, and taking from him 14 s on the 15th of march last.

He was a 2d time indicted for Assaulting Jacob [?] on the Highway, putting him in Fear, and taking from him 6 d on the 15th of March last.

He was a 3d time indicted of S. Pancras for assaulting William Tolfield in a Field near the Highway, putting him in fear, and taking from him a Watch, a Wig, coat waste-coat, Neckcloth, and 4 s on the 18th of April last he was the 4th time indicted with James Little for assaulting of William Taylor and Elizabeth his Wife, on the Highway with an intention to rob them, on the 22d of April last, he said he was about 29 Years of Age was born of honest tho' poor Parents they instructed me and used all they could to bring me up in the Fear of God and always took me to Church with them but i had no sooner got into one door than i went out at the other to meet some of my Companions and went to Gaming in the middle of Divine Service but at last fell into Company with one Susanna Coleman a Common Woman of the Town and at last finding i could not get Money enough to supply her [?] i got in Company with one James Little and some others not here taken and so we went up on the Highway.

Robert Harpham of S. George's in Hanover Square, was Indicted for high-Treason, in Counterfeiting the Currant Coin of this Kingdom, on the 26th of April last he said he was 22 Years of Age and was by Trade a Carpenter and some Time Trading in Timber but [?] October last a Statute of Bankrup was issur'd against me and i being very Extravagant I made it my Business Continually Coining of all sorts of Money. I ask'd him how long he had been guilty of Counterfeiting the Currant Coin of this Kingdom he told me he had been guilty of the Crime upwards of 3 Years but not so much as he had done within this Twelve Months.

Jonathan Wild, of S. Andrew's holborn, was indicted, for that whereas 50 Yards of Lace, value 40 s. was privately stoln in the shop of Katharine Stretham, by Persons unknown, on the 22d of January last; he the said Jonathan Wilde, on the 10th of March last, did feloniously receive of the said Katharine Stretham ten Guineas, on Account and under colour of helping the said Catharine Stretham to the said Lace again; and did not then nor any time since, discover or apprehend or cause to be apprehended and brought to Justice, the Persons that committed the Felony, he said he was about 38 Years of Age born at Woolverhampton and was by trade a Buckle Maker and followed my trade some time he was attended in the Condemn'd hold by the Rev. Mr. Nicholson which he often ask'd him if ever he had been guilty of Receiving of stolen goods and not prosecuting the thieves, he sayed very little to that but told me that his Life was swore wrongfully away by henry Kely and Mrs. Murphy but he hoped the King would give him a Reprieve for the good service he had done the Government in Discovering, and apprehending of so many highwaymen and house breakers.

The behaviour at the Place of Execution,

On Monday the 24th of May Jonathan Wild William Sperry and Robert Sanford was convey'd from Newgate between eleven and twelve a clock to Tyburn and harpham was drawn on a hurdle to Tyburn when they came to the Place of execution they had some time allow'd for their private Devotion which they behaved themselves very Devoutly in singing of Psalms and othe Ejaculations but a little before they was turned off Jonathan Wild and harpham desired the spectators to take warning by their untimely and ignominious Death harpham hanged about a quarter of an hour and then cut down and his [?] taken out and burnt near the Gallows.

This is all the Account that can be given by me T. Purney Ordinary of Newgate.

London Printed by John Applebee in the black Fryars near Bride wel bridge.

———

3.2

From James Guthrie, *The Ordinary of Newgate his Account, of the Behaviour, Confession, and Dying Words of the Malefactors, Who Were Executed at Tyburn, on Monday the 11th of this Instant November, 1728.*

Stephen Burnet, alias *Barnet*, alias *Barnham*, which last was his true Name; he said he was near nineteen years of Age, of creditable Parents, who gave him good Education at School, which he did not mind [but] in his Childhood apply'd himself to Thieving; for being acquainted with that famous Robber *Blueskins*, who cut *Jonathan Wild's* throat, when *Jonathan* visited him at the *Old-Bailey*, as he was going to be try'd; and was Executed about four years ago. *Barnham* waited on *Blueskins* in his Rounds, and attended the famous *Jonathan Wild's* Levy, when he should have gone to School. He own'd, that he had been abandon'd of God, and addicted to all manner of Wickedness, from his Infancy and Childhood; that when he was not Tall enough to reach up to a Man's Pocket, he stood up on a stool and pickt some Men's Pockets and that at other times *Blueskins* with some of his Companions, would have taken him upon the *Sneak* to Shops, and that he crept in behind their backs to the lower part of the Shops, and stole Goods to the value of 5, 6 or 10l. *Blueskins* and the rest going [out] upon the buying of a Pair of Stockings for the value of 7 s. for such Services. *Blueskins* made much of this young Proficient, giving him Fruit, or a Shilling or two, and then he thought himself well-pay'd. He was taken up with *Blueskins* and tried in the Country, where he was acquitted. He said that he was bound Apprentice to several Trades, and that also he went to Sea some times, but that he was of so perverse and wicked a Disposition that he would stay at nothing, as loving idleness and unwilling to Work. As he grew in Years, so he advanced in all manner of Vice, till he became one of the most audacious, impudent and unthinking Thieves that ever was. He took Pleasure in recounting his Adventures, and said, if it were not for the great Sin, then there was as much Pleasure in robbing People, considering the accidents and comic Rencounters which frequently fall out, as in any Game or Diversion whatever . . .

N. B. About two days before he was Executed, he sent for the *Printer* of the *Dying Speeches*, and requested him to insert in this Paper a SONG he was then making, in Commemmoration, and Commendation of himself, *Levee, Featherby* and *Vaux*, which having finish'd, he sent it accordingly to Mr. APPLEBEE, in expectation of its being inserted herein according to his Request; but upon per-suing the same, it appear'd to be compos'd in Vindication of his own, and his Companions wicket Exploits, and villainous Actions, and an earnest Exhorta-tion to their Confederates (who are at Liberty) to persue their illegal Proceed-ings, and glorying in the Perpetration of their abominable Actions, for which Reason it was Refused to be Inserted. This *Barnham* in all his exploits, appears to have been a most Impenitent, and audacious Criminal. He was sometime since try'd at *Kingston* Assizes, but then acquitted for want of sufficient Evidence; upon which, he immediately return'd to his *Old Trade*, and committed several Robberies on the other side of the Water, and about three Months since, being in *Little Britain*, (where he was Born) he shewed publickly to several Persons openly in the Streets, a silver Spoon, and about 15*s*. in fives and declar'd, that to be the produce of the Days Work; after which, he climb'd up one of the Lamp-Potts, and putting his Head thro' the Iron Ring in which the Lamps are usually plac'd, he loudly Swore before four Months were expir'd, he would perpetrate some Action; that he might be Hang'd in that Place, in which as to Time, he has been as good as his Word, tho' by the Lenity of our Laws, he suffer'd at the usual Place with the other Malefactors.

6

CUSTOM AND THE CALENDAR:
THE GREGORIAN REFORM AND
ITS OPPONENTS

THE Bill for correcting the calendar, a major item of reform which in one way or another touched the lives of the entire population, excited remarkably little discussion in parliament. Introduced in the Lords by the earl of Chesterfield in February 1751, it failed to provoke a single voice of dissent in either House. For its advocates (and, the evidence suggests, for much of polite society) it was a self-evidently necessary and long overdue measure of modernization. The advantages of a reform of the calendar had indeed been debated intermittently for more than 150 years. The long delay in introducing the New Style suggests that its implementation was regarded as a matter of some sensitivity, best avoided at times of political uncertainty or social crisis. The comparative stability of the early 1750s, with peace abroad and with major dynastic issues apparently resolved by the recent defeat of Jacobitism, seemed to have created an unusually favourable climate for domestic reform. However, some of the principal Pelhamite reforms—the Jewish Naturalization and Marriage Bills, for example—met with strong opposition.

The purpose of the Gregorian reform, proclaimed by Pope Gregory XIII in 1582, was to rectify errors brought about by the Julian calendar's miscalculation of the length of the solar year. Because the Julian year (introduced by Caesar in 46 BC) was eleven minutes too long it increasingly fell out of step with the seasons, so that by the middle of the sixteenth century the spring equinox was occurring ten days earlier than its official calendar date. In order to realign calendrical and natural time the Gregorian reform omitted ten days from October 1582. The intense suspicion of Roman Catholic influence in England in the 1580s was not conducive to the adoption of what was widely perceived as a 'papist' measure.[1] Britain's retention of the Julian calendar had put it at odds with most of continental Europe. By 1700, when even many Protestant

---

[1] In March 1583 a Bill proposing an alteration to the calendar was introduced into the House of Lords, but did not proceed beyond a second reading. See *Tudor Royal Proclamations*, ed. Paul L. Hughes and James F. Larkin, 3 vols. (New Haven, Conn., 1964–9), II. 497–9.

states had embraced the New Style, Britain's position looked increasingly anomalous.

By the mid-eighteenth century the disadvantages of this anomaly were widely felt in polite diplomatic and commercial circles. The principal parliamentary sponsors of the 1751 Bill were prominent figures in the political and cultural establishment. The fourth earl of Chesterfield, who led the proceedings in the Lords, was an experienced statesman and diplomat, as well as the exponent of a certain style of politeness. The second earl of Macclesfield, a leading mathematician and astronomer who was elected president of the Royal Society in November 1751, lent scientific authority to Chesterfield's proposal. Macclesfield particularly recommended the Bill as a measure which would remove the inconveniences to which 'all those who have any intercourse with other parts of Europe, and such as are any ways concerned in foreign trade and commerce' were exposed.[2]

The majority of the population, however, had no direct experience of intercourse with Europe and knew little of the inconveniences which exercised the reformers. What they did know was that a reform of the calendar would bring a degree of disruption to their own lives and customary practices. The 1751 Act (24 George II, *c*.23) introduced two major changes to the structure of the year. The first, and less controversial of the two, directed that from 1752 the official beginning of the year would be 1 January rather than 25 March, a measure which confirmed what had become widespread practice. The second followed the precedent of the original Gregorian reform by enacting that September 1752 would be a month of nineteen days only, with the second day to be followed by the fourteenth. The legislators went to considerable lengths to spell out the consequences of these provisions for the dates of both fixed feast-days and markets and fairs. From 2 September 1752 fixed feast-days, such as the Nativity and the Annunciation, and state holy days, such as the Gunpowder Plot and the Martyrdom of Charles I, would be observed on the same 'nominal' days (that is to say, the same days of the month) as before. Thus in 1752 Christmas Day would, as usual, be celebrated on 25 December, but as a consequence of the change in the calendar it would occur eleven 'natural' days earlier than would otherwise have been the case. In the case of fairs or markets for the sale of goods or hiring of servants, fixed by custom to particular dates, the Act directed that after 2 September 1752 they should be held on the same 'natural' day: in other words, a fair traditionally held on 11 November would henceforth be held on 22 November. It was further declared that the dates governing customary arrangements for such matters as the opening of land to common use and the time of payment of

---

[2] *The Parliamentary History of England, from the Earliest Period to the Year 1803*, ed. William Cobbett, 36 vols. (1806–20), xiv. 983.

rents and annuities and of the expiration of apprenticeships should not be brought forward but should fall on their respective natural days. As the final quarter of 1752 would be eleven days shorter than usual, tables for the recalculation of quarterly rents and wages were provided.

Despite the efforts of the parliamentary draftsmen to clarify the provisions of the Act, sceptics such as the duke of Newcastle (who reportedly urged Chesterfield '*not to stir matters* that had long been quiet')[3] rightly anticipated anxiety and confusion and a degree of resistance to its measures. Newspapers, periodicals, and pamphlets carried learned explanations of the change, as well as satirical comment on the folly and ignorance of those who refused to accept it. Clergymen lent their spiritual authority to the cause: sermons, intended to allay the religious scruples of parishioners, were sold at discounted prices in order to encourage a wide circulation. Although these efforts may not have amounted to an orchestrated campaign, organized from the centre, they do indicate anxiety on the part of both the religious and political authorities at a quite widespread reluctance to adopt the new calendar, especially in so far as it affected key dates in the ritual year.

Robert Poole's recent study, *Time's Alteration* (see 'References and Further Reading' below) is the first account to look seriously at opposition to the 1751 Act. Most general histories of the eighteenth century refer in passing to popular disturbances organized around the rallying-cry of 'Give us our eleven days!', and by repeating this slogan tend to reinforce the urbane perception of the 'anti-Gregorians', as they were occasionally known, as the uncomprehending representatives of rural stupidity in an enlightened age. In fact, the slogan is almost entirely absent from contemporary reports. It seems to owe its influence almost exclusively to the first of Hogarth's *Four Prints of an Election* (1755–8), where it is associated with the Tory cause in the hotly contested Oxfordshire election of 1754. That there was opposition to the New Style there is no doubt, but it was a quieter, more persistent, and in some ways more principled kind of resistance, which saw the 1751 provisions not, irrationally, as the theft of time, but as an assault on custom.

Contemporary newspaper accounts suggest that it was the date of Christmas rather than the supposed 'loss' of eleven days that became the focus of discontent. The refusal of rural parishioners to observe the festival on 25 December and instead to postpone worship and celebration until 5 January, which they regarded as the true date, was widely reported. The force of opinion was such that in some parishes ministers were persuaded, against their better judgement, to preach Nativity sermons on what came to be known as 'Old Christmas Day'. To the irritation of the reformers, almanac-writers, while officially adopting the

---

[3] *The Letters of Philip Dormer Stanhope, Earl of Chesterfield*, ed. J. Bradshaw, 3 vols. (1892), iii. 1424.

New Style, sometimes continued to record the dates on which, according to the supposedly defunct Julian scheme, festivals would have fallen. It is clear that in some parts of the country the official and unofficial calendars remained in competition as rival systems of time. 'I understand though not like yᵉ Newstile', wrote John Jackson in his journal on 5 January 1756 (New Style), which in accordance with the Julian calendar he persisted in calling 25 December (5.1).

These responses and events are indicative of the peculiar sensitivity of calendar reform. For Chesterfield and his supporters the calendar was a contrivance of human reason which might be adjusted and improved by legislative provision in the light of scientific knowledge. This attitude tended to overlook the deep historical meanings of the calendar or, to put it another way, tended to overlook the extent to which a belief in the integrity of the calendar as both the record and guarantor of custom allowed experience to find meanings. Any disruption to the calendar, however justifiable as a measure of rational correction, risked offending those who understood the ritual year as in some senses a sacred order of things.[4] Bob Bushaway, who stresses the specificity of local calendars in the eighteenth century, describes the calendar as an interlocking of 'various customary events' which 'was made up of many different types of repeated experience, that of work, of leisure, of the church, of parish or manor administration, and of the established gentry families'.[5] Thus the calendar enshrined a collective experience and perception of time. It accommodated both secular and religious activities: the rhythm and economy of rural work and the changing faces of the seasons were linked with the celebration of holy days and church activities, while founding moments in the history of the nation (the Restoration and the accession of the reigning monarch, among others) were also integrated into its memorial structure.

During the reign of Elizabeth the English calendar became significantly politicized and in the seventeenth century it was frequently the subject of controversy. The official celebration of key events in the national past gave the calendar a specifically English and Protestant identity, while Puritan reformers attacked the commemoration of saints' days and festivities which they saw as tainted by their Catholic origins. The 1751 reform may have stirred historical memories of these conflicts and debates. Clergymen who sought to break their parishioners' attachment to old Christmas Day sometimes echoed arguments deployed in the 1640s (for example, that there is no biblical authority for the celebration of Christ's nativity), or revealed a puritanical hostility to religious

---

[4] 'For the old account of time is the true' (*Jubilate Agno*, B, 367) declared Smart, whose devotion to the order of the ritual year is apparent in his *Hymns and Spiritual Songs for the Fasts and Festivals of the Church of England* (1765). See *The Poetical Works of Christopher Smart*, vol. i: *Jubilate Agno*, ed. Karina Williamson (Oxford, 1980), and vol. ii: *Religious Poetry 1763–1771*, ed. Marcus Walsh and Karina Williamson (Oxford, 1983).

[5] *By Rite: Custom, Ceremony and Community in England 1700–1880* (1982), 34.

festivities as such (3.1). The fear that the alteration in the calendar, however slight a deviation it may have appeared to the reformers, might lead to a dislocation of customary experience may not have been groundless. In 1784 the Yorkshire antiquarian Josiah Beckwith reported that

Since the alteration of the style, the *Wassail Bowl*, or *Wassail Cup*, as it was more commonly called, is so much gone into disuse in this part of the country, that I have scarcely seen it introduced into company these thirty years.—Indeed the festival of Christmas is not celebrated since that period as it used to be in my remembrance.[6]

As Poole has argued, the calendar episode illustrates some of the ways in which the nature of time was contested in the eighteenth century. Broadly speaking, an experience of time shaped by custom and social practice came into conflict with a scientific (and ultimately Newtonian) view which conceived of time as an abstract, linear, and 'impersonal' flow. There were other points of conflict, of course, especially where changing attitudes towards time imposed new disciplines on customary patterns of work. This is the theme of E. P. Thompson's classic essay on the rise of 'clock time' in the eighteenth century. Citing evidence from the so-called 'Thresher Poet' Stephen Duck, Thompson shows that 'timed labour' became a fact of life for the agricultural as well as the industrial worker. Thompson also cites Mary Collier's trenchant reply to Duck, which makes the point that, however regulated his labour may be, the woman's labour is more onerous because it is differently related to time. Her varied and exhausting tasks—housekeeping, gleaning, child-rearing, washing linen at the great house—endlessly cut across the boundaries between workplace and home and between labour and leisure which increasingly defined the male farm-worker's existence.[7]

Because so much of the surviving commentary on the reception of calendar reform was written from the perspective of those who supported reform it is difficult to draw firm conclusions about the social identities or cultural allegiances of those who opposed it. Repeatedly they are represented in London newspapers and periodicals as a laughably ignorant, superstitious, and clownish multitude. It was in terms of such stereotypes, constructed on the basis of a conventional opposition between urban refinement and rural stupidity, that critical observers defined and confirmed their own polite identities. Clearly these stereotypes are unreliable as evidence, but they nonetheless highlight some of the calendar episode's more important historical themes: the relations between town and country, the strength of custom in rural popular culture, and

---

[6] *Gentleman's Magazine*, 54 (1784), 98–9.
[7] See E. P. Thompson, 'Time, Work-Discipline and Industrial Capitalism', in id., *Customs in Common* (1991), 352–403. See also *The Thresher's Labour by Stephen Duck; The Woman's Labour by Mary Collier: Two Eighteenth-Century Poems*, ed. E. P. Thompson (1989).

the persistence of a sense of the miraculous and the non-rational in a supposedly enlightened age.

REFERENCES AND FURTHER READING

The most detailed study of the calendar affair is Robert Poole, *Time's Alteration: Calendar Reform in Early Modern England* (1998). For a helpful earlier essay see Paul Alkon, 'Changing the Calendar', *Eighteenth-Century Life*, 7 (1982), 1–18. References to the persistence of the Old Style in customary celebrations can be found in the three volumes of *British Calendar Customs: England*, ed. A. R. Wright (1936–40), and are scattered through many studies of regional folklore: see, for example, Kingsley Palmer, *The Folklore of Somerset* (1976), 161. The best account of the importance of national and local calendars in the eighteenth century is Bob Bushaway, *By Rite: Custom, Ceremony and Community in England 1700–1880* (1982). For instructive surveys of the calendar in earlier periods see David Cressy, *Bonfires and Bells: National Memory and the Protestant Calendar in Elizabethan and Stuart England* (1989); Ronald Hutton, *The Rise and Fall of Merry England: The Ritual Year 1400–1700* (Oxford, 1994); and Leah Marcus, *The Politics of Mirth: Herrick, Milton, Marvell, and the Defense of Old Holiday Pastimes* (Chicago, 1986). Hutton's recent survey, *The Stations of the Sun: A History of the Ritual Year in Britain* (Oxford, 1996), provides a richly informative overview. E. P. Thompson, 'Time, Work-Discipline, and Industrial Capitalism', in his *Customs in Common* (1991), 352–403, is a rewarding account of some related themes.

1. CHRISTMAS 1752

The first reports of resistance to the new calendar came early in 1753, immediately after the first Christmas to be affected by the Act. Accounts in several newspapers drew attention to the part played by custom and popular belief in focusing opposition to reform. The legend of the Holy Thorn, which was said to have sprung from Joseph of Arimathea's staff when he thrust it into the ground at Glastonbury, was of particular importance in the controversy over the true date of Christmas, since it was believed that the Glastonbury Thorn came into blossom on the anniversary of Christ's nativity. Opponents of reform claimed that the failure of the thorn to bloom on 25 December 1752 (New Style) showed that the new calendar lacked divine authority. Thorns at a number of sites, mostly in the southern and western counties of England, were said to be scions of the original at Glastonbury and the custom of watching for the flowering of the thorn on Christmas Eve appears to have been widely practised, continuing well into the nineteenth century. In writings concerned with the new calendar the custom was frequently ridiculed (1.5, 1.7), but, like other customs which came to be derided as manifestations of popular ignorance, it had once enjoyed polite and courtly recognition. Traditionally the monarch was presented with a sprig of the Holy Thorn on Christmas morning. Although the original Glastonbury Thorn was apparently cut down by parliamentary soldiers as part of the Puritan campaign against idolatry, the custom was revived and is indeed observed by the present monarch.[8]

1.1 *The London Daily Advertiser* (Friday, 5 January 1753)

We hear from Quainton in Buckinghamshire, that upwards of two thousand People came on the 24th of December at Night, with Lanthorns and Candles, to view a Black Thorn, which grows in that Neighbourhood, and which was remembered (this Year only) to be a Slip from the famous Glastonbury Thorn, that it always budded on the 24th at Night, was full blown the next Day, and went all off at Night: But the People finding no Buds, nor the Appearance of any, it was agreed by all, that the 25th of December N.S. could not possibly be the right Christmas Day, and accordingly refused going to Church, and treating their Friends on that Day as usual. At length the Affair became so serious, that the Ministers of the Neighbouring Villages, in order to appease the People, thought it prudent to give Notice, that the old Christmas Day should be kept holy as before.

1.2 *The Worcester Journal* (Thursday, 11 January 1753)

Worcester, *January* 11

Friday last being OLD *Christmas-Day*, the same was observ'd, in several neighbouring Places, by many of the *Anti-Gregorians*, full as *sociably*, if not so religiously, as usual; though, it seems, at some Villages, the Parishioners so *strongly* insisted upon having an OLD STILE *Nativity Sermon*, (as *they* term'd it) that their Ministers could not well avoid preaching to them: And, we are told, That, at some Towns, where the Markets are held on Friday, not a *Butter-Basket*, nor even a GOOSE, was to be seen in the Market-Place the whole Day.

---

[8] Roy Vickery, *A Dictionary of Plant-Lore* (Oxford, 1995), 182–7.

To the Printer of the WORCESTER JOURNAL

S<small>IR</small>,   *Samborn, Jan.* 3, N.S. 1753

T<small>HERE</small> has long dwelt in our Country (1), an antient *Gentleman* (2), near *Fifteen Hundred* Years old, who has always been *Sheriff* (3), and has all that Time been accounted a *True* Man, a noble Housekeeper, and a great Friend to the Poor. This Man has, of late, (and not till of late) been accus'd of making *false* and *erroneous Returns*; which Slander the old *Gentleman* laid so to Heart, that Grief (as is suppos'd) has occasion'd a *Stroke of the Palsy* (4), which took away the Use of his Body. Application was made to the——. They made him worse: So that many thought he had been dead; his *Heir* (5) seiz'd on his Office; his Friends lamented; nay, a certain *P——n* (6) made a *Funeral Sermon* for him; his *Passing Bell* rung (7). But, O wonderful! a certain *Old Woman* (8) sent for Doctor *Goodfellowship*, a Physician, then of small Account (because apt to get *drunk*) who by his Skill has perfectly recover'd his Senses, and the Use of more than half his Body. Since which, I hear, his Adversaries accuse him of *Obstinacy of Spirit*, and *Contempt of Government* (9), and fearing that should throw him into his old *Disorder* and *kill* him, I can do and say to his Character, That he is far better than his *Heir* they are so fond of; for I have frequently heard him toast Prosperity to his Majesty and all the Royal Family, and more frequently proclaim *Peace and Good Will towards Men* (10), and always found him to be a Friend to Peace and Good-nature, and very compliable to every Man's Humour; whereas his *Heir*, who is a *Foreigner* born, (they say at *Nice* (11)[)]; and a *Roman Catholick* (12), has already introduc'd a Spirit of Division, Contention, Inhospitality, and Ill nature, which is like to continue: Therefore, in Justice to my *Old Friend*, and in Recommendation of the *Doctor* to others in the like Case, your constant Reader desires you to make this publick.

                                                    Yours, J. c.

(1) *England.*
(2) *Old* C<small>HRISTMAS</small>.
(3) *The* Head *Festival.*
(4) *The late* A——.
(5) *New* C<small>HRISTMAS</small>.
(6) *Your Correspondent in one of your late Journals.*
(7) *Ringing on* N<small>EW</small> C<small>HRISTMAS</small>-D<small>AY</small>.
(8) *Old Use.*
(9) *Your same Correspondent.*
(10) *A* Carol *frequently sung.*
(11) *The Council of* N<small>ICE</small>, *where the* N<small>EW</small> S<small>TILE</small> *was first invented.*
(12) *Held under* P<small>OPE</small> G<small>REGORY</small>.

1.3   *The Public Advertiser* (Saturday, 13 January 1753)

By a Letter from Glastonbury we hear, that a vast Concourse of People attended the Thorn on Christmas-Eve, New-Stile; but, to their great Disappointment, there was no Appearance of its blowing, which made them watch it narrowly the 5th of January, the Christmas-Day, Old-Stile, when it blowed as usual, and in one Day's Time was as white as a Sheet, to the great Mortification of many Families in that Neighbourhood, who had tapp'd their Ale eleven Days too soon.

1.4   *The Ipswich Journal* (Saturday, 13 January 1753)

On Friday last Christmas-Day was kept, as before, about Windsor, &c. and in several other Towns nearer London, and for no other Reason, to speak in their own Terms, than because they won't have a Parliament Christmas.

1.5   George Woodward to George London (13 January 1753)

I find by ye News:papers, that several People have shewed a great Aversion to ye Alteration of ye Style, particularly with regard to ye Observation of Xmas Day; I think they c.^{d} not well have made more Disturbance, if the Day had been entirely Abrogated by act of Parliament: it's to very little purpose, to pretend to sett such obstinate ignorant People right, in this or any thing else; but it is evident enough, that upon ye true Principles of Astronomy, we have been wrong for some Hundred years last past in our Observation of That Day, & (if there is any thing at all in the Particularity of the Day of the month, wch. I think there is not,) the Gregorian Calculation, wch. we have now complied with, is most certainly the nearest: but ye Common People don't like it, because it has something of Popery in it, they say; I wish we had no other reason but Such as This, to find Fault with ye Church of Rome: some Folks in my Parish have been Fools enough, to give their Servants & Cattle a Holyday upon ye Old Xmas Day; who I suppose observ'd the Festival, as they usually do in most Country places, by getting heartily drunk; the Parish in general came to Church and ye Sacrament upon ye New Day; but not being satisfied with This, the Old Day (as I said before) was observ'd too, as far as Ringing of Bells & Carousing is thought to be a proper Celebration of it: but I hope by this time Twelvemonth they'll grow a little wiser,

& not be carried away with such a Zeal without Knowledge: I hear that a Clergyman in this Neighbourhood was weak enough, to drop the First Day, & observe the Last, by having Prayers, a Sermon, & ye Sacrament as usual; if it be known to his Diocesan, he perhaps may be call'd to account, for running Counter to ye Laws of ye Land . . .

I forgot to mention One Thing, whilst I was talking about Xmas, wch. makes some Talk in this Neighbourhood; a Man at Milton about 2 Miles off, having observ'd the great Zeal of ye Vulgar about keeping of Xmas, & the no small Stir that was made for ye Ascertaining of ye Right Day, thought he might make some Advantage by the general Superstition, that prevail'd amongst 'em; he had observ'd what Talk there was of ye Glastonbury Thorn, wch. by flowering upon Xmas Morning & going off again at Night was suppos'd to be ye proper Standard, whereby people might judge of ye Day: he therefore gave out, that he had a Flower in his Garden, that was of ye same nature with this Wonderful Thorn, & it w^d. accordingly make its Appearance very early upon Old Xmas Day, & close again at Night: Numbers of People got together at ye time, to see ye Opening of ye Flower, but none were admitted under a Penny a Piece; when they were all come with their Candles & Lanthorns, he rais'd the Ground with his Fingers, & shew'd 'em the Flower just opening, wch. was Satisfaction enough to Them; their Business w^d. not give 'em Leave to see the whole Progress of ye Day; so away they went fully convinc'd, that That was ye Right Day; the Man, they say got about Ten Shillings by his Stratagem; for it appears since that he had rais'd it under a Beehive to satisfy the Credulity of these People.

The Gloucester Journal (2 January 1753)   1.6

To all Tender Consciences,

That are afraid of Keeping Christmas-Day *according to the* New Stile, This is to Certify, That the *Glastonbury* THORN is in as Full Blossom This Day, the 25th of December, *New Stile*, as it was ever known to be the 25th of December, *Old Stile*; so that, I hope, for the future, nobody will doubt that the *New Stile* is the TRUE, tho' many have, *this Year*, refused to observe it. And, as it is probable that the *Old* may be soon forgot, I thought proper to give this Notice, for fear neither of them may be kept: And, if any Persons doubt the Truth of what is asserted, let them come away directly, and convince themselves by ocular demonstration.

1.7 *The Ipswich Journal* (Saturday, 20 January 1753)

Glastonbury, Jan. 13. We have been a good deal diverted lately by the Number of People that say they came here to see the Glastonbury Thorn (as they call it) blossom on Christmas-Day, a Thorn the Inhabitants of this Place are utter Strangers to; however, as these religious or curious People always spend some Money in the Town, they may depend upon being always welcome. The extraordinary Number of these Visitants this Year, we may suppose owing to the Alteration of the Stile.

1.8 *The Kentish Post, or Canterbury News-Letter* (Wednesday, 27 – Saturday, 30 December 1752)

To the Printer.

Sɪʀ, As the Alteration of the Stile has caused various Conjectures among the common People, (especially in this Part of the Country) And as several of them, thro' Ignorance and Obstinacy, have caused their Servants to work on the New Christmas Day, and not to keep it, but will keep Old Christmas Day, (as they call it;) It is greatly to be wish'd that some learned Gentleman would make the Reason of such Alteration more obvious to the Public, by inserting it in your Paper. It is likewise to be wish'd that some proper Method could be taken to hinder such Proceedings. I am, Sir,

Your constant Reader,

Dover, 27th December 1752.   P.S.[9]

1.9 *The Kentish Post* (Wednesday, 31 January – Saturday, 3 February 1753)

Extract of a Letter from Kettering in Northamptonshire, which shews the Incredulousness of the Country Folks in regard to the Old and New Christmas.

'According to Custom I send a Chin and a Cupple of Pullets; so now, Sir, I must tell you the Nuse of our Country; the People uss'd to ring a Midnight Peal on Christmas Day, but before they begin to ring they listen to the Bees to hear if they

---

[9] This hint was taken up in the *Kentish Post*, 13 Jan. 1753, which included a lengthy essay 'On Christmas Day' by John Barnett.

sung, but they did not sing on the New Christmas-Day, so they did not ring; but the Bees sung on Old Christmas Day and then the Bells rang; so wishing you all a happy New Year, and many of them.

H—K—

N.B. They will be in Town the 6th of January, Old Stile, 1753—Pray mind the Day.'

Berrow's Worcester Journal (Thursday, 16 January 1755)   1.10

To the PRINTER, &c.

Concerning CHRISTMAS-DAY.

WHEN one considers how little the People of *England* are disposed to submit to the Higher Powers, how tenacious of Ancient Usages, how jealous of Innovations, how high an Opinion they have of their own Private Judgment, and how little Complaisance for the Judgment of their Betters; it appears very amazing how any Improvements or Alterations have ever been introduced, but especially that Great One of the Reformation. The Methods of Human Policy could never have been able to have brought that Great Work to Perfection, without a superior Influence and Direction—What leads me to these Reflections is the surprising Obstinacy and Reluctance of some, and the real Scruples and Difficulties of others, about the late Alterations that have been made in the Form of the Year, by which Means the Fixed Feasts fall out something sooner than they did formerly. As to the Obstinate, there's no reckoning with them; but to the Scrupulous I have some thing to say which I hope may be of Service, and for their Sakes I have taken the Liberty to trouble the Publick with my Thoughts on that Subject.

First, then, I would recommend to them to consider that *Obedience is better than Sacrifice*, and that it is our Duty, whose Business it is to obey, not to make Laws, to study to be quiet, and to mind our own Business; not to intermeddle unnecessarily with what does not concern us, but especially with Things we don't understand, or are absolutely incapable of forming a true Judgment about . . .

When the Church-Doors are open, 'tis not the People's Choice whether they will come or not, it's Everybody's Duty to be there;—and if they have a Fancy to Mince-Pies and Baked Pudding upon *both* Days, let them invite the Author and the Printer to *Dinner*, and they will make no Difficulty of accepting the Favour.

2. CHAPBOOK AND ESSAY

Narratives of miraculous events, often of recent occurrence, were a stock feature of eighteenth-century chapbooks. The legend of the Glastonbury Thorn was related in an undated chapbook entitled *The Holy Disciple; Or, The History of Joseph of Arimathea*. In 1753 it was given specific topical application to the calendar controversy in *The Wonderful Works of God*, a crudely printed chapbook priced at 1*d*. (**2.1**). A correspondent in the *York Courant* (18 December 1753) reported that the chapbook had greatly increased popular belief in the legend, and protested that the itinerant sellers of such material should have 'a little more Regard to their Characters in what they distribute about amongst the lower Class of Mankind'. The intended readership and cultural values of *The World* (1753–6), a weekly periodical designed primarily 'to ridicule, with novelty and good humour, the fashions, follies, vices and absurdities of that part of the human species which calls itself the WORLD'[10] were clearly very different. Among its contributors was Chesterfield, prime mover of the 1751 Act. The tenth issue (**2.2**), one of the periodical's 'excursions into the country', an ironic defence of the Old Style and popular superstition, was written by Horace Walpole.

2.1   From *The Wonderful Works of God* (1753)

Shewing the Difference betweeo the Old Cdristmas and the New. Which appears by the holy *Thorn* that grows in *Glastonbury* Field in *Somersetshire;* which upon the 5th of *January* last, 1753, being old *Christmas Day*, was in the full Bloom, and there was a great many Gentlemen and Ladies from all Parts of *England* to see that beautiful *Thorn* where *Joseph* of *Arimathea* pitched his Staff, within two Miles of *Glastonbury*, to the great surprize of the Spectators, to see it bud, blossom, and fade, at the Hour of twelve, on Old Christmas Day, where a Sermon was preached at the same time, by one Mr. *Smith*.   Price One Penny

BUT what is now remarkable of the *White Thorne*, otherwise called the *Holy Thorne*, which to this Day is noted through all Enrope, for its budding on Christmas Day in the Morning, Blossoming at Noon, and fading at Night, the reason is,—It was the Staff of *Joseph of Arimathea*, which he used in travelling, and fixed

---

[10] 'Advertisement', *The World*, 4 Jan. 1753, p. 5.

it in the Eatth in the Place where the white Thorn now grows, it grew to what it is now; and tho' the Time of Popery in this Kingdom is now abolished, yet do thousands of People of different Opinions, go once a Year to see it, it being a most miraculous Curiosity, and brings many People from beyond Sea to see it, at its usual Time of budding, it being a Wonder supernatural, as being a matter contrary to the Course of Nature, and may make us cry out with the Psalmist, *O Lord, how wonderful are thy Way!*

This most holy Disciple, *Joseph of Arimathea*, was appointed and ordained by the Twelve to go and preach the Gospel in *England*; and according to his Mission given him, he took shipping at *Joppa*, a seaport Town in *Judea*, and sailing in many dangerous Storms through the *Mediterranean*, and other Seas, till at length he landed in *Burrow-bay* in *Somersetshire*, and then went eleven miles Eastward, that Day, which was to *Glastonbury*, where fixing his Pilgrim's Staff in the Ground, it was no sooner set in the Earth, but like *Aaron's* Rod, (which blossomed Flowers) when ther was a Contest between him and other learned Jews for the Priesthood, it was presently turned into a blossoming Thorn, which supernatural Miracle made the numerous Spectators, who came to see this Stranger, to be very attentive to hear his preaching the Gospel, which was concerning Christ crucified for the Redemption of Mankind.

At *Glastonbury* in *Somersetshire*, he arriv'd about three Years after the Death of our blessed Redeemer, being then th, 44th Year of his Age, doing wonderful Miracles, brought to the Conversion of Christ above 1000 Souls. He baptized at the City of *Wells*, four Miles from *Glastonbury*, above 5000 Persons in one *Day*: He piously persuaded them not to hazard the Salvation of their Souls, in the Worshiping the *Sun, Moon*, and *Strs*. Thus *Joseph of Arimathea* by his godly Life and good Behaziuor obtained the good Will of one *Ethelbertus*, a King, then reigning in the West of *England*; he converted many of his Nobles to the Christian Faith, & founded that famous Abby at *Glastonbury*, which, is said to be the first Christian Church . . .

On the 5th Day of *January* last 1753, being Old Christmas Day, the aforementioned Thorn was seen to bud, blossom, and fade, in the Presence of great numbers of Spectators; who by that were well assured the Old Christmas Day was right, (not the other) according to the new *Stile*; and at the same Time they heard a Sermon preached on that Occasion, by Mr. *Smith*.

On the Holy Thorn
GREAT *Joseph* to our Island came,
And piously liv'd in the same.
Three Pagan Kings converted he,
By preaching Christ most faithfully.
Lo, Faith and Charity was here,

And to this Day some Marks appear;
Which now, alas! we only show,
But most lament that do it know,
He there set up and laid him still,
But soon God's Wonders there were shown,
For Life and Death were quickly known.
A famous Tree sprung from the Staff,
Though modern Fools are apt to laugh,
Yet at Christ's Birth were Blossoms fair,
Which to this Day remaineth there.

2.2 From Adam Fitz-Adam [pseud.], *The World, For the Year One Thousand Seven Hundred and Fifty Three* (8 March 1753)

THE great men, who introduced the reformation into these kingdoms, were so sensible of the necessity of maintaining devotion in the minds of the vulgar by some external objects, by somewhat of ceremony and form, that they refrained from intirely ripping off all ornament from the drapery of religion. When they were purging the calendar of legions of visionary saints, they took due care to defend the niches of real martyrs from profanation. They preserved the holy festivals, which had been consecrated for many ages to the great luminaries of the church, and at once paid proper observance to the memory of the good, and fell in with the popular humour, which loves to rejoice and mourn at the discretion of the almanack.

IN so enlightened an age as the present, I shall perhaps be ridiculed if I hint, as my opinion, that the observation of certain festivals is something more than a mere political institution. I cannot, however, help thinking that even nature itself concurs to confirm my sentiment. Philosophers and freethinkers tell us that a general system was laid down at first, and that no deviations have been made to accommodate it to any subsequent events, or to favour and authorize any human institutions. When the reformation of the calendar was in agitation, to the great disgust of many worthy persons who urged how great the harmony was in the old establishment between the holidays and their attributes (if I may call them so), and what a confusion would follow if Michaelmas-day, for instance, was not to be celebrated, when stubble geese are in their highest perfection; it was replied, that such a propriety was merely imaginary, and would be lost of itself, even without any alteration of the calendar by authority: for if the errors in it were suffered to go on, they would in a certain number of years produce such a variation, that we should be mourning for good king Charles on a false thirtieth of January, at a time of year when our ancestors used to be tumbling over head and heels in Greenwich park in honour of Whitsuntide; and at length be choosing king and queen for Twelfth-night, when we ought to be admiring the London prentice at Bartholomew fair.[11]

COGENT as these reasons may seem, yet I think I can confute them from the testimony of a standing miracle, which not having submitted to the fallible authority of an act of parliament, may well be said to put a supernatural negative on the wisdom of this world. My readers no doubt are already aware that I have in my eye the wonderful thorn of Glastonbury, which though hitherto regarded as a trunk of popish imposture, has notably exerted itself as the most protestant plant in the universe. It is well known that the correction of the calendar was enacted by Pope Gregory the thirteenth, and that the reformed churches have with a proper spirit of opposition adhered to the old calculation of the emperor Julius Caesar, who was by no means a papist. Near two years ago the popish calendar was brought in (I hope by persons well-affected!) certain it is that the Glastonbury thorn has preserved its inflexibility, and observed it's old anniversary. Many thousand spectators visited it on the parliamentary Christmas-day—Not a bud was to be seen!—On the true nativity it was covered with blossoms. One must be an infidel indeed to spurn at such authority. Had I been consulted (and mathematical studies have not been the most inconsiderable of my speculations), instead of turning the calendar topsy-turvy by fantastic calculations, I should have proposed to regulate the year by the infallible Somersetshire thorn, and to have reckoned the months from Christmas-day, which should always have been kept as the Glastonbury thorn should blow.

MANY inconveniences, to be sure, would follow from this system, but as holy things ought to be the first consideration of a religious nation, the inconveniences should be overlooked. The thorn can never blow but on the true Christmas-day; and consequently the apprehension of the year's becoming inverted by sticking to the Julian account can never hold. If the course of the sun varies, astronomers may find some way to adjust that: but it is preposterous, not to say presumptuous, to be celebrating Christmas-day, when the Glastonbury thorn, which certainly must know times and seasons better than an almanack-maker, declares it to be heresy.

NOR is Christmas-day the only jubilee which will be morally disturbed by this innovation. There is another anniversary of no less celebrity among Englishmen, equally marked by a marvellous concomitance of circumstances, and which I venture to prognosticate will not attend the erroneous calculation of the present

---

[11] As a result of the alteration of the calendar the opening of Bartholomew Fair was moved from its traditional date of 24 August to 3 September. George Lillo's tragedy *The London Merchant* (1731) was reputedly sometimes staged there for the moral benefit of apprentices.

system. The day I mean is the first of April. The oldest tradition affirms that such an infatuation attends the first day of that month, as no foresight can escape, no vigilance can defeat. Deceit is successful on that day out of the mouths of babes and sucklings. Grave citizens have been bit upon it; usurers have lent their money on bad security; experienced matrons have married very disappointing young fellows; mathematicians have missed the longitude; alchymists the philosopher's stone; and politicians preferment on that day.

WHAT confusion will not follow, if the great body of the nation are disappointed of their peculiar holiday! This country was formerly disturbed with very fatal quarrels about the celebration of Easter; and no wise man will tell me that it is not as reasonable to fall out for the observance of April-fool-day. Can any benefits arising from a regulated calendar make amends for an occasion of new sects? How many warm men may resent an attempt to play them off on a false first of April, who would have submitted to the custom of being made fools on the old computation? If our clergy come to be divided about Folly's anniversary, we may well expect all the mischiefs attendant on religious wars; and we shall have reason to wish that the Glastonbury thorn would declare as remarkably in favour of the true April-fool-day, as it has in behalf of the genuine Christmas . . .

3. CLERICAL INSTRUCTION

The year 1753 saw the publication of a group of pamphlets and printed sermons specifically addressed to rural congregations, invoking the clergyman's spiritual authority to instruct his unenlightened flock in the merits of the new calendar. Like contemporary publications of the Society for the Promotion of Christian Knowledge, some of these tracts were subsidized with a view to securing a wide readership. *A Sermon Preached to a Country Congregation . . . To reconcile the People to the New Stile* (3rd edn., 1754) was sold at 'Price One Penny, or 6s. 6d. a Hundred to give away'. Such measures indicate the importance the Church attached to retaining control over the interlocking customary and ecclesiastical calendars, a control which the resistance to the 'new' Christmas may have seemed to put in doubt. Some writers saw the calendar controversy as an opportunity to pursue the old campaign against such loosely religious festivals as wakes. In so far as they originated as celebrations of the patron saint of a church, wakes could claim a spiritual function and a place in the local ecclesiastical calendar, but, as sermon writers complained, they had become primarily occasions for recreation—'a community's own petty carnival' as Robert Malcolmson puts it.[12]

3.1 From Francis Blackburne, *A Sermon Preached to a Large Congregation in the Country, on Friday January 5, 1753. Being the Day distinguish'd in the Almanacks for this present Year, by the Title of Old Christmas-Day. By the Vicar of the Parish.*[13]

GALATIANS iv. 9, 10, 11.

But now after that ye have known God, or rather are known of God, how turn ye again to the weak and beggarly Elements, whereunto ye desire again to be in bondage? Ye observe days, and months and times and years. I am afraid of you, lest I have bestowed upon you labour in vain.

IT gives me a most sensible pleasure, dear christian brethren, to see so many of you assembled together on this occasion; not because it is on *this* occasion, but because I am glad of *every* occasion that offers of ministring to your edification; and I rejoice in *this* no otherwise, nor upon any other account, than as it affords me an opportunity of preaching the truth to you as it is in *Jesus*.

But, however, as a very particular motive has brought a greater number of you together, at this time, than I have seen at this church for some years, it is proper that I should pay some regard to *that*; I will therefore answer your expectations so far as to give you *a Sermon on the day*, and the rather because I perceive you are disappointed of *something else* that you expected.

You are disappointed, I suppose, that the service for *Christmas-day* has not been read; and you will wonder the more at this, when you recollect that I have, on many occasions, complied with your little fancies and prejudices, in some things contrary to my own judgement, that, if possible, I might prevail with you, by such compliance, to consider, or, as the case required, to act for your own good in *other* things of more importance.

You may well expect, therefore, that I should give you some satisfactory account why I have not been so yielding now as at other times; and *that* I am now going to attempt, not without great hopes, that if I may but have an attentive hearing, and an impartial judgment, on your part, I shall dismiss you very well satisfied with *me*, and not dissatisfied with yourselves for attending at church

---

[12] *Popular Recreations in English Society 1700–1850* (Cambridge, 1973), 19.
[13] Blackburne (1705–87) was rector of Richmond, Yorkshire, from 1739 and archdeacon of Cleveland from 1750.

without performing that particular worship which you designed: *I speak to you as to wise men; judge ye what I say.*

The first reason I will give you why I have not read the service appointed in our liturgy and calendar for *Christmas-day*, but only the common prayers and service for the *fifth* day of *January* is, that I am forbidden to do otherwise by law, and by the strongest sort of human law in this kingdom, namely, an *act of parliament*, which is a law made by the king, lords, and commons in the supreme council of this nation, to whom both you and I have given a full power to act for us on all public occasions, and in matters of a thousand times more concern to us, than the keeping of *Christmas-day* . . .

Now I have it from good authority, as I will convince any of you that desire it, that our gracious sovereign king *George* gave his consent to this act of parliament most readily and willingly, as a law that would not do the least harm to religion, and would moreover be of great service to his own subjects, in carrying on their trading correspondence in foreign countries, where the time has been reckoned in *this* (which you think a *new*) way, for almost 170 Years; and you will agree with me, I am sure, that which is good for trade, cannot be bad for us, who are so much obliged to it for the necessaries of life . . .

I would not willingly give offence to the meanest man or woman among you, nor do I mean it; but as you have in a manner constrained me, I will speak my mind freely upon this occasion, not knowing when I may have another so proper for the purpose. To be plain, then, if it would have pleased you *as well*, it would have pleased me *much better*, if the king and parliament, instead of ordering us to keep *Christmas-day* eleven days before the usual time, had ordained that not only *that*, but any other festival (our weekly *Sundays* excepted) should not be kept at all.

My principal reason for saying this is, that it would be much better no religious respect should be paid to such times, than that this respect should be accompanied with so much riot and luxury, so many superstitious and profane sports and pastimes, together with so much gaming, cursing, swearing, drunkenness and debauchery as the yearly return of these times brings along with it.

I am at the best uncertain what authority we have (besides the statute law) for setting apart any times in honour of our Saviour and his apostles, save one day in seven: but I am as sure as the scriptures can make me, that such revels and disorders as are practised at *Easter*, *Whitsuntide*, and above all at *Christmas*, are most expressly contrary to the purity of the christian religion, and to the precept and example of the blessed and holy *Jesus*.

How can we possibly suppose that the formal devotions offered by certain persons at a particular season, with a pretence of honouring *Jesus Christ* more especially *then* than at other times, should be acceptable to him, when other portions of the same season are on the very same pretence employed in dissolute revels, in gluttony and drunkenness, and other vices and follies most contrary to the spirit and tenor of his whole gospel? Suppose, for want of more solid proofs of our obedience, any of us should say at the last day of account, 'Lord, Lord, have we not kept the feast of thy nativity every year in honour of thy name?' might he not, and will he not answer us with the greatest truth and justice; *'verily I say unto you, I know you not, depart from me ye workers of iniquity'* . . .

Now if any commandment of God, or any precept of *Christ* or his apostles had laid as good a foundation for keeping *Christmas-day*, as the fourth commandment has for keeping *Sunday*, I should have paid the very same respect to the one that I do to the other; but I can find no such thing, except in some catechisms which the papists have set out, wherein indeed they have put down this for one of the ten commandments, *viz. 'remember thou sanctify the holidays;'* which they do to cover their knavery and impiety in leaving out the second commandment, and at the same time, to mislead the common people into a belief that their superstitious institutions are of divine authority: thus do their wicked priests abuse the word of God first, that they may more easily abuse the poor people afterwards . . .

As it is, I own I don't see how we can get clear of the objection which the dissenters make to our celebration of these festivals, *viz.* that it is a remnant of popery; I have set myself about it twenty times, but could never find nor make any defence for them but on popish principles, for the ready reception of which in *other* articles, I have some reason to believe these *beggarly elements* prepare no small numbers of our common people.

I would not therefore have you, my brethren, to imagine that I charge these things upon *you*, as your own proper and peculiar fault; I am sensible you have been trained up and fixed in them by education, authority, and prejudices, the strength and force of which I very well know, having myself been under the bondage of them for no small part of my life . . .

4. THE NEW STYLE IN THE ALMANACS

As the form of publication most directly concerned with time, almanacs might have been expected to take a special interest in the new calendar. While a number of almanacs for 1752 and later years provide factual information concerning the implications of the change, one almanac-writer, Henry Season, offered a stream of comment in verse and prose on the reform well into the 1760s. As we saw in Chapter 4, the eighteenth-century almanac had a wide readership but was often looked down on for its supposedly low content and attacked for helping to perpetuate popular superstition. Season, however, claimed a scientific validity for his work. Far from sympathizing with the opponents of reform he carried on a regular assault on these 'conceited Peasants', as he called them (4.3). His irritation appears to have been strengthened by direct experience of resistance to the calendar in his own parish of Broomham, near Devizes in Wiltshire (4.4).

4.1 *Speculum Anni Redivivum: Or, An Almanack for the Year of Our Lord 1752. By Henry Season, Licensed Physician, and Student in the Asteral Sciences* (London: for the Company of Stationers)

[September]

Reader! more just now run Time's fleeting Sands,
Since *Caesar* has with *Gregory* shook Hands.
Shall *Britons*, fam'd for astronomic Light,
Still be reprov'd their Clock of Time's not right?
To mend that Fault, this Month is dock'd severe
Eleven Days, to rectify the Year.
With *Gallic* Tribes our future Time we'll trace;
But, for their Worship, that we'll ne'er embrace.

4.2 *Speculum Anni Redivivum* (1754)

[December]

The late establish'd *Christmas* don't refuse,
'Tis what the ancient Church did strictly use;
Then Virtue flourish'd, Holiness was Fame;
To seem and be a Christian was the same:
Shall Smiths, Mole-Catchers, th'unlearned Rabble,
True Time oppose with inconsistent Babble?
Cease idle Prate, who act in Pop'ry's Cause*,
Those that obey or break our Sov'reign's Laws?

    * As the Non-observers of new Time do.

Speculum Anni Redivivum (1755) 4.3

[December]

Methinks, I hear conceited Peasants cry,
Old *Christmas* shall be our's, Laws we defy;
Yet all the Zeal these artless Souls express,
Consisteth in their Drinking and their Dress:
Others there be, that stickle for the New*:
Amongst them all, alas! how very few
That praiseth God, or give the Poor their due.

* New *Christmas.*

Speculum Anni Redivivum (1763) 4.4

['OBSERVATIONS', December]

At the Request of some neighbouring Gentlemen, I shall employ the Remainder of this Page in animadverting on the Obstinacy of the Non-compliers with the New Style. I might use a Scripture Phrase to them, *viz. Light is come into the World, and Men love Darkness rather than Light*; but I know no Arguments from Scripture or Reason will convince or persuade such People as are merely swayed by their stupid Opinions, or follow the Whim of blind Custom. If Proofs were wanting, I myself could prove we are righter in our Time by 11 Days than before the Style was altered . . . But if no Proof could be found to vindicate the Justness of the New Style, the following Reasons should obligate People to observe it; for it is the King's Will and Pleasure to have it so: *Rom.* xiii. *Let every Soul be subject to the higher Powers; whosoever resisteth the Power, resisteth the Ordinance of God.*[14] Besides, it is a schismatic Discordancy, which weakens the Respect due to such a grand Festival. These, with other ill Consequences, must be sinful; and all Sin is from the Devil: Therefore these Dissenters must confess they are doing the Devil Service, when they break the Laws of the Kingdom, and in some sort imitate him too, who is the Author of all Discords: And some such Apes we have

---

[14] This text, much favoured by supporters of the new calendar, is also quoted by Peirson Lloyd, *The New Style the True Style* (1753), and E. Pullen, *The New and Old Stile Considered* (?Gloucester, 1760).

in my own Parish, who are altogether incorrigible, and whose Understanding is scarce a Degree above that of a *Hottentot*.

5. THE EXPEDITION OF JOHN JACKSON

In November 1755 John Jackson set out to travel on foot from his home at Woodkirk near Wakefield in Yorkshire to Glastonbury. The main purpose of his journey was to verify the story that the Glastonbury Thorn blossomed on old Christmas Day. His was consciously an eighteenth-century pilgrimage, marked by acts of worship along the way, and supported by pious gifts of charity. Jackson recorded his observations and experiences in a journal of some 20,000 words, which is dated throughout according to the Julian calendar. The festivals of the Church of England, a significant number of which fell during the period of his journey (November to early February), are scrupulously noted against their Old Style dates. For Jackson, and for others like him, the customary association between the old calendar and these key structuring moments of the ecclesiastical year was difficult to break. To understand the new calendar, and the arguments for it, as Jackson evidently did, was not necessarily to assent to it.

Little is known about Jackson beyond what can be gleaned from his journal. He is described elsewhere as 'a good mechanic, a stone-cutter, [and] land measurer, and I know not what besides', whose 'mechanical abilities were his chief excellency',[15] though he also wrote verse and apparently taught in a school. A long-distance traveller and local 'character', popularly known as 'Old Trash', he seems to have had a good deal in common with hawkers of printed material.[16] As one who repaired and constructed clocks (one for the use of the clothiers of Leeds on their way to market) he had a practical interest in the measurement and regulation of time. It is evident from his journal that he was a man of some learning, whose interest in topography and antiquities was informed by a prophetic sense of the spiritual destiny of Britain.

---

[15] Norrison Scatcherd, *The History of Morley* (Leeds, 1830), 220.

[16] A connection also suggested by his acquaintance with Robert Raikes, founder of the *Gloucester Journal*. On hawkers as 'characters' see Michael Harris, 'A Few Shillings for Small Books: The Experiences of a Flying Stationer in the Eighteenth Century', in Michael Harris and Robin Myers (eds.), *Spreading the Word: The Distribution Networks of Print 1550–1850* (Winchester, 1990), 83–108.

An Exact Journal, or, An Itenary from the Kedar Cabbin, in the Parish of   5.1
Woodkirk, Three Miles North West from Wakefield, in the West Riding of the
County of York, to Glaston, in Somerset, Containing an Account of All or Most
of Ye Antiquities of Glastenbury. And Particularly of the Holy Torn and the
Weary All Hill and the Torr (1756).[17]

THE INTRODUCTION

Gentlemen and good Neighbors.

To satisfy my curiosity I have been at Glastenbury, and am I bless God's Providence returned safe.

The noted Tree at Glaston I find is no fiction, and its Blossoming on
Christmas-Day, I think is truly supernatural. Miracles I find have not ceased, and
indeed I think our preservation and that of the whole Creation is the greatest
miracle of all, considering our present situation, in the midst of sinking nations;
and the wars of elements in the bowels of the earth; and thundring threatenings
of a proud and ambitious tyrant, who now spits fire at us; and is now making
chains for us.[18]

Is not our blooming state of prosperity a Divine miracle?

The Island we live in is only a Little Garden upon the Brittish Rock.

O! How wonderfull a miracle is our present existance. I pray God to make us
truly thankful for all His mercies.

> The bloody field the vacant stall,
> Have cry'd aloud repent.
> Diseases too repeat the call
> On the same errand sent.
> But earthquakes still speak louder yet
> And shake our guilty shore[19]
> Ye fools that slumber near the pitt
> Wake now or wake no more;
> When M and D and double CC,
> LU and double II.
> Do mark the year I greatly fear
> Strange alteration's nigh.

---

[17] We have been unable to trace the manuscript of the journal. The present text is extracted from *The Reliquary*, 15 (1874–5), 45–51, 73–80, 140–4, 201–6; 16 (1875–6), 19–27.

[18] Louis XV. The Seven Years War was not formally declared until May 1756, but French and British forces were already effectively at war in North America.

[19] The Lisbon earthquake of 1 November 1755 reportedly produced seismic sea-waves on the south-ern coasts of Britain. See C. Davidson, *A History of British Earthquakes* (Cambridge, 1924), 371–6.

The following is a true and faithful account of my tedious travels and exact observations &c.

That which gave me the first occasion and animated my desire of seeing ye town and Thorn of Glastenbury was ye many controversies I had about it amongst ye new up start sects of our modern Schismaticks who if we may believe em—are both newborn and sinless.[20] Both these and ye Old Puritans deny'd and scoffd at it. But their denials was of no weight with me, till I hearing some of our own Clergy tamper with it and would not allow it ye title of a supernatural miracle and witness of ye Gospels promulgation in England. Hereupon I formed a firm resolution of taking a Journey. And discovering my intention several encouraged and perswaded me to go and try ye truth of it and a gentleman gave me the following

ADVERTISEMENT.

Whereas. There is and has been an ancient story concerning the White Thorn at Glastenbury (to wit) that it Budded at morn, Blossomd at noon, and Faded at night yearly on Old Christmas Day. Now JOHN JACKSON ye bearer to be satisfied of ye truth of it himself, and for the satisfaction of others, is willing and desirous to undergo ye fatiegue of a journey thither upon proper incouragement and some small contribution towards his expences, and to get ye best accounts y^t he can amongst ye neighbours and inhabitants of ye place, and if he finds anything to answer his expectation if he lives till Christmas he intends to be an eye witness of it himself, and hopes however by making ye best observation he can of all ye passages, going and coming and committing them into writing; his pains will not be altogether needless nor himself accounted an idle spectator.

As witness &c.

Hereupon, *i.e.* upon ye strength of this Advertisement, I had some money given me both by neighbours acquaintance and others and afterwards by gentlemen and Clergy. And a neighbouring Clergyman presented me with a copy of verses not Ipertinent to ye purpose as followeth—

1

If all be true that Authors say
That every year on Christmas Day
Glastons white Thorn appears to sight
At noon in blossom dead at night.

2

Now ye Old Day is still ye same
Though one more early has ye name
But here's ye Question when ye tree
In blossom may expected be.

[20] Methodists?

3

On ye Old Day or on the New
To find ye truth, ye tree I'll view
To Glastenbury search my way
And at ye Abbey make some stay.

4

Old Ruins view, Inscriptions read,
As did our old Historian Speed;[21]
Old Relicks search, ye Span survey,
And bring some fragm^{ts} quite away.

5

And tho' I travel up and down
A stranger there to all unknown
Like Noahs Dove, if I'm distrest
Sine Argento[22] without rest.

6

What shall I do: I'll ask relief
And if deny'd, alas what grief
But tho' I traverse far and near
I neither thieves nor robbers fear.

7

Those mortals happy all allow
Who nothing borrow nothing owe
If I should crave pray wheres ye crime
Or take a token for my rhime.

8

Like a poor pilgrim home I'll trudge
And with ye hospitable lodge
Till I to Kedar Cabbin come
My humble cott, my welcome home.

9

Here would I live here would I dy
Where Princes prize less joy than I
And when my days are past and gone
I'd have this verse cut on my stone.

[21] John Speed (?1532–1629), author of *The Theatre of the Empire of Great Britiane* (1611).
[22] i.e. penniless.

10
In peace and quiet once did dwell
A harmless hermit in this cell
No causeless cares disturbd his rest
And now he's gone to endless rest.

The following is a faithfull and true account of all my Travels and Adventures, &c. during my tedious journey of which I kept an exact account and here follows A Diary or Memorandum for ye month of November, after ye Old English or Julian account the Old Style 1755.

Wednesday ye First Day of November, All Saints Day and Wakefield Winter Fayr, the Gig Fayr and Statiffs Day.[23] A sore heavy wet rainy day, and a north west cold wind all the day. This being ye day appointed to set on my journey to Glastenbury, I took my leave of ye neighbours and friends adjacent, and ordered things Ith Cabin, called at Woodkirk, and came to Milbank and lay there . . .

Saturday ye 24th day [of November] like as before. At morn leaving John Shakeshafts, I came away turnpike way for Birmingham . . . and having got thither I took up my lodging at Mr John Farringdons in Pinfold Street and there was ye first observation I had made on ye mischief of ye New Stile viz. y^t we never had any good weather since it began . . .

Munday ye 11th day [of December] the winter solstice. At morn sunshine and calm. About 11 o'clock I sett off for ye city of Bristol, and was told that ye villages I was to go through was Alleston, Ansbury, Patchway, Filton, Horvil and Stokes Croft. And I am told that at Patchway lives one Mr. William Barclat who got a sprig of ye Holy Thorn, and set it in his garden and it grows and thrives and blossoms &c. as that on Weary all Hill on Old Christmas Day and that many people come to see it. And y^t a man stands with a Hedge Bill to defend it that ye people do not come near it to pluck, or break it. And victuals and drink is given to such as come to see it. Barrels of drink given to strangers and poor and good victuals also . . .

Thursday ye 14th day, ye New Christmas Day, a gallant fine calm sunshine day, like Monday I went to St. Andrews; ye Minster, vulgarly called ye Colledge Church both ends oth day. And the Dean [of Wells] preached out of ye second chapter of Hagai and 7th verse. All ye day save Church time I was at Mrs. Winters, and lay there.

Friday ye 15th day the New St. Stephens Day as ye day before it. About noon I set off for Glastenbury over wet lanes and comons, and Hartly Bridge, and twixt

---

[23] Following the reform of the calendar the official date of Wakefield Fair was 11 November. A *statute* fair was a fair for hiring servants; a *gig* fair functioned primarily as a fair for amusements. See R. W. Malcolmson, *Popular Recreations in English Society, 1700–1850* (Cambridge, 1973), 20–4.

Hartly Bridge and Glaston I was sunk so deep in ye mire and clay holden fast by my left leg y^t I almost despaired of any getting out again without help, however at last with hard strugling I got out, and about 3 o'clock I got into Glastenbury, and was directed for lodging, to Widow Summers, in Nilot Street, a good civill religious old woman; and here I rested well, and without disturbance for there was no lodgers, but I, nor any family but herself, and a young woman. This day was calm and gloomy . . .

And now after a long digression I come to give account of what farther remarks I made from my coming into Glaston untill ye Old Christmas Day, thus it fell out, that as it is said before I got into Glaston on Friday ye 15 day of December Old Style I took up my lodging at Widow Summers's in Nilot Street and on Saturday the 16th day of December being the Old St. John's Day, I went and view'd the town and Torr &c. the Weary All Hill and it is a steep hill and is about 5 furlong in length and lyes oblong East and West and on one end toward the Tor and at ye West end on ye South side at ye skirt of the hill I found a young man graving and gathering red potatoes I stood and talked a good while with him and he told me where ye Holy thorn did grow, and pointed to the place, but said it was above 50 years since it was seen there and I heard afterward y^t the owner of the ground had ridded it from ye place to avoid ye strangers coming to see it. And y^t afterward nothing prosper'd but all he had went to ruin and he died a begar. I went to go to the place where it did grow and meeting another young man with much ado I got him to go with me to ye place where the old thorn had stood. And the young man said, here grew ye original thorn, there was a square place just like as if there had been a little garden, and in ye midst of it a little hole not a foot deep and about ye wideness of a little hat's crown, and there ye young man said ye old thorn stood but now it is at yonders house, and pointed to Mr. Buxton's house, which is vulgarly called Esquire Stroud's great Farm House, I asked the young man his name and he told me y^t his name was John Willis and that he lived at Street and so I thanked him and we parted and I went to Mr. Buxton's and Street and at Mr. Buxton's (y^t is Esquire Stroud's great Farmhouse) I saw the richest Fold of Manure y^t ever my eyes beheld I went and desired to see their Thorn and ye Mistris sent an old man with me into ye garden, and he bid me climb into it, and I did and got two or three of its twigs and came away and went into the house and thanked gentlewoman and she gave me Bread and Cheess and Small Beer so I came away to my Lodging to Mrs. Summers and lay there ye night . . .

Monday ye 25th day the Old Christmas Day a day as ye day before it. Cold rain and West wind till 9 o'clock in ye forenoon. And then I was for going to Esquire Stroud's great Farmhouse to view ye Holy Thorn in blossom but Mrs. Bartlett my hostess said it was needless for ye same was to be seen at ye far end of ye street at Mr. Downey's, and I heard 'em say y^t it begain to put out between 2 and 3 o'clock in the morning so I went to Mr. Downey's and Mrs. Downey went with me into ye orchard or garden I know not which and there it stands amongst ye large appletrees it is a large tall tree and ye body bole or trunk of ye tree is as thick as a man's body or thereabout. I got a small twig of it as it was partly in bud and hardly in blossom. I thanked ye gentlewoman and came away to my lodging house ye 7 stars, and about noon to Magdalen vulgarly Milin Street and to Chain-gate call'd William Ralls's house and he civilly gave me some Chaingate blossom of that Thorn and sent a young man with me to shew me the Holy Thorn there. It stands in an orchard at ye back-side of ye Chaingate water on a rising ground in ye North-west corner of ye Abbey grounds and like Mr. Downey's Thorn I got a twig of it in unopened blossom and we left it and we went into ye Abbey Yard and view'd several things, ye Abbot's old ruin'd House and desolate kitchin St. Joseph's Chappell &c. and I took up a stone in ye Chapell and 2 out of ye Abbey's Chancel and ye young man went wth me to ye Mayor's house in Chilquil, but found him absent gone where he was sent for to dine with a gentleman so we parted in ye High Street and I went to ye 7 stars in Nilot Street and wrote down ye passages . . .

And after I had ended this writing I went and finisht this Old Christmas Day at my lodging house viz. Mrs. Bartlet's in Nilot Street. I enquired whether ye thorn did ever bud or blossom on ye New Christmas Day, and they angrily answered me nay nor never will, and I understand though not like ye Newstile yet they say y^t we must not go to rebell against ye Government, and no Divine Service was read yet most of ye day ye bells rang as hard as they could at St. John's Church . . .

7

POPULAR POLITICS: JOHN WILKES
AND THE CROWD, 1768–1770

FROM the viewpoint of the parliamentary classes of eighteenth-century Britain, the unenfranchised mass of the people, lacking political rights, had no official political existence. Yet throughout the period there were frequent and sometimes spectacular manifestations of popular political opinion which the aristocrats and gentlemen who conducted the nation's business could not afford to ignore. In its various and developing forms this popular agitation was dynamic and often combustible. Its richest, though not its exclusive, terrain was the crowd. In contemporary reports, even those which are hostile to the expressions of popular sentiment, the symbolic energy of the crowd is almost as conspicuous as its capacity for violence. Far from being simply anarchic, it is apparent that the activity of crowds was often highly codified, governed by ceremony and convention even in the application of force. The crowd was the main arena of a politics of spectacle and performance; its theatricality was perhaps its most distinctive quality.

It would be unwise, however, to generalize about the political motives and functions, and even the social composition, of eighteenth-century crowds. Recent historical accounts have stressed the diversity of crowds, and the need to examine them in the light of their specific occasions and forms. Ideologically they were far from uniform, and their relationships with authority differed widely. It would be quite wrong, therefore, to assume that popular political activity in the eighteenth century was invariably excited by antagonism towards the privileged and polite. The hiring of crowds for the purposes both of intimidation and support at elections was by no means uncommon, especially in the earlier years of the century. In addition, much crowd activity, occasioned by a growing catalogue of political anniversaries (including the Gunpowder plot, the restoration of Charles II, the landing of William III at Torbay, and the coronation of George I), was celebratory or factional and sectarian in character, and hence not simply reducible to expressions of class consciousness or social protest. Even in cases where the political activity of the crowd was essentially generated from 'within'—where its forms and outlook were consciously plebeian—its social function was not necessarily subversive. While the traditions of popular festival could be appropriated by radical elements in the crowd seeking to mobilize the populace, the associations of such traditions (for example, their character as 'licensed' events) might persist, and even predominate.

There was, then, no 'typical' eighteenth-century crowd. Crowds assembled from a variety of motives: to protest against rises in the price of bread, to oppose contentious legislation, to attack chapels or meeting-houses, to disrupt elections, to obstruct turnpikes, to celebrate the triumphs of military heroes, and so on. In many respects the Wilkite agitation of 1768–70, from which the following extracts are drawn, was an exceptional outbreak, unusually widespread and sustained, and focused to an uncommon degree on fundamental constitutional issues such as the rights of election.

There were two major waves of popular Wilkite activity in the politically turbulent first decade of George III's reign. The signal for the first was Wilkes's arrest by general warrant in 1763 for authorship of the allegedly seditious forty-fifth issue of the *North Briton*, a satirical journal conducted by Wilkes and the poet Charles Churchill, which had consistently opposed the administration of the earl of Bute. Although the episode ended in apparent defeat, with Wilkes in exile in France, soon to be declared an outlaw, his stand against the forces of government, which he denounced in the language of radical patriotism as in equal measure autocratic, corrupt, and un-English, gained him considerable popular support. This support was reactivated on Wilkes's return from exile in February 1768. In rapid succession, he stood unsuccessfully in the parliamentary election for the City of London, was elected Member for Middlesex (March 1768), was sentenced to twenty-two months in the King's Bench prison in connection with the publication of *North Briton* no. 45 and the blasphemous parody of Pope, *An Essay on Woman* (June 1768), and was expelled from the House of Commons (February 1769). In defiance of his expulsion, Wilkes three times stood for re-election, and headed the poll for Middlesex in each contest, only for the result to be declared null and void (February–April 1769). In May 1769 Henry Lawes Luttrell, Wilkes's only serious rival (albeit heavily defeated in the poll) was declared to have been elected in his place.

In pursuing the major constitutional issues which were raised by these events, Wilkes and his supporters exploited the resources of the press and other means of shaping opinion with a professionalism and skill which were novel in extra-parliamentary politics. Yet for all these innovations in technique, Wilkite political culture retained many customary elements. Its symbolic acts—the illumination of windows, triumphal cavalcades, effigy-burning, feasting, the wearing of favours—were often identical with those practised, sometimes in quite different political contexts, by earlier eighteenth-century crowds. It reproduced, in circumstances of political crisis, existing popular idioms of misrule. The Wilkite crowd was a festive crowd, more remarkable, perhaps, for the energy than for the originality of its symbolic life, and apparently tireless in devising new applications for its slogans, signs, and ceremonies of solidarity. The figure 45, commemorating not only the *North Briton* paper which had occasioned Wilkes's first great confrontation with government but also the historic defeat of Jacobitism, absolute power, and a Catholic Pretender, inspired a multitude of visual puns, from the simplest of graffiti to the intricate choreographing, along numerical lines, of social events such as dancing and feasts (1.3).

While not necessarily contesting the legitimacy of established authority, the Wilkites, in common with other crowds of the period, took delight in parodying its ceremonies. As John Brewer has shown,[1] Wilkes was popularly depicted as a leading player in such burlesques. He was celebrated as a master of jest almost as much as he was honoured as a political martyr. Contemporary engravers tended to accentuate rather than play down his physical ugliness, notably his pronounced squint, making him a fittingly grotesque emblem for a self-consciously ungenteel crowd. Yet Wilkes's own cultural sympathies were polite rather than plebeian. His ability to move between different cultural milieux, and thereby to appeal to a broad social range of support, was an important factor in his political success. According to George Rudé,[2] his most active adherents belonged to the class of small tradesmen and shopkeepers—haberdashers, hatters, linen-drapers, saddlers, ironmongers, and the like—although he also numbered a significant body of wealthy City merchants and even some aristocrats among his followers. There was undoubtedly a very considerable—probably majority—plebeian presence in the Wilkite crowds. Thus Wilkite agitation was 'popular' in what we might think of as a characteristically eighteenth-century sense, mobilizing a diverse and temporary coalition of social forces rather than appealing to specific class interests. The extent to which it was divided along gender lines is unclear. In many ways Wilkite political culture, typified by a sort of alehouse conviviality, was self-consciously masculine, but this does not exclude the possibility that women sympathized with Wilkite causes or played a role in Wilkite crowds. Women were often prominent figures in eighteenth-century disturbances, especially, it seems, those which were mounted in order to contest the price of food. We might note that contemporary prints sometimes picture women at Wilkite demonstrations, and that George Rudé's research has found examples of women arrested on suspicion of involvement in Wilkite riots. As far as we know, Charlotte Forman (see Section 4) was no rioter, but her letters to Wilkes are an eloquent record of the terms in which one woman was able to identify with his life and causes.

[1] *Party Ideology and Popular Politics at the Accession of George III* (Cambridge, 1976).
[2] *Wilkes and Liberty: A Social Study of 1763 to 1774* (Oxford, 1962).

The extracts presented below are drawn from a range of genres: newspaper reports, pamphlets, trial records, letters, prints, and ballads. The likelihood of locating material which deals impartially with so controversial and much-despised a phenomenon as the Wilkite crowd is remote. None of the sources from which the extracts are selected can be regarded as 'untainted'. The voices from the crowd which they record do not speak freely but conditionally, according to the protocols and constraints of particular literary forms.

REFERENCES AND FURTHER READING

On the English crowd in the eighteenth century see George Rudé, *The Crowd in History: A Study of Popular Disturbances in France and England 1730–1848* (1964), and *Paris and London in the Eighteenth Century: Studies in Popular Protest* (1970); E. P. Thompson, 'The Moral Economy of the English Crowd in the Eighteenth Century', in his *Customs in Common* (1991), 185–258; and John Stevenson, *Popular Disturbances in England, 1700–1870* (1979). Nicholas Rogers, *Whigs and Cities: Popular Politics in the Age of Walpole and Pitt* (Oxford, 1989), 347–89, is an excellent overview of the crowd and problems in its analysis. On Wilkes and the Wilkites, the classic account is George Rudé, *Wilkes and Liberty: A Social Study of 1763 to 1774* (Oxford, 1962), importantly qualified by John Brewer, *Party Ideology and Popular Politics at the Accession of George III* (Cambridge, 1976), esp. pp. 139–200. John Sainsbury, 'John Wilkes, Debt, and Patriotism', *Journal of British Studies*, 34 (1995), 165–95, is a challenging account of the ambiguous character of Wilkes's popular appeal. Joel L. Gold, ' "Buried Alive": Charlotte Forman in Grub Street', *Eighteenth-Century Life*, 8 (1982), 28–45, gives an informative account of Forman's career and generous extracts from her letters to Wilkes. P. D. G. Thomas, *John Wilkes, A Friend to Liberty* (Oxford, 1996) is the most recent biography. Among other recent studies of popular politics and the Wilkite crowd see John Brewer, 'Theater and Counter-Theater in Georgian Politics: The Mock Elections at Garrat', *Radical History Review*, 22 (1979–80), 7–40; id., 'Commercialization and Politics', in Neil McKendrick, John Brewer, and J. H. Plumb, *The Birth of a Consumer Society: The Commercialization of Eighteenth-Century England* (1982), 197–262; and id., *The Common People and Politics, 1750–1790s* (Cambridge, 1986); Ronald Paulson, *Popular and Polite Art in the Age of Hogarth and Fielding* (Notre Dame, Ind., 1979), 24–30; and Linda Colley, 'Radical Patriotism in Eighteenth-Century England', in Raphael Samuel (ed.), *Patriotism: The Making and Unmaking of British National Identity*, 3 vols. (1989), i. 169–87.

1. THE WILKITE CAVALCADE

In April 1769 Wilkes was re-elected as Member for Middlesex for the third time in two months, in defiance of the decision by the House of Commons that his candidature was invalid. In the absence of Wilkes himself, who was serving a sentence in King's Bench prison, his supporters made the election the occasion for a series of elaborate political demonstrations. These events were widely reported in newspapers. The most detailed accounts appeared in the early issues of the *Middlesex Journal*, a tri-weekly publication founded in April 1769 which was consistently and outspokenly Wilkite in its sympathies, though at the same time careful to highlight the respectability of Wilkes's leading supporters. The following reports of the movement of Wilkite cavalcades towards Brentford, where polling for the Middlesex elections took place, illustrate the theatrical and visual character of popular political spectacle in the eighteenth century. As a political event, the Wilkite cavalcade drew on existing, even traditional, expressive devices, including conventions of emblem and music, and codes of dress. As the extracts indicate, however, it also had the capacity to generate new forms of political argument. Wilkes's release from imprisonment in April 1770 was marked by widespread, and sometimes violent, celebrations including, according to 1.3, one of the most elaborate of the many recorded variations on the theme of '45'.

The Middlesex Journal; Or, Chronicle of Liberty (11–13 April 1769)   1.1

Previous to the election, above 100 gentlemen voluntarily offered to take the poll for Mr. Wilkes; and the services of forty of these were accepted.

On Wednesday evening at five o'clock, Mr. Reynolds,[3] solicitor to Mr. Wilkes, and a few select friends, proceeded to Brentford in post-chariots and four.

This morning upwards of one hundred freeholders of the county of Middlesex breakfasted with Mr. Higley,[4] of Stanhope-street, Clare-market, and from thence proceeded in form towards Brentford.

This morning young Lord Mills[5] of Fleet-market, and Mr. John Deane of the Old Bailey, set off for the election at Brentford, in a coach and six, with flags and streamers. Lord Mills applied to a neighbouring b-r-net for his black servants and French horns, but unfortunately was disappointed, as the horns were left at the sign of the Three Balls in Fleet-market for safety.

The freeholders, and other friends to LIBERTY, began to move from London, Westminster, and other parts of the county, as early as half an hour after five this

---

[3] John Reynolds (b. 1728), attorney and custodian of the papers of the Society of the Supporters of the Bill of Rights (SSBR).

[4] A James Higley of Clare Market is included in a list of 'the spirited and independent FREEHOLDERS of MIDDLESEX, Enemies to ministerial Influence, and Court Despotism', *Political Register* (1769), 81–99.

[5] 'Lord Mills', a radical publican and active Wilkite; see Neil McKendrick, John Brewer, and J. H. Plumb, *The Birth of a Consumer Society* (1982), 246.

morning, having blue cockades, stamped with Magna Charta, and the Bill of Rights, in letters of gold.

By eight o'clock near 500 *honest* and *independent* freeholders were assembled at Brentford.

About the same hour near 90 *Luttrellites* passed through Hammersmith on horseback, preceded by 6 French horns—but at least 20 of these were servants in livery.

At half past eight a small party of the *friends* of *freedom*, passed through the same place, preceded by two french horns.

Before nine o'clock 1600 freeholders were arrived at Brentford.

At nine o'clock the sheriffs came upon the hustings. The writ was read to the sheriffs, mentioning the resolution of the house of commons, relating to the last election being void, on account of John Wilkes, Esq; been incapacitated. Then read the proclamation against bribery and corruption: then the sheriffs being sworn in, Mr. Sawbridge[6] addressed the freeholders in a very sensible manner; wherein he put in nomination John Wilkes. Esq; After, Mr. Townshend[7] addressed the freeholders in such a constitutional manner, as gave life and spirit to every true Englishman. The candidates put up were,

John Wilkes, esquire	{All hands up, and great huzzaing.
Luttrell[8]	{Great hissing, and no hands up.
Captain Roche[9]	Silent.
Serjeant Whitaker[10]	Silent.

From nine o'clock to eleven the friends of Mr. Wilkes thronged into Brentford immensely fast, and before noon the town was quite filled.

At a little after ten o'clock 200 of Mr. Wilkes's friends, preceded by music, and a flag, with the words—freedom! liberty! entered Brentford. This procession was closed by Mr. John Swan,[11] carrying a white wand.

Five minutes after this came a coach and six, the horses sumptuously adorned with blue ribbons; and persons were on the roof, bearing flags, inscribed, Bill of Rights—Magna Charta.

At half past ten o'clock 300 sons of liberty entered Brentford on horseback,

---

[6] John Sawbridge (1732–95), MP for Hythe, wealthy City supporter of Wilkes, and founder member of SSBR. Brother of the radical historian Catherine Macaulay.

[7] James Townshend (1737–87), MP for West Looe, supporter of Wilkes, and founder member of SSBR.

[8] Henry Lawes Luttrell (?1737–1821), persistent adversary of Wilkes; resigned seat at Bossiney in order to contest Middlesex election of April 1769 as ministerial candidate.

[9] David Roche, a supporter of Wilkes who aimed to push Luttrell into third place in the poll.

[10] William Whitaker, serjeant-at-law, and representative of moderate Whig opinion.

[11] Possibly the John Swan questioned in the Commons in February 1769 about the publication on Wilkes's behalf of a letter surreptitiously obtained from Lord Weymouth.

preceded by six French horns, and four silk flags, with the above inscription in letters of gold.

The candidates all stand the poll. A very great majority for Wilkes; few or no votes for the others. All things peaceable and quiet.

We this moment learn from Brentford, that the polling is just began, and there are four candidates, *Wilkes*, *Roach*, *Whitaker*, and *Luttrell.—*Wilkes polls near twenty to one.

The majority of Mr. Wilkes's friends travelled at their own expence, in coaches, chariots, landaus, chaises, and on horseback.

Many ladies (freeholders) were amongst the *friends* of *freedom*, and distinguished by breast-knots of blue and silver, with the motto above-mentioned.

We are informed that colonel Luttrell, with his *troop of horse*, rode over the people who were assembled at Hyde-park corner (to see the freeholders of Middlesex proceed to Brentford) One or more was killed, and many others so dangerously wounded, that they were sent to St. George's hospital.

By EXPRESS

Hounslow, April 13, ten o'clock. 'It was a pleasing sight this morning, to observe the drivers and horses of almost every stage adorned with ribbands, and to remark the joy in every countenance within and without the coaches, and the effusive expressions of *liberty* which fell from every tongue.'

Hammersmith, half past ten o'clock. 'Among other singularities, a poor man is this moment passed through this place, with a threepenny loaf stuck on the end of a pole, and adorned with blue ribbons.'

Brentford, Thursday 11 *o'clock.* 'You would have laugh'd to have seen the *paltry* and *contemptible* tools of the ministry sneak into this town, with *cockades* of the *Liberty Colour* in their *hats, shame* and *confusion* in their *faces*, and con*scious guilt* in their abandoned *hearts!*'

Three Pigeons, Brentford 12 *o'clock.* According to the best judgment we can form, there are at this moment in this town between fifteen and sixteen thousand persons; out of which number the open and secret enemies of Mr. Wilkes may possibly amount to six or seven hundred, but certainly not more.

Hustings, 2 *o'clock.* Agreed that the poll should close in an hour; and it accordingly did. The numbers then were, for Mr. Wilkes 1143, for Mr. Luttrell 296, for Mr. Whitaker 5.—Captain Roche declined.

At a quarter past five the sheriffs declared the number of votes for each candidate, and Mr. Wilkes duly elected.

About ten minutes before the close of the poll, Mr. Luttrell retired from the hustings. The populace notwithstanding the number of constables with staves shewed great dislike to him; and he would have been in danger, had not Mr. Townshend, Mr. Sawbridge, and the Rev. Mr. Horne,[12] &c. taken him under their protection, and conducted him to a friend's house near the poll booth.

1.2   *The Middlesex Journal* (13-15 April 1769)

Yesterday morning a grand cavalcade, consisting of about 300 horsemen, set out from Poplar, Mile End, &c. with colours flying, and musick playing, to the London Tavern where they were joined by many more. One body, instead of going through St. Paul's Church-yard, went down Newgate street, with an intent to call on Captain Allen;[13] and two persons were dispatched to acquaint him of the intended compliment. The captain came down accordingly to the hatch of the little lodge fronting the street, when the freeholders paid their respects to him, by bowing and huzzaing, which he politely returned. Their musick then struck up, and after playing some little time, they went down the Old Bailey into Fleet-street, on their way to Brentford, to poll for Mr. Wilkes.

The above body stopped in their way to the Royal Exchange, and called out for Mr. Dingley[14] to go along with them as candidate, but receiving no answer they gave three huzzas, and proceeded to the Mansion House, before which they drew in form. Their musick then played three times, after which three cheers were given, and then continued their route, amidst the acclamations of the people, who expressed their wishes that their choice this time might be final.

At night the bells of several parishes were rung, and the populace obliged the inhabitants of the city, and many streets in Westminster, to illuminate their windows.

Party began to appear very early in Brentford, for on Wednesday morning a man asked if 45,000 rolls would be sufficient, was answered by one of Mr. L——'s life-guardmen, No! there will want just one more; and having so said, he rolled him in the mud, adding, and you shall make that odd one.

Yesterday the publicans all the way from Knightsbridge to Brentford, sold their beer at 3d. per pot, which they said was in honour of Mr. Wilkes . . .

Yesterday the house of commons was very full, and sat late.

---

[12] John Horne [later Horne Tooke] (1736–1812), radical polemicist and philologist; founder member of SSBR who broke with Wilkes in 1771 over the application of its funds.

[13] Captain Miles Allen (d. 1791), prominent City supporter of Wilkes.

[14] Charles Dingley (d. 1769), wealthy saw-mill owner and supporter of the government; intended to stand against Wilkes in the Middlesex election of 16 March 1769, but was unable to find a nominator; organizer of the cavalcade of 'loyal' merchants in March 1769.

The election of John Wilkes, Esq; is declared null and void.

On Thursday night a party of the Horse-Guards patroled the streets, in the liberties of Westminster; and the Foot-Guards at St. James's were kept under arms the best part of the night, to prevent any riots or disturbance.

John Sawbridge, Esq; member for Hythe in Kent, in going to the election at Brentford on Thursday morning last, had his chariot windows broke to pieces with stones, brickbats, &c. by some malicious persons, between Knightsbridge and Kensington; but Mr. Sawbridge, by leaning back, happily received no hurt.

The person who was thrown down and trampled on by the horses, while Mr. Luttrell's cavalcade were going through Hyde-park on Thursday, and who was afterwards carried to St. George's hospital, happily was found to have received no hurt; for after having been recovered from the stupor which some blow and the fright had occasioned, by bleeding, and other proper treatment, he took an opportunity of quitting the hospital.

Mr. Luttrell's hat, his loss of which occasioned so much mirth among the mob, was the cause of two or three battles, numbers were so desirous of having it; wherefore the man who first took it up, seeing there was no possibility of keeping it with peace, cut it into slips, and sold them at various prices. It is said that the button alone sold for half a crown.—*Which is more than the value of his head*.

The Middlesex Journal (19–21 April 1770)   1.3

A linen-draper in Cheapside, to prevent his windows being broke on Wednesday night, as he did not intend to illuminate on Mr. Wilkes's release, had the sashes taken out in the afternoon; but the populace broke the window-shutters of the lower part of the house; and in all probability would have proceeded to farther violence; had not some of the neighbours gone in and put up candles; one fellow got into the house, and insisted that the lights should be put up by the gentleman himself.

Wednesday night the populace again broke some panes of glass in the house of Mr. Barclay, of Cheapside, for not illuminating his house.

The same night the windows of Mr. Angus, baker, in Newstreet-square, were broke.

A sword-cutler, who lives opposite the above baker's, refused to illuminate, and declared his resolution to shoot the first person who should attempt to break his windows: for this purpose he stood at his door with a loaded musket from dusk till half an hour after eleven; when he fired his piece into the air, and went into his house.

Wednesday, opposite the King's Arms, in Brentford, a platform was erected in the middle of the road, when a very lusty chimney-sweeper being come, he was hoisted by tackle ready provided for that purpose into a superb chair, and being seated, was afterwards attended by 44 more of the same profession, each of whom was also attended by one of their boys, and being likewise seated, a curtain was drawn, when a buttock of beef, (on which was stuck a flag, with Mr. Wilkes's head painted thereon) and a ham, decorated also with a flag, on which was painted the number 45, each weighing 45lb. was discovered; on the side of each was placed a loaf weighing 45 ounces; and likewise a pot of porter; after the necessary forms of saying grace, &c. were gone through, the President proceeded to the distribution of the meat, which he did in equal portions by compasses; that being done, they began to eat, and when they had occasion for bread, &c. it was handed to them by the boys attending, who afterwards feasted very sumptuously on what their masters had left. The scene caused much diversion to the inhabitants of that town.

2. POPULAR BURLESQUE:
THE MOCK ELECTION AT GARRAT

The tendency for Wilkes's supporters to parody the ceremonies and celebrations of the established order has been widely discussed. In developing their conventions of political travesty the Wilkites were in many ways indebted to existing forms of political burlesque, to which they gave a specific political content. A case in point, and one of the best-documented instances in the eighteenth century, is the ceremony of mock election held at the hamlet of Garrat, near Wandsworth.

According to John Brewer, upon whose detailed account and interpretation the following summary is based, the mock election was in its early eighteenth-century origins an exclusively plebeian occasion.[15] Contests for the fictitious office of 'mayor' of Garrat were arranged to coincide with the parliamentary elections which they parodied. The candidates engaged in an elaborate travesty of the official paraphernalia of the election process: oaths of qualification, election cavalcades, speeches from the hustings, and printed election addresses were all made the objects of popular ridicule. In preparing for their often impressive appearances, the candidates were sometimes

---

[15] 'Theater and Counter-Theater in Georgian Politics: the Mock Elections at Garrat', *Radical History Review*, 22 (1979–80).

assisted financially by brewers, who saw the festivities as an opportunity for an increase in sales. In the 1760s there was a significant development in the social and political character of the event. Partly as a result of the production of Samuel Foote's Haymarket comedy, *The Mayor of Garratt* (1763), the mock elections became more widely noticed, both by polite society, which tended to ridicule them, and by the Wilkites who attempted to appropriate the Garrat election of 1768 for radical political ends. According to the report in *Lloyd's Evening Post*, 8 June 1768, 'during the procession of the Candidates for the borough of Garrat, the cavalcade stopped near the King's Bench prison, when the drums, trumpets, hautboys, salt-boxes, &c. struck up; after which the Candidates made their compliments to Mr. Wilkes. The salt-boxes were painted blue, with No. 45, blazoned thereon, in gilt capitals.' The pamphlet *Description* of 1768 (2.1) contains many topical political references (most frequently to Wilkes and Bute), together with a critical commentary on the political establishment from the eyewitness observer, though the burlesque itself cannot be said to have constituted a coherent Wilkite spectacle. In more general terms, the question of the social function of such popular festivities—were they, to borrow Brewer's vocabulary, cathartic or subversive?—is posed with unusual clarity by the events at Garrat.

From *A Description of the Mock Election at Garrat, On the Seventh of this* 2.1 *Month. Wherein is Given Some Historical Account of its First Rise, the Various Cavalcades of the Different Candidates, the Speeches They Made Upon the Hustings, the Whimsical Oath of Qualification, and an Authentic Copy of their Several Droll Printed Addresses. Collected, for the Amusement of a Country Friend, By a Person on the Spot* (1768)

Garrat is a village near *Wandsworth*, in the neighbourhood of *London*. It was formerly a small borough, and sent two members to parliament; the mayor of which taking part in the civil wars against *Cromwell*, was by him sent to prison, and the corporation deprived of its charter. However, they have, since that time, kept up the spirit of electioneering; and that with no small degree of humour; it being the highest degree of burlesque you can possibly conceive. The expences are defrayed by a subscription of the people of *Wandsworth*, and the friends of each particular candidate.

The candidates at this general election, under their assumed titles, with their respective professions, were,

LORD TWANK'EM, a Cobler.
SIR THOMAS NOBLE ROUNCE, a Fellowship-Porter,[16] and Corn-meter.
SIR JOHN HARPER, an Inkle-weaver.[17]
SIR WILLIAM AIREY, a Waterman.
SIR CHRISTOPHER DASH'EM, *ditto*.
SIR TRINCALO BOREAS, a Cryer of Fish.
And
GENERAL WADE, a Setter of Colours.[18]

The voters were sworn upon a brick-bat, besh-t, and the oath administered, is as follows:

The Oath of Qualification for the ancient Borough of *Garrat*, according, and as it stands on the old record, handed down to us by the *grand Volgee*, by order of the great *Chin Kaw Chipo*, first Emperor of the Moon. *Anno Mundi*, 68.

That you have been admitted, peaceably and quietly, into possession of a free-hold thatched *tenement*, either black, brown or coral, in hedge or ditch, against gate or stile, under furze or fern, on any common, or common field, or enclosure, in the high road, or any of the lanes, in barn, stable, hovel, or any other place within the manor of *Garrat*; and, that you did (*bonâ fide*) keep (*ad rem*) posses-sion of the said thatched tenement (*durante bene placito*) without any let, hin-drance, or molestation whatever; or, without any ejectment, or forcibly turning out of the same; and, that you did then, there, and in the said *tenement*, discharge and duty pay and amply satisfy all legal demands of the tax that was at that time due on the said premises; and lastly, did quit and leave the said premises in sound, wholesome, and good tenantable repair, as when you took possession, and did enter therein.

So help you—

Sworn (*boram nobis*) at our great Hall on *Garrat* Green, covered with the plen-teous harvest of the goddess *Ceres*, and dedicated to the jovial god *Comus*.

Happy would it be for the future well-being of many individuals, was the oath administered at elections, of no greater consequence than this!

After parading the town of *Wandsworth* in true taste and spirit of borough candidates, bowing and saluting the ladies &c. at the windows on both sides, they proceeded on to *Garrat*, and approached the hustings in the following order . . . [Cavalcade of Wade described.]

Next advanced,

---

[16] A member of the fellowship of the Porters of Billingsgate, a guild having certain monopolies in the City of London (*OED*).
[17] A weaver of linen tape.   [18] Presumably a dyer.

The *cavalcade* of SIR THOMAS NOBLE ROUNCE.
Colours.
Two *blacks* blowing French horns, dressed in
white liveries with red lace.

Descriptive of the inward disposition of the present times: black *and* noisy
LIBERTINES.

A man grotesquely habited, with a fool's cap on
his head, playing on a salt-box painted
blue, with *liberty* emblazoned on it in
gold letters, riding on a mule.

This figure was truly emblematical of modern liberty, *it being at present
little better than a* fool's-cap *to such as wear it, of a* mulish *disposition, a*
mongrel *breed, between freedom and licentiousness, and attended with a*
clattering *noise.*

Two brother porters with staffs, on the top of
which were little figures, resembling
fellowship-porters, in blue, holding
in their hands a label, on which was
written *freedom.*

*This puts me in mind of a porter I saw once sinking under a heavy load,
with the number* forty-five *scrawled upon his knot, in chalk;* free *in a state of
slavery.*

A man carrying by way of pageant the city
arms, with a wheat-sheaf on the top.
A contrast.
Sir Thomas on horseback, in boots; dressed
in blue and silver, and a tye wig;

*which was so laden with oil and powder, that, with the heat of the day, so soiled
his coat, that I hear* Sir Thomas *is in a peck of troubles; the salesman of whom he
borrowed it, having refused to take it back; and what is worse, his wife severely
drubbed him for it.*

Two other porters with staffs, as before.
Colours.
A large party of horsemen with favours,
blue and gold.

When on the hustings Sir *Thomas* was struck speechless at the universal cry, *No boots—No boots*,[19] having no resource but pulling them off, which he could not do, having holes in his stockings, and thinking it inconsistent with the dignity of *liberty* to head the hustings *barefoot*.

The following was his printed address to the people.

To all and every of the free-born, free-thinking, free-speaking, free-drinking, free-men, free-holders, free-voters, blest with the *freedom* of the most ancient, loyal, and thrice renowned borough of GARRAT, *greeting*.

GENTLEMEN,

As the *Garret* inhabitants are *above* all others in point of situation, even so it becomes you, at this time to make choice of men, whose *garrets* are well furnished with genuine *English* materials.

From such representatives (only) you may expect an extension of LIBERTY and full securities of your properties; therefore, in order to enable you to transmit these blessings to posterity, I *Sir Thomas Noble Rounce*, thus nobly offer myself a candidate to represent you in next barley-mint, with full confidence in your unanimous concurrence on the day of election.

Gentlemen, were I to proceed according to the present mode of candidates (who promise a thousand good things, with little abilities, and less intentions to perform any promise so made) I should have addressed you with, 'Gentlemen, be assured that all the egg-size for the future, shall be laid on foreign pictures only: and, furthermore, that the meanest cobler in the borough of *Garrat*, shall be invested with a power of lowering the *tacks* with five hundred *et caeteras* more.'

But although I do not promise to *do* any thing, yet I here give my *word* and *honour*, that nothing shall be left *undone*, by

GENTLEMEN,
Your most faithful,
And most humble Servant,
SIR THOMAS NOBLE ROUNCE...

[Cavalcades of Harper, Airey, and Dash'em described.]

Next came on,

---

[19] A popular satirical emblem of the 1760s, representing John Stuart, third earl of Bute (1713–92), First Lord of the Treasury (1762–3), who was commonly believed to exercise improper political influence through his connection with the king's mother, Princess Augusta.

The *cavalcade* of S I R T R I N C A L O B O R E A S.
Colours.
Drums.
A man on horseback, in a Hungarian dress,
with a drawn sabre in his hand.

Designed to ridicule the growing taste of having foreigners in our retinue, while our countrymen are perishing for want.

Six boys whimsically dressed, on horse-back,
two and two.
Sir Trincalo, dressed in blue and gold, in
something of a triumphal car, formed
upon a tumbril, drawn by six horses,
two a-breast, and two black postilions,
in drab liveries, having two field pieces
mounted in front, and banners displayed
behind. In this car were seated, besides
others, six performers on wind music,
dressed in scarlet.
Colours.
Partizans on horseback, with scarlet favours.

This hero, on the hustings, with the voice of a *Stentor*, bellowed forth the following speech.

Gentlemen,

After having considered of what I shall say, notwithstanding my belly[20] may give my *tongue* the lie, I think 'twill be best, in order to be looked upon as *somebody*, to declare myself *nobody*: this may seem a little *doxical*, but I'll make it plainly appear; they say to be *great* in the eyes of the world, we should be *little* in our own: and woful *sperience* tells us, that now-a-days, the *less* a man is thought on in public, the *greater* he is in his own opinion. In hopes then to become *great*, I will make myself *little*; and in order to be *somebody*, I will, in fact, be *nobody*. I will not open my mouth in politicks; for here I am sure, the *less* I say, the *less* offence I can give—*Wilkes* for that—I will not move in *religion*, for here, the more we *stir*, the more we *stink*.—*W-stl-y* and *Squintum*[21] for that.— And as to trade, or *mercial* matters, I shall not *enterfere* there; and why? the

---

[20] 'Being a very corpulent man' (note in original).
[21] *W-stl-y* presumably stands for 'Wesley'. 'Squintum' was the nickname of the leading Methodist minister, George Whitefield.

reason's plain—because, at present, there's little or none to *enterfere* in. Thus, gentlemen, I hope to meet your *approbation*; for if I do *nothing*, I can do no *harm*. Permit me to say, gentlemen, 'twould have been well for this country had many of our first ministers taken the same step; for the misfortune is, in doing *many things* they have done *ill*, whereas had they done *nothing*, they'd have done *well*.

Nobody for ever! *Nobody* for ever! long live *Trincalo*! was the continued noise for several minutes, and convinced the public that Mr. *Nobody* was a man of some importance.

Thus he appeared in print.

To the worthy gentlemen and free voters of Richmond in Surry, and it's environs.

GENTLEMEN,

As the general election is drawing near, to make choice of members for that ancient borough of *Garrat*, emboldened by the solicitation of many gentlemen, my good friends and countrymen, I shall offer myself a *candidate*; as well knowing my rights to the freedom of that ancient place for more than thirty years past.

The gentlemen of *Garrat* would have found the name of GOFF[22] on their books of record long ago, but his majesty (whom God preserve) having great occasion for such gentlemen, I went voluntarily into the royal navy, where, by fortune in war, defeat of battles, and other atchievements of honour, I became great in promotion, and dropt my old title of D—r Goff, which has been memorable and respectable for thirty years in the royal navy; for which services, by the mutual consent of *Mars* and *Neptune*, I was made a knight of the never-failing billows, and bear the title of,

SIR TRINCALO BOREAS;

in which character I hope to shine on the day of the poll; as I am not in the least conscious of any guilt by bribery, fee, reward, or any other corruptible method. No, gentlemen, I would as soon part from life as my honour; and I wish every member that has been returned, could put his hand to his heart, and say with Sir *Trincalo*, 'Here lies the good of my country.' If, therefore, gentlemen, I have the honour of being returned, my utmost endeavours shall be exercised in the discharge of so important a trust committed to me, in protecting the rights and liberties of this ancient borough, and causing discord to cease, and unity and love to take its place.—For *freedom and liberty are the blessings we true Britons* should *enjoy* . . .

---

[22] 'This man's name is *Goff*' (note in original).

5. *Sir Trincalo Boreas* (1768). Goff, the fishmonger of Richmond, standing at the Garrat election. © The British Museum

3. THE SYMBOLISM OF RIOT

The political crises of 1768–70 were marked by frequent episodes of violence. While the sheer brutality of some of these occurrences should not be underestimated, it is also evident that such violence had a rationale and even a discipline of its own. Often it was the culmination of a contest for urban space or of a series of symbolic statements and counter-statements. A turning-point of the most serious outbreak, the 'Massacre of St George's Fields' of 10 May 1768, which resulted in several fatalities, was the removal, by order of the magistrates, of a handbill which had been pasted to the wall of the prison in which Wilkes was held.

The previous night had also witnessed disturbances, though of a lesser degree of savagery, outside the Mansion House, the official residence of the lord mayor of London. In the report of proceedings at the Old Bailey against two men accused of involvement in the riot (3.1) the Wilkite crowd engages in a kind of satirical performance. In a parody of executive justice, it parades a mock gibbet, bearing a jackboot and a petticoat, symbolizing the supposed liaison between the earl of Bute and the king's mother, the Princess Dowager Augusta. The contending forces struggle for possession of this satirical machine.

The second set of extracts (3.2–3.4) concerns the so-called 'Battle of Temple Bar' of March 1769 when a cavalcade of City merchants carrying an address professing loyalty to the king was intercepted by a Wilkite counter-demonstration. Again the opposing forces engaged in a contest of symbols. Outside St James's Palace, the royal residence, a grotesquely decorated hearse, commemorating some of the victims of the events at St George's Fields, intruded into the remnants of the loyal procession (3.3), while in a deliberately symbolic act the ensign of the steward of the king's household was broken (3.4).

3.1   From *The whole Proceedings on the King's Commission of the Peace, Oyer and Terminer, and Gaol Delivery for the City of London and . . . for the County of Middlesex* (1768)

William Hawkins and Joseph Wild were indicted, for that they, together with divers other persons to the number of an hundred or more, being malefactors and disturbers of the peace, on the 9th of May with force and arms near the Mansion-house of the Right Hon. Thomas Harley,[23] Lord Mayor of the city of

[23] Thomas Harley (1730–1804), banker, MP, and lord mayor of London (1767–8); one of the most prominent City opponents of Wilkes.

London, unlawfully, riotously, and tumultuously did gather together, in order to disturb the peace of our Lord the King; that he the said Hawkins did threaten to knock down the said Lord Mayor acting in the execution of his office, and in and upon one Philip Pyle, being one of the servants of the Lord Mayor, assisting, and by his commands, and in his presence, him the said Pyle with a certain flambeau and a large stick over his head and divers other parts of his body, did beat and strike, so that his life was greatly despaired of, &c. &c.

Mr. Way. About eight o'clock in the evening of the 9th of May, going from Swithin's-alley to Batson's coffee-house, I saw a croud of people carrying a gibbet, on which hung a boot and petticoat, going down towards the Mansion-house; I stopped to observe whether they made any stand at the Mansion-house, I observed they halted there; there were great hissing and hallooing; I went to the Mansion-house, and had not been there above a minute or two before I saw my Lord Mayor come out of the gates of the Mansion-house, making his way towards the people that supported this gibbet; I believed when I saw them in Cornhill, there did not seem to be more than fifty or sixty; seeing my Lord go out by himself I made my way up to him; before I got to him, I saw the prisoner laying about him with a stick, which I afterwards observed had some nails in it; he had struck one or two people, which afterwards I found to be my Lord Mayor's servants; they had hold of him, endeavouring to bring him into the Mansion-house at the little gate by Charlotte-row; while the scuffle was between him and my Lord's servants, I heard several people cry, knock him down, knock him down; the prisoner had disengaged himself from them, and was making towards the corner of the Poultry by the linen-draper's; I stepped very briskly cross the kennel and laid hold of him by the collar; I drew him back, and with the assistance of the other servants he was lodged in the Mansion-house; the mob was by that time increased to I believe 150, making a noise, hollooing and hissing.

Philip Pyle. I am servant to my Lord Mayor; I was attending my Lord Mayor on the 9th of May about eight o'clock in the evening, my Lord and Lady were going out in a coach; some persons brought in notice that there was a large mob coming down Cornhill; I was standing in Charlotte-row with a flambeau in my hand, I went to see who they were; my Lord Mayor in the mean time came down the steps, as the gibbet was brought to the Mansion-house; there might be 150 of the mob, the street was all full from Cornhill to the Poultry, they were hissing and crying Wilkes and liberty; I observed one in particular had a blue cockade in his hat, the same as Mr. Wilkes gave at the election; my Lord Mayor said, bring back that thing, throwing out his hand; I believe there might be a dozen or fourteen had hold of it, carrying it along; it was a pretty formidable thing when it was together; they turned their heads many of them, but made no halt; I followed the gibbet as far as the pastry-cook's; I got hold

The Rape of the Petti-coat.

He valiantly seiz'd the Petti-coat and Boot at the Portal of his own Mansion.

Daily adv.

6. *The Rape of the Petti-coat* (1768). The central figure is Thomas Harley, lord mayor of London. © The British Museum

of it and gave it such a shake they were obliged to quit it; I turned with it in my hand, and was pulling it back towards the Mansion-house; there was one man came to me, I believe not the prisoner, and catched the flambeau out of my hand (it had not been lighted) and laid it about my head, and broke my head in several places; I let drop the gibbet which I had in my left hand, in order to defend myself against the mob; I twisted the flambeau out of the man's hand, and I believe I did return it, I believe I did not strike above once; I believe there were two or three about me striking of me; I thought I must make a retreat, fearing they should get me down, which if they had, they certainly would have murdered me; I made my way into Charlotte-row, I thought some of my fellow-servants might see me, and I might be relieved; just as I was turned the corner they fell upon me again; I received several violent blows on my head, I did not see from whom I received them; my coat was torn; I turned and saw the prisoner on my right-hand, the stick flew out of his hand, and my fellow servant picked it up; he defended himself with his hands as well as he could, but I pulled him I dare say twenty yards through the mob; the mob had hold of him and me likewise; when I got within ten yards of the Mansion-house the mob rescued him from me; I catched at him again, but missed him, and I believe I was not three yards from him when Mr. Way took hold of him, then we brought him into the Mansion-house.

Q. Did you see any thing throwed?

Pyle. No, I did not; then after that the windows were broke; that was an hour and a half or two hours after this.

Q. Did not the croud disperse upon these people being apprehended?

Pyle. No, so far from that, they said they would have them out again; there was a single pane in one window, and another in another broke, when the prisoner was in the Mansion-house; he said he was coming by and had not touched any body, and that he did not think of any riot at all.

Thomas Woodward. I am servant to my Lord Mayor. On Monday the 9th of May about eight in the evening, my fellow servant and I were standing at the Mansion-house back door in Charlotte-row, waiting for my Lord and Lady who were going out; the people were coming down with a gibbet, with a boot and two petticoats; my fellow-servant said, here is something coming, we will go to the corner and see what it is; my Lord came out from the steps and called out, what is that, bring it back; they had halted, but were moving on; my Lord said something to my fellow servant; he went to the gibbet and pulled it down; I saw the people take his flambeau out of his hand, and give him one or two blows with it, I could not see who struck him; afterwards the prisoner Hawkins took a piece of wood from the gibbet and struck my fellow servant, (*produced in court a large piece of timber about four feet long with nails in it;*) he struck him with it more than once, twice, or three times; I received one blow upon my head and shoulder with it; I received a blow or two from some other person, but do not know who: as we were conveying the prisoner Hawkins to the back door, the people came on so fast, if I had not had this stick the prisoner would have been rescued from Mr. Way and my fellow servant; I struck at one or two, one I knocked down, I believe in the kennel;

when we got the prisoners in, I was left in a room with them; all that I know of Wild, I did not see him before he entered the door, I can give no account of him; I asked him how he could do so; Hawkins said he was sorry for it, but said he did not know he had struck any body.

Q. Did any of you see where my Lord Mayor was in the time of the scuffle?

Woodward. I saw him on the steps, and afterwards I saw him out in the mob near the pastry-cook's; I think he had a scarlet coat on and green silk waistcoat.

Edward Stinton. I am also a servant to my Lord Mayor; my Lord Mayor stood upon the steps of the Mansion-house; he came down and desired the mob to disperse, and not breed any riot; he said he wondered what he had done that he could not rest in his house; he came out at the front gate, and came round upon the broad stones, the gibbet and boot were taken down then; I with the rest ran into the mob to see that nobody used my Lord ill; I saw a stick throwed at him, it came within two or three yards of him; I heard the prisoner Wild say, there he is, pointing to my Lord Mayor, knock him down, knock him down.

Q. What was my Lord doing?

Stinton. He had desired them to disperse.

Q. How far might Wild be from my Lord Mayor?

Stinton. About half a dozen yards or more from him.

Q. Was there a number of people round Wild at the time?

Stinton. There were a great many; I laid hold of him, and I think I said, d-m you, what do you mean by knock him down; he said, I did not know who to knock down.

Q. Did you know Wild again?

Stinton. Yes, very well; I took him in myself, and my Lord was at the door at the same time.

Pyle. When Hawkins was examined at Guildhall, he acknowledged he took the stick from the gibbet, though before he had denied having any stick at all.

Hawkins's defence.

Best part of what is charged against me is very wrong; I am a lighterman, and came from the water-side; about five o'clock I left the Custom-house and came to Bear-key, I live in Old-street; coming home I saw a great mob going along Cornhill; I followed the mob, I saw my Lord's servant lay hold of the gibbet on a man's shoulder, and haul it down; I saw several people strike him with a flambeau; the mob hauled me in among them; the gallows was lying under foot, he had got hold of one part of it, hauling it away; he laid hold of me by the collar twice; I took hold of a piece of wood, but this is not the piece, it was a broomstick, and I throwed it out among the mob, who it hit I cannot tell; he got hold of me as I was making off from among the mob; then Mr. Way collared me, and brought me into the Mansion-house, there the footman ran his fist into my face three times, and said, I wish I had no more to do than to lick you and half a dozen such.

Wild's defence.

I saw a man in a white coat in the croud; I asked what he had done, I was told he was a pick-pocket; I heard others say, knock him down, and I believe I said so; they laid hold of my collar and asked me who I would have knocked down; I said, nobody, friend; he said he heard me say, knock him down; I said, I said no such word; he said he did insist upon my going into the Mansion-house; I made no resistance, but went; I am very wrongfully accused, I was not there three minutes; there was no gibbet, no boot, no nothing when I came there.

Hawkins Guilty. Imp[risoned]. Wild Acquitted.

The Public Advertiser (23 March 1769)   3.2

Yesterday at Noon about six hundred of the principal Merchants of this City, set out from the Royal Exchange, in their Carriages, in order to present an Address to his Majesty, attended by the City Marshal and Constables. Before they got to Cheapside, the People shewed them many Marks of their Resentment, by hissing, groaning, throwing Dirt, &c. but when they arrived in Fleet-street, the Multitude grew quite outrageous, broke the Windows of the Coaches, and threw Stones; and the People on the other Side Temple-bar shutting the Gates, the Cavalcade was obliged to stop. Mr. Cook, the City Marshal, and his Attendants going to open the Gates, were pelted with Mud. The Populace then attacked the Gentlemen in their Carriages; Mr. Boehm and several of his Friends being covered with Dirt, were obliged to take Shelter in Nando's Coffee-house. Some of the Coaches then drove up Chancery-lane, Fetter-lane, and Shoe-lane; but the greatest Part of the Gentlemen, finding it impossible to proceed, returned home.

The Address, however, did at length reach St. James's, but the People threw Dirt at the Gentlemen as they got out of their Carriages at St. James's Gate. There were about one hundred and fifty of the Merchants came into the Drawing Room, and at Four o'Clock the Address was read by Mr. Watkins, an eminent Merchant.—His Majesty was pleased to return a most gracious Answer, and they had all the Honour to kiss his Majesty's Hand.—A Hearse, with two white Horses and two black, joined in the Train at Exeter 'Change, and followed all the Way to St. James's.

The Riot Act was twice read at St. James's-Gate, and the Mob not dispersing, but still continuing to be riotous, seventeen of the most active were laid hold of and secured.

A Correspondent informs us, that it was observed by a Wag at a Coffee-house West of St. Dunstan's Church Yesterday Afternoon, that the Merchants and principal Traders of London received a Compliment at Temple Bar, which was never paid to any but a Crown'd Head, viz. the Gate being shut against them.[24]

3.3   *The Political Register* (1769), 255

When some of the coaches got to Exeter Exchange, a hearse came out of Exeter street, and preceded them, drawn by a black and a white horse, the driver[25] of which had on a kind of rough coat, resembling a skin, with a large cap, one side black, the other white, whose whole figure was very grotesque: On one side of the Hearse was painted on canvas, a representation of the rioters killing Mr. Clarke at the Brentford election; and on the other side, was a representation of the soldiers firing on young Allen in the cow-house.[26] The hearse attended the cavalcade to St. James's, and made a short stop at Carleton House, the duke of Cumberland's, and Lord Weymouth's,[27] in Pall-mall, where they made also a short stay, and then went off up St. James's and Albermarle street.

3.4   *The Public Advertiser* (29 March 1769), extract from an unsigned letter

When the great Body of Merchants, and other principal Gentlemen of the City of London, were proceeding in a grand Cavalcade with their loyal and season-able Address to present it to his Majesty, they were attacked in their March by various Bodies of Ruffians, in so outrageous a Manner that it exceeded all

---

[24] Alluding to the ceremony performed at Temple Bar since the reign of Elizabeth I whereby the sovereign requested permission of the lord mayor to enter the City.

[25] Reportedly Henry Redmond Morres, second Viscount Mountmorres (*c.*1743–97), a young Irish aristocrat and supporter of Wilkes.

[26] George Clarke, a Wilkite lawyer, was killed during clashes between supporters of Sir William Proctor (1722–73) and Serjeant John Glynn (1722–79), the radical candidate, at the Middlesex by-election, 8 December 1768. William Allen, a publican's son, was shot by soldiers during the 'Massacre of St George's Fields', 10 May 1768.

[27] Thomas Thynne, third Viscount Weymouth, and first marquis of Bath (1734–96), statesman. His letter of April 1768 urging magistrates to act firmly in cases of civil unrest was construed by Wilkites as an incitement to murder.

the Riots and Disturbances of former Times. These abandoned Wretches were so well instructed in their Business, that they singled out the chief Persons in the Cavalcade, to treat them with every Kind of Indignity which Malice could invent;—persisting in, and renewing their Attacks for the Space of two Miles. Nay, when Part of this Cavalcade had reached the Royal Residence (other Parts having been obliged to fly for their Lives) yet even there, and in the Face of M[ajesty] itself, they were so far from desisting, that their Fury and Insolence broke out afresh; and a Band, as if chosen for the Purpose, began to pelt the Gentlemen with Dirt, as they alighted out of their Coaches to enter the Palace. Moreover, the Lord Steward of his Majesty's Houshold[28] had the Wand, the Ensign of his Office, broke to-pieces; and was himself personally assaulted, while he was endeavouring to discharge the Duty of his Station in quelling the Rioters.

4. A FEMALE WILKITE

Wilkes's notoriety as a rake and a spendthrift was only one element in a complex political identity. No less important in winning him popular support was his favoured role as a martyr in the cause of liberty, a self-image which his extended (if comfortable) term in prison seemed to confirm. It was his reputation for political virtue, as the protector of the poor and down-trodden, that drew Charlotte Forman to correspond with him. A journalist and translator, Forman was probably the author of a series of political essays which were published in London newspapers under the name of 'Probus' in the period 1756–60 (a second series appeared in 1773–5). By 1768, when she began writing to Wilkes, Forman had fallen upon hard times. In 1764 her annual allowance of £50 was withdrawn and in 1767 she was imprisoned for debt. When a second such disaster seemed imminent she appealed success-fully to Wilkes (himself in prison at the time) for assistance. The extract we give below is a striking instance of her personal identification with Wilkes as someone who, like herself, had suffered social injustice. Forman's education may have distanced her from the popular culture of domestic servants and the labouring poor, but her economic circumstances put her (like many an impecunious eighteenth-century writer) on much the same level.

---

[28] William Talbot, first Earl Talbot of Hensol (1710–82), Lord Steward of the Household (1761–82). Ridicule in *North Briton* no. 12 of his horsemanship at George III's coronation led him to challenge Wilkes to a duel in 1762.

4.1   Charlotte Forman to John Wilkes (2 March 1769), British Library Additional MS 30870, fos. 117–18

Sir,

I was going to write to you last week, but as soon as I took up the pen, my thoughts, impatient to break loose after a long confinement, crowded so fast upon me, all striving for precendency, that unable to manage the headstrong crew, I dashed a handful of them on a piece of paper to cool their courage, 'till I should be at leisure to bring them to order: but as I find them still refractory, I must be content to let them have their own way this time.

Since the 16th of January last, I have been in a profound reverie. 'Tho the event of that day was nothing more than what I expected, yet the untoward progress of your affairs since, has absorbed all my thoughts.[29] I must own I had some hopes that the House of Commons would have done you justice. I cannot express the anxiety I felt whilst your cause was depending there. My spirits were continually fluctuating, according to the news of the day; and every report had the same influence on me as the weather has on the Thermometer. But when I heard the result of the late Council, my heart failed me. I exclaimed, what! King, Lords and Commons united against him? I conceited I saw a Giant armed with a mountain in each hand to crush you. Alas, said I, is this the fruit of my hopes? Is this what I have so earnestly wished, so fervently prayed for?—Hope whispered in my ear, 'God is all-sufficient.' I then called to mind David's words, and applied them to you: Cadent a latere tuo mille, et decem millia a dextris tuis: ad te autem non appropinquabit.[30]—I shall pay you no compliments of condolance on this reverse of fortune. I am not equal to the task, neither do you stand in need of comfort. Your great soul is proof against the shafts of the fickle goddess. Nor wealth nor titles add any thing to the intrinsic worth of any person. You are still the same man; still that homme unique, in all your actions inimitably great! . . .

It is now Sir, seven weeks since I had the honour of seeing you. The time seems long. Fearful to intrude while your affairs were depending, I stayed away; and now, necessity which has no law, forbids me to go. Evils that cannot be cured must be endured: such are mine; they are the consequences of my situation. If my sufferings could in the least alleviate yours, I would bear them with pleasure; but as the case stands, I feel all the weight of yours, without being able to ease you of a load, which added to my own, is become insupportable. I cannot boast

---

[29] On 16 Jan. 1769 the Lords turned down Wilkes's attempt to reverse judgments brought against him by the court of King's Bench; see *Journals of the House of Lords*, 32 (1768–70), 222–3.

[30] Joel L. Gold, '"Buried Alive": Charlotte Forman in Grub Street', *Eighteenth-Century Life*, 8 (1982), 44 n. 25, identifies this as a quotation from the Vulgate, Ps. 90: 7: 'A thousand shall fall at thy side, and ten thousand at thy right hand: but it shall not come nigh thee.'

of un courage mâle, but if there is such a thing as female fortitude, I believe I have a spice of it. Sometimes I laugh at my fate, and think my case something similar to that of Sisyphus, condemned to roll the stone up the hill to no purpose. At other times I compare myself to the poor wretches in Holland, who for certain crimes are let down into a deep hole half full of water, where a cock is turned upon them to let in more; on the other hand, there is a pump, which they are obliged to keep going, in order to escape drowning. So in like manner, as long as I am able to earn a shilling, I may escape starving and no longer, for all my endeavours answer no other end than barely to keep me alive to undergo more misery. I often wish I had been brought up at a green stall, for I have known people get estates that way. Even at this time of day, if I was able to manage a mop, I would fling away the pen, for I am positive there is not a servant of four pounds a year but what lives far better than I do. 'Tis a saying, that when things come to the worst, they mend. Now, if I may be allowed to compare lesser matters with greater, I shall beg leave to observe, Sir, that your troubles and mine keep pace, with this difference that yours take the lead, and mine follow; therefore 'till yours mend, mine cannot. I make it out thus. The year 1763, that fatal aera of all your misfortunes, is also the aera of mine: 'till then I had a sufficiency. With fifty pounds a year, I kept even with the world, and could spare something upon occasion. Your troubles began in the spring of that year, mine followed in the autumn. In 1764, whilst England was lamenting that her Patriot was gone, death snatched away my brother, my only and last support. Your 41st and 42^{d} year are very memorable, so were mine. The year 1757 was my 41st year, I was then confined to my room, yet travelled almost as far as the gates of eternity, (would to God I had reached them!) I was three months going and coming, and the remainder of that year and all the next was spent in recovering the fatigue of the journey. This answers to your present confinement. Since October last, (your Birth-month and mine) your troubles are encreased, so are mine in various shapes, but I shall not trouble you with a detail of them. I shall only mention that my hopes are dashed with regard to the Gazetter, for Mr Say told me last Tuesday to translate no more for it, as it was of no use to him. I suppose he intends to take the news from the evening papers as he used to do, to save expences. I have had nothing for it yet, reste a savoir whether I ever shall. It is a grievous stroke to me, because I had nothing else to depend on to pay my lodging. I beg Sir, you will not be offended at the contents of the third page of this letter, I wrote it meerly for amusement. I have not room to add any more than that I have the honour to be with great respect and acknowledgemen^t,

Sir

Your most humble and
most obedient Servant.
Charlotte Forman

Thursday night March 2^d 1769.

I hope to have the honour of waiting on you as soon as I am able to bear the walk.

5. POPULAR PROJECTIONS OF WILKES

One of the most remarkable developments in the political culture of the 1760s was the forging of Wilkes's popular identity. His exploitation of the resources of the press and his understanding of the techniques of political campaigning were exceptionally shrewd. Yet the political beatification of Wilkes was not achieved solely through the management and manipulation of popular opinion. The Wilkite crowds were themselves participants in his political construction—in the production, adaptation, and dissemination of a distinctive popular iconography. They were celebrants and guardians of the features encoded there: his rebelliousness, his wit, his sexuality, and his Englishness. Sharpening and politicizing the traditional functions of the Fool, he was the emblem as much as the organizer of a self-consciously grotesque counterworld of riot.

The transgressive quality of this Wilkite counterworld is represented in **5.1**, an audacious parody of the Book of Common Prayer. Sold in both inexpensive and more costly editions, this hagiography presents Wilkes as the saviour of the artisan and commercial classes of London: the printers and bookbinders, who benefit from the market for Wilkite writings, the glaziers and candlemakers, who benefit from Wilkite demonstrations, and the street-singers of Wilkite ballads, one of whom is reported as saying that 'he earned from 18 shillings to a Guinea almost every Day during the late City Election, singing Songs upon Wilkes and Liberty, and No. 45' (*Public Advertiser*, 4 April 1768). Extracts **5.2** and **5.3** are examples of Wilkite street culture, two of the numerous broadside ballads sung and sold in celebration of Wilkes's exploits in the late 1760s; **5.3** associates Wilkes and his followers with the spirit of 'rough music', a customary form of collective punishment meted out to those who had broken unwritten social codes.

5.1   From *Britannia's Intercession for the Deliverance of John Wilkes, Esq. from Persecution and Banishment*, 4th edn. (1768)

¶   *At the beginning of this intercession, the orator shall pronounce, with an audible voice, one of these passages.*

WHEN B*** turneth from the error of his way, and doeth that which is seemly and good, he shall wear his plaid in peace. *Scots Journ.*

To Wilkes belong freedom and greatness of spirit, though many have devised against him, and complied not with the words of his mouth. *North Briton.*

Through the spirit of Wilkes we are yet in the land of freedom, because his exertion in that point faileth not. *Polit. Regist.*

Give thanks, O ye people, give thanks unto Wilkes, for he is mighty amongst us. *Let. to H——y.*

O let the wickedness of a favourite come to an end, but establish the upright and free-born. *No. 45.*

We waited patiently for Wilkes, and he came unto us, and he heard our moan. *Gaz.*

DEARLY beloved countrymen, Wilkes's speeches urgeth us in several places to acknowledge and confess our gratitude and praises, and that we should not dissemble or hide them before the face of our country, but confess them with a joyful and merry heart, to the end that we may enjoy a continuance of the same, through his fortitude and plainness. And although we ought at all times to acknowledge our favours from great men, so ought we especially so to do when we come together, to render thanks for the great benefits we have received from Wilkes's hands, to speak in his praise, to hear every speech, and to plead those things which are constitutional and requisite both for freedom and liberty.

¶ *Then the orator shall say,*

O Wilkes! be thou our strength.
>   *Answ.* And we shall sound forth thy name abroad on the earth.
>   *Orat.* O Wilkes! continue thy aid.
>   *Answ.* O Wilkes! continue thy aid.

¶ *Here all standing, the orator shall say,*

Honour be to thee, O Wilkes!
>   *Answ.* As thou wert in the beginning, thou art now, and ever will be, liberty without end, Amen.

¶ *Then the people shall chaunt,*

>   O Come, let us sing unto Wilkes, let us rejoice in the spirit of his writings.
>   Let us thank him with our lips, and shew ourselves glad in him with huzzas.
>   For Wilkes is a great writer, and a writer above all writers.
>   In his brain are all the quirks of the law, and their effects are known to him also.
>   The N**** B***** is his, and he made it, his head prepared the matter thereof.
>   For he is the man that sheweth wonders, and we are the people that read the work of his hands.
>   If you would hear him speak, turn not away, as in his provocation, when an exile, and as in the day of tribulation in the King's Bench prison.

When our great men tempted him, proved him, and saw him staunch.

Several years was he grieved with this set of wretches, and said, It is a people who want slavery and famine. They know not my worth.

Unto whom I swear by magna charta that they should not gain their end.

Honour be to thee, O Wilkes!

As thou wert in the beginning, thou art now, and ever shall be, liberty without end. Amen.

¶ *Then shall follow these verses, one verse by the orator, and another by the people.*

O Give thanks unto Wilkes, for he is sensible, and his sensibility continueth for ever.

Let all them give thanks whom he hath defended, and delivered from the power of arbitrary seizures.

Many a time have some men fought against him, after the writing of number Forty-five.

Yea, many a time have they vexed him, but they have not utterly prevailed over him.

They have spread their net to destroy him without a cause, yea, even without a cause did they put him afar off.

They laid a net for his feet, and have happily fallen into it themselves.

Great is his courage, and great his perseverance, yea, and his capacity is wonderful.

Wilkes sitteth up the falling poor, and bringeth down oppressors to the ground.

Let your voice be for the man of your right-hand, and upon the man who hath supported you in the time of your trouble.

We will not go back from thee, O Wilkes! O let us be free, and we will sing forth thy name.

Honour be to thee, O Wilkes!

As thou wert in the beginning, thou art now, and ever will be, liberty without end. Amen.

WILKES, thou hast been our glory from one tribulation to another.

Before the Essay was brought forth, or the North Briton was made, thou wast the man of liberty who defendest our cause, and stood up in our behalf.

Thou turnest B*** to distraction, and again thou sayest, Rise no more to perplex this free people.

For all thy intrigues were in my sight, they are but as yesterday in mine eyes.

But behold, thou shalt dread my displeasure, and be afraid of my spirited indignation.

I have set thy misdeeds before thee, and thy secret fawnings in the light of thine own eyes.

Behold, who regardeth the power of thy wrath? it is even as a weapon without sharpness.

Thou art full of nothingness, and art empty for lack of true knowledge.

Honour be to thee, O Wilkes!

As thou wert in the beginning, thou art now, and ever will be, liberty without end. Amen.

¶ *The lecture appointed for this intercession, is taken out of the Chronicles, the twelfth chapter, beginning at the forty-fifth verse.*

Now there was in the reign of G***** the king, a mighty spirit of tribulation. And the great men of the land were laying upon the people burthens of great weight, yea, heavier burthens than were borne by their fathers, or their fathers fathers before them. And they cried out unto the elders, and complained for lack of relief. (Now the elders were deaf to their cries, and they minded not the daily lamentation which they made.) And they cried yet louder and louder, so that the whole land was pierced with the sound thereof. And behold, in process of time, that there arose up a man, (who was also an elder, and a colonel of the guard, in the land of Buckingham) who had compassion upon them; and he opened his mouth, and said, Of a truth I perceive that you are oppressed and agrieved, and that your task-masters lay upon you more than you are able to bear. Behold, I myself will speak unto this people who do evil continually; and will require a reason for that which they now do. Be ye, therefore, patient, having peace amongst yourselves, and you shall be filled. Now it came to pass that after a short time this good man did as he promised unto the people. And he spoke time after time of their tribulation, and wrote even letters with his own hand, complaining of the rulers in a free country. And behold, they were affronted thereat, and they were full of envy against this man, because he had spoken well of the people. And when it was so that he had wrote even a forty-fifth letter unto them, that they took him out of the house of his habitation, and put him into a fast place, which place is called a tower even unto this day. And they looked into his dwelling, and searched for his papers, and all his secret workings, and they took them every one. And behold, when they had found these, that they took him from the fast place, and banished him afar off beyond the sea. And he was left there, and commanded not to return; for behold it was seemly unto the elders that he should be put away from amongst them.

Thus ends the first lecture.

O All ye people, praise ye Wilkes, bless him, and huzza him for ever!

O ye printers of the land, praise ye Wilkes, bless him, and huzza him for ever!

O ye printers devils, and their agents of whatsoever denomination, praise ye Wilkes, bless him, and huzza him for ever!

O all ye booksellers, pamphlet-stitchers, and bookbinders, praise ye Wilkes, bless him, and huzza him forever!

O Williams,[31] praise Wilkes, bless him, and huzza him for ever!

O Bingley,[32] praise Wilkes, bless him, and huzza him for ever!

O all ye glaziers of the city, praise ye Wilkes, bless him, and huzza him for ever!

O ye chandlers of grease, praise ye Wilkes, bless him, and huzza him for ever!

O ye uncorrupted, non-bribed, and independent electors of the city, praise ye Wilkes, bless him, and huzza him for ever!

O ye glorious and ever-famed freeholders of Middlesex, praise ye Wilkes, bless him, and huzza him for ever!

O all ye ballad-singers, hawkers, and pedlars, praise ye Wilkes, bless him, and huzza him for ever!

Honour be to thee, O Wilkes!

As thou wert in the beginning, thou art now, and ever will be, praised without end. Amen.

5.2 'Wilkes, and Liberty. A New Song. To the tune of, *Chevy-Chace*' (1768?)

I

In *George-street*, *Westminster*, there liv'd,
    A Man of patriot Fame,
And there perhaps he liveth still,
    And JOHN WILKES is his Name.

II

To all the *Scots* he Hatred bore,
    Which grew to such a Pitch,
He would not with Ld B*** shake Hands,
    He would not catch the ITCH.

[31] John Williams, bookseller, who published many Wilkite tracts, including the *North Briton*, for which he was pilloried in 1765.

[32] William Bingley (d. 1799), bookseller and printer of the second series of the *North Briton*; confined in King's Bench prison in November 1768 for refusing to answer questions relating to a published attack on the Lord Chief Justice.

III

His Pen was like a two-edg'd Sword,
   His Wit was sharp and pat;
And *keen North Britons* he could write,
   But not a Word of that.

IV

The Muckle [great] *Laird* grew wan at this,
   And try'd a thousand Ways,
But could not win him to himself,
   As ev'ry *Briton* says.

V

This touch'd his Pride.—All in the Night
   His *Mirmydons* he sent,
To take the *Culprit* safe in Hold,
   He order'd; and they went.

VI

The TOWER then receiv'd the Guest,
   But he car'd not a F——t a,
They soon were glad to let him go,
   By Dint of MAGNA CHARTA.

VII

The muckle *Laird* then gang'd his Gait,
   Alas, he could not stay!
A *Cat* will mew, as Shakespear says,
   A *Dog* will have his Day.

VIII

Beware, *gude Laird*,—for tho' this Work
   By other's Hands is done;
So bunglingly 'tis brought about,
   We ken 'tis all thine own.

IX

God prosper long our noble King,
   And keep us bold and free;
So quaff the Bowl, and let us sing
   To WILKES and LIBERTY.

5.3 'A New Song' (1769?)

Come let's laugh at dull malice for who the duce knows,
Tho' the house wilkes expelled, yet again in may be chose
And still be the Envy of those that's his foes.

CHORUS

wilke's has ever been true to old England
For wilkes sing for ever huzza

wilkes twice in the city was chose alderman.
Tho once was rejected deny it who can
Yet Farringdon ward did elect him again

May Middlesex county by wilkes do the same
And in spite of all courtiers elect him again,
For wilkes your sweet Liberty'll ever maintain

Now P[roctor?], no more dares the hustings come near
[Fo]r that murdering v——n the halter does fear
i hope he'll be hang'd if he ever comes here

There's B-t gone to Rome, and P—— to France
[a]nd M—— to Germany'll quickly advance[33]
Tis wilkes's rough musick[34] that's led them a dance

as tis wilkes' put a stop to these devils let's hope
B——t's head may come off, p—'s neck in a rope
with grief the she devil she quickly will croak

Then each hearty freeholder let's merrily sing
all [?] success to brave wilkes not forgetting staunch glynn
and [?] wherever they poll we'll elect them again

---

[33] Possibly references to Bute, who went to Italy in 1769 for reasons of health, the Princess Dowager Augusta, who visited the continent in 1770, and George III who was Elector of Hanover (though he never in fact visited the Electorate).

[34] For discussions of 'rough music', see Martin Ingram, 'Ridings, Rough Music and the "Reform of Popular Culture" in Early Modern England', *Past & Present*, 105 (1984), 79–113; id., 'Ridings, Rough Music and Mocking Rhymes in Early Modern England', in Barry Reay (ed.), *Popular Culture in Seventeenth-Century England* (1985), 166–97; and E. P. Thompson, *Customs in Common* (1991), 467–531.

8

POPULAR PERCEPTIONS OF EMPIRE:
NATIVE AMERICANS IN BRITAIN
IN THE 1760s

THE eighteenth century is rightly seen as the period which witnessed Britain's emergence as Europe's leading colonial power. By 1763 Britain controlled vast tracts of land in North America as well as valuable possessions in India, Africa, and the Caribbean. Yet, as P. J. Marshall has shown, the process by which what came in time to be understood as an empire was acquired was a complex and uneven one.[1] The colonial presence took quite different forms, ranging from commercial supremacy to territorial expansion and settlement, in different parts of the globe. In these circumstances the unifying idea of empire as a distinctive and inclusive political entity was slow to develop and take root. In particular, it is unclear how far those outside the political élite thought of themselves as the beneficiaries of an imperial state, or derived their sense of national identity from that perception.

Recent historical work has begun to explore this question of the extent of a popular consciousness of empire in the eighteenth century. Kathleen Wilson has argued that 'There were strong material reasons . . . for ordinary English people to be avidly interested in imperial affairs.'[2] In their everyday production and consumption of goods they were implicated in a system of commerce which was increasingly sensitive to, and indeed driven by, imperial imperatives. Of equal and related importance in the forging of a consciousness of empire was the experience of war. In the course of the century Britain's wars with her foremost continental rival, France, turned increasingly on competition for colonial possessions and the control of overseas trade. Wilson argues that the popularity of naval heroes like Admiral Edward Vernon in the 1740s, celebrated in a range of cultural products (including prints, ballads, medals, and ceramics), helped to

---

[1] 'The Eighteenth-Century Empire', in Jeremy Black (ed.), *British Politics and Society from Walpole to Pitt, 1742–1789* (1990), 177–200.

[2] 'Empire of Virtue: The Imperial Project and Hanoverian Culture c.1720–1785', in Lawrence Stone (ed.), *An Imperial State at War: Britain from 1689 to 1815* (1994), 129.

shape 'a nascent imperialist sensibility'.[3] A decade later the Seven Years War (1756–63), in which Britain achieved unprecedented military successes and territorial gains, helped to create, as Marshall puts it, 'a new and much wider awareness of a world outside Europe'.[4] As we saw in the Introduction, newspaper reports of British triumphs in India, North America, and the Caribbean were greeted by widespread popular rejoicing, bringing home the message that the nation's destiny was being decided in remote lands and among unfamiliar peoples.

Narratives and representations of the non-European peoples caught up in the struggle for empire were widely circulated in the period. Native Americans, the focus of the material presented here, were portrayed in a wide range of printed forms and performances: travel writing, captivity narratives, broadside ballads, magazine poetry, novels, plays, children's entertainments, engravings, and newspaper reports. These representations, which paid little regard to the diversity of Indian nations and cultural identities, were structured by an underlying opposition between Indian savagery and European civilization. The opposition could be turned to a number of uses (for example, by bringing new perspectives to bear on familiar customs and institutions) without calling into question its originating hierarchical premiss. Sometimes the American Indian was presented as simply savage, predisposed to violence, and devoid of human feeling. Alternatively, the Indian's savagery and lack of culture could be understood as a form of innocence. The uncomprehending Indian, cast adrift in foreign courts and unwittingly exposing the artificiality of European manners and the corrupting effects of luxury, was both a familiar vehicle for, and secondary object of, eighteenth-century satire.[5] Indian difference was also interpreted as a form of noble savagery: the supposedly warlike, democratic, and masculine character of Indian society was thought capable of sustaining a republican virtue lost to a Europe enfeebled by its pursuit of commerce and refinement. This interest is closely related to the eighteenth-century fascination with the cultural products of 'primitive' societies which we documented in Chapter 1. Native Americans were particularly envied for their possession of a power of eloquence which could not survive in a modern commercial society. European observers admired the vividly metaphorical character of Indian oratory, and associated it with what they thought of as a state of social simplicity. Yet while they sometimes lamented the lack of such rhetorical resources in their own speech, they nonetheless regarded this figurative abundance as incompatible with the language of modern

[3] *The Sense of the People: Politics, Culture and Imperialism in England, 1715–1785* (Cambridge, 1995), 164.

[4] Marshall, 'The Eighteenth-Century Empire', 200.

[5] See, for instance, John Cleland's comedy, *Tombo-Chiqui: Or, The American Savage. A Dramatic Entertainment* (1758).

politeness. To have lost the natural fertility of Indian eloquence might be regretted, but it was a price worth paying for the benefits of living in a society dedicated to the pursuit of economic improvement and refinement in the arts.

Ambiguities of this kind colour much of the material presented below. The documents record two colonial encounters of the 1760s: the embassy of Cherokee leaders to London in 1762 and the fund-raising tour of Britain undertaken by the Mohegan convert and preacher Samson Occom in 1766 and 1767. Such visits, widely reported in the influential and expanding newspaper press, played an important part in stimulating popular interest in non-European peoples. The best-known of these 'exotic' visitors was the South Sea Islander known as Omai, who was brought to Britain by Captain Cook's second expedition in 1774 and stayed until 1776. The subject of both a heroic portrait by Joshua Reynolds and a successful Covent Garden pantomime (*Omai; or, A Trip round the World*, 1785) he was conducted on an extended tour of sights and receptions which in many ways followed a pattern established by earlier eighteenth-century visits.[6] In 1710 four leaders of the Iroquois confederacy, which held extensive territories in the present New York State, had been invited by colonial officials to visit London. Like a number of later visits, the Iroquois mission had serious military and political objectives. For the Indian nations the consequences of European settlement in North America were mostly dire: disease, dispossession, slavery, and war. But for much of the eighteenth century their control of valuable natural resources such as fur (much prized in European markets) and their military prowess still made them desirable allies. As the British and French colonists struggled for supremacy in North America they also struggled to secure the support of auxiliary Indian forces. The Iroquois visit of 1710, the Cherokee visits of 1730 and 1762, the visit of the Creek Indian chief Tomochichi in 1734, and the visit of the Mohawk war leader Theyendanegea (also known as Joseph Brant) in 1776 were all official, or semi-official, delegations, arranged for the purpose of concluding trading agreements, military alliances, or treaties of peace.

From the British point of view an important objective of these embassies was to impress the American visitors with a sense of the nation's public splendour and military strength (1.5). Typically, an audience with the reigning monarch was followed by inspections of the troops and naval forces at the Artillery Ground and royal dockyards, and visits to the Houses of Parliament and Westminster Abbey. As the *Royal Magazine* frankly reported to its readers in 1762, the Cherokee leaders were 'conducted to the most eminent places in and about this city, in order to give them some idea of the English wealth and power'. By such means, it was believed, 'the false ideas they have conceived of the English nation,

---

[6] See William Huse, 'A Noble Savage on the Stage', *Modern Philology*, 33 (1936), 302–16; Pat Rogers, 'The Noblest Savage of Them All: Johnson, Omai, and Other Primitives', in *The Age of Johnson*, 5 (1992), 281–301.

by the unjust and artful representations of the French, will be effectually obliterated'.[7] In this role the native Americans were granted a certain dignity. They were official visitors, men of eminence among their own people, who in theory merited the respect owed to other ambassadors of independent nations. Yet the visits were organized on the assumption that they were, indeed, savages, culturally inferior and naively susceptible to shallow shows of strength. This duality was reflected in the struggles of newspaper accounts to settle on a vocabulary which would be appropriately indicative of rank. The visitors were commonly described as Indian 'kings', 'princes', 'chiefs', or 'generals', but there was often at least a suggestion of irony in the use of such terms and a hint of ridicule at the Indians' failure to live up to them. Occasionally it was acknowledged that these titles were European impositions which could not accurately reflect native American social and political structures (1.1).

In their ambassadorial function the Indian visitors were primarily cast as observers, but their unfamiliarity, as well as their public visibility, also made them the objects of popular attention. In addition to inspecting official institutions and attending grand ceremonies of state they were introduced to many of London's venues for entertainment, where they could be seen by ordinary onlookers as well as members of the political and social élite. The Cherokees who came to Britain with Sir Alexander Cuming in 1730 viewed, and were viewed at, such places of public resort as Bedlam (where, according to the *Grub-Street Journal* of 27 August, they were 'attended by a great number of the populace'), Sadler's Wells, the theatre at Lincoln's Inn Fields (where they were present at performances of Thomas Southerne's *Oroonoko* and of the farce *The Emperor of the Moon*), and several of London's fairs, including Bartholomew Fair where, as *Fog's Weekly Journal* reported on 5 September, 'the Indian Kings . . . saw the Droll, called Wat Tyler, or Jack Straw, with which Performance they seem'd greatly pleas'd' (see Chapter 3, 2.1).

As Richmond Bond puts it of the Iroquois delegation of 1710, on such occasions the native Americans 'were themselves a spectacle to the city's mobile populace'.[8] A surviving playbill of 1710, announcing a performance of Martin Powell's puppet show 'for the Entertainment of the Four Indian Kings', depicts the curtained stage at 'Punch's Theatre' occupied not by Powell's puppets but by the crowned Iroquois ambassadors, with a key identifying them by name. According to one account, when the Iroquois were taken to the theatre at the Haymarket for a performance of *Macbeth*,

the curtain was drawn, but in vain did the players attempt to perform—the Mob, who had possession of the upper gallery, declared that they came to see the Kings, 'and since we have paid our money, the Kings we will have'—whereupon Wilks came forth,

---

[7] *Royal Magazine*, 7 (1762), 16.   [8] *Queen Anne's American Kings* (Oxford, 1952), 3.

and assured them the Kings were in the front box—to this the Mob replied, they could not see them, and desired they might be placed in a more conspicuous point of view—'otherwise there shall be no play'—Wilks assured them he had nothing so much at heart as their happiness, and accordingly got four chairs, and placed the Kings on the stage, to the no small satisfaction of the Mob, with whom it is a maxim to have as much as possible for their money.[9]

There were many later instances when visiting Americans were exploited as marketable attractions (see, for example, 1.5-1.7) or even frankly exhibited as exotic curiosities (3.1 and 3.2). What exactly this material tells us about popular attitudes to non-European peoples is open to interpretation. The point of view adopted in many of the newspaper accounts is self-consciously polite, and as derisive of the 'mob' as the mob is said to be of the Indians. The texts present a layered and hierarchical structure of observation, with the polite observer observing a mob which in turn observes the native Americans. 'When the four *Indian* Kings were in this Country [in 1710] . . . I often mix'd with the Rabble, and followed them a whole Day together, being wonderfully struck with the Sight of every thing that is new or uncommon', opens *Spectator* no. 50, where the pleasurable novelty may be provided by the prospect of the Indians, or the rabble, or by the conjunction of the two.[10] Occasionally (as later in the same *Spectator* paper) an 'Indian' outlook is imagined, though the focus of interest remains the European culture defamiliarized by means of this projected view. By way of contrast, the writings of the Mohegan preacher Samson Occom (4.1) offer a perspective which, though mediated through the forms and values of European systems of belief, remains that of a genuine Indian outsider, a fact of which he was himself on occasion forcibly reminded.

REFERENCES AND FURTHER READING

The most authoritative account of the Cherokee visit of 1762 is John Oliphant, 'The Cherokee Embassy to London, 1762', *Journal of Imperial and Commonwealth History*, 27 (1999), 1–26. Richmond P. Bond, *Queen Anne's American Kings* (Oxford, 1952), is a richly documented survey of the 1710 visit. A broader view is provided by Carolyn Thomas Foreman, *Indians Abroad 1493–1938* (Norman, Okla., 1943). Richard Altick, *The Shows of London* (Cambridge, Mass., 1978) is helpful on the commercial exploitation of visiting native Americans.

Leon Burr Richardson, *An Indian Preacher in England* (Hanover, NH, 1933), reprints diaries and correspondence relating to Samson Occom's visit of 1766–8. Additional information can be found in W. D. Love, *Samson Occom and the Christian Indians of New England* (Boston, Mass., 1899), and Harold Blodgett, *Samson Occom* (Hanover, NH, 1935).

---

[9] Cited ibid. 4.   [10] *The Spectator*, ed. Donald F. Bond, 5 vols. (Oxford, 1965), i. 211.

On Native Americans and British culture in the period see P. J. Marshall and Glyndwr Williams, *The Great Map of Mankind: British Perceptions of the World in the Age of Enlightenment* (1982), and G. S. Rousseau and Roy Porter (eds.), *Exoticism and Enlightenment* (1989). Peter Hulme, *Colonial Encounters: Europe and the Native Caribbean, 1492–1797* (1992), provides a model analysis of colonial discourse and its anxieties. See also David Murray, *Forked Tongues: Speech, Writing and Representation in North American Indian Texts* (Bloomington, Ind., 1991), and Helen Carr, *Inventing the American Primitive: Politics, Gender and the Representation of Native American Literary Traditions, 1789–1936* (Cork, 1996). P. J. Marshall, 'The Eighteenth-Century Empire', in Jeremy Black (ed.), *British Politics and Society from Walpole to Pitt, 1742–1789* (1990), 177–200, is an overview by the leading authority on the subject. Kathleen Wilson's recent work, 'Empire of Virtue: The Imperial Project and Hanoverian Culture *c.*1720–1785', in Lawrence Stone (ed.), *An Imperial State at War: Britain from 1689 to 1815* (1994), 128–64, and her *The Sense of the People: Politics, Culture and Imperialism in England, 1715–1785* (Cambridge, 1995) is particularly illuminating on the popular consciousness of empire in the period.

1. THE CHEROKEE EMBASSY OF 1762

The American background to the visit of the three Cherokee leaders in 1762 is complex, involving conflict between the British and French in North America, differences between the colonies of South Carolina and Virginia, and political rivalries within the Cherokee nation itself. When war with France broke out in the mid-1750s the Cherokees entered into an alliance with Britain, but relations between the two deteriorated rapidly and an already difficult situation was made worse by the hostile and punitive stance adopted by the authorities in South Carolina. By 1759 the Cherokees were in open conflict with their former allies. This bitter and costly war, which pitted Cherokee warriors against regular British troops as well as colonial forces, was not concluded until November 1761.

In the immediate aftermath of the war the Cherokee leader Ostenaca (also known as the Man Killer of Tomotly) sought opportunities to restore good relations with the British. It was Ostenaca who, with two Cherokee companions, led the 1762 embassy to London. As John Oliphant has explained, Ostenaca's aims in visiting Britain were twofold: he wished both to obtain prestige for himself at the expense of rivals such as Attakullakulla (or Little Carpenter) who had been a member of Sir Alexander Cuming's delegation to London in 1730, and to improve trading relations with the colony of Virginia.[11] With the blessing of the Virginian authorities the

---

[11] 'The Cherokee Embassy to London, 1762', *Journal of Imperial and Commonwealth History*, 27 (1999), 1–26.

Cherokees sailed for Britain in May 1762. Officials in London had no prior warning of their departure and the responsible Secretary of State, the second earl of Egremont, who took an enlightened interest in native American affairs, was obliged to improvise an official programme of events.

Escorting the Cherokees, and assisting as their interpreter, was a young Virginian officer, Henry Timberlake, who had been sent as an envoy to Cherokee country in 1761 to promote negotiations for peace. In a detailed narrative of the embassy which he published in 1765 Timberlake defends himself from the charge that he profited financially from the visit by putting the Cherokees on display in London. Conscious of the Cherokees' dislike of 'the continual crowds of visitors' who flocked to their lodgings, he 'resolved to admit none but people of fashion'. Yet 'So far from these orders being complied with, the whole rabble of the town was ushered in the next day . . . they pressed into the Indians dressing room, which gave them the highest disgust, these people having a particular aversion to being stared at while dressing or eating.'[12] Whatever the truth about his personal involvement, Timberlake's memoir usefully illustrates the extent of popular demand for exotic spectacle. The almost daily accounts which appeared in the newspapers give further evidence of this interest. The encounters are often reported in such a way as to accentuate or construct boundaries between polite observers, whose interest in the native Americans is informed, rational, and properly respectful of rank and the crowd, whose thirst for novelty and outlandish spectacle simply reflects its own savagery.

The Public Advertiser (Monday, 5 July 1762)   1.1

The Cherokee Chief who is now here is the second Person in Point of Consideration of his People. The Cherokees are the most considerable Indian Nation with which we are acquainted, and are absolutely free; so that when we call any of their Chiefs Princes or Kings, it is to accommodate their Manners to our Ideas; for this Chief, or any other, has not the smallest Power or Prerogative, or even Property, more than any other Man of his Country. It is Courage and Ability that constitutes a Chief amongst the Cherokees, who are led by him indeed in Time of War, and take his Advice in Time of Peace, but without allowing him any Authority or Preheminence, except in such Circumstances as the Good of the Community requires. The Strength of an Indian Nation consists in their Warriors; and of these, according to the best Accounts, there may be about three thousand amongst the Cherokees.

[12] *The Memoirs of Lieu. Henry Timberlake (Who accompanied the Three Cherokee Indians to England in the Year 1762)* (1765), 120, 123.

1.2 *The St. James's Chronicle; or, The British Evening-Post* (Saturday, 3–Tuesday, 6 July 1762)

When the Cherokee Chief and his Attendants were at Vauxhall Gardens last Week, they had a very sumptuous Entertainment. The Wines first set before them, were Burgundy and Claret, which however they did not seem greatly to relish. Others were then placed on the Table, when they fixed upon Frontiniac, the Sweetness of which highly hit their Palates, and they drank of it very freely.

The Cherokee Chiefs are sitting for their Pictures, to Mr. Reynolds.

1.3 *The St. James's Chronicle; or, The British Evening-Post* (Saturday, 10–Tuesday, 1[3] July 1762)

Yesterday the Cherokee King, with his two Chiefs, in consequence of an Invitation sent them by the Right Hon. the Lord Mayor on Saturday last, went to the Mansion-House and dined with his Lordship. They seemed greatly pleased with the numerous Concourse of Ladies and Gentlemen, who crowded to the Windows, &c. to see them pass.

1.4 *The Public Advertiser* (Saturday, 17 July 1762)

MR JOHNSON will perform his HORSEMANSHIP on Tuesday Evening, at Seven o'Clock, as usual, at the Star and Garter at Chelsea; and as the Chiefs of the Cherokees have a particular Pleasure in seeing his Performance, they intend to be present, and will indulge the Company with their Appearance upon the Green for a sufficient Time to satisfy the Curiosity of the Public, in hopes that they may receive the like Politeness from the Populace, in their Retirement to the Apartment appointed for them.

1.5 *The Public Advertiser* (Friday, 23 July 1762)

The King of the Cherokees, and his two Chiefs, will be this Evening at Vauxhall Gardens.

This Day, the King of the Cherokees, and his two Chiefs, will go to see the Curiosities at the Dwarf's Tavern, Chelsea Fields, where they will likewise dine and drink Tea. Tickets at 1s. each, will be taken in the Reckoni[n]g, either for Wine, Punch, Tea, &c. The Tea this Day will be 1s. a Head, which will be an excellent Sort on purpose. Dinner will be on the Table at Three o'Clock.

This Day the Cherokees will go in the Admiralty Barge to Deptford, Greenwich, and Woolwich, to see the Military Stores, &c. And as there are now six Capital Ships on the Stocks, it must give them a high Opinion of our Strength and Grandeur, which is the rather to be wish'd, as the French and Spaniards had always intimated to them that we were an inconsiderable People, and unable to protect them in case of a War.

The London Chronicle: or, Universal Evening Post (Saturday, 24-Tuesday, 27 1.6 July 1762)

To the PRINTER

CURIOSITY is certainly no censurable disposition in a people, while it is, as all dispositions should be, under the guidance of reason. But when it passes the bounds of reason, it becomes a mark of great levity; and when indulged to the greatest excess, is certainly to be deemed madness . . .

What, for example, can apologize for peoples running in such shoals to all public places, at the hazard of health, life, or disappointment, to see the savage Chiefs that are come among us? Are time, expence, and danger, of so very little consequence to us, that we cannot wait for so poor a sight till opportunity can gratify us, as it very soon will do, without our suffering from either of them? These poor creatures make no more than theatrical figures, and can be seen with no satisfaction from the pressures of a throng: why then are people mad in their avidity to behold them?

I own it caused mirth in me, but it was with a mixture of contempt, to read in the papers, how these poor wild hunters were surrounded by as wild gazers on them at Vauxhall, and that three hundred eager crouders were made happy by shaking hands with them; and have wondered from what motive that familiarity could arise, whether it was with a design to do honour, or receive it; or whether it was from hearty good fellowship, on a supposition of equality.

The greatest curiosity I can wish to have satisfied about them (for I have not yet indulged mine with running any where to behold them) would be to hear what judgments these poor creatures really form of our behaviour. I should like to read a letter (if they could write one) on that subject, to their friends at home, in order to learn what they think of the mad savages of Great Britain; as they certainly must have seen in us what they never before had an idea of, and must consider our kindnesses to be as strange as our customs; and, savages as they are, I doubt not but they think them alike stupid and unnatural. Yet savages though they be, I dare venture to stake my credit, for their not throwing down a pipe to run and gaze at any of us, or that the wisest man among us, with all the powers of his eloquence, will not persuade them to believe that any of the human species could ever have been so foolish as to run in throngs, and give money to see a man get into a quart bottle.[13]

1.7   *Lloyd's Evening Post, and British Chronicle* (Monday, 26–Wednesday, 28 July 1762)

> Growing concern about the exploitation of the Cherokees prompted the publication of this presumably fictitious but well-informed letter, written in the persona of a London alehouse-keeper.

To the EDITOR *of* LLOYD'S EVENING POST.

SIR,

I BEG leave, by means of your Paper, to lay my case before the Publick. I keep a little snug Publick-house as any in town; and, though I say it, sell as good beer as need be drank; I make shift to pick up a little money, and think myself happy so to do, in an honest way: But, Sir, I have a wife! a wife, Mr. Editor, who is never satisfied, and who wants to get money at any rate; she has heard that Mr. **** has got money by shewing the Cherokees at his house, and nothing will serve her turn but she will have them at ours. I have taken great pains to shew her how unchristian-like it would be to make a shew of our fellow-creatures, and to convince her, that, though in a different dress from ours, they are really men, and most probably men who in their own country are treated with the greatest respect; but all won't do, if there is but money to be got by it, that is all my wife cares for. I was obliged, for the sake of a quiet life, to go on Sunday last to the Dwarf Tavern, to see in what manner they were exhibited there; and whether it would be worth our while. The first thing I observed was two papers affixed one to the outer gate, and the other to the sign-post, containing these words:

---

[13] A reference to the so-called 'Bottle Hoax' of January 1749 when a large audience was lured to Haymarket theatre by an advertisement announcing that, among other feats, a man would get inside a quart bottle. When he failed to appear, the crowd rioted, and the hoax became a by-word for public credulity.

'*July* 25

This day the King of the Cherokees and his two Chiefs drink Tea here.'

I went in, paid my shilling, and drank tea, which at another time is no more than sixpence; but, it seems, upon this occasion, there was a particular sort of tea provided. I saw only the two Chiefs, the King being not well, as I was told by the Master of the house; these were shewn to some hundreds of people; and, if their looks or behaviour may be believed, not from their own choice; and what served to confirm me in that opinion was, that, upon the people's crowding in, a man who was within the rail with them told them, that if they would have a little patience they should be brought down into the garden. I was too much shocked to stay long, so came away, reflecting upon a very just, though shocking remark, made by a vulgar fellow, in the room whilst I was present; They are brought here, says he, to be shewn like wild beasts.

I gave my wife a faithful account of what I had seen, begging of her, at the same time, not to think any more of so inhuman a project, but to no purpose: she is making the necessary preparations, and has already railed off one corner of the tap-room, where the club-chair is to be placed for the King. A blanket is to be thrown over the rail. I think that at the Dwarf it is a quilt; but my wife says, as ours is an ale-house, a blanket will do very well. Our beer is to be sold for six-pence per pot, and we are to have a particular sort for that day; which, to say the truth, is to be worse than we usually sell, as people will be too much taken up with the Cherokees to mind their liquor. We are not to put up bills, but to have a man stand at the door with a Constable's staff, who is to cry, *Walk in, Gentlemen, see 'em alive!* Now, Sir, as I cannot in conscience agree to so shameful a proceeding, I beg you will, by publishing this, convince the world it is without my consent.

OLD HONESTY.

P. S. I have been assured that his Majesty King George has honoured the Cherokee King with his protection; and if that be the case, I think no man has a right to make a property of him.

The St. James's Chronicle; or, The British Evening-Post (Thursday, 29–   1.8
Saturday, 31 July 1762)

The Intemperance of his Cherokee *Majesty* and his Chiefs, and the selfish Views of the Proprietors of our public Gardens, in so plentifully treating them with strong Liquors, give Occasion to the Considerate, sincerely to wish them safely shipped off for their own Country. At Vauxhall, on Thursday last, it is supposed that no less than Ten Thousand Persons crouded thither to obtain a Sight of these Indians. At the same Time, a Songstress of the Grove attempted the Honour of traversing the Walks with the swarthy Monarch dangling on her Arm; but the Press was so much, as to oblige him to retire, with his Chief, (and many Ladies of the Town) into the Orchestra, where they entertained themselves and the gaping Multitude, by sounding the Keys of the Organ, scraping upon the Strings of a Violin, clapping their Hands in Return for the Claps of Applause bestowed upon them, and swallowing, by Wholesale, Bumpers of Frontiniac. Between Two and Three in the Morning their Cherokeeships began to think of departing, and, being duely supported, made Shift to reach their Coach for that Purpose. The Chief, who was in his best Plight, stepped in first, with his Friend; but the Garment of *his Majesty* unluckily falling foul of a Gentleman's Sword-Hilt, in the Croud, a Sort of Scuffle mistakenly ensued, the Sword by some Accident was drawn, and broke, and the Indian's Hands in a pretty bloody Condition, were exposed to the Spectators with much seeming Remonstrance and Complaint. He then threw himself into a Fit of Sullenness or Intoxication, or both, on the Ground, and obstinately remained there for a considerable Time. Force however effected what Persuasion could not, for he was Neck and Heels lifted in, and laid along the Bottom of the Coach. Soon after, his Legs which had obstructed the shutting the Door, being carefully packed up with the rest, the Coachman, by driving away, put an End to this wretched Scene of British Curiosity and Savage Debauchery.

1.9 *The St. James's Chronicle; or, the British Evening-Post* (Thursday, 5–Saturday, 7 August 1762)

To the PRINTER *of* The ST. JAMES'S CHRONICLE.

MR. BALDWIN,

I HOPE it will not be thought *crimen laesae majestatis*, or HIGH TREASON in me to censure the Behaviour of his *Cherokee* Majesty, and to say such Practices as he was guilty of in this Nation would have subjected him to have been deposed in his own Country, like his mad drunken Brother, the Czar of Russia. But perhaps after all, it ought to be a Maxim in this Case, that the King can do no Wrong, as it may be averred, that his Most Ignorant Majesty cannot distinguish between Right and Wrong: The whole Blame therefore must lie upon his Prime Ministers, or whatever you please to call them, who led him into Actions so highly unbecoming the Seriousness of Majesty. Could our News-Papers be translated

into the Cherookean Language, and could the Cherokees read, what must they
think of their great Warriour, when they are told, that he spent his Time in
England in getting Drunk at one Place, picking up common *Squaws* at another,
and making himself Ridiculous and Contemptible wherever he went? And must
they not look upon the English People as a Pack of Idiots, Beasts, and
Barbarians, when their King shall relate to them, at his Return, that he was
exposed to publick View as a Monster? It has been pretended, that the Reason
for bringing over this outlandish Monarch to be stared at, was in order to give
the Savage Americans an high Opinion of our Nation. Had his Conductors,
indeed, carried him only to the Parliament-House, to see the Graces of Action
and Elocution displaid there, or to Westminster-Hall, to observe the Gravity of
the Judges, as well as of the Council, to Sir John Fielding, my Lord-Mayor, or
before the Sitting Alderman, to remark with what Sagacity our Magistrates
examine Criminals, to a Review of the City Militia, to conceive the Fierceness of
our Soldiers, to Whitfield's Tabernacle,[14] to learn the Excellencies of our Religion,—then indeed might his Cherokeean Majesty have entertained a wonderful
Opinion of our Wisdom: But what could he gather from Sadler's Wells, but that
Wine and Punch was the best of the Entertainment? or from Vauxhall, but that
the *Squaws* were very tempting, and the Usquebaugh too strong for his kingly
Head? For my own Part I am apt to suspect, that there was a deeper Scheme of
Politics in bringing this Indian Monarch over than is generally imagined. Our
Nation is remarkable for its Greediness after Novelty, which requires continually
to be fed with fresh Matter. It does not signify what engages our Curiosity at the
Time, whether a Riot at home or a Battle abroad, a Gypsy or a Lord Mayor, a
Murderer or a Minister. May it not therefore be conjectured, that this strange
Sight was exhibited, like a Tub thrown out to a Whale, to divert our Attention
from the present political Squabble? At least, I am sure it would have been made
a Plea against Mr. P—,[15] had he continued in, and brought as a Proof of his
republican and aristocratian Principles, that his Cherookean Kingship was suffered to expose himself among the Dregs of the People, in order to inspire them
with a dislike to Monarchy.

But it is said in one of your Papers, Mr. Baldwin, that 'three Men, in Imitation
of the Cherokee King and the Chiefs, having their Faces painted like them, have
been shewn at many of the publick Places for the real Indians.' This perhaps is
a Banter; but I hope it is true, for the Honour of both Nations. English Curiosity is easily imposed upon: It is sufficient to dress up a common Grenadier with
high-healed Shoes and a lofty Turband, and Numbers of Fools will walk in to see

---

[14] See the introduction to Section 4, below.
[15] William Pitt had resigned as first minister in 1761.

the Outlandish Giant. Every Puppet Show will put off King Henry and Fair Rosamond, &c. for the King of Prussia and his Court; and I cannot but admire the Quickness of Thought in the noted Yeates, who has got the Start of his Brother Wire—[?] by clapping a Pair of Whiskers upon Punch, blacking his Face, and dressing him in a strange Robe, has already passed him off through half the Country for the Cherokee King. We know what Crowds of People 'By their Majesties Command' prefixed to the Top of our Play-Bills, have drawn to the Play-House Doors; and the Proprietors of our public Gardens, and Places of Entertainment, have practised the same Decoy with no less Success in the present Instance. No Matter what the Object is; let it be an uncommon one, it will draw a Crowd of Gapers together: And I remember, a certain Comedian, so long ago as when Goodman's-Fields was opened [1733], was very sensible of our Love for Curiosity: Accordingly, at the Time of his Benefit, he advertised in all the Papers, *for the Entertainment of the Morocco Embassador and his Retinue*, who were just then come over. To represent these illustrious Personages, he hired four of the most ill-looking, hard-featured Irishmen he could get, made their Countenances more fierce with Whiskers, and improved the sallow Hue of their Complexion with Walnut-Juice. These he drest up in Character, and placed them in an odd-fashioned Coach with three or four of the same Country, metamorphosed in like Manner, behind it. The Cavalcade, as it passed through the City, drew along with it a great Concourse of People, which answered the Intent of the Contriver: For the Play-House was crowded from Top to Bottom. The four Chiefs were placed conspicuously in the Stage Box, with their Attendants behind them, to the Admiration of the Audience. They sat quietly for some Time, till at last they could not help jabber to one another in the Irish Language, which, however, passed off very well to those within Hearing for the right genuine Morisco Tongue. At last they grew impatient for Want of Drink, till they were supplied with repeated Pots of Porter, which they tossed off to the great Joy and Astonishment of the Spectators, who said one to another—*Mind how they swig our* English *Beer—they have none such in their own Country.*—Towards the End of the Play, the Fumes of the Liquor made them so far forget the Dignity of their Characters, that they began to fall out among themselves, and imagine they were quarrelling about a Fare. Nothing was now heard but—Tunder O Noons— Arrah by Jesu—&c. and the Ambassador called out,—'If Maaster will give Base [?], by St. Patrick we'll have a tight Set-to upon this Stage before all the Paple.' I need not tell you the Consequence: The Audience was enraged at the Affront put upon them, tore up the Benches, cut the Scenes, thrashed the Performers; and the sham Ambassador, together with his mock Retinue, were carried before a Magistrate, and sent to Clerkenwell Bridewell.

I am your humble Servant,

YOU KNOW WHO.

The Public Advertiser (Friday, 6 August 1762)   1.10

Tuesday last an Order was sent from the Secretary's-Office, to prevent the Cherokee King and his Chiefs being taken to any more Places of public Entertainment, as it has been productive of much Rioting and Mischief.

It is said that three Men, in Imitation of the Cherokee Kings, and having their Faces painted like them, have been shewn at many of the public Places for the real Indians.

The Public Advertiser (Saturday, 7 August 1762)   1.11

To the PRINTER.

SIR,

As the Public are greatly imposed upon by the many Accounts published in the Papers, relative to the Cherokee Indians. I think it my Duty to undeceive them, by assuring your Readers that few of those Accounts are true; but especially, that Gentleman who entertained them with the Intemperance and Amours of the swarthy Monarch and the Songstress of the Grove, has rather mistaken the Matter; for the King of the King of the King of the Cherokees was not at Vauxhall that Night. It is very true, the two Chiefs were there, and intoxicated; the Reason of which was, the ungovernable Curiosity of the People, who would force in upon them, and oblige them to drink; and, for the future, I shall take particular Care to confute any unjust Paragraphs I may hereafter meet with in any of the Papers.

Suffolk-street, Aug. 4, 1762   H. TIMBERLAKE.

2. SONGS AND THEATRICALS

The strangeness and theatricality of these reported encounters made them a valuable source for ballads and stage performances. A lengthy verse narrative of the supposed courtship of an English gentlewoman by one of the Iroquois visitors of 1710 became, according to Bond, 'one of the most popular ballads of the eighteenth century', running to 'at least fifteen different printings'.[16] In

---

[16] *Queen Anne's American Kings*, 72.

contrast to the romance idealism of this ballad, Henry Howard's broadside song (2.1) is salacious and crudely satirical, offering the home reader both the frisson of imagined sexual contact between savage masculinity and refined femininity and the patriotic prospect of British womanhood's unmanning of the Indian warrior. The ballad was headed by an engraving of the three Cherokee leaders posing in ceremonial dress.

Three months after the Cherokees departed the first performance of *The Witches; or, Harlequin Cherokee* took place at Drury Lane. The text of this pantomime (written by James Love, formerly known as James Dance) was never printed, but according to the advertisement it concluded 'with the Return, Landing and Reception of the Cherokees in America'. It was performed regularly as an afterpiece at Drury Lane between 1762 and 1766. At least one performance appears to have been attended by a Cherokee. The advertisement for the performance of 30 October 1764 announced that it was 'By desire of Chukatah, the Mankiller of Settico, a great warrior of the Cherokee Nation', a reference to the leading member of a second group of Cherokees accompanied to Britain by Timberlake.[17]

Although Robert Sayer's children's book, *Harlequin Cherokee* (2.2), was not published until 1772 it is clearly based on some of the events of the 1762 embassy (including the visit to Vauxhall), and it seems probable that it was suggested by the earlier pantomime. Sayer was a pioneer of the 'turn-up' book.[18] His Cherokee harlequinade is an engraved sheet divided into four panels, each of which has upper and lower flaps which can be folded back to reveal different images below. By this means a narrative progresses through a series of surprising juxtapositions and changes of scene: a structure interestingly suited to the book's theme of cultural difference.

2.1   A New Humorous Song, on the Cherokee Chiefs. Inscribed to the Ladies of Great-Britain. By H. Howard (1762)

To the Tune of, *Caesar and Pompey were both of them Horned.*

I

WHAT a Piece of Work's here, and a d——d Botheration!
Of Three famous Chiefs from the *Cherokee* Nation;
Who the Duce wou'd ha' thought, that a People polite, Sir,
Wou'd ha' stir'd out o' Doors to ha' seen such a Sight, Sir?
Are M[onste]rs so rare in the *British* Dominions,
That we thus shou'd run crazy for *Canada Indians*.

Are M——rs so rare, &c.

[17] *The London Stage 1660–1800,* pt. 4: *1747–1776,* ed. George Winchester Stone, Jr., (Carbondale, Ill., 1962), 964, 1080.
[18] See George Speaight, *Juvenile Drama: The History of the English Toy Theatre* (1946).

II

How eager the Folks at *Vauxhall*, or elsewhere, Sir,
With high Expectation and Rapture repair, Sir;
Tho' not one of them all can produce the least Reason,
Save that M——rs of all Sorts are always in Season.
If so, let the Chiefs here awhile have their Station,
And send for the whole of *Cherokee* Nation.

If so, let the Chiefs, &c.

III

The Ladies, dear Creatures, so squeamish and dainty,
Surround the great *Canada* Warriors in plenty;
Wives, Widows and *Matrons*, and pert little *Misses*,
Are pressing and squeezing for *Cherokee* Kisses,
Each grave looking Prude, and each smart looking Belle, Sir,
Declaring, no *Englishman* e'er kiss'd so well, Sir.

Each grave looking Prude, &c.

IV

That *Cherokee* Lips are much softer and sweeter,
Their Touch more refin'd, and their Kisses repleter,
The fair ones agree—nay, I mean not to flatter,
For who like the Ladies can judge of the Matter?
Ye Nymphs then, who like 'm, indulge your old Passion,
Be sw[ive]d by the Chiefs of the *Cherokee* Nation.

Ye Nymphs then, &c.

V

Ye Females of *Britain*, so wanton and witty,
Who love even Monkies, and swear they are pretty;
The *Cherokee Indians*, and stranger *Shimpanzeys*,
By Turns, pretty Creatures, have tickl'd your Fancies;
Which proves, that the Ladies so fond are of Billing,
They'd kiss even M——rs, were M——rs as willing.

Which proves, that, &c.

VI

No more then these Chiefs, with their scalping Knives dread, Sir,
Shall strip down the Skin from the *Englishman*'s Head, Sir;
Let the Case be revers'd, and the Ladies prevail, Sir,
And instead of the Head, skin the *Cherokee* T——l, Sir.

Ye bold Female *Scalpers*, courageous and hearty,
Collect all your Force for a *grand Scalping Party*.
                              Ye bold Female Scalpers, &c.

VII

For Weapons, ye Fair, you've no need to petition,
No Weapons you'll want for this odd Expedition;
A soft Female Hand, the best Weapon I wean is,
To strip down the Bark of a *Cherokee P—s*.
Courageous advance then, each fair *English* Tartar,
Scalp the *Chiefs* of the *Scalpers*, and give them no Quarter.
                              Courageous advance then, &c.

2.2   *Harlequin Cherokee or the Indian Chiefs in London.* London. *Publish'd as the Act directs Feb. 24th. 1772 by Robt. Sayer, Map & Printseller. No 53 in Fleet Street.* 6d. Plain. 1s. Colour'd. Book 12

Panel 1

Here Harlequin that artful thief
You see is like an Indian Chief
What can his meaning be for this
Since Europe all is known for his
Must Savage Wilds become his prey
Turn up and then attend the lay.

Panel 1a

Here Harlequin that artfull Elf
Behold just half like to himself
With Magic Sword and Comic mask
No doubt he's got a heavy task
Yet further you shall see and hear
If you turn down it will appear.

Panel 1b

Here Harley's Seen at his full length
With all his magic Power and Strength
And two strange Indians staring at him
Who wonder at his meaning rat him
His meaning you shall know a non
In part the Second—pray go on.

Panel 2

Here's a Ship—likewise a Cargo
By fancy brought without Embargo
For it is known to all the Nation
No Duty's paid for Frolickation
The Young & Old may laugh and play
But turn it up and then away.

Panel 2a

Sly Harley here has made a Capture
Of which in time youll be in rapture
To England they must sail with speed
It is by Fortune so agreed
What other things we've got to shew
Pray turn it down & you shall know.

Panel 2b

Again you see we change the Scene
To view obsequious Harlequin
Who to his new got booty landed
Appears quite free and open handed
For you may guess nay almost swear
He'll make a penny of such ware.

Panel 3

See here in pleasures ample round
The strange Americans are found
Tho' they seem odd to stare & Grin
Yet we as Wildly stare at them
It is the Custom of each Nation
Which causes all the Consternation.

Panel 3a

But now the Orchestra we view
Which is to them a subject new
For ne'er to them was seen before
On all the vast atlantick shore
A scene to yield so much delight
As what they here behold to night.

7–9. Robert Sayer, *Harlequin Cherokee or the Indian Chiefs in London* (1772), Panels 3, 3a, 3b. The scene is Vauxhall Gardens. By permission of the Osborne Collection of Early Children's Books, Toronto Public Library

See here in pleasures ample round
The strange Americans are found
Tho' they seem odd to stare & Grin
Yet we as Wildly stare at them
It is the Custom of each Nation
Which causes all the Consternation.

But now the Orchestra we view
Which is to them a subject new
For ne'er to them was seen before
On all the vast atlantick shore
A scene to yield so much delight
As what they here behold to night.

See here in pleasures ample round
The strange Americans are found
Tho' they seem odd to stare & Grin
Yet we as Wildly stare at them
It is the Custom of each Nation
Which causes all the Consternation.

But now the Orchestra we view
Which is to them a subject new
For ne'er to them was seen before
On all the vast atlantick shore
A scene to yield so much delight
As what they here behold to night.

Another scene is here display'd
They now behold the fine cascade
Astonishment has struck them dumb
Yet pray a little forward come
We'll have another frolick bout
In the next part you'll see it out.

Panel 3b

Another scene is here display'd
They now behold the fine cascade[19]
Astonishment has struck them dumb
Yet pray a little forward come
We'll have another frolick bout
In the next part you'll see it out.

Panel 4

Here Harlequin you see again
No doubt he's something in his brain
For I have heard with Fun and Frolick
He never yet has had the cholick
And if still further you would know
Pray Turn it up and we will shew.

Panel 4a

The Indian chiefs you see once more
Are destin'd for their native shore
With british follies in their mind
Again they brave the waves & wind
'Tis so ordain'd by Harlequin
And now turn down & close the scene.

Panel 4b

Now Harlequin has made his market
They on the Ocean must embark it
To Woods and Wilds proceed again
No more to see young Harlequin
Of whom they tell such tricks & stories
Which swell no doubt old Englands Glories.

---

[19] According to *A Description of Vaux-Hall Gardens* (1762), 'by drawing up a curtain is shewn a most beautiful landscape in perspective of a fine open hilly country with a miller's house and a water mill, all illuminated by concealed lights; but the principal object that strikes the eye is a cascade or water fall' (p. 9).

3. MOHAWKS ON SHOW

The events of the Seven Years War increased public interest in native Americans. Occasionally this interest took a crudely exploitative form, with exhibitions of Indians being advertised in the newspaper press. The paying audience was also susceptible to exploitation, however, and we cannot be sure that the Mohawk Warrior shown in 1759 (3.1) was not the white impersonator described in the *Grand Magazine* of that year as 'being come to London, where he exhibits himself in Indian dress, displaying and explaining their method of fighting'.[20]

The authorities in Britain did not encourage such exhibitions, partly because they thought them politically injudicious but also because they considered them inhumane. In a wider context the parliamentary intervention of 1765 (3.2) can be understood as an example of the distancing of the polite from the world of popular amusements.

3.1 *The Public Advertiser* (Wednesday, 3 January 1759)

Just arrived from AMERICA,
And to be seen at the New-York Coffee-house in Sweeting's Alley,

A Famous Mohawk Indian Warrior; the same Person who took M. Dieskau, the French General Prisoner, at the Battle of Lake George, where General Johnston beat the French, and was one of the said General's Guards; he is dressed in the same Manner with his native Indians when they go to War, his Face and Body painted, with his Scalping-knife, Tom-ax, and all other Implements of War that are used by the Indians in Battle. A Sight worthy the Curiosity of every True-Briton.

Price One Shilling each Person.

The only Indian that has been in England since the Reign of Queen Anne.

3.2 *The Parliamentary History of England, from the Earliest Period to the Year 1803*, ed. William Cobbett, 36 vols. (London, 1806–20), xvi. 50–2

Proceedings in the Lords on a Complaint of advertising Two Indian Warriors to be shewn. March 5 [1765]. Notice being taken to the House, and complaint made,

[20] Cited in Carolyn Foreman, *Indians Abroad 1493–1938* (Norman, Okla., 1943), p. xxii.

of an advertisement in the printed newspaper, intituled, 'The Gazetteer and New Daily Advertizer, Monday, March 4th, 1765,' 'That there is to be seen, at the Sun Tavern, facing York Buildings in the Strand, two Indian Warriors of the Mohawk nation, from ten in the morning till six in the evening; each person to pay one shilling.' Ordered, That the person who keeps the Sun-tavern facing York Buildings in the Strand to attend this House to-morrow.

March 6. The House being informed, 'That John Schuppe, who keeps the Sun-tavern in the Strand, where the two Indians are shewn, and Hyam Myers, were attending without, pursuant to their lordships' order.'

The Earl of Sandwich acquainted the House with the purport of a letter which he received from sir Joseph Yorke, his Majesty's ambassador in Holland, relating to the said Indians, when they were there; and the directions given by his excellency for their being brought to England, in order to their being carried back to America. Then the said John Schuppe and Hyam Myers were called in, to the bar.

And the said John Schuppe, being examined in relation to the shewing of the said Indians, acquainted the House, 'That the said Hyam Myers hired a room of him for eight days, in order to shew two Indian Warriors he had brought from America; that they have been shewn there for eight days, at 1s. each person; that they have their meals regularly, and drink nothing stronger than small beer.'

The said Hyam Myers being also examined, acquainted the House, 'That, about eleven months ago, he was at New York; and being about to come to England, the two Mohawks that are now with him came down to New York, and desired him to bring them to England to see their father; but, having no money to pay their passage, he first consulted his friends about it, who advised him to bring them over, as he might reimburse himself the expence of their passage by shewing them; that accordingly he brought them to England, and landed at Bristol, where he left them with their interpreter while he came up to London; that, during his absence, the interpreter carried one of them to Amsterdam, and there sold him; that, upon the first knowledge of this transaction, he immediately went to Amsterdam, in order to recover him, and took the other Mohawk with him; but, notwithstanding all his endeavours, he could not get him again, being cast in a cause which he instituted there for that purpose; that, upon this, he went to the Hague, and applied to sir Joseph Yorke, desiring him to procure the said Mohawk's release; that, some time afterwards, he was directed by sir Joseph Yorke to return to Amsterdam, and he would have the Mohawk delivered to him; and at the same time, sir Joseph desired him to carry them back to their own country, by the way of England, telling him, he would write in his behalf to the Secretary of State, to whom he directed him to apply on his arrival in England: that he accordingly brought them to England, but, being distressed for money, he had shewn them in order to reimburse himself the expence he had already been at, and also to enable him to carry them back to their own country; but acknowledged he had made no application either to the Secretary of State, or to the Board of Trade.'

Resolved, 1. That the bringing from America any of the Indians who are under his Majesty's protection, without proper authority for so doing, may tend to give great dissatisfaction to the Indian nations, and be of dangerous consequence to his Majesty's subjects residing in the colonies. 2. That the making a public shew of Indians, ignorant of such proceedings, is unbecoming and inhuman.

Then it was moved, 'That the said John Schuppe and Hyam Myers be called in again, and ordered not to shew the said Indians from this time, but to detain them, taking proper care of their maintenance, till a proper person should be sent by the commissioners for trade and plantations to receive them, in order to their being returned to America.' Which being agreed to; they were called in again accordingly, and acquainted therewith by the Lord Chancellor.

4. SAMSON OCCOM, MOHEGAN PREACHER

Three years after Ostenaca returned to Cherokee territory Samson Occom (1723–92), a native American from a quite different background, set out from Boston on a religious mission to Britain. Occom's people, the Mohegans, occupied lands in the area of New London in present-day Connecticut. According to Occom's own account of his early life, his parents were 'very Strong in the Customs of their fore Fathers, and . . . led a wandering Life up and down in the Wilderness,' raising him in their 'Heathenish Notions' until the activities of evangelical preachers persuaded him 'to think about Religion' and to learn to read.[21] At the age of 19 Occom entered Eleazar Wheelock's Indian charity school at Lebanon, Connecticut where he studied for four years, preparing himself for service as a teacher and itinerant missionary among the native American peoples of New England. He was ordained a Presbyterian minister in 1759.

The idea of sending Occom on a preaching tour of Britain to raise funds for Wheelock's school was probably suggested by the leading English Methodist George Whitefield, who spent extended periods in North America in the course of his evangelical career. Although some of Wheelock's associates expressed concern that Occom might not be sufficiently 'polished' for such a mission, others were convinced of his value 'as a Specimen of the benefit of ye School'.[22] As Wheelock observed in a promotional

---

[21] Leon Burr Richardson, *An Indian Preacher in England* (Hanover, NH, 1933), 70.
[22] Ibid. 227.

pamphlet which was distributed in the course of the mission, 'as none but Samples of uncivilized *Indians* have ever been sent over, and exhibited to public View on this Side of the Water, the Britons are naturally led to form a more despicable Idea of them, and consequently to hold them in far more sovereign Contempt'.[23] It was Occom's role to alter that perception. In the event the tour, which lasted from 1766 to 1768 and took Occom and his companion Nathaniel Whitaker through much of England as well as to parts of Scotland and Ireland, proved a considerable financial success, raising the large sum of £11,000 in contributions for Wheelock's school.

Occom's first official appearance in London seems to have been planned as a sort of *coup de théâtre*. Although his arrival had been anticipated by newspaper reports, he was screened from public view until he delivered his first sermon at George Whitefield's Tabernacle. Occom's diary account of this event (4.1) is frustratingly terse, but the location suggests that the congregation he addressed would have been both large and socially mixed. Whitefield's followers included a number of aristocrats (notably Selina, countess of Huntingdon, a leading Calvinistic Methodist, and the earl of Dartmouth), but he originally made his name as a field preacher, addressing huge London crowds in disreputable areas such as Moorfields, the site of both Bedlam and Grub Street. These impolite associations, together with his enthusiastic appeal to his congregations' emotions, earned him a place in the revised *Dunciad* (II. 258). Whitefield's Tabernacle, situated just to the north of Moorfields, was originally erected on a temporary basis as a large booth, but this was replaced in 1753 by the brick structure in which Occom preached.

Occom seems generally to have been received with interest and respect during his time in Britain, where he met a number of leading figures in and outside the Anglican Church: Thomas Secker, archbishop of Canterbury, Philip Doddridge, an influential religious writer and minister at Northampton, John Newton, vicar of Olney and friend of the poet William Cowper, William Romaine, rector of St Anne's, Blackfriars, and Martin Madan, minister of the Lock Hospital near Hyde Park. In retrospect, however, Occom seems to have been unable entirely to throw off the suspicion that he was valued primarily as a 'specimen' of the civilizing process. He attracted attention, his biographer contends, 'not because his words were mighty but because they were the words of an Indian, a picturesque character in a dramatic rôle'.[24] Certainly Occom's acculturation did not prevent him from being occasionally ridiculed as a sort of popular exhibit. As he later observed bitterly in a letter to Wheelock, with whose educational schemes he had become thoroughly disillusioned, 'I was quite willing to become a Gazing

---

[23] *A Brief Narrative of the Indian Charity-School in Lebanon in Connecticut, New England: Founded and Carried on by that Faithful Servant of GOD the Rev. Mr. Eleazar Wheelock. The Second Edition, with an Appendix* (1767), 7.

[24] Harold Blodgett, *Samson Occom* (Hanover, NH, 1935), 90.

Stocke, Yea Even a Laughing Stocke, in Strange Countries to Promote your Cause'.[25] Occom's surviving writings offer us a perspective which is rarely recorded in the eighteenth century: the literate voice of an ethnic outsider, reporting the manners of high and low in England while remaining firmly attached to his own excluded and threatened culture.

4.1   Extracts from Samson Occom's Diary (1766)

Saturday, Febru^r 8 [1766]: Was at Mr Whitefield's Conceil'd—and on *Sabbath 9th Feb^r* was Still Conceil'd. *Monday, Febru^r ye 10th* Mr Whitefield took Mr Whetaker and I in his Coach and Introduc'd us to my Lord Dartmouth, and apear'd like a Worthy Lord indeed. Mr Whitefield Says he is a Christian Lord and an unCommon one—after We Pay'd our Compliments to my Lord—Mr Whitefield Caried us to my Lady Hotham's, and She receiv'd us with all Kindness. She is an aged Woman, and a Mother in Israel, and We rode about Both in the City and out, the Land about the City & in the Country is like one Continued Garden. Last Sabbath Evening walk'd with Mr Wright to Cary a letter to my Lord Dartmouth and Saw Such Confusion as I never Dreamt of—there was Some at Churches, Singing & Preaching, in the Streets some Cursing Swaring & Damning one another, others was hollowing, Whestling, talking gigling, & Laughing, & Coaches and footmen passing and repassing, Crossing and Cross-Crossing, and the poor Begars Praying, Crying, and Beging upon their kness,—*Tuesday* Din'd with Mr Savage, and in the even'g Mr Whitefield and his people had Love Feast at the Chappel. Mr Whetaker and I Join'd with them. *Wednesday Feb^r 12* rode out again. *Thirsday Feb^r 13* Mr Whitefield Caried us to the Parlament House—there we Saw many Curiosities, from thence went over Westminster Bridge a Cross the River Thames made all of Stone—thence went to Greenwich, and had a glance of Hospital there. But a Tedious Cold rainy Day it was,—We were Introduc'd by Mr Whitefield to Mr Faudagel a Quaker—Got home again in the Evening—*Fryday Feb^r 14*—Early in the morning Mr Whitefield Carried us to Mr Romains and Introduc'd us to him and to Mr Madin (Maden) and to Mr Singenhagan and old Apostolec German Minister,—and return'd Home again—

Mr Whitefield *takes unwearied* Pains to Introduce us to the *religious Nobility* and others, and to the best of men in the City of London—Yea he is a tender father to us, he provids everything for us, he has got House for us—ye Lord reward him a thousand and Thousand fold—He is indeed a father in God, he has made him a Spiritual Father to thousands and thousands, and god has made

[25] Harold Blodgett, *Samson Occom* (Hanover, NH, 1935), 123.

him a Temporal father to the poor—His House is Surrounded With the poor, the Blind, the Lame, the Halt and the mamed, the Widow, & the Fatherless, from Day to Day, God continue his useful Life.

Sabbath Feb' 16, I Preach'd in *M' Whitefield's Tabernacle* to a great Multitude of People; I felt [blank in Mss] *Monday Feb' 17*—M' Whitefield presented us to *D' Gifford* a famous Baptist Minister, and were receiv'd Extreamly Well—and Dined with him—*Tuesday* we Stay'd Home—*Wednesday, Feb' 19* we were Conducted to See the Kings Horses, Carriages and Horsemen &c—and then went to the Pt. House and went in the Robing Room and saw the Crown first, and saw the King, had yᵉ Pleasure of Seeing him put on his Royal Robes and Crown.— He is quite a Comly man—his Crown is Richly adorn'd with Diamonds, How grand and Dazling is it to our Eye,—if an Earthly Crown is So grand—How great and glorious must the Crown of the glorious Redeemer be, at the right hand of the majesty on High—tho' he was once Crown'd with Thorns—The Atendence of King george is Very Surprizing, as he went to the House of Parlament he & his glorious Coach was atended with footman Just before and behind them all round, and the Horseman Just behind and before the footmen, and the Bells & all Sorts of Musickal Instruments Playing, and the Cannon Firing, and Multitudes of all Sorts of People Throning all Round—if an Earth King With his attendᶜ is So great. How grand, how Dreadful and glorious must the appearing of the Son of god be—When he Shall Desend from Heaven, to Judge the World, He will Desend with Cherubem and Serephems, with Angels and Archangels and with Sound of the Trumpet and with great Power and glory,—with Thunder & Lighteng,—and the Family of Heaven, and Earth, and Hell Shall appear before him, and the Eilments Shall melt with fervent Heat—Lord Jesus prepare me for thy Second Coming—

We went Emediately from Seing The King, to Dine with a Nobleman My Lord DartMouth, a most religious Noble-man and his Lady also, the most Singular Cupple amongst Nobility in London—This Day also went to Westminster Abey, and had a fuler Vew of the Moniments—saw Bedlem also—in the Evening we return'd again to M' Whitefield's—

Thursday, Feb' 20—This is the Queen Chalottes Birth-Day, was Conducted to St. James's where the Royal Family and the Nobility were to be together to keep a Joyful Day—but we were too late, however we Saw some of the Nobility in their Shining Robes and a throng of People all around,—the Sight of the Nobility put me in mind of Dives and the Rich Gluton, and the poor reminded me of Lazarus—What great Difference there is Between the Rich and the Poor— and What Diference there is and will be, Between God's poor and the Devil's Rich, &c—

o Lord God Amighty let not my Eyes be Dazled with the glitering Toys of this World, but let me be fixt and my Soul Long after Jˣ Who is the only Pearl of great

Price—This evening Went into our House which Mr Whitefield Provided for us and all the Furniture also—and a Made to Wait on us—Blessed be god, that he has Sent his Dear Servant before us—

Fryday Feb^r 21: was Conducted to the Tower, saw the Kings Lions Tiggers Wolf and Leopards &c—Saw the Kings Guns and the Muniments of antient Kings on Horse Back and their Soldiers on foot with their Antient Armour of Brass and Tin—Din'd with Mr Keen, and then went to a funeral, Mr Whitefield gave an Exhortation to the People and then Pray'd— . . .

Tuesday, April 22: Preach'd in the Evening at Mr Whitefield's Tottenham Court C[h]apel, to a great Multitude, and the L^d was present with us I hope

Sabbath, April 27: Preach'd at Little St. Hellens and Devenshare Square—and I [had] of a freedom in the after Noon,—*Monday, April 28:*, Went to See Several Gent^n—Mr Dilly gave me 4 Books for my own Use—Din'd with Mr Barber a good Disenting Minister—then went with Mr Whitaker to Mr Bailey's, and Mr Whitaker Baptiz'd a Child for him,—and then went home.

Wednesday, April 30 We went to Wait upon his grace the Arch Bishop of Canterbury and he appear'd quite agreable and Friendly—In the evening I Preach'd at Mr Whitefield's Tabernacle to a Crowded Audience and I believe the L^d was with us of a trouth— . . .

Saturday, June 7: I went to North Hampton, got thence Just before Night, and was receiv'd with all kindness—

Sabbath June 8: Preach'd at Mr Riland's Meeting House to a throng'd Congregation, & the L^d gave me Some Strength and the People attended with great Solemnity and affection and was told afterwards one young Man was Converted and hopefully Converted—in the after Noon Preach'd In Riland's Yard to about 3000 recken'd—

Monday June 9: Mr Newton of Olney about 15 miles off Came to fetch me to his Place, after Breakfast we Sot off, rode in a Post Chace, there a little after 12: this Mr Newton is a Minister of the Church of England, he was a Sailor, and god marvellously turn'd him and he is a flaming Preacher of the Gospel,—at Evening I Preach'd at one of the meetings in the Place, to a Crowd of People,—Lodg'd at Mr Newton's,—a Number of good people live in this place, but very poor in this World—*Tuesday, June 10:* Mr Newton and I took a walk towards Northampton about [blank] miles—and then Breakfasted,—and then we parted, he went Back a foot, and I went on Horse to Northampton, got there about 12: Din'd with Mr Hextal, one of the Desenting Ministers of the place, at 6 in the Even'g I Preach'd the Meeting House where great Doc^r Doddrege was Minister, and there was a great Concourse of people and attended with great Solemnity—Lodg'd at Mr Riland's—there is a number of warm Christians in this Town—

Wednesday June 11: got up a little after 3 and was in a Coach before 4: and return'd to London—Got there a little after 6:—found my friends well—Thanks be to god for his goodness,—

Sabbath June 15: Preach'd in the morning at Mr Burford's Meeting, had some freedom—in the after Noon I preach'd at Mr Pitts, with Since of Divine things in the Evening Preach'd at Shakespeare's walk—and Sup'd with Mr Waren this Evening—

Monday June 16: Went to Mr Thornton's at Clapham and was Entertain'd with all Kindness. he is a gent^n of emense fortune, and he is the right Sort of Christian and a very Charitable man—Lodg'd with him this Night—*Tuesday Morning* Mr Thornton took me in his Chariot and Caried me to my Lodgings—

Wednesday June 18: I went in the Morning to See Mr Guinap, a Baptist Minister of Saffron Walden, Breakfasted with him—

Thursday June 19: Preach'd in Mr John Wesley's Foundry to a Crowded Audience, begun at 7 in the Evening—

Saturday June 21: Mr Whitaker and I went to Saffron Walden, got there before Night, Lodg'd at Mr Fuller's—

Sabbath June 22: Went to Meeting, Mr Whitaker Preach'd and in the after Noon I Preach'd to a Crowded Congregation, and I was very Poorly, but I belive the L^d was with us of a truth and in the evening Preach'd again to great Assembly and I had Some Strength, and the People made a Collection—

Monday June 23: we return'd to London, got there Some time before night—the L^d be Prais'd for all his goodness to us—this Evening I heard, the Stage Players, had been Mimicking of me in their Plays, lately—I never thought I Shou'd ever come that Honour,—O god woul'd give me greater Courage—

The 'Stage Players' to whom Occom refers may well have been the company which performed Samuel Foote's *The Minor* at the Haymarket Theatre on 18 and 20 June 1766. The play was well known for its satire of Methodism in general and for Foote's mimicry of Whitefield's preaching style in particular. This was not the only occasion that Occom was chosen as the target of such ridicule. In a letter to Occom's companion, Nathaniel Whitaker, a Dr Wood reported from Norwich at the end of September 1767 that 'On Friday last was a Grub-street penny Paper publish'd in Norwich aiming foolishly (but without Wit) to expose the Institution & good Mr Occom in particular—A very low Affair it is & utterly below Notice—I'm sure Mr Occom is Soldier good enough to despise a Squib.'[26] Judging from surviving printed evidence[27] whoever wrote this Norwich 'Catchpenny' (4.2) seems to have had some knowledge of Occom's career and preaching style. The interjection 'Hawke', which repeatedly interrupts the sermon's flow, is probably intended as an onomatopoeic rendering of the process of clearing the throat

[26] Richardson, *An Indian Preacher in England*, 303–4.

[27] *Extracts of Several Sermons, Preached Extempore at different Places of Divine Worship, in the City of Bristol, by the Rev. Nathaniel Whitaker . . . and the Rev. Mr. Samson Occom, An Indian Minister . . . As taken down by a Youth* (Bristol, 1766).

or spitting, and as a reminder to the reader of the Indian convert's inherent lowness and savagery.

4.2   From *A Cry from the Wilderness: Or, A Converted Indian's Address to a Xn. Congregation*. Norwich: Printed in the Year 1767. [Price One Penny.]

I Beg leave to drop a few Words among you, by Way of Apology for this Application.—H-a-w-ke.—

'Till the Age of seventeen, I lived a poor blind Heathen, like the rest of my Countrymen, in a State of Darkness and Ignorance and Poverty.—H—ke.—I had lived easy and contented in this wretched Condition, 'till about thirty Years ago it pleased the Lord to rouse me from this dangerous Security to a Sense of my lost and miserable Condition: then I became regenerate, was cleansed from all Filthiness of Flesh and Spirit, and have been ever since a new Creature.—H—ke.—

I'll tell you how it happen'd, in a few Words.—Good Mr. MAMMON was the Instrument the Lord chosed for this Work. He saw me one day wandering in the Wilderness of Sin, and called me by an Interpreter, and lovingly asked me to taste a Cup of his Liquor.—I drank—and drank again—and verily thought I in my heart, the Way of this People is good—it is a good Way—and blessed are they that walk therein.—H—ke.—He invited me to stay with him; and let me to know, if I wou'd follow his Directions, he wou'd put me in the way to drink of this blessed Cup every day.—The Lord inclined my Heart to yield to the good Motion, and with his Blessing on my earnest Endeavours I soon learned to read, and conformed myself to the holy Ordinances in all things.—H—ke.—

After I had once tasted that the Lord was gracious, I grew in his Grace daily, and was made sensible of the dark and forlorn Condition of my poor barbarous Countrymen; who are ignorant of the Value of Money and Trade, and don't know what is good, neither for Soul nor Body.—H—ke.— . . .

May a Spirit of Liberality prompt you to employ the Talents entrusted to you, in promoting the Work of the Lord; that all may be subject to his Kingdom—that his Kingdom may come unto all Mankind, and that all may come into one Fold and under one Shepherd. In this Way and Manner may ye employ your worldly Pelf to the greatest Interest and most lasting Advantage.—H—ke.—What can I say?—As the Load-Stone draws Iron by a secret Charm, so let the Word of Power in my Mouth melt your hard Hearts and draw forth more precious Metals from your Purses.—H—ke.—

Lastly, give me leave to beg the Assistance, not only of your Money, but your earnest and hearty Prayers for the Success of this great Work. *Paul* may plant and

Apollos water; but God must grant the Increase: which he can do to the abundant Emolument of the Dispensers. He that giveth to the Poor, in a proper Way and Manner, lendeth to the Lord; and his Charity shall be returned upon him an hundred-fold.—Not only so, but many are the Benefits to be expected from the Conversion and Attachment of the *Indians*. Ye will acquire a prodigious Extent of Territory—promote your Trade among Nations, who shall learn to want your Commodities, and be glad to take off your Ware—procure a numerous body of lusty Slaves, a Mine of Wealth and Prop of Empire—and finally ye shall redeem Hundreds, yea Thousands I may say, Millions I may say, of strong and hardy People, from the Idolatry of Satan, to the Service and Glory of our Lord, and to the everlasting Interests of his Kingdom.

    Amen.

CHORUS of *SATYRS.*
At such Farce-Actors, who pretend
These pious Means, for wicked End,
We laugh amain, and keep our Pence
From spoiling Indian *Innocence.*

                            Anon.

INDEX

References in **bold** are to material in the selections. References in *italic* are to illustrations. Passing references to places in London are not included.